The Future of Multilateralism

The Future of Multilateralism

Global Cooperation and International Organizations

Edited by Madeleine O. Hosli,
Taylor Garrett,
Sonja Niedecken
and Nicolas Verbeek

ROWMAN & LITTLEFIELD
Lanham • Boulder • New York • London

Published by Rowman & Littlefield
An imprint of The Rowman & Littlefield Publishing Group, Inc.
4501 Forbes Boulevard, Suite 200, Lanham, Maryland 20706
www.rowman.com

86–90 Paul Street, London EC2A 4NE, United Kingdom

Copyright © 2021 by The Rowman & Littlefield Publishing Group, Inc.

British Library Cataloguing in Publication Information Available

Library of Congress Cataloging-in-Publication Data Is Available
ISBN: 978-1-5381-5528-8 (cloth : alk. paper)
ISBN: 978-1-5381-5792-3 (pbk : alk. paper)
ISBN: 978-1-5381-5529-5 (electronic)

Contents

Foreword

This book comes at a critical time for global cooperation. The year 2020 was supposed to be a moment of reflection on the achievements and challenges of multilateralism, and an occasion for renewed commitment to finding common solutions to urgent global issues. And it was, but in a way what we had not predicted.

On 24 October 2020, the United Nations (UN) turned 75. We had prepared for a birthday with something to celebrate, most notably a long period of relative peace between nations, unknown to the past centuries, and a few decades when an unprecedented number of people were being lifted out of poverty and hunger, also with the help of the UN and other multilateral organizations. It was however also a time to look at the challenges that multilateral cooperation faces, with the climate and environmental crisis unfolding faster than our capacity to respond, growing inequalities within and between countries, and persisting conflicts and humanitarian crises affecting the Global South. The year 2020 launched a "Decade of Delivery" at the UN General Assembly in New York, to ask renewed commitment to the leaders of all country to the 2030 Agenda and its Sustainable Development Goals (SDGs), which they signed five years before, and whose implementation is still lagging behind, risking to fail to deliver on our promises for a greener, fairer and more peaceful world.

As this process unfolded, the global pandemic struck. In some countries, the health crisis hit first, taking millions of lives of the most vulnerable and bringing medical systems on the brink of collapse. In others, including many fragile economies and societies in Africa and elsewhere in the Global South, it was the socio-economic crisis, which struck the hardest, destroying the jobs of millions of people lacking social protection, closing schools and leaving countless children without education (and school meals) and triggering a tragic raise in acute hunger in dozens of countries.

The crisis we are living goes well beyond the health dimension. The world risks losing many of the hard-won improvements towards sustainable development. COVID-19 is bringing about the worst collapse in per capita incomes since 1870. It is leading to tens of millions of new people unemployed worldwide and hundreds of millions suffering from acute hunger. It is striking the most vulnerable hardest: women, children, disabled, people lacking social protection and those in the informal sector.

The crisis gave us a painful yet clear answer to the questions we were about to discuss in 2020: yes, global cooperation and multilateralism are needed today more than ever. Failures in defining common solutions to the challenges we face today result in the loss of lives, livelihood and the progressive destruction of our environment. Tragically, as reminded by the UN Secretary-General, multilateralism is under fire precisely when we need it most: when we need the world leaders and citizens to come together to achieve the SDGs, fight inequalities and ensure a more inclusive and sustainable world.

This means that the reflection on the state and future of global cooperation is ever more relevant.

For this reason, academic contributions like this book on the future of multilateralism are fundamental to provide an analysis of the current state of global cooperation and governance and to indicate the way forward in providing solutions to the pressing challenges ahead.

For the same reason, as the UN, we sought to maintain and adapt our original plan to make of UN75 a moment of collective reflection, by organizing a global conversation[1] with more than 1,000 dialogues held across the world, a one-minute survey that was filled in by over one million people in all UN member states, and two large independent polls. What came out of these surveys is that people overwhelmingly support global cooperation as a vital way to deal with today's challenges. People across the world expect their leaders to deliver answering the big challenges of our time collectively, with the immediate priority of improving access to basic services and enabling global solidarity in the COVID-19 crisis, and the longer-term commitment to finding solutions to the climate crisis, ensuring greater respect for human rights, settling conflicts, tackling poverty and reducing corruption.

While much more work is needed, the UN, its member states, and key multilateral partners like the European Union continue to define and deliver global solutions to these problems. This is being done in response to the COVID-19 crisis to support countries, especially developing and fragile ones, in coping with the immediate health, humanitarian and socio-economic consequences of the crisis. And this will require continued and increased efforts in the longer-term recovery from COVID-19, to ensure that the investments made to restart our economies are focused on creating a greener, fairer and more sustainable socio-economic model. One where people's fundamental rights are put at the centre and no one is left behind, in line with the commitments taken by world leaders in the 2030 Agenda.

To be successful in recovering from this crisis and getting back on the track of sustainable development, we need a whole-of-society approach. We need an alliance where international organizations, the public and private sector, academia, civil society and all individuals play their part in supporting cooperative solutions and ambitious goals in defence of environment, equality, human rights and peace. Global cooperation is about people, not empty institutional settings, and today's technologies and our globalized world offer new avenues for the participation of those who want to make their voice heard.

With this in mind, I want to wish all readers of this book an enriching experience. Thorough research and studies give us a stronger understanding of the world we live in and show us how we can contribute to make it better.

Many thanks also to Prof. Madeleine O. Hosli for inviting me to share these opening words.

—Barbara Pesce-Monteiro

Director, United Nations in Brussels

Barbara Pesce-Monteiro is the director of UNDP's Representation Office in Brussels. She is also the United Nation Secretary-General's Representative towards the European Union (EU) and the Belgian authorities.

Before this appointment, she was the UN Resident Coordinator in Cuba for four years. From 1990 to 2010, she worked with UNDP in Colombia, Guatemala, Nicaragua, Angola and Mexico. In addition, she covered the Sahel with UNCDF. She holds a master's degree in rural development planning (UK) and completed her degree in international political science at La Sapienza University (IT).

NOTE

1. https://www.un.org/en/un75/presskit.

Foreword

International organizations are actors that have been present in international relations for long times. The present situation in the world, which is characterized by shifting power relations and the COVID-19 pandemic, is not the first time that international organizations have been pressured and seriously challenged. In previous situations, these organizations have shown to be resilient in the sense that, in spite of the problems, they try to move forward and adapt to the new circumstances. They don't give up easily in difficult situations. Both the leadership of global and regional multilateral organizations and their member states need to explore how to meet today's challenges. This requires analysis, creativity and diplomatic expediency in order to demonstrate that international organizations still have value and are able to innovate, adapt where necessary and continue the work for which the organizations were originally created, but now in new arrangements.

Madeleine Hosli and her collaborators have decided to analyse the future of multilateral organizations while both the shift in power relations between states and the pandemic remain unfinished. The authors focus on the United Nations and some of its specialized entities (the Bretton Woods institutions, UN Women, UNICEF, the World Health Organization and the World Trade Organization), several major regional organizations (the African Union, the Asian Infrastructure Investment Bank, the Association of Southeast Asian Nations, the European Union and Mercosur in Latin America) as well as some significant regimes (e.g. climate change and development cooperation). Their work resulted in a series of pictures of the present situation in these organizations and regimes, which help to understand what kind of problems, threats and challenges exist and matter. For instance, the WHO problems discussed are restricted autonomy over resources, continuous influence by international politics and weak leadership in and around the organization;

the problems of ASEAN are the lack of response to the Rohingya humanitarian crisis and the impact of a more assertive China in the region. Since the authors are not only interested in the state of the art of the organizations but also forward looking, they likewise try to analyse and show where and how potential improvements can be found. They look for new dynamics, how the agenda can be developed further and mention possible future developments. The Mercosur chapter, for instance, proposes a reform in the presidency of the highest organ. The UNICEF and UN Women chapter depicts the pandemic as an opportune moment for a substantial reform of the humanitarian agenda, better coordination and the inclusion of new civil society actors. The book's forward-looking focus makes the included chapters useful means for assessing the future of multilateralism.

—Bob Reinalda

Dr Bob Reinalda is a fellow and senior researcher at Radboud University, Nijmegen, Netherlands. He was trained at the University of Amsterdam as a political scientist, focusing on international relations, and as a social historian. He holds a PhD in social sciences from the Rijksuniversiteit Groningen (1981). His research focuses on leadership by executive heads of IOs and the development of international secretariats of IOs and multilateral conferences. His book *International Secretariats: Two Centuries of International Civil Servants and Secretariats* has been published by Routledge in its Global Institutions Series (2020). His article "Institutional Development of the United Nations Secretariat" appeared in the special issue for the seventy-fifth anniversary of the UN in the journal *Global Governance* in 2020 (volume 26, issue 2). He participates in the Aarhus University Project "Organizing the World—International Organization and the Emergence of International Public Administration, 1920–1960s" and the Cambridge History of International Law Project, focusing on IOs in the Age of Empire (1860s–1919).

Introduction

Madeleine O. Hosli

Multilateralism has been a tool used to solve a variety of challenges facing the international community notably since the end of World War II. The establishment of the United Nations (UN) and of various of its specialized agencies, programmes, funds and other entities are examples of this trend. Prominent global multilateral organizations are the International Monetary Fund (IMF) and the World Bank, as well as—since 1995—the World Trade Organization (WTO) as a follow-up to the earlier General Agreement on Tariffs and Trade (GATT).[1] But several international organizations were already established much earlier, such as the International Labour Organization (ILO), headquartered in Geneva, set up to enhance social and economic justice and to establish adequate international labour standards. In fact, some of the international governance institutions well-known today, including the ILO, have been created already in the beginning of the twentieth century (the ILO in 1919); some were even established at the end of the nineteenth century, including—in 1874—the Universal Postal Union (UPU), which coordinates member state postal services. A thorough analysis of multilateral governance institutions created before the twentieth century can be found in Ruggie (1993). By comparison, Muldoon et al. (2010) provide an in-depth overview of the evolution and establishment of multilateral governance institutions in the early years of the new millennium. A thorough overview of the history of multilateralism, nationalist impulses of member states and the problem-solving capacities of international organizations can be found in Lavelle (2020).

An early contribution to the analysis of the role and function of international organizations in the framework of global interdependence is of Jacobson (1984); Shanks et al. (1996) explore the establishment and continuation of international organizations over time, whereas Goetz and Patz (2017) analyse patterns of resourcing of international organizations.

Like global multilateral institutions, regional organizations are often based on an explicit commitment to the principle of rules-based multilateralism. For example, the European Union (EU) has advocated 'effective multilateralism' in several of its documents.[2] Similar to the United Nations itself, it has as main goals and norms principles such as the defence of the rule of law, democracy and human rights on the global level. Other regional organizations are similarly committed to the principle of multilateral governance, although the extent and depth of their own patterns of integration varies across organizations. For example, the African Union (AU) has a conflict management system institutionally similar to the one used by the United Nations Security Council (UNSC) and strongly developed patterns of institutional interaction with the United Nations. The Association of Southeast Asian Nations (ASEAN) may have a somewhat less active agenda of regional political integration, but it is still of high relevance to actions based on multilateralism in a regional context, not least in terms of combatting the effects of the COVID-19 pandemic. Moreover, regional organizations can be important actors in international negotiations and global governance (e.g. see Panke et al., 2019) and conversely, international organizations such as the United Nations increasingly rely on regional institutions to implement their goals, including partnerships in peace missions and implementation of the Sustainable Development Goals (SDGs).

Clearly, patterns of multilateral governance can be of crucial importance to regional integration schemes as well as efforts on the global level to combat threats facing the international community. However, what is 'multilateralism'? According to Robert Keohane (1990, p. 731), the core of multilateralism is 'the practice of coordinating national policies in groups of three or more states, through ad hoc arrangements or by means of institutions.' This definition clearly incorporates several of the existing international and regional mechanisms of cooperation. Similarly, John Gerard Ruggie (1992, 1993) in essence conceives the multilateral system as a (social) construction managing international life based on solidarity among its members; moreover, in his perspective, it has the potential to resolve potential conflicts due to the promise of dispersion of the gains of state cooperation over time. Core principles to his understanding of multilateralism hence are 'indivisibility' and 'diffused reciprocity'; moreover, central to international institutions is 'their multilateral form' (Ruggie, 1992, p. 565).

For example, climate governance, to be effective on a global scale, depends on multilateral patterns of negotiation and decision-making to arrive at common outcomes and the protection of respective common goods (e.g. the reduction of harmful emissions, mitigation of global warming and adaptation to rising sea levels).[3] Many international organizations or entities related to the UN deal with a specific threat to global 'public goods' provision, including, UNHCR—for the protection of refugees worldwide—UNICEF (protection of children globally), and UN Women (protecting the rights and wellbeing of women on the international level). The UN itself is currently in a process of reform—not least based on the agenda of 'one UN'—aiming to achieve more consistency across its various institutions. Nonetheless, the many UN-specialized agencies, programmes, research institutions and other entities still play particularly important roles in combatting common threats and addressing challenges to the wellbeing of humans worldwide; they explicitly operate based on the principle of multilateral governance.

For example, in the current system of global governance, the World Health Organization (WHO), as a specialized agency of the United Nations, plays a very important role not least in the context of the COVID-19 pandemic. The health crisis broke out in December 2019 in the Chinese city of Wuhan, but spread to other regions in the first half of 2020 (notably to Europe and the United States and, thereafter, to Africa, Latin America, Oceania and several countries across the world). The WHO's function as a monitoring and information-sharing institution on the global level has certainly played a crucial role in combatting effects of this crisis. The U.S. administration claimed in spring 2020, however, that the operations of the WHO were biased, in favour of China, which allegedly withheld crucial information on the numbers and the severity of the outbreak of COVID-19 within China.[4]

Global governance nowadays is characterized by patterns of multilateral negotiations and decision-making, in the framework of a variety of international institutions. At the same time, some institutions are based on 'plurilateralism.' Prominent examples of this are the G-20, dealing with preeminent issues concerning the maintenance of global economic and financial stability. The North Atlantic Treaty Organization (NATO) may, similarly, be seen as a plurilateral construct, focusing on the provision of (regional) security, encompassing large parts of the EU, Turkey, the United States, as well as a range of newer member states, including Montenegro (since 5 June 2017) and North Macedonia (since 27 March 2020). The WTO as an international organization, moreover, is experimenting with 'plurilateral' trade agreements, as collective agreements have proven increasingly difficult to establish, given the complexity of issues dealt with and membership size.

With shifts in changing global power constellations, however, patterns of multilateral decision-making are likely to be modified. For example, the shift of power to Asia,[5] notably China's considerable economic growth, has already led to the creation of alternatives to the 'traditional' multilateral postwar system, for example, by the 2015 establishment of the Asian Infrastructure Investment Bank (AIIB). The AIIB is still more committed to traditional forms of multilateral collaboration than other fora created recently, which are rather based on 'quasi-multilateralism,' such as the Forum on China-Africa

Cooperation (FOCAC) or the Cooperation between China and Central and Eastern European Countries (China-CEE, or 17+1). Nonetheless, China can also be viewed as a 'status quo power,' for example, in the framework of the United Nations Security Council (UNSC) where it holds one of the permanent seats. Its aspiration, however, is more of being a 'responsible stakeholder' in global governance, while its actual engagement in the multi-lateral order is under debate, not least due to its position on international legal agreements such as the future of Hong Kong. By comparison, Russia notably aims to preserve its current institutional influence globally and largely supports the international institutions created after World War II. In this sense, it is more of a 'status quo power' within the UNSC and within the multilateral global order. Clearly, several powers on the international level—including Brazil and India—are increasing in economic importance, but their influence is not yet reflected fully in current patterns of global governance. The EU, due to Brexit, loses one member holding a permanent seat and may well aim to increase its role again within the UNSC.

The outbreak of the COVID-19 pandemic has demonstrated how a global health crisis can lead to explicitly national-oriented measures, including the closing of geographical borders of several affected states. The crisis has rendered pressures on multilateral governance highly visible, on the regional as well as the global levels. Nonetheless, given the scale of many threats and challenges globally, multilateral, rule-based governance still seems the only way to effectively provide international 'common goods,' including human wellbeing, environmental protection and global as well as regional peace and stability.

Many national-level Ministries of Foreign Affairs are embedded into structures of regional as well as global cooperation. For example, they actively participate in UN-related institutions and activities, while simultaneously being a member of their own regional integration schemes. This is true for the many states embedded in the African Union (AU) as a regional governance structure, but also for member states of MERCOSUR or of the EU. It seems there can be valuable synergies between operations within a regional integration scheme and governance on the global level, within international institutions, including the United Nations and its various specialized agencies, programmes and funds. Many member state delegates are trained to defend their states' interests in global fora such as the United Nations General Assembly (UNGA), while operating in partially comparable ways within their own regional integration scheme.

In recent years, many international and regional organizations have been faced with what seems to be a 'crisis of legitimacy.' While trust of citizens even within older democracies in their own governments seems to be decreasing, so is trust in regional and global institutions. There appears to be a 'crisis of multilateralism,' reinforced by populist and nationalistic tendencies (e.g. see Moreland, 2019), a prominent example being the attitude of the Trump administration in the United States towards international institutions and multilateral governance (Gowan, 2018), which was partially reversed by the Biden administration. However, other large powers in the current global system are, similarly, partially working against current ways of multilateral global governance; Russia, for example, has been in breach of international legal agreements and China appears to circumvent global multilateral governance by creating new, 'quasi-multilateral' institutions, with the aim to actively refine multilateralism in accordance with its own priorities.

Despite such trends, many regional and global challenges can simply not be addressed in effective ways without encompassing international governance, as they naturally transcend borders. This is true for challenges to the environment in terms of cross-border emissions and pollution as much as for problems related to the maintenance of a rules-based system for global trade.

This book provides an overview of different organizations within the current system of global governance, addressing challenges they are facing in terms of pressures on multilateralism, and the opportunities to still effectively use such channels to solve common threats. The title *The Future of Multilateralism* reflects the contents of the book: the various chapters focus on pressures on—and opportunities provided by—multilateral governance.

The first part of the book deals with international organizations. We discuss pressures on the UN itself, but also on some of its specialized agencies, programmes and funds.

Chapter 1, by Madeleine O. Hosli, focuses on the United Nations, its specialized agencies, programmes, funds and related entities and discusses how the organization aims to address recent challenges to multilateral governance. Pressures on funding, combined with nationalistic tendencies in several of its member states, are complicating the operations of the organization. The COVID-19 pandemic, moreover, risks delaying the implementation of the SDGs. The chapter discusses how the UN deals with such challenges and still preserves the 'principle of multilateralism' as a core element of global governance. It explicates how various entities within the United Nations system cope with the dual challenge of pressures on multilateralism and the effects of the COVID-19 pandemic, while their very role is quintessential to solving the problems and complications caused by the pandemic.

Dimitra Protopsalti, in chapter 2, focuses on humanitarian aspects regarding the future of multilateralism. As is the case in conflict situations, in the middle of a global crisis such as the one caused by the COVID-19 pandemic, women and children constitute potentially highly vulnerable groups, not least in view of increases in cases of domestic violence. The chapter explores two UN entities that are directly affected by such trends: UNICEF and UN

Women. It is explicated how these two organizations, embedded into the United Nations system, respond to the current crisis and possible future approaches regarding the provision of humanitarian assistance and support in situations of crisis and conflict are presented.

Chapter 3 of this book, written by Yue Han, discusses the role of the WHO in view of the 'crisis of multilateralism' and notably, the COVID-19 pandemic. It explores the role of the organization within the global system of governance and the ways in which it copes, as a multilateral institution, with global public health emergencies. Being based on multilateral governance as a core principle, while serving the international community with expert advice, the WHO as a specialized agency of the United Nations plays a core role in the governance of global health. It has been criticized by some actors as 'biased,' but is of core importance to combat the current crisis.

Chapter 4, by Morgane De Clercq, focuses on the WTO as a multilateral institution within the global governance structure that has been highly affected by recent nationalistic trends. For example, the pressures on its dispute settlement mechanism (DSM)—core to the organization's functioning—reflect challenges to patterns of multilateral governance that were cherished by member states over a time span of several decades.[6] The chapter also deals with problems related to free riding, clashing perspectives between developing and developed states, new trade agreements, dynamics of two-level games and bilateral compared to multilateral patterns of member state engagement.

Finally, the last chapter within Part I of the book—chapter 5, by Nicolas Verbeek—deals with the future of the International Monetary Fund (IMF) and of the World Bank. It discusses challenges to multilateralism in view of changing global power relations, globalization, international crises as well as shifting power constellations, such as the rise of China and the gradual economic strengthening of African states within the global system of governance.

Part II of the book focuses on regional institutions and organizations in the context of global governance.

The focus of chapter 6, by Nandi Makubalo, is on the AU. Of notable interest is how the organization interacts with the global level of governance, including the UN and how it aligns its activities with this preeminent global governance institution in the face of crises and challenges to peace and security in its member states. The chapter explores how, in view of recent developments, including the COVID-19 pandemic, the AU may still be able to work, in cooperation with the United Nations, to strengthen multilateralism and to—directly or indirectly—achieve the SDGs.

Chapter 7, by Sonja Niedecken, discusses the future of EU foreign policy and external relations. It demonstrates how EU development aid, partnerships, humanitarian aid and EU diplomacy have developed in recent years and how they are likely to further develop in the future, given recent trends within the EU and challenges as well as opportunities related to multilateralism. Clearly, the EU is a regional integration scheme based on, and advocating, multilateralism. But how does the organization deal with recent pressures?

Chapter 8, by Carolina D'Ambrosio, discusses the economic and financial consequences of the COVID-19 crisis on the multilateral relations of EU member states. Specifically, it addresses the suspension of the Growth and Stability Pact (GSP), and the possible reactions by the European Commission in order to sustain southern European states (i.e. the European instrument for temporary Support to Mitigate Unemployment Risks in an Emergency, SURE, or any further financial instrument that may be developed). The reaction of EU institutions will be of crucial importance for the future of multilateralism among the EU's member states: the formation of two opposed blocs appears to develop—northern European versus southern European states. These blocs differ strongly on the fiscal-economic approaches to be undertaken to face the economic recession likely to result from the crisis. The chapter further asks how economic choices may impact the future of the EU in the next five to ten years and which financial scheme, created based on multilateral agreement, is likely to prevail.

Chapter 9, by Rizwan Togoo, focuses on the ASEAN, which has turned into an important player in the Asia-Pacific region. It discusses how ASEAN, however, faces challenges in terms of legitimacy, notably due to power shifts in the region and the organization's response to the Rohingya humanitarian crisis.

Amber Schoele, in chapter 10, turns to the Latin American context. The chapter explores how a Latin American integration scheme—MERCOSUR—operates in view of challenges to global governance and to multilateralism. It looks into the ways the organization has been set up and operates at the moment and reflects on how the COVID-19 pandemic might affect the organization's capacity to deal with challenges on the regional level.

The last part of the book focuses on a selection of other multilateral organizations and regimes, offering insights into case studies on the AIIB, multilateral development cooperation and the UN climate regime, respectively.

Chapter 11, by Taylor Garrett, focuses on the future of global multilateral leadership by looking at the potential of China and the AIIB. Due to the withdrawal of the United States from multilateral leadership positions and other trends, opportunities for other states to lead global collaboration efforts through multilateral institutions opened up. Discussing Chinese leadership, the Belt and Road initiative, non-western led multilateralism, and shifting global dynamics, the chapter focuses on the role of the AIIB in the context of the global multilateral shift.

In chapter 12, Gulnara Abbas discusses patterns of global development cooperation. She analyses institutional structures and shifts in policies over time, while also addressing potential effects of the COVID-19 pandemic on development cooperation and foreign aid. The chapter emphasizes the need to implement partnerships, allowing for balanced patterns of collaboration between donors and receivers of development aid.

Chapter 13, by Juliana Cubillos, Frederik Heitmüller and Irma Mosquera Valderrama, deals with patterns of multilateral governance in international tax law. The authors show how multilateral cooperation in international tax law has developed notably since the 2008 financial crisis and how international tax standards have been introduced by OECD and non-OECD countries to tackle challenges such as tax evasion, harmful tax competition and aggressive tax planning. The authors address the standards focusing on the interaction between different international and supranational organizations (mainly at the EU level) in this process.

Finally, chapter 14 turns to the institutionalization of global efforts to combat climate change, as an example of multilateral environmental cooperation. Susann Handke, in this chapter, examines the prospects of the 2015 Paris Agreement and the decisions of the 2018 Katowice Rulebook for fostering multilateral climate cooperation. The chapter argues that the UN climate regime is equipped with tools and an interactional space that, if used wisely, can facilitate a multilateral process and attend to several layers of governance.

While the current system of global governance encompasses many more institutions and multilateralism is core to many other (regional) organizations and actors, with the selection of organizations analysed, this book aims to provide insights into how multilateral governance works at present and how it might develop in the future, given challenges and opportunities arising from recent trends. Each chapter provides a brief overview of the organization or regime focused on, demonstrates how it operates within current structures of multilateral governance, and addresses ongoing and potential new challenges it faces, including those emanating from the COVID-19 pandemic. Moreover, the chapters focus on potential future avenues and ways forward for the organization or regime to counter respective pressures, offering insights into 'The Future of Multilateralism.'

We hope the volume might provide valuable insights into current challenges to multilateral governance, the ways various organizations deal with them and some 'food for thought' as to how multilateralism may be preserved as a valuable tool of global governance. Multilateralism may be challenged—and evolving—but it clearly serves a quintessential role in terms of combatting collective global problems and supporting efforts to maintain peace, human wellbeing and the preservation of global and regional stability.

NOTES

1. The IMF and the World Bank Group—consisting of the International Bank for Reconstruction and Development (IBRD), the International Development Association (IDA) and the International Finance Corporation (IFC)—are specialized agencies of the UN. The WTO is a 'related organization' of the United Nations. On this, please see the chapter by Nicolas Verbeek in this volume.

2. On the EU and the strategy of effective multilateralism, for example, see Kissack (2010), Bouchard et al. (2013) and Drieskens and Schaik (2018).

3. For classic work on collective goods provision, see Olson (1965); on institutional arrangements to protect them, see Ostrom (1990).

4. The role of the WHO and related tensions in global politics are addressed in the chapter by Yue Han in this volume.

5. On shifts in global power relations and multilateralism, see Jørgensen (2013).

6. For example, see Ikenberry (2015).

REFERENCES

Bouchard, Caroline, John Peterson and Nathalie Tocci (eds.). (2013). *Multilateralism in the 21st Century: Europe's Quest for Effectiveness*. London: Routledge.

Drieskens, Edith and Louise G. van Schaik (eds.). (2018). *The EU and Effective Multilateralism: Internal and External Reform Practices*. London: Routledge.

Goetz, Klaus H. and Ronny Patz. (2017). Resourcing International Organizations: Resource Diversification, Organizational Differentiation, and Administrative Governance. *Global Policy*, 8(S5), 5–14.

Gowan, Richard. (2018). Multilateralism in Freefall? New York: United Nations University Centre for Policy Research (CPR). Available at https://cpr.unu.edu/the-multilateral-freefall.html.

Ikenberry, G. John. (2015). The Future of Multilateralism: Governing the World in a Post-Hegemonic Era. *Japanese Journal of Political Science*, 16(3), 399–413.

Jacobson, Harold K. (1984). *Networks of Interdependence: International Organizations and the Global Political System*. 2nd edition. New York: Knopf.

Jørgensen, Knud Erik. (2013). 'Prospects for Multipolarity and Multilateralism in World Politics,' in Thomas Christiansen, Emil Kirchner and Philomena Murray (eds.), *The Palgrave Handbook of EU-Asia Relations*, 45–58. Basingstoke: Palgrave Macmillan

Keohane, Robert O. (1990). Multilateralism: An Agenda for Research. *International Journal*, 45(4), 731–764.

Kissack, Robert. (2010). *Pursuing Effective Multilateralism: The European Union, International Organisations and the Politics of Decision Making*. Basingstoke: Palgrave MacMillan

Lavelle, Kathryn C. (2020). *The Challenges of Multilateralism*. New Haven: Yale University Press.

xxii   *Madeleine O. Hosli*

Olson, Mancur. (1965). *The Logic of Collective Action: Public Goods and the Theory of Groups*. Cambridge, MA: Harvard University Press.
Ostrom, Elinor. (1990). *Governing the Commons: The Evolution of Institutions for Collective Action*. Cambridge: Cambridge University Press.
Moreland, Will. (2019). *The Purpose of Multilateralism: A Framework for Democracies in a Geopolitically Competitive World*. Washington, DC: Brookings Institution.
Muldoon, James P. Jr., JoAnn Aviel, Richard Reitano and Earl Sullivan (eds.). (2010). *The New Dynamics of Multilateralism: Diplomacy, International Organizations, and Global Governance*. London: Taylor & Francis.
Panke, Diana, Stefan Lang and Anke Wiedemann. (2019). *Regional Actors in Multilateral Negotiations*. Lanham, MD: Rowman & Littlefield.
Ruggie, John Gerard. (1992). Multilateralism: The Anatomy of an Institution. *International Organization*, 46(3), 561–598.
Ruggie, John Gerard. (1993). 'Multilateralism: The Anatomy of an Institution,' in John Gerard Ruggie (ed.), *Multilateralism Matters: The Theory and Practice of an Institutional Form*. New York: Columbia University Press.
Shanks, Cheryl, Harold K. Jacobson and Jeffrey H. Kaplan. (1996). Inertia and Change in the Constellation of International Governmental Organizations, 1981–1992. *International Organization*, 50(4), 593–627.

Abbreviations

AAA	Accra Agenda for Action
ACDEG	African Charter on Democracy, Elections and Governance
ADB	African Development Bank
ADB	Asian Development Bank
AfCFTA	African Continental Free Trade Area
AICHR	ASEAN Intergovernmental Commission on Human Rights
AIIB	Asian Infrastructure Investment Bank
AMIS	African Union Mission in Sudan
AMISOM	African Union Mission in Somalia
APRM	African Peer-Review Mechanism
APSA	AU Peace and Security Architecture
ASA	Association of Southeast Asia
ASEAN	Association of Southeast Asian Nations
AU	African Union
AUDA	African Union Development Agency
BEPS	Base Erosion and Profit Shifting
BRIC	Brazil, Russia, India, and China
BRICS	Brazil, Russia, India, China, and South Africa
CCM	Council of the Common Market
CJEU	Court of Justice of the European Union
CSO	Civil Society Organisation
DDG	Deputy Director-General
DG DEVCO	Directorate General for International Cooperation and Development
DG ECHO	Directorate General for European Civil Protection and Humanitarian Aid Operations
DG NEAR	Directorate General for Neighbourhood and Enlargement

DG Trade	Directorate General for Trade
DSA	Debt Sustainability Analysis
DSB	Dispute Settlement Body
DSDG	Division for Sustainable Development Goals
DSU	Dispute Settlement Understanding
EB	Executive Board
ECB	European Central Bank
ECOFIN	Economic and Financial Affairs Council
ECOSOC	Economic and Social Council
EEAS	European External Actions Service
EIB	European Investment Bank
EMU	European Monetary Union
ERCC	Emergency Response Coordination Centre
ESF	Environmental and Social Framework
ESM	European Stability Mechanism
EU	European Union
FAO	Food and Agriculture Organization
FCTC	Framework Convention on Tobacco Control
GATT	General Agreement on Tariffs and Trade
GCM	Global Compact for Safe, Orderly and Regular Migration
GLoBE	Global Anti-base Erosion
GPEDC	Global Partnership for Effective Development Cooperation
GSP	Growth and Stability Pact
G20	Group of Twenty
G7	Group of Seven
HL	Humanitarian Logistics
HLF4	4th High level Forum on Aid Effectiveness
HLPF	High-Level Political Forum on Sustainable Development
HSC	Humanitarian Supply Chain
IADB	Inter-American Development Bank
ICSU	International Council for Science
ICT	information and Communications Technology
IDA	International Development Association
IFC	International Finance Corporation
IFI	International Financial Institutions
IHC	International Health Conference
IHR	International Health Regulation
ILO	International Labour Organization
IMF	International Monetary Fund
IMST	Incident Management Support Team
IOAC	Independent Oversight and Advisory Committee
IPR	Intellectual Property Rights

ISSC	International Social Science Council
ITO	International Trade Organisation
LDC	Least developed country
LIC	Low-Income Country
MDB	Multilateral Development Bank
MDG	Millennium Development Goal
Mercosur	Southern Common Market *Mercado Común del Sur*
MFN	Most Favoured Nation
MNE	Multinational enterprise
MPIA	Multi-Party Interim Appeal Arbitration Arrangement
MS	Member States
MIC	Middle-Income Country
MSF	Médecins Sans Frontières
MSME	Micro, Small and Medium Enterprises
MSP	Multi-Stakeholder Partnership
NAM	Non-Aligned Movement
NATO	North Atlantic Treaty Organization
NDB	New Development Bank
NDC	Nationally Determined Contribution
OAU	Organisation for African Unity
ODA	Official Development Assistance
OECD	Organization for Economic and Social Development
OHCHR	Office of the United Nations High Commissioner of Human Rights
OIC	Organization of Islamic Cooperation
PAHO	Pan American Health Organization
PCD	Policy coherence for development
PD	Paris Declaration
PHC	Primary Health Care
PHEIC	Public Health Emergency of International Concern
PPI	Policy on Public Information
PTA	Preferential Trade Agreement
QMV	Qualified Majority Voting
R2P	Responsibility to Protect
SAA	Stabilisation and Association Agreements
SCO	Shanghai Cooperation Organization
SADC	Southern African Development Community
SDG	Sustainable Development Goal
SDR	Special Drawing Right
SDT	Special and Differential Treatment
SEAFET	Southeast Asia Friendship and Economic Treaty
TAC	Treaty of Amity and Cooperation in Southeast Asia

TFEU	Treaty on the Functioning of the European Union
TIFA	Trade and Investment Framework Agreement
UN	United Nations
UNDESA	United Nations Department of Economic and Social Affairs
UNDP	United Nations Development Programme
UNFCCC	UN Framework Convention on Climate Change
UNGA	United Nations General Assembly
UNESCO	United Nations Educational, Scientific and Cultural Organization
UNHCR	Office of the United Nations High Commissioner for Refugees
UNICEF	United Nations International Children's Emergency Fund
UNOAU	United Nations Office to the African Union
UNOCHA	United Nations Office for the Coordination of Humanitarian Affairs
UNSC	United Nations Security Council
UN Women	United Nations Entity for Gender Equality and the Empowerment of Women
VNR	Voluntary National Review
WB	World Bank
WTO	World Trade Organization
WHA	World Health Assembly
WHO	World Health Organization

Part I

INTERNATIONAL ORGANIZATIONS

Chapter 1

The United Nations and Challenges to Multilateralism

Madeleine O. Hosli

1. INTRODUCTION

The United Nations (UN), based on the principle of 'one state one vote' as its decision-making principle in the General Assembly (UNGA), is a core example of a truly international organization, fully based on patterns of multilateralism. The United Nations Security Council (UNSC) uses a different principle, where the winning nations at the end of World War II essentially gained a permanent seat as powerful members of the global community that could safeguard international peace and security.[1] But both can be seen as reflections of a 'multilateral global governance system', dealing with important challenges from an international perspective. They are cornerstones of the post–World War II multilateral system.

At the end of the nineteenth and in the beginning of the twentieth century, based on various negotiations and agreements between states, the foundations have been laid for a global governance system that would regulate areas such as trade, finance, shipping and communication (Ikenberry, 2015, p. 403).[2] After the end of World War I, the first global intergovernmental organization resembling the UN was created: The League of Nations. But after some early successes, the organization turned out to be unable to face the political pressures emanating from power politics and to prevent the aggression and developments that ultimately led to the start of World War II.

It was only in 1945, at the end of World War II—after a period of aggression, destruction and a true collapse of the multilateral system of governance—that the UN was established as an international intergovernmental organization. The UN began its operations in October 1945. The organization was explicitly set up to 'save succeeding generations from the scourge of war' (Preamble, United Nations Charter).

Over time, the organization has grown significantly, not only in terms of member states (MS) but also as regards the number of specialized agencies, programmes and funds it encompasses. Among the UN's specialized agencies today are the Food and Agriculture Organization (FAO), the International Labour Organization (ILO), the International Monetary Fund (IMF), the International Telecommunications Union (ITU), the United Nations Educational, Scientific and Cultural Organization (UNESCO), the World Health Organization (WHO), the Universal Postal Union (UPU) and the International Bank for Reconstruction and Development (IBRD). Among its funds and programmes are the United Nations Development Programme (UNDP), the United Nations Environment Programme (UNEP), the United Nations Human Settlements Program (UN-HABITAT) and the United Nations International Children's Emergency Fund (UNICEF). Other entities (linked to the UNGA) are the Office of the United Nations High Commissioner for Refugees (UNHCR) and the United Nations Entity for Gender Equality and the Empowerment of Women (UN-Women).[3]

Many of the specialized agencies, programmes and funds face similar challenges as regards ensuring a sound financial basis for its operations and respective challenges to multilateral governance. This is true as much for UNICEF, focusing on the wellbeing and rights of children as it is for UNHCR, supporting refugees and vulnerable persons globally.[4] Clearly, each of the United Nation's specialized agencies and programmes works fully based on the principle of multilateralism, in terms of decision-making and membership composition. But simultaneously, pressures on multilateralism can imply that the respective specialized agency or programme faces challenges as regards funding, rendering it more dependent on the preferences and priorities of state actors and donors in times of lower financial contributions to the organization. Without a doubt, the recent outbreak of the COVID-19 pandemic has strongly influenced the agendas and activities of essentially all entities incorporated into the UN system. Due to delays in membership contributions, some institutions and agencies have increasingly engaged in obtaining funding from non-state sources, including from businesses and philanthropic organizations. While this enhances the funding base, it moves the organizations away from activities led and supported by a state-based intergovernmental system.

The UN as an entity is nonetheless dependent on the support of its member states, not least in financial terms. Some larger actors within the UN are steady and stable contributors to its budget, among them the member states of the European Union (EU). Similarly, important contributions to the UN budget are paid by large or financially powerful member states such as the United States, China and Japan. Other member states, by comparison, are strongly involved in sending troops for UN peace missions, making them important actors in the global maintenance of peace and security, including outside the more institutionalized frameworks of the UNSC and the UNGA. Among the top troop contributing countries (TCCs) in spring 2020—in terms of troop and police contributions—were Ethiopia, Bangladesh, Rwanda, Nepal, India and Pakistan.[5] Accordingly, member states can be of core relevance to the UN, either in terms of general financial contributions or support specifically to peace missions, based on actual troops sent to the organization.

In recent years, enhanced efforts have been made to 'reform' the UN, not least by moving back more clearly to the concept of 'one UN'. This development aims to avoid fractionalization and the building of 'small empires' within the—by now large—UN system. It was originally initiated in a 2005 report on the initiative of the then United Nations Secretary-General Kofi Annan, titled 'Delivering as one', aiming to more closely align the UN's activities in areas such as development, humanitarian aid and environmental protection (e.g. see UNGA resolution A/RES/60/1). But it is similarly a high priority—not least in financial terms—of Antonio Gutierrez, United Nations Secretary-General since January 2017.

While the UN itself is in a process of reform and dependent on financial and other support by its member states, it is a core example of an international governance institution and the practice of multilateralism across its system. However, challenges to the latter, including nationalistic tendencies in several of its member states, put pressures on the organization, to the point of rendering the work of its specialized agencies and programmes highly challenging in practice.

The COVID-19 pandemic has put new pressures on the UN as an organization. Not only did the UN itself need to switch to online communication among most of its staff and hold meetings of, for example, the UNSC and the various committees of the UNGA in digital formats, but the pandemic has similarly created additional strains for the work of several of its specialized agencies, programmes and funds.

For example, the UNHCR, while already needing to be creative as regards funding opportunities in the past, had to generate additional means to fund its programmes, given the consistently high need to protect refugees, migrants and people of concern, not least in war zones. But the COVID-19 pandemic creates additional dangers for the affected communities, and for UN staff serving in these organizations. With this, the pandemic puts severe additional burdens on these UN entities (while a programme such as the UNHCR already has a full job and programme of activities to combat the worst challenges facing the groups it aims to protect).[6] The pandemic has complicated logistics and the organization of respective missions, further increasing the workload and pressure on its employees in the field.

Similarly, UNICEF, focused on the rights and wellbeing of children, is affected by the pandemic: the crisis deteriorates the situation of children due

to lockdowns, enhanced risks of violence, the geographical spread of the illness and related economic hardship. Such trends further complicate the work
of UN officials serving in the organization, while their work is needed more
than ever in view of the pandemic. Clearly, the COVID-19 crisis, in addition
to this, risks delaying the implementation of the SDGs, which will affect children as well as vulnerable groups more generally.[7] The pandemic and related
lockdowns risk excluding disadvantaged children from education, meals provided at schools and other schemes supporting their situation.

Many of the SDGs will risk delayed implementation due to the effects of
the pandemic. For example, SDG 1 ('no poverty') will be more difficult to
attain if several segments of the population in underdeveloped areas of the
world are unable to work, earn some kind of income and secure a living.
Implementation of the goal is also complicated by the additional pressures
international organizations are facing due to COVID-19, including the UNDP,
which experiences several new challenges to its work aimed at increasing
perspectives for development and human wellbeing. Similarly, SDG 2 ('zero
hunger') is more difficult to attain, as the pandemic complicates the situation
of countries already affected by, for example, malnutrition. Economic pressures due to lockdowns will make it difficult for vulnerable groups, including
migrants and illegal workers, to secure a living in several countries across the
world. The pandemic, moreover, can endanger food security, which further
complicates attainment of SDG 2.

Clearly, SDG 3 ('good health and well-being') is a goal directly endangered by the pandemic. Healthy lives are difficult to achieve in view of the
many threats related to the effects of COVID-19, notably in areas where
adequate health systems and medical facilities are weakly developed. Similarly, implementation of SDG 4 ('quality education') is bound to suffer from
pressures related to COVID-19: many schools across the globe have closed
temporarily in the wake of lockdowns, leading to delays in education and
enhancing the risk that vulnerable segments of society will be unable to
obtain education: For children living in poverty, online alternatives to education are often impossible, as there is a lack of adequate (online) infrastructure
and no means available for many to attend education remotely. Clearly, SDG
8 ('decent work and economic growth') will be severely endangered by the
economic recession the pandemic is likely to generate. Economic pressures
and financial hardship will probably lead to considerable delays in the implementation of SDG 8.

These are just some examples of how the pandemic may enhance pressures
on the UN to act and how implementation of the SDGs is likely to be delayed
by the various effects of COVID-19.

Accordingly, pressures on multilateralism, amplified by the COVID-19
pandemic, put challenges to the UN as an organization, which is, in turn,

desperately needed to act in the global common interest and safeguard the situation of vulnerable people across the globe. This chapter will deal with such challenges, first reflecting on the UN, multilateralism and changing global power structures (section 2), then moving on to how the COVID-19 pandemic may create additional pressures for multilateral organizations (section 3). Section 4 reflects about possible ways forward in view of current pressures and section 5 offers final reflections and concludes the chapter.

2. MULTILATERALISM AND CHANGING GLOBAL POWER STRUCTURES

Since its establishment at the end of World War II, the UN as an organization has always had to adapt to changing global realities and power structures. Conversely, when it was created, it reflected the power structures at the time in its institutional setup; this can notably be seen in the composition of the UNSC, where the 'P-5' (currently France, the UK, the United States, China and Russia) hold a permanent seat.

The United Nation's first decades were strongly characterized by the East-West division that split the globe into pro-Western and communist entities. Clearly, debates in the UNGA reflected this division; it constituted the major 'dimension of contestation' within the organization (e.g. see O'Neill, 1996). In essence, many resolutions discussed within the UNGA reflected the tensions between the 'Western' and the 'communist' world for decades; this included resolutions related to international security, disarmament and those focused on the Middle East.[8]

Similarly, the UNSC has been characterized by stalemates between the 'East' and the 'West' for several decades,[9] slowing down or hampering decisions on peace missions where rivalries between the communist and the 'Western' world were at stake. A short phase of revival, however, seemed to materialize after the fall of the Berlin Wall in 1989. This time span appeared to provide a strong new impetus for the UNSC's ability to interfere and to establish peace missions in various conflict areas, based on gradually stronger mandates. It seemed like the breakdown of the 'old' East-West division would allow the organization to start a new, intensified phase of action in which the UNSC could truly act to uphold its mandate to maintain international peace and stability.

But unfortunately, this new phase of revival soon turned again into a more confrontational mode—for example, splitting Russia from the European UNSC members as well as the United States after the annexation of the Crimea in 2014. This reinforced stronger, underlying divisions between mainland China and Russia on the one hand, and the other UNSC members on the other. The 'stalemate' over Syria in recent years, and similarly over Yemen, are examples of this impasse, where the organization seemed paralyzed and unable to intervene in the sense of upholding the organization's mandate to secure peace and defend human rights—largely due to 'power politics' at the highest international level.

Similarly, over the course of several decades, the UNGA has been characterized by the process of decolonization. Leading to the establishment of large entities working for the concerns of the 'developing world', the G-77 was created in 1964, as were other large groups within the UNGA, such as the Non-Aligned Movement (NAM) in 1961. While this division seemed to determine the dynamics somewhat less within the UNSC, it was clearly dominant within the UNGA.

Hence, both the operations of the UNSC and of the UNGA were affected by changing global power structures and dynamics. Their agendas often reflected these changes—an example being the many UNGA resolutions focused on topics related to decolonization. In this sense, the UN and its various entities largely constituted a 'mirror' of global politics.

In the more recent past, a confrontational attitude and partial withdrawal of a larger member from the organization, not least in terms of funding, posed additional challenges to the United Nation's explicit modus operandi as a multilateral, international organization: The Trump administration in the United States acted as a force against multilateralism,[10] by withdrawing funding and support from respective entities, in contrast to earlier phases where the United States was strongly involved in the establishment of core principles underlying the work of the UN. Examples of the latter are the role of the United States in the issuing of the Declaration of Human Rights in 1948 and the establishment of various specialized agencies and programmes working alongside the UN to maintain global stability, including the IMF and the World Bank (WB; see the chapter by Nicolas Verbeek in this book) and the World Trade Organization (WTO; see the chapter by Morgane De Clercq). Without a doubt, the attitude of the Trump administration has had repercussions for the United Nation's reputational legitimacy and accountability on the global level, although the organization has gone through difficult times before—including the Cold War period—and has been remarkably resilient to respective pressures.

With the distancing of main founding powers of the UN from the organization itself, alongside shifts in global economic relations, actors in Asia—most notably China—have gradually gained power and influence. While China remains within the UNSC as a permanent member, it has established other ways of acting that circumvent the 'traditional', Western-led principle of multilateralism; the AIIB is an example of this (see the chapter by Taylor Garrett in this book). Similarly, the Shanghai Cooperation Organization

(SCO), with Russia and China as crucial actors, demonstrates the ties of affinity in this area (in spite of old animosities) and the gradual development of 'alternative centres of power' globally.[11] The SCO aims to strengthen the economic and security ties among its members and has China as an active, core member of the organization. There is little doubt that an initiative such as the Chinese Belt and Road Initiative may further enhance such structures, based on economic investment and development potential that also affects political realities. Maybe the global community, with such changing global power structures, gradually moves into some kind of 'competitive multi-lateralism' (e.g. see Moreland, 2019). Clearly, emerging powers—next to China and potentially Russia, India, Brazil and South Africa as well as other quickly growing states on the international scale—need to be incorporated into a (new) global governance structure, more adequately reflecting current influence in global politics (e.g. Ikenberry, 2015). However, these powers are nonetheless often represented in fora such as the UNSC, albeit as non-permanent members, based on elections by the UNGA for a two-year time span.[12] Largely due to a sense of insufficient representation in international organizations given their actual political weight, the BRICS has been created as a group advancing similar priorities on the global scale. This is also true for other multilateral patterns of collaboration operating outside the formal UN framework—including the G-20—partially strengthening a perception that the UN itself might have reached the limits of global multilateral coordination. However, it is also true that such groups tend to have strong ties with the UN itself, in this sense rather adding to, instead of replacing, its role.

Despite various challenges to the UN, however, the organization enjoys the support of its member states in many different forms. Several of them are strongly upholding the principle of multilateral rules-based governance and patterns of international, collective decision-making, in spite of nationalistic, inward-looking trends in political terms in a variety of UN member states. Clearly, the members of the EU, for example, as collectively strong financial contributors to the organization, are themselves embedded into 'multilateral-ism' as a regional governance principle. Japan as a significant (financial) power for the organization upholds its values and norms explicitly and the African Union (AU) is based on strong links to the overarching goals of the UN (see the chapter by Nandi Makubalo in this book). Despite criticism tar-geting the organization or multilateralism, de facto, many UN member states strongly support its overarching norms, principles and modes of operation.

Nonetheless, the organization and its various entities are clearly affected by changing global power structures. To a certain extent, this is a logical con-sequence of the ways in which the organization has been set up and operates. While formal change, such as UNSC reform, is almost impossible to achieve due to institutional constraints—notably the required decision-making hurdles to alter its composition—in more informal ways, global emerging powers have increasingly gained a stronger 'voice'. This is true, for example, for debates within the UNGA and its committees as well as informal exchanges between permanent and non-permanent members within the UNSC.

3. THE COVID-19 PANDEMIC AND CHALLENGES TO MULTILATERALISM

The outbreak of the COVID-19 crisis in early 2020 has demonstrated how vulnerable multilateral structures can be, on the global as well as the regional levels, to new pressures (see the chapters by Carolina d'Ambrosio and Sonja Niedecken on the European Union in this book, the chapter by Rizwan Togoo on ASEAN and the chapter by Amber Scheele on Mercosur, respectively). Even within a highly integrated regional integration scheme such as the EU, efforts—at least in the beginning of the COVID-19 pandemic—seemed to be fully focused on domestic environments; border closings further demonstrated the tendency to nationalism. This has put severe pressures on the EU as an organization, which was only gradually able to respond and develop common answers, based on initiatives by the European Commission and related intergovernmental agreements. But the EU is only one of the regional organizations in which such tendencies and challenges to possible multilaterally agreed solutions were felt. Similarly, in other parts of the world, the almost 'instinctive reaction' to close borders and care for the own citizens first was clearly visible (e.g. in Latin America and on the African continent), while a pandemic 'does not respect borders' and would probably best be tackled by swift collective decision-making and activities based on multilateral action.

With the UN, as well as many regional organizations, having to conduct meetings at the highest political levels online, patterns of decision-making have changed. For example, the UNGA has met digitally as a response to the outbreak of the pandemic, changing the patterns of informal networking that usually characterizes meetings at the highest levels of the organization. Similarly, for the first time in history, the 75th Session of the UNGA did not take place 'live', but was largely conduced online. Generally, the severity of the crisis in New York has jeopardized the usual patterns of work of the organization, enhancing the need for a quick shift to digital negotiations and decision-making. It remains to be seen how the shift to 'digital' will affect the modus operandi of the organization in a medium-term perspective and how it may affect negotiations and decision-making, not least within the UNGA and the UNSC. It might well be that in the future, even when the COVID-19 pandemic has come to an end, digital ways of interaction, replacing a variety of face-to-face meetings, might be preserved. The advantage of this could be efficiency gains, for example, due to lower international travel costs and a lower related 'carbon footprint'; but it could also imply that delegations from countries with sound and stable internet connections and more of a habit to work digitally could have an advantage in the framework of multilateral negotiations over those less used to online communication or with less developed digital infrastructures, enhancing a potential 'digital divide' not least in international diplomacy.

Pressures on multilateralism, in the wake of the pandemic, could probably most clearly be seen with the U.S. administration's spring 2020 threat to withdraw its funding for the WHO—the UN specialized agency dealing at the forefront with the prevention of global diseases and pandemics (see the chapter by Yue Han in this book). The threat even implied a potential withdrawal of the United States as a member from the WHO altogether. Whether such measures would be feasible in practice—as this would, in essence, imply a redirection of funds approved by U.S. Congress—remained to be seen. But the leading rationale for the administration to consider such drastic steps was a sense that the organization might be 'biased' in favour of China; the accusation entails that China has not correctly transmitted information and figures on the crisis when the COVID-19 outbreak started. In a sense, this is again a repercussion of potential 'changing global power structures' that find their reflection in the ways multilateral governance works and international organizations operate (or are perceived to operate).

Quite serious are the pressures that are likely to emanate from the economic slump which will follow the COVID-19 pandemic. The seriousness of the economic recession is yet to be seen, but it will definitely lead to enhanced pressures on the finances of the United Nation's member states and with that, their ability and willingness to support the organization and its various entities. This is true for the global level, reflected in the operation of the UN system, but also on regional levels, including at the one of the EU.

Hence, while complicating the operation of the WHO, but also of programmes and entities such as UNICEF, UNHCR or UN Women, the pandemic aggravates the situation for the most vulnerable groups globally, while it takes away the capacity of member states to fund these very institutions. In this sense, the pressure on multilateralism is 'double'. Similarly, the pandemic risks affecting the financial and reputational capacities of these organizations, while their actions are needed more than ever to combat the worst effects the situation has generated.

Resilience and robustness of the institutions will probably make them get through the crisis, but the effects of the pandemic, in economic and financial terms, are likely to continue in the years to come. The potential effects range from decreased financial contributions to—and partially related to this—lower trust in their operations and activities. Innovation and new financial support structures, not least via contributions by large businesses and other entities globally, could constitute ways out of the enhanced challenges generated.

4. POSSIBLE WAYS FORWARD

Pressures on multilateralism that were already existing, combined with the effects of the COVID-19 pandemic, are likely to strengthen nationalistic—and populist—trends on a global scale, as there will be more strains on financial resources. But the UN and its specialized agencies, programmes and funds tend to be 'resilient', as they have already survived major geopolitical shifts and political tensions since they started. It seems states, on a global level, still largely prefer—and defend—a multilateral world order based on rules-based patterns of governance. According to Ikenberry (2015: 400), states still have deep (and growing) interests in an international order which is open and 'at least loosely rule-based, i.e. a system of multilateral governance'. What will probably be needed, however, is greater creativity to reduce costs (e.g. to possibly shift meetings from live to online also in the years to come, without the need for social distancing complicating the pattern of face-to-face meetings), while expanding the funding bases for these organizations. The COVID-19 pandemic, similarly, puts pressures on the financial wellbeing of companies globally. But a further diversification of funding sources—while avoiding asymmetric dependence on donors—and new approaches to their ways of operation can help international organizations move forward, also in times of pressures on their institutional foundations and multilateral decision-making capacities. This might, however, be paralleled by a gradual shift away from state-based multilateralism to new patterns of collective governance that encompass a wider range of actors.

The pandemic has induced nationalistic trends, but their very existence may also demonstrate clearly that problems facing humanity do not respect borders. In times of pressures on international trade, resorting to domestic policies and closing-off to exports has demonstrated that over time, economic losses are also pertinent to the nation that shields behind protectionism: strengthening the position of domestic producers—while other nations may produce the same product more cost-effectively—is likely to strip the protectionist country of income from trade based on the principle of 'comparative advantage'. Protectionism is 'costly' to its citizens. Early liberal economic thinkers, including Adam Smith and David Riccardo, have shown how the 'invisible hand'—based on constrained government intervention—and the alleviation of restrictions on mutual trade will benefit both an exporting and an importing nation. New barriers to trade and hurdles to international exchange lower the potential benefits of economic interaction, with negative repercussions for consumers and the general wellbeing of the public, also in the country that establishes (economic) barriers. Of course, a pandemic such as COVID-19, however, has led to serious shortages globally of specific goods—including medical appliances needed to treat the illness, such as ventilators—implying that many states started up production of such goods on the domestic level, no matter whether they had a 'comparative advantage' in economic terms concerning the product. The COVID-19 pandemic, moreover, has demonstrated how distrust in a specific government may prevent nations from importing goods produced in that same country, with the reluctance of the United States to rely on Chinese products constituting a clear example of this trend. In this sense, domestic security concerns and trade—as regards production of COVID-19 testing material or medical appliances to treat the illness—are certainly interrelated.

Clearly, protecting the environment and prevention of global warming cannot be achieved without collective action. Effects of environmental degradation cross borders and necessitate efforts and coordination on the international level. Ideally, a pandemic like COVID-19 would, similarly, be tackled by collective endeavours, by common strategies between conglomerates of businesses across borders, by trans-national research endeavours and by shared sources and medical supplies within regional entities or even internationally. In a time of a pandemic as serious as COVID-19, resorting to 'my nation first' strategies can be as harmful as protectionism is to the wellbeing of a nation's own citizens. With an end to the pandemic, it is likely that losses due to nationalism will be displayed more clearly *ex post*. The UN and its specialized agencies, next to global governance institutions such as the WTO, will be strongly needed, in times of changing global power constellations, the threat of populism or nationalism and decreasing funds available to support international organizations and their activities. Accordingly, in the face of a severe crisis, a rules-based, multilateral global governance system may be even more important and pertinent to maintain stability on the global level and ensure the wellbeing of potentially severely affected citizens, compared to more 'regular' phases in global affairs.

5. ADDITIONAL REFLECTIONS AND CONCLUSIONS

This chapter has reflected on how the UN moves forward in view of challenges to multilateralism, caused by, for example, nationalistic tendencies in several of its member states which have only been aggravated by the COVID-19 crisis. As experience teaches us, economic recession—such as the one probably being caused by the pandemic and its consequences—is likely to lead to a further 'my nation first' attitude. It may equally lead to increasing protection of domestic producers and more economic barriers being established towards third countries—in parallel to enhanced hurdles materializing for potential immigration by 'foreigners', as a result of the crisis. In other words, 'inward-looking trends' encompass both economic elements (in terms of protectionism) and political ones (in terms of trends to render immigration more difficult or to actually 'close' borders for citizens with other nationalities). But 'inward-looking' attitudes pose challenges to the international community, which, in turn, is clearly the only one able to provide collective goods on the global level—in a framework of actual 'global governance'. This equally applies to common measures to combat COVID-19 as a serious health policy challenge as well as its effects in economic terms. The challenges do not stop at borders; they are of a genuinely international character. The COVID-19 health crisis has affected some parts of the world more than others—and is likely to further aggravate existing inequalities[13]—but the reach of the crisis is global in scope. It is impossible to combat global challenges on the domestic level and the increased focus of several of the member states of the UN on their own domestic situations and the wellbeing of their own citizens to the detriment of others is likely to worsen the situation for all. Hence, it is crucial to return to patterns of problem-solving on the level of international governance institutions such as the UN. While the need is large, the forces against this are also extensive. More than ever, anti-international, anti-regional trends put 'multilateralism' and its effects in danger, while multilateralism simultaneously seems the only way forward to effectively address the respective challenges (in terms of both the causes and the effects of the crisis). This is a paradox difficult to address; but it does need to be resolved to avoid the worst effects of both 'the crisis of multilateralism' and the crisis generated by COVID-19.

Certainly, each UN specialized agency, programme and fund is affected in different ways by challenges to multilateralism and pressures based on the COVID-19 pandemic. Clearly, WHO is very directly affected in terms of international health policy and respective repercussions; moreover, it is strongly affected by nationalistic and protectionist trends on the level of trade relations and current economic developments. The work of UNDP faces additional challenges in view of increasing inequalities generated by the pandemic, by poverty and economic pressures and ensuing hurdles to development. UNHCR faces an even more threatening situation for refugees and people of concern, as they are among the least protected not least in the framework of a global health crisis. UN Women sees the need of its work increase even further, as COVID-19 has also led to situations in which women, for example, due to increased domestic violence in connection with lockdowns, need additional protection. UNICEF is needed more than ever to effectively address the situation of children living in poverty, being faced with malnutrition, with violence or with school closures and the connected lack of educational possibilities, caused by COVID-19. Clearly, if the many SDGs and their indicators are to be attained, even more efforts are needed by international organizations, supported by their member states, to address the root causes preventing their implementation.

By comparison, for example, UN Environment, while affected by the crisis, sees some of its goals realized in partial ways, as the crisis has led to a lowering of emissions in several countries, including large parts of China and Europe.[14] This may also partially facilitate implementation of SDG 13 ('Climate action'). The patterns of communication among UN staff and institutions, the modes of negotiation and of intergovernmental agreement, committee work and research led by such global entities, have all been affected by digitalization—with effects not to be overseen yet. Some of these trends, however, may partially generate 'positive' effects that came in unexpectedly. For example, online patterns of communication and negotiation can lower costs of travel and accommodation related to international meetings, reduce transaction costs and with this, render intergovernmental negotiation processes more cost-effective, while lowering emissions related to (international) travel. In this sense, the challenges stemming from the global health crisis may, for some aspects of UN work, create some (small) benefits as regards the modes of operation, easier achievement of some environmental targets and the reduction of costs for the respective institutions. Simultaneously, digitalization may create new 'biases' in international negotiation, with UN states more adapted to digital forms of communication and better infrastructures potentially being privileged in multilateral processes based on online formats. However, it will lower levels of harmful emissions, as many international meetings—including the Annual Sessions of the UNGA itself— are related to extensive international travel.

Nonetheless, it is likely that these 'positive developments' are strongly outweighed by the pressures generated by COVID-19 as a global health crisis, in social, economic and political terms, in a global perspective. While the challenges caused by the pandemic are not unique to the UN, but in fact apply to governments, firms, (higher) education institutions and other organizations internationally, the combination of ongoing challenges to multilateralism with those emanating from the COVID-19 crisis put extensive pressures on the UN as an organization. Simultaneously, the need for the organization—as well as its various specialized agencies, programmes, funds and other related entities—to act is even more important in view of the effects of the crisis. This dilemma also concerns regional organizations, including the EU, where a common governance approach—in terms of combatting the crisis itself, as well as the (economic) effects it generates—is strongly needed. The challenge of 'pressures on multilateralism', while the very (rules-based) system of multilateral global governance seems the only way forward to address the causes of these pressures, is a paradox difficult to solve. But if a risk of outright confrontation, nationalism and closing of borders is to be avoided, multilateralism needs to be revived, including the institutions underpinning it.

NOTES

1. On representation in the UNSC, possibilities for and hurdles to reform, for example, see Russett (2005), Voeten (2008) or Hosli and Dörfler (2020).

2. See Ruggie 1993 for institutions created before the twentieth century.

3. For a full overview of the UN System, see https://www.un.org/en/pdfs/un_system_chart.pdf.

4. On recent challenges to UNICEF and to UN Women, see the chapter by Dimitra Protopsalti in this book.

5. For figures of March 2020, see https://peacekeeping.un.org/en/troop-and-police-contributors.

6. For an overview of challenges to the work of the organization due to COVID-19, see, for example, http://reporting.unhcr.org/covid-19.

7. For example, see https://www.unicef-irc.org/covid19.

8. For a full overview of votes cast by UN member states on UNGA resolutions, for example, see Voeten (2009). The dataset has been updated on Dataverse for votes cast in the time span 1946 to 2015.

9. This division was reinforced by the shift of the permanent UNSC seat from Taiwan to mainland China in 1971.

10. On respective effects, see Gowan (2018).

11. On this organization, for example, see Scott-Smith (2020).

12. For patterns of representation in the UNSC in terms of permanent compared to non-permanent membership, for example, see Hosli and Dörfler (2020).

13. This will negatively affect implementation of SDG 10 ('Reduced inequalities').

14. For an in-depth analysis of the global climate regime and recent pressures due to nationalism and to COVID-19, see the chapter by Susann Handke in this book.

REFERENCES

Gowan, Richard. (2018). Multilateralism in Freefall? New York: United Nations University Centre for Policy Research (CPR). Available at https://cpr.unu.edu/the-multilateral-freefall.html.

Hosli, Madeleine O. and Thomas Dörfler. (2020). 'The United Nations Security Council: History, Current Composition and Reform Proposals', in Madeleine O. Hosli and Joren Selleslaghs (eds.), *The Changing Global Order: Challenges and Prospects*. Cham: Springer. 299–320.

Ikenberry, G. John. (2015). The Future of Multilateralism: Governing the World in a Post-Hegemonic Era. *Japanese Journal of Political Science*, 16(3), 399–413.

Moreland, Will. (2019). The Purpose of Multilateralism: A Framework for Democracies in a Geopolitically Competitive World. Washington, DC: Brookings Institution. Available at https://www.brookings.edu/research/the-purpose-of-multilateralism/.

O'Neill, Barry. (1996). Power and Satisfaction in the United Nations Security Council. *The Journal of Conflict Resolution*, 40(2), 219–237.

Ruggie, John Gerard. (1993). 'Multilateralism: The Anatomy of an Institution', in John Gerard Ruggie (ed.), *Multilateralism Matters: The Theory and Practice of an Institutional Form*. New York: Columbia University Press.

Russett, Bruce. (2005). Security Council Expansion: Can't, and Shouldn't. In Reforming the United Nations for Peace and Security. Proceedings of a Workshop to Analyze the Report of the High-level Panel on Threats, Challenges, and Change. New Haven: Connecticut: Yale Center for the Study of Globalization. 153–166.

Scott-Smith, Giles. (2020). 'The Shanghai Cooperation Organization', in Madeleine O. Hosli and Joren Selleslaghs (eds.), *The Changing Global Order: Challenges and Prospects*. Cham: Springer. 177–191.

Voeten, Erik. (2008). 'Why No UN Security Council Reform? Lessons for and from Institutionalist Theory', in Dimitris Bourantonis, Kostas Ifantis, and Panayotis Tsakonas (eds.), *Multilateralism and Security Institutions in an Era of Globalization*. London, New York: Routledge. 288–305.

Voeten, Erik, Strezhnev, Anton and Bailey, Michael. (2009). United Nations General Assembly Voting Data. Available at https://doi.org/10.7910/DVN/LEJUQZ, Harvard Dataverse, V27, UNF:6:d0mGNR+Qja/nNTgUCC5xAA==[fileUNF]

United Nations. (2018). Summary of Troop Contributing Countries by Ranking. Available at https://peacekeeping.un.org/sites/default/files/2_country_ranking_report.pdf

Chapter 2

UNICEF and UN WOMEN in the Post-COVID-19 Era: How the Pandemic Is Expected to Reshape the Humanitarian Agenda

Dimitra Protopsalti

1. INTRODUCTION

The 2010s constitute a milestone in the field of international relations and consequently in the way global cooperation is practised. More specifically, even before considering the weight of the global pandemic, multilateral cooperation has been heavily impacted by the United States' behaviour under the Trump administration which had openly cast doubts on and in some cases even withdrew from various international fora. A prime example of the United States' new multilateral attitude was President Trump's warning of a potential U.S. withdrawal from the UN Human Rights Council based on the former's claim that the UN shields regimes it should rather be condemning (Prakash & Dolšak, 2017). In turn, this new attitude has rippled throughout multilateral networks triggering states around the world to adopt more unilateral approaches as global leaders challenge the legitimacy and efficiency of multilateral organizations.

Undoubtedly, the dawn of the 2020s was overwhelmed by the COVID-19 pandemic which altered the global landscape once again and tested the adequacy of major multilateral entities.

As a result, many countries put in place general lockdown measures and travel restrictions. The present chapter sets out to highlight the different ways in which the global crisis has deepened issues for populations in need, such as the access to proper healthcare, in regard to women and children in conflict ridden areas. Unfortunately, this unprecedented phenomenon has created unique challenges while intensifying already-existing issues to the future of multilateral cooperation in the humanitarian field.

As stated in the UN Charter, humanitarian aid constitutes a crucial part of international cooperation. As one of the most robust global governing organizations today, the UN strives to solve international economic, social, cultural and humanitarian issues (UN Charter, art. 1, para. 3). Amidst the COVID-19 pandemic, women and children remain the most vulnerable groups since they are severely affected by humanitarian crises (Carpenter, 2005, p. 296) which directly calls on the UN to respond under the mandate of the UN Charter. The need for UN humanitarian action is additionally clear taking into account the significant increase in cases of domestic violence worldwide due to self-isolation and general lockdown measures in many affected countries (Phumzile Mlambo-Ngcuka, 2020). Furthermore, the closure of school units left almost 91% of children out of schools, the biggest percentage of simultaneous physical absence ever recorded (Miks & McIlwaine, 2020) which will have unforeseen effects on the future of child development.

Taking the above into consideration, it is essential to discuss how this newly experienced situation is expected to affect women and children and which steps need to be taken by the respective international organizations that are entitled with this mandate. UNICEF and UN Women form the two UN bodies that deal with the protection of children rights and women respectively with a long-established action plan. Considering the number of people living below the poverty level and in conflict-stricken areas, UN WOMEN and UNICEF classified humanitarian action as an imminent need long before the occurrence of the pandemic. Thus, humanitarian entities need to gather their resources and join with cooperative global networks—both governmental and non-governmental—to obtain the highest degree of flexibility and impact, which will ultimately allow them to offer assistance in a faster and more effective way.

Therefore, the aim of this chapter is to analyse UNICEF and UN Women's operations in their handling of crises as they work to provide humanitarian aid and protect the rights of women and children worldwide. In addition, the chapter will explore how these UN entities will evolve through the current crisis and which strategies they have implemented so far. Moreover, it examines the likelihood these tactics will be integrated as future approaches of institutional humanitarian action plans. The chapter also scrutinizes general challenges that arise in UNICEF and UN Women's line of humanitarian action from a micro-perspective. Next, the chapter shifts the focus to a macro-perspective addressing specific challenges to the humanitarian agenda, including the politicization of aid, the gap between humanitarian needs and available resources and the inefficiency of humanitarian logistics (HL). All of these issues intensified with the COVID-19 dynamic which this chapter will discuss. The last part of the chapter will discuss potential options for reform which target a vertical approach that would potentially assist humanitarian entities to address these issues and respond effectively. In this regard, it emphasizes that multilateral cooperation still forms an effective means to tackle humanitarian crises. The chapter proposes a customized humanitarian response based on each case, by a better mapping of the needs and the integration of local resources, including the skills and knowledge of the communities. Moreover, it suggests better coordination and reform of HL to achieve maximum potential. It concludes that a holistic approach to the humanitarian crises is necessary while simultaneously, the COVID-19 pandemic provides an opportune moment to reshape the humanitarian agenda and increase its effectiveness.

2. UNICEF—'FOR EVERY CHILD A FAIR CHANCE'

2.1. UNICEF's Working Pillars

International actors in the early twentieth century not only acknowledged the need for global cooperation in regard to children's welfare but also created specific organizations to act on these issues. The League of Nations, the predecessor of the UN, became the main party responsible for the formation of educational and child-related networks (Fuchs, 2007, p. 397). UNICEF was established in 1946—along with UNESCO—under resolution 57(I) (UNGA, 1946), of the United Nations General Assembly (UNGA) in the aftermath of World War II with a further aim to offer relief and assistance to children in need. Its initial operational role was related to material aid and fundraising with an extended reliance on child-related non-governmental organizations (NGOs), which not only supported the implementation of UNICEF's programmes but also contributed to the Declaration of the Rights of the Child (ibid., p. 402; Jones, 2004, p. 144).

UNICEF's elementary scope fell under the UN guidelines. In 1959, the UNGA proceeded with the adoption of the Declaration of the Rights of the Child (UN General Assembly Resolution, 1386 (XIV), 1959) whereby UNICEF obtained its own mandate. The Declaration was an extended version of the initial five-point Geneva Declaration of the Rights of the Child (1923) which was endorsed by the League of Nations in 1924. In 1989, the UN adopted the Convention on the Rights of the Child, according to the UNGA 44/25 resolution on 20 November of the same year, which was also declared as World Children's Day (United Nations, 1989). The core organization of UNICEF derives from the UNGA and its main three characteristics remain consistent up to the present. These include: (1) UNICEF's practical operations, (2) an in-country presence and (3) its reliance on voluntary contributions from public and private sector entities (Jones, 2004, p. 137).

Since then, UNICEF has taken serious steps in order to assist children in need and has further expanded its action plan to shield children's rights for protection, education, healthcare and shelter. With its mission *'For every child a fair chance'*, UNICEF operates on a vast action plan which targets emergency response and humanitarian aid centred on the essential needs of children across the globe. UNICEF's operational backbone is extended but not limited to child protection, inclusion and survival, education and social policy, gender equality and emergency responses. UNICEF strives to be the safeguard of migrant and displaced children as well as children with disabilities who constitute the most marginalized and excluded groups in society. It promotes gender equality since often especially girls are found in the least favourable situations, finding themselves as recipients of less support than boys. At the same time, their basic safety, hygiene and sanitation needs are often neglected (UNICEF, 2020). In addition, various obsolete educational techniques and materials perpetuate gender gaps in regard to learning and skills development leading to 25% of girls excluded from employment and education or training in contrast to just 10% of boys at a global scale.

Moreover, UNICEF conveys policies aimed at adolescent development by supporting investments in youth with an end means of establishing strong and inclusive societies. It is driven by the fact that in the present, the adolescent population exceeds one billion (the biggest percentage so far related to the overall global population) possesses an unprecedented level of education, yet it is often ignored by policy makers. Adding the factors of poverty, gender inequality, climate change, economic turmoil and conflict, the equilibrium leans against the adolescent growth and their ability to reach their full potential.

Last but not least, UNICEF is responsible for establishing strategies to relatively new challenges such as climate change since environmental deterioration thwarts children's rights, especially those who live in high-risk areas. Several natural phenomena worldwide (e.g. droughts and floods) have a heavier impact on poorer populations, in turn increasing food insecurity and nutritional deprivation for children (UNICEF, 2020).

The year 2019 constituted a year-landmark for UNICEF, following the thirtieth anniversary of the Convention. Throughout this time, UNICEF made concrete steps to tackle issues related to children in need and simultaneously adhered to the respective Sustainable Development Goals (SDGs). UNICEF even released optional protocols targeting specific challenges as supplements to the Convention. The protection of children involved in armed conflicts (child-soldiers) as well as their defence against trafficking, prostitution and pornography form vivid examples. In addition, an optional protocol allows children to submit complaints, appeals and petitions should their national legal system have not responded accordingly to any rights violation. The only condition is that their country of origin must be amongst those which ratified the protocol (UNICEF, 2019a, p. 9).

2.2. Humanitarian Action—COVID-19: Impact and Response

According to the Humanitarian Action for Children Overview (2020), there is currently one out of four children living in a conflict affected area, while the number of dispute and disaster zones is the highest recorded since the adoption of the Convention of the Rights of the Child. Millions of children have been displaced, while others still remain without official immigration statuses. Global data indicate that children have always constituted not only the most vulnerable group but also the most severely affected by humanitarian crises. Nevertheless, the various challenges still exist and steadily increase. Natural disasters, deadly diseases and the increasing activity of armed conflict groups deprive children of their fundamental rights, and compromise the efforts for humanitarian support. UNICEF's goals for 2020 were rather optimistic and expanded to various sectors such as education, water, sanitation and hygiene, nutrition and health. Simultaneously, its aims targeted the mitigation of multifaceted crises (health, socio-economic, armed conflict and refugee) (UNICEF, 2019b, p. 5). Currently, the additional pressure to combat the effects of COVID-19 has sharpened the challenges UNICEF needs to respond to under its mandated mission and purpose.

From an educational perspective, through joint efforts such as the 'Learning Passport' on behalf of UNICEF and Microsoft, a great deal of children is able to continue their education from home. Ukraine and Timor-Leste, for example, are among those who embraced this strategy. Other cooperative initiatives include partnerships with broadcasting agencies in order to air the classes and self-learning programmes throughout countries, such as in Rwanda. Some of these programmes even provide children with books and allow them to continue their education remotely. The COVID-19 pandemic has affected almost every area worldwide. To this end, UNICEF is closely working with national governments and Ministries of Education in order to adjust the learning experience with the assistance of technology. It has even expanded in the digital world with the '#LearningAtHome' initiative in order to provide a more holistic learning approach that targets children's physical health and mental wellbeing while continuing to support children with limited online access and those with learning difficulties (UNICEF, 2020).

The COVID-19 pandemic has impacted the health and safety of children, posing an additional challenge UNICEF. Conflict perpetuation has been the main reason for providing humanitarian aid, even so, the pandemic outbreak constitutes a significant factor for the designing and implementation of future action plans. UNICEF largely depends on the funding of donors, the United

States being one of the largest; yet, its funding deficit lies at 43%. More than half of its resources are directed towards conflicts in the Democratic Republic of the Congo (dealing additionally with the Ebola outbreak), South Sudan, Yemen, the Syrian Arab Republic, Syria's neighbouring countries hosting Syrian refugees and areas hit by natural disasters such as Mozambique (UNICEF, 2019b, p. 12). However, in 2020, UNICEF had to divert its previous effort to target resources at combatting the more immediate issues triggered by the pandemic.

Coronavirus has been classified as a pandemic and the specialists speculate that its behavior from now onwards will resemble this of the seasonal flu (Begley 2020). Consequently, it will become an integral part of the usual illnesses the globe faces, and it will pose an additional threat to the already disadvantaged regions. With President Trump's accusations to the WHO for belated responses, as Yue Han further elaborates in chapter 3, as well as the United States' withdrawal from the funding of the institution, multilateral humanitarian organizations are facing a serious threat of legitimacy and efficiency. This might hamper their potential to fulfil their cause. Adding the predicted upcoming economic recession following the mitigation of the pandemic, it is highly likely UNICEF's funding resources will deteriorate. Consequently, its operational work will be even more challenging, considering the deepening of the financing and response gap, contrary to the severity of humanitarian needs, which seem to soar.

3. UN WOMEN—'*ONE WOMAN*'

3.1. UN WOMEN's Working Pillars

UN Women is the entity of the UN, established in 2010, which is responsible for promoting gender equality and the empowerment of women, as part of the UN reform agenda. Its main goals focus on the support of intergovernmental institutions in the shaping of their policy process, assisting member states to adhere to certain standards while providing necessary technical or financial support. Moreover, UN Women's mandate entails the monitoring of the commitments of the UN to gender equality and the forging of effective partnerships with civil society within the member states. Their working pillars include the advocacy over women's underrepresentation in leadership positions and political participation, despite the fact of their proven efficacy as leaders. UN Women strives for economic empowerment of women who are often unequally affected by poverty, exploitation and discrimination while they are entitled with the greatest part of household work which impedes their quest for economic opportunities. What is more, women are proven to contribute to a longer and more sustainable peace after a conflict, when they are engaged to the peace processes, considering the greater degree to which women are affected by war. Since women are underrepresented or even excluded by peace processes and negotiations, UN Women is working towards women's full and equal participation at all levels of these procedures for preventing conflict, building and sustaining peace.

UN Women's work for terminating gender-based violence is also worth mentioning. It is working both at a global and a national level to establish an international framework and assist governments to adhere to it. UN Women's tasks entail partnership with civil society and other entities in order to prevent and respond to violence, the development of action plans that target safety, health justice and prevention. In fact, the latter is considered the most effective tool to end violence, in terms of cost and sustainability (UN Women, 2020a, p. 9).

As a response, UN Women stresses the importance of multilateral cooperation in order to tackle the multi-layered issue of women's underrepresentation. An initial, yet important step has been the Convention on the Elimination of All Forms of Discrimination against Women (CEDAW) (United Nations, 1979, p. 13). The UNGA adopted it in 1979 and it has 99 signatory states. Although there is still further work to be done in order for the Convention to be endorsed by more states, it is a clear sign of the importance of global cooperation. An additional initiative, strengthening the Convention, was the Beijing Platform for Action (1995). Today, it counts its twenty-fifth anniversary, providing a more inclusive framework with 12 critical areas of concern, including but not limited to, health, violence, environment, poverty, education and training. Therefore, it still remains a powerful tool. UN Women is working towards these goals, and through these multifaceted grids, it supports training for female political candidates, offers voter and civic education and endorses sensitization campaigns on gender equality.

For economic empowerment, UN Women is working through the aforementioned structures along with the ILO guidelines and in cooperation with fundamental organizations or with civil society, stressing the importance of multilateralism with the inclusion of regional actors. This aspect of UN Women's operation focuses on highly marginalized groups such as rural women, domestic workers, migrants and low-skilled women. A significant aspect, which is currently a priority both in the national and the international agenda, is violence against women which has a tremendous and long-term impact on their health and wellbeing. Moreover, violence also has an overall toll for society in relation to health care, legal systems, productivity and budget development. In that regard, CEDAW and the UN Convention support the improvement of the international normative framework and reinforce governments to adopt and enact legal reforms aligned with international standards. Last but not least, UN Women endorses the Women Peace and Security (WPS) agenda (2000) guided by ten UN Security Council resolutions—1325, 1820, 1888, 1889, 1960, 2106, 2122, 2242, 2467 and 2493—in order to enhance women's presence and inclusion in all aspects of peace processes. Through its interventions in more than 50 countries, UN Women endeavours to implement the WPS agenda from policy to practice and to harness uprising threats such as violent extremism, climate change, protracted conflict, human trafficking and refugee crises (UN Women, 2016, p. 3).

3.2. Humanitarian Action—COVID-19: Impact and Response

As described earlier, UN Women highlights the importance of global cooperation through its operational framework which confirms the hypothesis that joint efforts are proved to be fruitful in tackling serious humanitarian challenges. In addition to what has formerly been addressed, UN Women has a supplementary factor to take into consideration and integrate into its future action plan, namely the COVID-19 pandemic. This unprecedented challenge poses a significant threat to gender equality by exposing deep pre-existing inequalities and vulnerabilities—social, political and economic—hence amplifying the impacts of the pandemic and risking the gains of the past decades.

The outbreak of the global health crisis has brought a different reality to all aspects of life. Nonetheless, for a lot of women, the general lockdown put in force in many countries impacted their physical and mental health, since the rates of domestic violence increased. The 'Stay-Home/Stay-Safe' campaigns launched globally had rather the opposite effect on them. Hence, the COVID-19 crisis, which augmented the burden of care for women and girls, obtained a gender dimension and the way that UN Women will respond to this crisis is crucial for the future. Despite the progress in the human rights sector, these groups still remain more vulnerable to emergency conditions and consequently suffer more by the consequences of the pandemic. First of all, women's own health and safety is currently at risk due to the exact measures taken to combat the spread of COVID-19. The isolation, the limited movement and the social distancing form the factors that contribute to the higher levels of domestic violence. The current circumstances provide open space for their abusers to take action, making them suffer not only by the disease itself but also from emotional and physical exploitation which undermines their well-being or even their life. It is also worth mentioning that women suffer more in comparison to men, from the economic and social impacts of the health crisis. While women constitute a major part of the labour force and assume three times as much unpaid care work as men—even before the COVID-19 pandemic—they still lack social safety with female-headed households being notably vulnerable (Bhatia, 2020). What is more, while the pandemic is still raging, women comprise the majority of front-line health workers making their infection possibility rate rise (ibid.). Henceforth, a provision for their needs (e.g. protective equipment and hygiene products) is essential in order for them to execute their duty effectively. Last but not least, even now and despite women's proven abilities and efficiency in leadership positions, they are still underrepresented in the designing and response processes of the international health fora to battle the pandemic. It is rather disappointing to witness that while women constitute 70% of the health and social workforce, they still lack equality of participation in crucial decision-making procedures (Sharma et al., 2020, p. 1). Only 30% of women have leading positions in the global health sector which pursues to shape the future of the global community after the pandemic (Dhatt, 2020).

UN Women highlights the gender aspect of the COVID-19 crisis while it joins forces with the WHO in an attempt to mitigate the gender gap. In order to propose more effective and targeted policies, it incorporates the public sector as well as NGOs towards a data collection campaign which focuses on knowledge gathering and accounting for all the vulnerable groups. UN Women highlights the fact that the best practice to respond to the pandemic is the collection of qualitative sex-disaggregated information in addition to quantitative data, in order to determine the evolution of the situation. This consists of including differing rates of infection, differential economic impacts and care burdens, not excluding the incidence of domestic violence and sexual abuse. To this end, it works with domestic statistical offices with further aim to enhance their collection-data capacity and gender responsiveness (UN Women, 2020b). Additionally, UN Women has included in its operational framework the aspect of boys' education from an early age towards the opposite gender as a means to tackle the issue of gender violence at its roots. Building on this guideline, it has launched the 'HeForShe' initiative in order to inspire men to unite with solidarity against women's sexual harassment, hence making gender equality initiatives more inclusive and, consequently more effective (UN Women, 2017). Taking the COVID-19 factor into account, the aforementioned initiative is advanced to a campaign level with the quote '#HeForSheAtHome' and endeavours to motivate men to acknowledge that the household burden needs to be equally shared (UN Women, 2020c). Cumulatively, all the efforts, recommendations and guidelines of UN Women stress for gender equality and multilateral participation in order to reap the most benefits possible for the groups concerned.

4. CHALLENGES OF MULTILATERAL ORGANIZATIONS IN REGARD TO HUMANITARIAN SUPPORT AND WAYS FORWARD

4.1. Issues of the Humanitarian Agenda

The chapter has demonstrated so far that UNICEF and UN Women, through their vast action plan are trying to address serious global challenges and assist vulnerable groups in need, namely children and women. In addition, they are taking into account the new dynamic of the COVID-19 pandemic which has imposed a significant trial on their operational framework. Both UN entities are in favour of inclusiveness and they are working towards multilateral cooperation, engaging governmental and non-governmental actors, civil society and various regional parties. Nonetheless, the humanitarian field, which is extensively based on multi-layered collaboration, has yet to face additional operational burdens.

Having analysed the humanitarian challenges on a micro-level through the lenses of the two UN agencies, this section continues to expand the focus at a macro-level. It addresses the challenges multilateral organizations face in regard to humanitarian crises and later, the section moves to identify how the COVID-19 pandemic is expected to influence the future of their action.

Traditionally, humanitarian actors play a crucial role in war-torn areas, hot conflicts, or after the signing of peace agreements by providing support and aid to vulnerable peoples. One of the serious challenges humanitarian actors face today is the threat to the physical security of humanitarian workers, especially in increasingly hostile environments. In fact, there are several cases where multifarious crises have raised severe security concerns to the humanitarian entities, causing them to withdraw from the field (McGoldrick, 2011, pp. 969–970). Adding the complications inspired by the COVID-19 pandemic, their roles and responsibilities have become more difficult to manage. Humanitarian workers on the frontlines of the response, are not only placed within the most challenging context but also face a higher infection risk which would potentially lead to their stigmatization in the community (Sharma et al., 2020, p. 1). What is more, the very nature of armed-violence has been transformed, turning conflicts into multi-layered and complex crises both internally and internally, impeding their mitigation. At the same time, local actors are distrustful towards humanitarian entities working in the field. The latter are often perceived as 'Western' institutions and face accusations of leading vast political strategies or being used as sound boards for the West's foreign interests (McGoldrick, 2011, p. 973).

Moreover, in cases where multifarious mechanisms are involved in the same region, humanitarian organizations are challenged to maintain their operational independence, considering the fact that each actor wants to reap the benefits of a successful humanitarian intervention for its own constituency. Simultaneously, humanitarian actors operate based on fundamental principles, such as impartiality, independence and neutrality (ibid., p. 976). However, the lines are often blurred among the combatants, with vulnerable populations in need of humanitarian aid and other actors operating in the same area, thereby hampering efficiency and credibility of humanitarian aid work. This is the case where humanitarian entities seem to contradict the very principles they are defending, when the humanitarian support is turned into a tool for major powers of the region to reach their political goals (Stoddard, Harmer & Haver, 2006, p. 24).

The politicization of humanitarian aid is also a major issue facing the integrity and competency of humanitarian organizations (Grandi, 2018). These situations are often exploited for political purposes at the expense of peoples' suffering. Witnessing the extended division created within the EU and the rise of nationalistic approaches around the world (e.g. Hungary's border closure, Trump's advocacy for the wall at the US border with Mexico), one can hypothesize that the current health crisis might become a political tool for promoting unilateral interests. Counterintuitive to their collaborative nature, multipolar entities are often used as vessels for power distribution and rival interests among states which strive to promote their national goals. To this view, international cooperation is highly compromised and its lacking competency in the prevention and resolution of conflicts is more than apparent (Grandi, 2018, p. 182). The political game that unravelled simultaneously with the COVID-19 outbreak poses significant higher demands for emergency humanitarian action. The example of the United States ceasing funding for the WHO is a clear sign of the decline of support for international organizations that are concerned with global public health or humanitarian aid.

Another crucial challenge humanitarian organizations face is the availability of resources. Research shows that the global capacity for responding to emergencies is lower than the actual needs for humanitarian support (Daar et al., 2018). Based on data by the UN Office for the Coordination of Humanitarian Affairs (UNOCHA), more than 140 million people are affected by humanitarian crises, including civil wars and violent conflicts, which continues to add to the currently great number of displaced people, refugees and asylum seekers. It is also worth mentioning that these people are also severely affected by natural disasters which torment areas where humanitarian crises unravel and tend to worsen due to climate change, another global challenge of the international agenda. On top of that, the breakout of the COVID-19 pandemic still affects the most vulnerable groups and deepens the crisis and inequity which they are experiencing. For instance, children's exposure to poverty affects their health and wellbeing and if poverty persists during adulthood, it lurks a greater difficulty for these individuals of accessing health services (Xafis, 2020, p. 3). Following the spread of COVID-19, vulnerable populations were forced to confront the virus with an already-compromised health status due to their lack of access to proper health care amongst other factors which ultimately perpetuated global inequalities (ibid.).

Arguably, UNICEF and UN Women rely heavily on external donations; however, the current funding resources are not sufficient to cover growing demands, a gap which has further expanded since the global health crisis

(Daar et al., 2018, p. 169). Thus, these organizations need to provision current funding so as to redirect it towards innovative solutions which assist in resolving the ongoing financial issues which hinder their capacity to aid the populations who are giving purpose to their work (ibid.). To this view, research suggests the use of technology and know-how from other sectors, the forging of new partnerships (including public, private and non-governmental entities) as well as the favourable inclusion of the ideas of the local populations affected by crises (ibid., p. 172).

Adding to the aforementioned context, a serious challenge seems to be the deficit in HL. According to Kovacs and Spens (2009, p. 507), apart from the lack of resources, money, supplies, technology, transportation capacity and staff, there are a variety of issues that continue to be topical and relevant to the response in the COVID-19 crisis. First of all, no one could have predicted the degree to which the virus spread would extend, not to mention its high and fast rate of contagion. Hence the unpredictability of demand in terms of timing, location, type and size combined with the suddenness of the occurrence and the high demand in large amounts of health and sanitary equipment impeded the humanitarian response of the respective agencies (ibid.). Taking into account the increase in states' nationalist attitudes following the outbreak of COVID-19, several states have imposed bureaucratic obstacles and actively restricted humanitarian responses on their territories. For example, grassroots organizations in Myanmar—where the army offensives continue to increase the displacement rate—mobilized to distribute basic health supplies such as thermometers and hand sanitizers and organized quarantine facilities in various areas, including internally displaced camps. However, the military blocked these organizations' actions, following the government's commitment to distribute food supplies to vulnerable populations, which unfortunately revealed to be a public relations strategy (Franco, 2020). Thus, the already-difficult tasks performed by humanitarian entities have become much more complex and ineffective (McGoldrick, 2011, p. 973). This factor, in combination with governmental and institutional relief package launches for battling the economic standstill, highlights governments' enduring reluctance for directing resources the tackling of the roots of social inequality, which humanitarian organizations cannot face alone (Xafis, 2020, p. 4). A possible explanation for this phenomenon would be the supremacy of state sovereignty which surpasses the power of humanitarian organizations, leaving them fighting against all odds.

All the circumstances described earlier create a rather disappointing image for the future aspects of humanitarian response and aid for UNICEF and UN Women. Serious steps need to be taken since the existing status quo in the humanitarian field along with the COVID-19 crisis will deepen inequalities and further challenge the livelihoods of many vulnerable groups. The next part of the chapter will present possibly efficient means that would assist the humanitarian entities in their work and combat the current situation amidst the COVID-19 pandemic.

4.2. Means for Effective Humanitarian Response and Reform

Undoubtedly, the COVID-19 pandemic constitutes one of the biggest global challenges since World War II since it is not only a health crisis but has shaken the already-turbulent international agenda to the core as well. Nevertheless, like in most emergency situations, there are political factors and interests at stake. Examples vary and diversify, starting from China—the initial location of the COVID-19 outbreak—which is trying to rebrand itself by sending medical assistance, supplies and human resources to the affected areas. Once the country mitigated the infection curve, it potentially tried to compensate for the damage done by failing to disclose crucial information about the virus (Verma, 2020). Another vivid example is the United States blaming China for the pandemic and accusing the WHO itself for coverage of the Chinese government at the earlier stages of the outbreak (McNeil & Jacobs, 2020). Trump's rhetoric, followed by the US funding withdrawal from the WHO, whilst its administration took no responsibility for the death of thousands of citizens, proves how humanitarian aid can become a political tool to favour certain interests.

At this point, the chapter outlines possible ways that humanitarian entities, including UNICEF and UN Women, could respond to the current crisis and inspect policies that would be effective in tackling future challenges. The measures implemented to mitigate the spread of the virus, such as the restriction of refugee movement, the enforcement of border control and the lockdown of displacement camps, have caused restricted access to the affected populations as well as the suspension of various humanitarian operations (Sharma et al., 2020, p. 1). Building on the argument of resource deficits, which is expected to amplify in the post-COVID-19 era, Matopoulos, Kovacs and Hayes (2014) argue in favour of better understanding and mapping of the necessary conditions to integrate local resources in the humanitarian supply chain (HSC) and its configuration. The latter, as the researchers explain it further, describes the way the supply chain is structured and organized taking into consideration key elements such as 'the number and type of organizations involved, the source locations and products, the production sites and methods, the logistics activities (e.g. delivery channels and inventory deployment), and the financial flow' (ibid., p. 622). This will allow for a customized approach based on the necessities of each affected area, hence develop a more efficient humanitarian response. Through their proposed framework, they highlight physical (use of local materials), human (use of local staff) and organizational (local decision making, sourcing, supplies, partners, etc.) resources in order to surpass various barriers to aid programmes such as language, customs and domestic political issues. As such, the aid intervention is more likely to meet the needs of the beneficiaries and reach substantial goals (ibid., pp. 628–630).

However, the gender gap as part of the humanitarian process should not be overlooked. As stated previously, women comprise both a vulnerable group which is affected by the pandemic to a greater degree and a major percentage of the health workforce worldwide. To this view, when it comes to immersing local staff in the earlier-described HSC framework, the women's percentage of engagement as health workers needs to increase (Fuhrman et al., 2020, p. 3). From an organizational perspective, the Matopoulos et al. (2014) framework should include local women in leadership positions in order to reinforce trust in health systems. This is because women are disproportionately affected by health diseases, while in many humanitarian settings, women and girls are the last to receive medical treatment (Fuhrman et al., p. 3). Moreover, women are often stigmatized by social norms that point out internally displaced people, refugees, members of certain ethnic or racial groups or those of different sexual orientation, thus preventing them from receiving proper medical assistance. Hence, women are more than capable of understanding the actual extent of health needs and as such their incorporation in leading roles within the health systems is crucial (ibid.). Applying these ideas, it is more likely that the responses to COVID-19 will effectively address the needs of women, girls and other vulnerable groups in each community (ibid.).

Additionally, a potential way forward in the humanitarian field would be the adoption of alternative tactics, endorsed by organizations (UNICEF, UNOCHA, etc.) and NGOs (Save the Children, etc.). Heaslip, Kovacs and Haavisto (2018) argue over a different approach in the humanitarian context which expands further than a traditional 'top-bottom' strategy. The latter usually focuses on the improvement of organizational responses. On the contrary, they propose a 'bottom-up' tactic which allows the proliferation and the diversification of new actors by including local ownership and partnership. In addition, it endorses community participation by engaging the skills, talents and aspirations of the beneficiary populations, therefore maximizing the benefits on both ends of this equation. This approach targets a better reform and a shift in notions about humanitarian aid by advocating for the active participation of relief recipients in the humanitarian process rather than the treatment of them as passive receivers of aid (ibid., pp. 1177, 1183).

Further observations converge to the fact that poor or miscoordination of the humanitarian aid process hinders the effectiveness of the agencies involved. Likewise the need for improvement of the humanitarian system is widely acknowledged. Despite the development of cooperative behaviour among the humanitarian actors, their combined efforts for the assessment of situations and the mapping of possible responses, there are barriers to be surpassed, such as the competition among humanitarian agencies. The latter tend to view the field as an increasingly competitive industry and their presence in the field seems to depend on their adequacy in engaging the media, raising funds and lobbying political actors (McGoldrick, 2011, p. 977). A possible way out of this deadlock could be the re-prioritization and reform of HL. HL constitutes a vast operational framework which entails 'procurement, transportation and relief materials warehousing from the origin point to the beneficiaries' locations' (Khan, Lee & Bae, 2019, p. 2). Therefore, it plays a significant role in all segments of humanitarian support. Nonetheless, humanitarian organizations do not accredit great importance to the HL, which in combination with the politicization of aid and the inequity between humanitarian needs and available resources, further hinders their effectiveness. In fact, HL comprises 80% of the operational totality and is a decisive factor for the success or failure of a humanitarian operation. Yet, it is still a low priority issue for the humanitarian organizations who often do not employ sufficient staff or do not dedicate enough time for their training. Although still contrary to the prioritization of staffing logic in most humanitarian organizations, an efficient supply chain constitutes a crucial bridge between the following dyads: (1) disaster preparedness and response, (2) distribution and procurement and (3) headquarters and field (ibid.; Tatham & Kovacs, 2010, p. 36).

Research emphasizes the importance of transparency in the humanitarian field and consequently also in HL. Transparency is seen as a major tool for tackling serious issues including but not limited to 'corruption cases, misuse, theft, fraud, power abuse, nepotism, favouritism and clientelism' (Khan, Lee & Bae, 2019, p. 4). Khan et al.'s approach splits transparency into two categories: (1) information transparency which is related to disclosure, accuracy and clarity, and (2) organizational transparency, which entails corporate governance, decision making and accountability. The inclusion of these dimensions in institutional practice leads to accountability and public trust, key elements in the humanitarian sector. People need to trust that humanitarian entities fulfil the purpose they were created for, allocating the donated resources—part of which come from the wider public—mindfully. Likewise, in cases of misuse of power—for example, the Haiti UN peacekeeping mission scandal—the perpetrators need to be held accountable for their actions and dismissed from their positions. Consequently, the implementation of efficient HL can be an effective tool for the design and implementation of humanitarian operations (ibid., p. 4).

Combining the alternative 'bottom-up' strategies and the reform of HL in relation to the COVID-19 response, aid processes should first aim at protecting the front-line workforce including groups with special needs—for example, pregnant women—within it. In addition, the operational procedures should battle mistrust, disinformation and stigma towards humanitarian workers in partnership with local communities in order to mitigate the incidents of harassment and violence. On the basis of a customized approach depending on each situation, special attention needs to turn to displaced populations. Since the COVID-19 pandemic had adverse health effects on vulnerable women and children, their needs should be prioritized along with the safety and security of the respective humanitarian workers of the field, in order for the latter to execute their duties effectively. Last but not least, the fostering of professional standards is crucial in tackling gender biases and elevating the position of female humanitarian workers. In this way, the humanitarian response strategies can take women's insights and specific needs into consideration as well as promote female leadership and participation in decision-making processes (Sharma et al., 2020, p. 2). To conclude, at a national level, governments should incorporate effective means to deal with violence against women in their COVID-19 responses. To this end, health and other front-line facilities ought to integrate local resource supply channels for situational and future needs for communities' sustainability, such as shelters, counselling services, support hotlines or crisis centres (Roesch et al., 2020, p. 1).

5. CONCLUSION

Taking everything into consideration, the humanitarian field benefits immensely from multilateralism, but at the same time, it is being severely challenged by the repercussions of the COVID-19 pandemic. Especially in these complicated times, it is crucial that humanitarian organizations redefine their values and priorities to target better responses for those in need. This chapter has described the vast action plan of UNICEF and UN Women, the two UN entities that aim to secure the rights of the two historically most affected groups by humanitarian crises, namely children and women. The pandemic, in most cases, only magnified pre-existing threats to the physical and mental health of these two demographics. Additionally, the analysis of the chapter underlined the way that these UN agencies have responded to the current health crisis, and which steps they have integrated in their action plan in order to tackle this issue. UNICEF strives through joint initiatives to battle the closure of the school units worldwide in order for children to continue their learning. However, its funding deterioration hinders its efforts and amplifies the resources gap. Further, UN Women battles women's under-representation in crucial political processes and endeavours to combat the rise of domestic violence and women's greater suffering by the pandemic. To this end, it launches campaigns, targeting both boys' and men's awareness over gender inequalities. What is more, the chapter has scrutinized the challenges that humanitarian organizations face, namely the politicization of aid, the disparity between humanitarian needs and the available resources and the inefficiency of HL, all intensifying with the COVID-19 dynamic. These challenges undermine the operational efficiency of the humanitarian entities and they have a further impact on the populations in need of humanitarian support.

In the last part of the chapter, it is argued that multilateral cooperation in the humanitarian field is still an efficient tool; nevertheless, substantial changes need to be made for the benefit of all shareholders involved in this process. The changes proposed focus on a vertical transformation rather than a traditional horizontal strategy. To this view, the local integration of resources in HL is suggested in order to reduce the documented resource deficit, especially considering the fact that humanitarian organizations—such as UNICEF and UN Women—rely heavily on donations. Building up on this argument, humanitarian efficacy could be improved via a 'bottom-up' approach which targets the engagement of skills, talents and aspirations of local communities. UNICEF and UN Women have a strong presence worldwide, hence the adoption of this approach would be beneficial to their work. The mitigation of the gender gap is a crucial step to make moving forward considering the percentage of both vulnerable women and women on the front-line of the workforce as UN Women underlines. Last but not least, the chapter concludes in favour of the re-prioritization of HL which can help increase the efficiency and effectiveness of projects. This will more likely lead to greater public trust in the humanitarian network. Though, this will not be possible without incorporating women in key decision-making positions—as UN Women strives for—not only because they are such a large part of the constituency but also because they are unequally affected by humanitarian or health crises. Cumulatively, the COVID-19 pandemic constitutes an opportune moment for humanitarian entities to adopt a holistic approach towards emergency situations. UNICEF and UN Women are vivid examples of agencies relying heavily on multilateral cooperation in order to reach their goals and provide humanitarian support to children and women worldwide. Multilateral cooperation in the humanitarian field could therefore strengthen and remain an effective means for the support, relief and aid to the most vulnerable groups.

REFERENCES

Bhatia, A. (2020). Women and COVID-19: Five Things Governments Can Do Now. Retrieved from https://www.unwomen.org/en/news/stories/2020/3/news-women-and-COVID-19-governments-actions-by-ded-bhatia

Begley, S. (2020). Experts envision two scenarios if the new coronavirus isn't contained. Retrieved from https://www.statnews.com/2020/02/04/two-scenarios-if-new-coronavirus-isnt-contained/

Carpenter, R. (2005). 'Women, Children and Other Vulnerable Groups': Gender, Strategic Frames and the Protection of Civilians as a Transnational Issue. *International Studies Quarterly, 49*(2), 295–334. Retrieved 22 June 2020 from www.jstor.org/stable/3693516

Daar, A., Chang, T., Salomon, A., & Singer, P. (2018). Grand challenges in humanitarian aid. *Nature, 559*(7713), 169–173.

Dhatt, R. (2020). Global health security depends on women. Retrieved from https://www.devex.com/news/opinion-global-health-security-depends-on-women-96861

Franco, J. (2020). 'If the virus doesn't kill me . . .': Socioeconomic impacts of COVID-19 on rural working people in the Global South. *Agriculture and Human Values, 12*(1–2). doi: 10.1007/s10460-020-10073-1.

Fuchs, E. (2007). Children's rights and global civil society. *Comparative Education, 43*(3), 393–412. Retrieved from https://doi.org/10.1080/03050060701556356

Fuhrman, S., Kalyanpur, A., Friedman, S., & Tran, N. (2020). Gendered implications of the COVID-19 pandemic for policies and programmes in humanitarian settings. *BMJ Global Health, 5*(5), 1–5.

Grandi, F. (2018). Forced Displacement Today: Why Multilateralism Matters. *The Brown Journal of World Affairs, 24*(2), 179–189.

Harmer, A., Haver, C., & Stoddard, A. (2006). *Providing Aid in Insecure Environments: Trends in Policy and Operations.* (Report No. 23, 2006–09). Humanitarian Policy Group. Retrieved from https://www.odi.org/sites/odi.org.uk/files/odi-assets/publications-opinion-files/269.pdf

Heaslip, G., Kovács, G., & Haavisto, I. (2018). Innovations in humanitarian supply chains: The case of cash transfer programmes. *Production Planning & Control, 29*(14), 1175–1190.

Jones, Phillip, W. (2004). 'UNICEF', in D. Coleman, & P. W. Jones (eds.), *The United Nations and Education: Multilateralism, Development and Globalisation,* 137–186. London: Taylor and Francis.

Khan, M., Lee, Y. H., & Bae, J. H. (2019). The role of transparency in humanitarian logistics. *Sustainability, 11*(7), 1–27.

Kovács, G., & Spens, K. (2009). Identifying challenges in humanitarian logistics. *International Journal of Physical Distribution & Logistics Management, 39*(6), 506–528.

Matopoulos, A., Kovács, G., & Hayes, O. (2014). Local Resources and Procurement Practices in Humanitarian Supply Chains: An Empirical Examination of Large-Scale House Reconstruction Projects. *Decision Sciences, 45*(4), 621–646.

McGoldrick, C. (2011). The future of humanitarian action: An ICRC perspective. *International Review of the Red Cross, 93*(884), 965–991.

McNeil, D., & Jacobs, A. (2020, May 29). Blaming China for Pandemic, Trump Says U.S. Will Leave the W.H.O. Retrieved 27 June 2020 from https://www.nytimes.com/2020/05/29/health/virus-who.html

Miks, J., & McIlwaine, J. (2020, April 20). Keeping the world's children learning through COVID-19. Retrieved from https://www.unicef.org/coronavirus/keeping-worlds-children-learning-through-COVID-19

Mlambo-Ngcuka, P. (2020, April 6). Violence against women and girls: The shadow pandemic. Retrieved from https://www.unwomen.org/en/news/stories/2020/4/statement-ed-phumzile-violence-against-women-during-pandemic

Prakash, A., & Dolšak, N. (2017). International organizations and the crisis of legitimacy. Retrieved from https://www.openglobalrights.org/international-organizations-and-crisis-of-legitimacy/

Roesch, E., Gupta, J., & García-Moreno, C. (2020). Violence against women during COVID-19 pandemic restrictions. *BMJ, 369*, M1712.

Sharma, V., Scott, J., Kelly, J., & VanRooyen, M. (2020). Prioritizing vulnerable populations and women on the frontlines: COVID-19 in humanitarian contexts. *International Journal for Equity in Health, 19*(1), 1–3.

Tatham, P., & Kovács, G. (2010). The application of 'swift trust' to humanitarian logistics. *International Journal of Production Economics, 126*(1), 35–45.

UNICEF. (2019a). For Every Child, Every Right: The Convention on the Rights of the Child at a crossroads. Retrieved from https://www.unicef.org/reports/convention-rights-child-crossroads-2019.

UNICEF. (2019b). Humanitarian action for children 2020. Retrieved from https://www.unicef.org/reports/humanitarian-action-children-2020-overview.

UNICEF. (2020, April 20). UNICEF and Microsoft launch global learning platform to help address COVID-19 education crisis [Press release]. Retrieved from https://www.unicef.org/press-releases/unicef-and-microsoft-launch-global-learning-platform-help-address-COVID-19-education.

United Nations Children's Fund UK. (1989). The United Nations convention on the rights of the child. Retrieved from https://downloads.unicef.org.uk/wp-content/uploads/2010/05/UNCRC_PRESS200910web.pdf?_ga=2.78590034.795419542.1582474737-1972578648.1582474737.

United Nations, Beijing Declaration and Platform for Action, Fourth World Conference on Women: Action for Equality, Development and Peace. (1995 October 27). International Human Rights Law Documents, 428–431. https://doi.org/10.1017/9781316677117.051.

United Nations (n.d.). United Nations Charter Retrieved from https://www.un.org/en/sections/un-charter/chapter-i/index.html

UN General Assembly, Convention on the Elimination of All Forms of Discrimination against Women, (1979 December 18). United Nations, Treaty Series, vol. 1249, p. 13. Retrieved from https://www.refworld.org/docid/3ae6b3970.html [accessed 20 May 2020].

UN General Assembly. Declaration of the Rights of the Child. (1959, November 20). A/RES/1386(XIV). Retrieved from https://www.refworld.org/docid/3ae6b38e3.html [accessed 20 May 2020].

UN General Assembly, Establishment of an International Children's Emergency Fund. (1946, December 11). A/RES/57(I). Retrieved from https://www.unicef.org/about/history/files/UN_resolutions_UNICEF_1940s.pdf [accessed 20 May 2020].

UN Security Council, Security Council resolution 1325 (2000) [on women and peace and security]. (2000, October 31). S/RES/1325 (2000), Retrieved from https://www.refworld.org/docid/3b00f4672e.html [accessed 20 May 2020].

UN Women. (2016). Peace and Security [Issue Brief]. Retrieved from https://www.unwomen.org/-/media/headquarters/attachments/sections/library/publications/2013/12/un%20women%20briefthematicpsuswebrev3%20pdf.pdf?la=en

UN Women. (2017, December 20). Are you #HeForShe [Press release]. Retrieved from https://www.unwomen.org/en/news/stories/2017/12/press-release-heforshe-international-human-solidarity-day

UN Women. (2020a). COVID-19 and Ending Violence against Women and Girls. (EVAW COVID-19 briefs). Retrieved from https://www.unwomen.org/en/digital-library/publications/2020/04/issue-brief-COVID-19-and-ending-violence-against-women-and-girls

UN Women. (2020b). COVID-19: Emerging gender data and why it matters. Retrieved from https://data.unwomen.org/resources/COVID-19-emerging-gender-data-and-why-it-matters

UN Women. (2020c). HeForShe launches #HeForSheAtHome campaign. Retrieved from https://www.unwomen.org/en/news/stories/2020/4/news-heforshe-launches-heforsheathome-campaign

Verma, R. (2020). China's 'mask diplomacy' to change the COVID-19 narrative in Europe. *Asia Europe Journal 18*, 205–209. https://doi.org/10.1007/s10308-020-00576-1

Xafis, V. (2020). 'What is inconvenient for you is life-saving for me': How health inequities are playing out during the COVID-19 Pandemic. *Asian Bioethics Review, 1–12.*

Chapter 3

The World Health Organization under COVID-19: Behind the Crisis

Yue Han

The WHO, as the largest inter-governmental organization specializing in international public health, was founded in Geneva on 7th April 1948. It is one of the specialized agencies of the UN. So far, with 72 years of development, WHO now has 194 member states across the world and is regarded as the leader in global public health provision.

However, as the world entered into the second decade of the twenty-first century, the WHO and all people around the world met huge challenges. On 30 January 2020, the WHO announced a public health emergency of international concern (PHEIC) due to the quick spread of COVID-19. This pandemic has spread over all populated regions in the world, including Asia, America, Europe and Africa, and caused much loss there. No doubt, more than ever, we need people around the world to cooperate together and we need WHO's coordination and guidance. Especially, since this is a pandemic that happens in a deeply globalized world and the spread of virus is not restricted by territories, religions or ideologies. A single state alone will not solve this problem; therefore, this is really the time that we urgently need multilateralism. Moreover, on 14 April, President Donald Trump of the United States declared to stop funding to the WHO, accusing its belated actions. What challenges were brought to the WHO by the global outbreak and this incident? Are there any long-standing problems behind these new challenges? What can be done to tackle these problems as the boost for a better WHO? And ultimately, are we witnessing a broader dilemma of multilateralism that questions what the future of multilateralism will be like? In the following sections, this chapter will explore the answer to these questions in regard to the WHO.

2. ABOUT THE WORLD HEALTH ORGANIZATION

2.1. Establishment

Since the fourteenth century, with the continuous improvement of technology and social productivity, the scope of human activities has gradually expanded, constantly accompanied by several epidemics that have caused huge losses. In the face of new diseases or viruses, humans have never been more vulnerable. To this day, although we have achieved impressive economic and technological development, we still face a huge health crisis. Every epidemic has left us with hard lessons and experience. Therefore, we have also gradually gained new knowledge about how to prevent and control epidemics and how to understand health and strive to put them into practice.

In the 1450s, a plague swept across Europe. With the exception of Finland and Iceland, it claimed the lives of around 25 million people (Britannica, 2020). This plague has a more well-known name, the Black Death. In this epidemic, in order to control the spread of the disease more effectively, the then Venetian authority announced that all foreign people suspected to be infected and ships must be quarantined for 40 days before being allowed to enter Venice. This practice is the source of what we call "quarantine" today (UNESCO, 2020). During the fifteenth and sixteenth centuries, with European colonists entering the Americas, many fatal diseases and viruses also stepped onto the continent, especially the smallpox, which caused the local indigenous people, who had no immunity to such diseases to die in large numbers. In 1980, through the not Smallpox Eradication Programme of the WHO, this infectious disease that has infested humans for hundreds of years, was finally declared eradicated (WHO, 2010). In the first half of the nineteenth century, cholera broke out in Europe that was once again shrouded in the shadow of an epidemic. This time, people realized the importance of cooperation to cope with the crisis. In 1851, the International Sanitary Conference was held in Paris, which was also the first formal attempt to carry out disease prevention and control through a global cooperative mechanism (McCarthy, 2002, p. 1111). Between 1918 and 1919, almost 50 million people worldwide died from the flu virus (Britannica, 2020). It is also known as the Spanish flu, but in fact its origin has not been confirmed. This epidemic was the most serious outbreak in the twentieth century, but at the same time, it provided the impetus to further develop the international public health system after this crisis. The establishment of the Ministry of Health in France and the United Kingdom (UK) is largely due to this experience (Cotter, 2020).

From the beginning of the twentieth century, the development speed of the global public health system began to increase, and all countries reached a consensus to resolve global problems and crises in this field through international cooperation. In 1902, the world's first international health organization, the Pan American Health Organization (PAHO), was established. After the WHO was founded, PAHO was kept and became a regional office of the WHO. The functions of the L'Office International d'Hygiene Publique and the Pulque Health Organisation of the League of Nations, which were established in 1907 and 1919, respectively, were subsequently integrated by WHO. These two can be regarded as predecessors of the WHO. In 1945, the appeals from some developing countries brought the global health issue formally onto the agenda of international discussions (Cockerham, 2018, p. 33). Subsequently, the United Nations Conference on International Organizations voted to establish a new international health organization. In 1946, the International Health Conference (IHC) adopted the Constitution of the WHO (McCarthy, 2002, p. 1111). During the transition period from 1946 to 1948, the interim committee was composed of 18 countries that took over global health affairs. On 7 April 1948, the WHO was officially established as a specialized agency of the UN and the prime leader in the global public health system.

2.2. The Development of the WHO

As an agency that based in Geneva promotes and coordinates global public health cooperation, the WHO has 194 member states, as well as six regional offices, respectively, responsible for the affairs in Africa, the Americas, South-East Asia, Europe, the Eastern Mediterranean and the Western Pacific. These offices operate within a unified WHO framework but also have a degree of autonomy and decision-making power, with the aim to increase flexibility in the setting of different regional health priorities according to the circumstances of different regions (White, Stallones, & Last, 2013, p. 252). In addition, the WHO also has country offices, but not every country has it. If a country can conduct high-level health policy and projects, in that case, the WHO will play a smaller role in this country; therefore, the United States and some developed countries in Europe often do not have a country office, and instead, they are directly in contact with regional offices or the headquarters. In contrary, the country offices in undeveloped countries sometimes assume a more important role than their own health ministry (White et al., 2013, p. 253). The regional and country offices, to a certain extent, ensure the flexibility of the implementation of projects, which are adapted to local conditions for better results. However, this setting also brings some problems, which will be discussed in the following parts.

According to the Constitution of the WHO, which was adopted in 1946, the internal structure of the organization (including the World Health Assembly [WHA], the Executive Board [EB] and the Secretariat) remains unchanged until today. The WHA is the main decision-making body, responsible for determining general policies issued by WHO, and has the authority to manage the budget and appoint the Director-General. Each member states has at least one representative in the WHA, who must be a medical professional. In addition, the WHA has the power to set regulations and standards, which are binding on all states. According to the Article 19 of the Constitution, the WHA also has a legislative power, namely the treaty/convention-making power, which was first used in the case of the Framework Convention on Tobacco Control (FCTC) of 2003 (Cockerham, 2018, p. 35). The WHA adopts the principle of majority voting, in which each member states has a fair vote and at least two-thirds of the votes are required for approval.

The EB is primarily responsible for implementation and may also provide advice and proposals to the WHA. It has only 34 members who are elected by the WHA, and are medical experts as well. Geographical equity must be taken into account in the election of members (Cockerham, 2018, p. 36). The Secretariat is the bureaucracy of the WHO, consisting of the Director-General and other technical and administrative staff. According to the Constitution, the Director-General, nominated by the EB and appointed by the WHA after the election, is the head of the Secretariat and the WHO. His main responsibilities include the preparation of financial reports and staff appointments, as well as to decide whether a disease is to be declared as a PHEIC. The central working principle of Secretariat and the Director-General is neutrality, which means they shall not be biased by nationality backgrounds. They are committed to the WHO, rather than their home country, and as a result, the Director-General has much informal power and prestige, which regularly affects the EB to support his initiatives (Cockerham, 2018, p. 36). Moreover, the personal orientation and leadership style of different Director-Generals and the level of support from member states also influence the external role of the WHO in the global public health system.

2.3. The Role of the WHO

The WHO's functions and roles in the global health system are mainly defined by the constitution. However, its status in the real world is sometimes changing and its authority could be challenged. This COVID-19 pandemic is likely to become an important dividing point on its development path.

According to the Constitution, the WHO has a total of 22 functions that almost cover all aspects of global health, among which the primary function is to direct and coordinate international health work, which is also the fundamental definition of the WHO's role. This highlights the expectation in the post-war era, that it is supposed by its founders to assume a leading role (Cockerham, 2018, p. 32). Specifically, the WHO has the following six core functions: "providing leadership on matters critical to health and engaging in partnerships where joint action is needed; shaping the research agenda and stimulating the generation, translation and dissemination of valuable knowledge; setting norms and standards and promoting and monitoring their implementation; articulating ethical and evidence-based policy options; providing technical support, catalysing change, and building sustainable institutional capacity; and monitoring the health situation and assessing health trends" (WHO, 2014). Through these functions, the WHO aims to achieve "the attainment of by all peoples of the highest possible level of health," which is a grand goal clearly written in the constitution. The WHO's creation was meaningful from the very start, which is not only because it integrated all the functions of previous health organizations but also because it entails a fundamentally comprehensive interpretation of health. According to the Preamble of the Constitution, "Health is a state of complete physical, mental and social wellbeing and not merely the absence of disease or infirmity." Thus, health is not only affected by biological factors but also the result of social factors, corresponding to two orientations to promote health, which will be further described further. In addition, in the 1946 Constitution, health was also regarded as a basic human right; thus, the legal obligation of states to protect the health of people was confirmed (WHO, 2017). At the 73rd WHA on May 19, the WHO once again recalled its authority and leadership and reiterated its constitutional definition of health as the fundamental human right for all people (WHO, 2020).

3. COVID-19 AND THE TWO-LEVEL CHALLENGE

3.1. The WHO in the COVID-19 Pandemic

In 2020, just at the beginning of the second decade of the twenty-first century, the international community is confronted with a huge test—the COVID-19 crisis, with outbreaks in many countries and regions. In addition to the country as the main actor fighting against the epidemic, the WHO, as the prominent authority in the field of global public health, plays a significant and irreplaceable role. This is because the spread of disease is not blocked by borders, and pandemic control and resolution require practical international cooperation and information sharing, as well as real-time surveillance and professional guidance at the macro level. What's more, when developed countries focus on the domestic epidemic affairs, developing countries with a poor medical level face a greater crisis and the role of WHO is more indispensable in these countries and regions.

So how is WHO responding to this crisis? I have selected the most important actions. For a more detailed timeline, it might be necessary to visit the official website.

According to the WHO (2020), on 31 December 2019, the Municipal Health Commission of Wuhan, China, reported an unidentified pneumonia case, and the WHO set up the Incident Management Support Team (IMST) the next day. The WHO announced this on a social media platform on 4 January 2020, followed by official news of the event on the following day, which included risk assessment and recommendations. On 10 January, the WHO released a series of technical guidance online; on 14 January, it indicated that there might be a limited human-to-human transmission of the coronavirus; on 20 January, experts from the WHO regional office arrived at Wuhan for a field visit. On 30 January, the Director-General announced that the novel coronavirus (2019-nCoV) was a PHEIC. Prior to that, the Director-General had convened an Emergency Committee to discuss whether the outbreak constituted a PHEIC, but could not reach an agreement; in February, WHO conducted a series of plans and meetings, and organized a mission of experts from different countries to China; on 11 March, it expressed concern about the transmission rate and severity of the epidemic and assessed that COVID-19 can be considered a pandemic; since then, the WHO has continued its work in response to the outbreak. Generally, the WHO has been playing following roles during the outbreak: monitoring of the development of the global epidemic; timely release of authoritative information to prevent the spread of misinformation; provision of professional advices and guidance for countries; organization of experts to study about the virus and the pandemic; coordination of efforts of different actors at all levels (including countries, other international organizations, NGOs, etc.) to better manage COVID-19 and provide assistance to countries with weak medical abilities. The WHO expresses an optimistic attitude that the outbreak can be controlled and its impact mitigated through its leadership and continued global cooperation and solidarity (WHO, 2020).

3.2. The First-Level Challenge: From the Pandemic

Although the WHO has expressed optimism, there is no doubt that this outbreak of COVID-19 is a huge test that every step matters. If it fails to perform its functions well, people's attitude towards it may deteriorate, and its influence and authority will be affected. After all, the premise for international organizations to carry out their work is largely based on consensus and recognition. Before an outbreak becomes a global crisis, the WHO's ability and sensitivity to unusual situations is critical. Of course, this also relates to our current level of science and technology: new diseases or virus mean that our understanding about it is limited; therefore, measures are also limited, but that doesn't mean we are completely incapable, as we can draw lessons from previous experience, and carry out studies on the new virus at the same time. All this requires the WHO to have quick reaction speed and an effective mechanism.

In addition, after the outbreak, the ways to coordinate and direct the global response are crucial. Since the severity of the epidemic is different in countries and regions, attitudes and practices vary widely, which makes it more difficult for the WHO to achieve its goal of controlling the pandemic at the global level. Just as the WHO declared, different actors play different roles in the response to the epidemic: WHO is only the key leader in catalysing and coordinating the comprehensive global response, and member states still make central efforts (WHO, 2020). However, the role of the WHO in underdeveloped regions is relatively more important because of the low level of medical technology and the fragile local health systems. In general, due to the different outbreak times in different regions, imbalances of medical resources and levels around the world and different measures taken by countries, it has become more difficult than ever for the WHO to coordinate and guide global health work.

3.3. The Second-Level Challenge: From the Trump Administration

It was at this difficult time of pandemic that the WHO encountered an unprecedented institutional crisis. On 29 May 2020, U.S. President Donald Trump announced that the United States will terminate relations with the WHO. Prior to this, the Trump administration had stated that it would stop funding the WHO (CNN, 2020). As early as in the 1950s, the Soviet Union had also boycotted the UN system, including the WHO (Cockerham, 2018, p. 37); however, the absence of the Soviet Union was only temporary, and it did not mean that it had any strong complaints about the WHO specifically. This time the United States announced that it will withdraw from the WHO and stop funding it, to an extent, that symbolizes the Trump administration's pro-denial attitude towards the WHO's work. Considering its previous withdrawal from the Paris Agreement and the Iran nuclear agreement, it is a reasonable doubt that the Trump administration does not hold a positive attitude further to multilateralism.

President Trump believes that WHO is mismanaging the pandemic, and believes that it has failed to fulfil its "basic duty" (BBC, 2020). He also accused the WHO of being China-centric, though he did not give any clear evidence. After announcing the cessation of funding for the WHO in April, President Trump wrote to the Director-General, Dr Tedros, asking the WHO to make substantial reforms. However, this request was not approved by the WHO. Therefore, the United States announced that it will end its relationship with the WHO permanently.

There is no absolute standard to judge whether its behaviours are correct or not, but those series of allegations from the Trump administration may have following impacts on the WHO. First, WHO's leadership and authority in the global public health system will be affected. Brazilian President Jair Bolsonaro also threatened in May that Brazil may also withdraw from the WHO (Reuters, 2020). At the same time, President Trump claimed to redirect funds to other needed places. If the United States turns to support other organizations or wants to establish a new one to replace WHO in the future, then the status of WHO will be endangered. Second, the Trump administration's accusation of WHO's overreliance on China could damage the WHO's reputation, because one of the principles of WHO is to maintain independence and neutrality, and the reason why WHO can obtain supports from various countries is also largely based on the recognition of this principle. Finally, under the current situation where the pandemic is still serious, if the United States ceases financial support for WHO, from the current point of view, this will not be conducive to the control of the global epidemic, and could weaken WHO's capabilities in the long run. Especially for undeveloped countries that rely heavily on the WHO, this move will directly affect the health safety and the development in these places. Therefore, WHO has called on its member states to provide sustainable funding (WHO, 2020).

Dr Richard Horton, the editor-in-chief of the authoritative medical journal— the *Lancet*—remarks that these allegations are unfounded, and the halting of funds is "a crime against humanity"; global health and safety require a strong WHO, and the WHO needs strong support from the United States (Horton, 2020).

4. THE LONG-STANDING PROBLEMS

In fact, although the COVID-19 pandemic has brought WHO challenges on two levels, it also reflects to some extent, some of the inherent problems that have long existed in WHO and other similar international organizations. These problems are not necessarily independent of each other but often affect or interact with each other. This pandemic has exposed these problems and highlights the urgency of solving them.

4.1. The Financial Problems

First, the WHO's financial and budgetary problems have always existed, and if the WHO loses U.S. financial assistance, it may further undermine its role in global system. Compared with other actors that have a global public health mandate, WHO's budget size (excluding voluntary extra-budgetary donations) is not large, even smaller than the budget of some major hospitals in Western Europe and the United States (Cueto, Brown, & Fee, 2019, p. 327), and member states are in arrears of contributions from time to time. In the 1990s, the WB's health loans even exceeded WHO's regular budget (Clift, 2013, p. 7), which undoubtedly impacted the WHO position. Tight budgets can cause many problems, such as hampering the achievement of short-term and long-term goals. After the 2008 economic crisis, the WHO was considered to be "under-resourced" (Cueto, Brown, & Fee, 2019, p. 324). It suffered budget and staff reductions, especially in emergency responses. This is partly related to WHO's slow response to the Ebola outbreak in 2014. Once the Ebola epidemic was over, the WHO launched a series of new emergency projects in order to better promote its ability to respond to emergencies in the future. Yet, many people are now worried that WHO will still encounter funding problems because of the lack of monetary support from member countries (Hayden, 2016, p. 494), and this will directly affect WHO's emergency responses.

In addition to its budget, WHO funding sources have also caused some problems. The funding of the WHO mainly stems from assessed contributions and voluntary contributions. Assessed contributions must be paid by each member states, while the amount varies according to wealth and population of the respective country. According to the WHO, the proportion of assessed contributions has declined in recent years: the proportion in 2018–2019 has only been about 17.02% (WHO, 2020). Voluntary contributions are extra-budgetary but account for two thirds or more of all annual spending (Cueto et al., 2019, p. 326). These funds come from different countries, mainly developed countries. They also come from some organizations or private foundations, such as Bill and Melinda Gates Foundation. Why does the composition of WHO's funding sources also cause problems? This is because compared to voluntary contributions, the WHO has greater autonomy over assessed contributions and can decide how to spend this part of money more independently. However, the WHO has been relying heavily on voluntary donations from the beginning, even though the assessed contributions also gradually increased with the joining of the new member states. A large part of voluntary donations can only be used for a specific programme, and more than half of the funds come from developed countries. Moreover, developing countries may perceive and rank the health agenda and priorities differently (White et al., 2013, p. 253), which may lead to the imbalance of funds between different programmes. Take the ongoing COVID-19 pandemic as an example, Developed countries may pay more attention to vaccine research and production because they already have the ability to cope with the domestic epidemic. However, undeveloped countries with poor health levels may have difficulties responding to the epidemic and WHO's technical assistance and financial supports are even more needed. In addition, since voluntary contributions are not mandatory, this part of funds entails potential instability and volatility. Overall, according to Cueto, Brown and Fee (2019), the weak and unstable funding situation of WHO will make the leadership of the global health system fragmented, and other better-funded bilateral institutions, such as USAID, multilateral organizations such as the WB, and private foundations could all challenge the WHO. If the United States really withdraws from the WHO and ceases funding, this problem will likely become more serious.

4.2. On the Web of International Politics

The second problem is that the WHO is hard to be completely independent of international politics. Since Global order changes and power politics have always exerted influence and pressure on the WHO. For sure, this is also a problem that many other international organizations encounter. Specifically, to further understand this issue, we need to understand the two orientations of the WHO, because it is the development of these two orientations that is mainly affected by international political flows.

As mentioned earlier, the definition of health by the WHO is not only biological but also involves social factors. Therefore, WHO's programmes and initiatives can be roughly divided into two orientations. The first is a biomedical orientation, which is mainly reflected in direct vertical intervention projects, such as disease control and eradication programmes, which are mainly supported by developed countries, because they are usually short term and less complicated to implement. In addition, people or countries that receive assistance are usually considered passive and cannot actively participate in the programme (Cueto et al., 2019, p. 337). The second is a socio-medical orientation. This view believes that promoting health should be achieved not only through technical means but also through the development of basic health systems. This orientation involves health equality and the promotion of a broader improvement of the social environment (Cueto et al., 2019, p. 2), which is often more concerned by undeveloped countries. From the beginning of the WHO's establishment, conflicts between these two orientations have occurred from time to time. People who support socio-medical orientation have been criticized for being too idealistic because they asked the WHO to do something beyond their capabilities, such as solving poverty; while biomedical is regarded as a tool for pursuing national interests, where poverty and diseases are described as "natural" (Cueto et al., 2019, p. 339).

Before the establishment of the WHO, the United States and the Soviet Union reached a consensus on the establishment of an international organization dedicated to public health, but they had divergent ideas. The United

States believed that this organization should focus on the monitoring and control of infectious diseases. It also believed that the socio-medical approach is a criticism of capitalism; but the Soviet Union was more inclined to the socio-medical orientation, and believed that the WHO should bear more social work (Cockerham, 2018, p. 33). In the early days of its establishment, WHO was under tremendous pressure from the United States and the Soviet Union. But because the Soviet Union was temporarily absent from the UN, it lost the power at the WHO during that period. In the 1950s, the United States largely influenced the WHO, so that the biomedical vertical programmes dominated. In the 1970s, the relationship between the United States and the Soviet Union eased. They then reached an agreement on the Smallpox Eradication Programme (1967–1977). This project achieved success through vaccines and surveillance, which greatly improved people's confidence in disease control and vertical projects, as well as WHO's prestige (Cockerham, 2018, p. 38). At the same time, during this period, newly independent former colonial states joined the UN system, and developing countries gradually formed a force in the UN, persuading the UN General Assembly to pass the Neo International Economic Order (Neo International Economic Order). Correspondingly, within the WHO, the United States' dominance and biomedical orientation have been challenged, socio-medical has begun to rise, and developing countries have called for greater attention to the development of basic health needs. In 1977, WHO passed a resolution on "Health for All by the Year 2000"; in 1978, the "Alma-Ata Declaration" with the Primary Health Care (PHC) as the core was proposed, and PHC is the main way to realize the "health for all."

From the 1980s to the early 1990s, developed countries led by the United States and Britain advocated neoliberal economic policies. They emphasized the role of market, advocated for reducing government intervention in the economy and called on other countries to open markets and engage in free trade. The WB and the IMF appeared on the world stage at this time more and more frequently. Neoliberalism believes that health is more of a commodity than a human right, and that market regulation is more important than state behaviour. This view poses a huge challenge to the socio-medical-oriented PHC (Cockerham, 2018, p. 41). Therefore, the WHO suffered a double crisis during this period. Financially, more and more countries began to decrease the funding of the WHO, with a tighter and tighter budget. Therefore, the WHO was increasingly relying on donations from the extra-budgetary resources of developed countries, and the influence of developed countries on WHO was surging. From the leadership perspective, the unique advantages that the WB and the IMF can provide in regard to funding have also made them more and more important in the global health system and shaken WHO's leadership comparatively. Affected by the economic crisis in 2008, neoliberalism began to decline. The WHO also turned from being affected by neoliberalism to attaching more importance to the social medical approach in order to promote global health, and reemphasized the importance of PHC and health equity.

4.3. WHO's "Relatively Weak Leadership" and the Lack of Power

Due to the dual impacts of financial problems and international politics, WHO presents a relatively weak leadership style both internally and externally, which is mainly due to a fundamental problem: the lack of power. In the context of this article, power is defined as the ability to let others (mainly the state) do something and the ability to refuse things that one doesn't want to do. This interpretation is mainly influenced by classical realism. According to Morgenthau (1973), power is the ability to control the actions of others.

Externally, WHO's leadership in the global public health system is sometimes challenged by other actors. Due to the rise of neoliberal economic policies since the 1980s and the rapid development of economic globalization later on, public health is also considered to have important links with economic development. Other actors are gradually participating in global health work, such as the WB, the WTO, the IMF and other, which have strong competitiveness. UNICEF and UNDP in the UN system also have health-related mandates (White et al., 2013, p. 252). In addition, the WHO is often under pressure from major powers, and even criticized and questioned, just as the United States does in the pandemic. Internally, the WHO is different from other UN agencies through the establishment of its regional organizations (Clift, 2013, p. 7). Each regional branch enjoys a certain degree of autonomy. Therefore, the effective communication between Geneva and regional offices becomes crucial. In reflection of the criticized response to the 2014 Ebola epidemic, we found that the relationship between the headquarters and local offices is sometimes "confrontational" (Cueto et al., 2019, p. 323). Some countries are worried that their economic development will be negatively affected by WHO's health assessments.

Fundamentally, this relatively weak leadership style of WHO still stems from its lack of power. The mandate of the WHO is the role of directing and coordination, which means that many of its decisions are often not mandatory but only for reference and guidance, and the main subject of global public health practice is still each country. During the COVID-19 pandemic, governments still assumes the primary responsibility (WHO, 2020). As an intergovernmental organization, WHO's establishment is based on the consensus of all member states. If this consensus does not exist, the WHO will face the potential risk of being abolished or replaced. From a realist perspective, states are still the main actor of the international system and politics, and the founder of major international organizations. The change of international politics is determined by the state's pursuit of power and interests. Besides, due to the lack of a central power over the powers, the international system is anarchic, and therefore the influence of the international institutions on state behaviour is limited (Mearsheimer, 1995, p. 7). Instead, these institutions sometimes reflect the interests of powerful countries and even become a tool to pursue national interests. According to hegemonic stability theory, in order to maintain status or pursue interests, hegemons often establish an international order or systems, and promote international cooperation; for example, after the end of World War II, the United States supported the Bretton Woods system (Cockerham, 2018, p. 8). In general, many of the WHO's dilemmas derive from its lack of powers, so that it cannot be fully independent of international relations. At the same time, it has limited enforcement power on powers, which is a problem shared by many similar international organizations.

5. THE FUTURE OUTLOOK

In the face of the COVID-19 crisis, it is necessary to pay attention to those problems behind and trying to solve them is essential not only to overcome the current crisis but also to the development in the long run. In fact, the fundamental power-related problem will exist for a long time, and is difficult to be solved thoroughly, but it does not mean this situation cannot be improved. To address surface problems, WHO can further improve its operational capabilities and functions continually at all levels under the 2005 Constitution. What's more, WHO can also strengthen its independence by continuously calling for adjustments. However, this depends to a great extent on the international community, especially the leaders or leading groups of powerful countries' awareness of the global crisis and their faith in multilateralism.

First of all, the WHO should keep strengthening its functions and optimizing its working process, to win over more sustainable support and trust from member states for itself. Specifically, the WHO should try to strive for best performance in the six core functions mentioned earlier, and it must ensure its absolute professionalism and authority in the global public health system. At the same time, the WHO should also improve its ability to respond to global emergencies, and gradually form a mature emergency response system. The more urgent the situation is, the more efficient the WHO has to lead global cooperation. Furthermore, we must pay attention to the role of the Independent Oversight and Advisory Committee (IOAC) (WHO, 2019). By thoroughly monitoring, reviewing and reflecting on each performance, the WHO may continuously benefit from experience. Finally, WHO should try to balance the biomedical orientation and sociomedical orientation. Technical assistance through vertical programmes is as important as promoting global health equality, and these two are not conflicting; especially in underdeveloped areas, this is even more important. If only short-term vertical intervention projects are undertaken, and the local fundamental health level cannot be promoted, the limited results achieved may also be compromised.

As for financial issues, in the face of the current situation, WHO should first try to continue to negotiate with the U.S. government to explore the possibility of not terminating relations and continuing its financial support. After all, the United States, as one of the most important actors in the international system, and one of the founding countries of WHO, is also the biggest contributor. If negotiations fail to achieve good results, the WHO should actively seek more than one sources of funding to fill this gap. In the long term, the WHO still has to work hard to increase the proportion and amount of assessed contributions, so as to enhance its control and autonomy over its money. In order to achieve this goal, the WHO needs to strengthen its operational capabilities and provide better "services" to member states, in order to further consolidate the support and trust of member states.

Finally, to solve these problems, we still need to call on the international community, especially nation states, to pay attention to public health issues, effective multilateralism and global governance, as solutions. According to realism, global governance depends on state power. Global governance, represented by international rules and regulations and international organizations, is itself established and developed by the state, therefore it needs long-term support from the state (Cockerham, 2018, p. 20). However, because the state behaviour in the international community is driven by the pursuit of national interests, the most basic national interest is national security (the independency, and territorial and sovereignty integrity) and the importance of global health issue is sometimes overlooked. This COVID-19 pandemic has reminded the international community that we cannot wait until every crisis erupts. Second, as the leadership in global public health governance, WHO's status and power should be guaranteed, which can be further ensured by improving relevant international laws and regulations.

6. CONCLUSION

Overall, the global health system and WHO have encountered huge challenges during the COVID-19 pandemic, but the problems we have witnessed so far actually reflect many long-standing problems behind the scenes and solutions to these problems are of crucial importance to overcoming current crisis and to its future development. The two main issues of the WHO are the financial problem and the influence of international politics. To a certain extent, other similar international organizations often encounter the same problems. From a deeper perspective, multilateralism represented by international organizations is sometimes in dilemma. Both multilateralism and global governance emphasize the importance of extensive cooperation between countries to solve problems. However, due to the anarchy of the international system, the state is the main actor in this system. It is hard for organizations that are established based on multilateralism to operate without being influenced by international relations. However, global problems and crises, such as the COVID-19 or climate change, can only be controlled or resolved through extensive global cooperation, since all human-being shares a common destiny and future. As time goes by, I firmly believe people will pay more and more attention to these global issues, and recognize and value the importance of multilateralism in the future.

REFERENCES

BBC. (2020, April 15). Coronavirus: US to halt funding to WHO, says Trump. Retrieved 7 June 2020 from https://www.bbc.com/news/world-us-canada-52289056.

Britannica, T. Editors of Encyclopaedia (2020, November 9). Black Death. Encyclopedia Britannica. https://www.britannica.com/event/Black-Death.

Britannica, T. Editors of Encyclopaedia (2020, July 7). Influenza pandemic of 1918–19. Encyclopedia Britannica. https://www.britannica.com/event/influenza-pandemic-of-1918-1919.

Cédric, C. (2020, April 23). From the "Spanish Flu" to COVID-19: Lessons from the 1918 pandemic and First World War. Retrieved 22 June 2020 from https://blogs.icrc.org/law-and-policy/2020/04/23/spanish-flu-covid-19–1918-pandemic-first-world-war/.

Clift, C. D. (2013). The role of the World Health Organization in the International System. Retrieved 22 June 2020 from https://www.chathamhouse.org/sites/default/files/publications/research/2013-02-01-role-world-health-organization-international-system-clift.pdf.

CNN. (2020, May 29). Trump announces end of US relationship with World Health Organization. Retrieved 7 June 2020 from https://edition.cnn.com/2020/05/29/politics/donald-trump-world-health-organization/index.html.

Cockerham, G. B. (2018). *Global governance and public health: Obstacles and opportunities.* 1–66.

Cueto, M., Brown, T., & Fee, E. (2019). *The World Health Organization: A history (Global health histories (Series)).* 1–9, 320–340.

Hayden, E. (2016). Major rethink for outbreak response. *Nature,* 540(7634), 494–495.

Horton, R. (2020). Offline: Why president Trump is wrong about WHO. *The Lancet,* 395(10233), 1330.

McCarthy, M. (2002). A brief history of the World Health Organization. *The Lancet,* 360(9340), 1111–1112.

Mearsheimer, J. (1995). The false promise of international institutions. *International Security,* 19(3), 5–49.

Morgenthau, H. (1973). *Politics among nations: The struggle for power and peace* (5th ed. rev., reset. ed.). New York: Knopf; distributed by Random House.

Reuters. (2020, June 5). Bolsonaro threatens WHO exit as COVID-19 kills "a Brazilian per minute." Retrieved 7 June 2020 from https://www.reuters.com/article/us-health-coronavirus-brazil/bolsonaro-threatens-who-exit-as-covid-19-kills-a-brazilian-per-minute-idUSKBN23C1TF.

UNESCO. (2020, March 31). Black Death: How can we learn from the spread of disease along the Silk Roads. Retrieved 2 June 2020 from https://en.unesco.org/news/black-death-how-can-we-learn-spread-disease-along-silk-roads.

White, F., Stallones, L., & Last, J. (2013). "Global public health, ecological foundations" in *Public Health Organization and Function in Evolving Health Systems.* Oxford University Press.

WHO. (2010, May). The Smallpox Eradication Programme—SEP (1966–1980). Retrieved 1 June 2020 from https://www.who.int/features/2010/smallpox/en/.

WHO. (2017, December 29). Human rights and health. Retrieved 26 May 26 2020 from https://www.who.int/news-room/fact-sheets/detail/human-rights-and-health.

WHO. (2019, December 19). WHO's role in emergencies. Retrieved June 9 2020 from https://www.who.int/news-room/q-a-detail/who-s-role-in-emergencies.

WHO. (2020, April 27). WHO Timeline—COVID-19. Retrieved 23 June 23 2020 from https://www.who.int/news-room/detail/27-04-2020-who-timeline—covid-19.

WHO. (2020, May 19). Covid-19 Response. Retrieved 22 June 2020 from https://apps.who.int/gb/ebwha/pdf_files/WHA73/A73_R1-en.pdf.

World Health Organization. (n.d.). *Assessed contributions.* WHO. Retrieved 8 June 2020 from https://www.who.int/about/funding/assessed-contributions

WHO. (n.d.b). The role of WHO in public health. Retrieved 1 June 2020 from https://www.who.int/about/role/en/.

Chapter 4

The Multilateral Trading System in a Changing World: The WTO and Current Threats Challenging Its Survival

Morgane B. De Clercq

INTRODUCTION

The WTO was founded in 1995 as a final product of the Uruguay Round and operates as a successor of the General Agreement on Tariffs and Trade (GATT). The GATT and subsequently the WTO were created as an institutional solution to the Prisoner's Dilemma in trade to foster international trade by reducing tariffs and limit the use of non-tariff barriers. Initially, the GATT was established as a post–World War II agreement in 1947 in a world with the United States acting as a hegemon to promote and spread American values such as trade liberalisation, multilateralism and a legal approach to international trade (Capling & Trommer, 2017, p. 116). The GATT was formed as a temporary agreement until the International Trade Organisation's (ITO) charter was implemented, which was blocked by the non-ratification of the United States and ultimately never came into effect. The ITO was intended to complement the Bretton Woods institutions, the WB and the IMF (Capling & Trommer, 2017, p. 117).[1] The GATT, however, came into force. In tandem with its principle of liberalisation were principles of non-discrimination, reciprocity, development and safeguards (Zacher & Finlayson, 1981). Several rounds of trade negotiations have been organised since the establishment of the GATT and ultimately the Uruguay Round, finalised in 1994, led to the creation of the WTO in order to strengthen the rules of the international trading system.

The WTO has expanded ever since and as such, it has become the largest and most important international organisations regulating global trade. It currently consists of 164 members and several states are currently in the process of accession (WTO, n.d.a). The main goals of the WTO have been expanded to include six themes (1) reducing discrimination; (2) promoting market access opportunities; (3) formulating rules of conduct for goods and services; (4) promoting transparency of national laws and regulations; (5) promoting dialogue and understanding on trade matters, and (6) settling trade disputes (Capling & Trommer, 2017, p. 127). These goals must be accomplished in accordance with the WTO's main principles: (1) non-discrimination, based on the "most favoured nation" (MFN) principle indicating that all countries should be treated the same (2) transparency, (3) reciprocity, (4) flexibility and (5) consensus, a principle shaped during the Uruguay Round implying that all members must agree unanimously (Baldwin, 2016, p. 97). These principles can be traced down to the overarching principle of the WTO. The constitutional principle entails that the WTO is an organisation that is rules-based and not results-based (Baldwin, 2016, p. 97). This is auspicious in theory, though in practice, it has been proven that globalisation affects its effectiveness. Globalisation, in this context, is defined by the Peterson Institute of International Economics (PIIE) as "the growing interdependence of the world's economies, cultures, and populations, brought about by cross-border trade in goods and services, technology, and flows of investment, people, and information" (Kolb, 2019). A first example that will be further explored in this chapter is the rise of populism which changes the playing field of the WTO and challenges the multilateral nature of the organisation. It appears to be impossible to align all members which subsequently leads to a shift from multilateral towards plurilateral agreements.

This chapter will analyse the current challenges the WTO faces in this rapidly changing world and explores how ongoing trends will shape the future of the WTO and consequently, multilateralism. The chapter is structured as follows: firstly, an in-depth analysis of the WTO today will be made focusing on its current functioning, its advantages and its main challenges: (1) the failure of the Doha Round, (2) the Dispute Settlement Body (DSB) and President Trump, (3) the new Sino-American reality and (4) the 2020 COVID-19 pandemic terrorising the entire world. Secondly, based on the challenges previously discussed, a most likely scenario for the organisation's future will be outlined with the focus on plurilateral agreements, a parallel DSB, a post-COVID-19 world and the importance of the least developed countries (LDCs).

1. THE WTO TODAY

1.1. The Disappearance of the Sense of Belonging: Change in Playing Field

To understand the implications of the advantages and challenges, an overview of the current playing field of the WTO will be outlined. The WTO has always been a member-driven organisation with its secretariat only carrying out a limited supporting function towards WTO members (WTO, n.d.b). This implies that members bring new initiatives to the negotiation table and negotiate the terms of agreements, which apply the single undertaking principle, themselves. According to Patrick Low (2011), Chief Economist at the WTO, the single undertaking principle was initially created to "prevent parties from 'cherry-picking' results or 'harvesting' early outcomes from the negotiations unless all parties agreed" (p. 4). Later, the meaning of the single undertaking principle as a negotiation strategy shifted towards the stimulation of inclusiveness to encourage the signature of an agreement (Low, 2011, p. 4). According to Hoekman (2012), the single undertaking principle is that "nothing is agreed until everything is agreed" (p. 746). However, the Uruguay Round already showed that aligning the interest of all members was a challenging task and, due to global changes, these difficulties only increase.

A current trend that influences the working of the WTO is the rise of populism. The rise of populism prevents the WTO from properly executing its initial function of creating rules for freer trade and enforcing compliance of these rules. Instead the WTO firstly needs to concentrate on aligning the diverging interests of the two groups created due to the populistic trends and thus act as a referee before it can execute its main function: the first group of states comprises the states with populistic leaders who mainly operate in self-interest and the wellbeing of their own country (e.g. protectionist policies) and do not thrive for international cooperation and the second category of states includes states who value cooperation and believe in the interest of a global, interdependent multilateral trading system which facilitates smooth, predictable and freer trade flows (WTO, n.d.a). This change in playing field will directly and indirectly influence the working of the WTO and the current challenges it faces. The next sections will analyse the benefits and challenges of the WTO.

1.2. Factors Leading to Sustained Cooperation within the WTO

The WTO's most significant advantage is closely related to its goal: providing freer trade to all members, which reflects the inclusiveness of the organisation. Generally, the WTO has achieved this goal relatively well due to several values which direct the effectiveness of the organisation.

The first one is the previously mentioned *consensus* that must be reached between the member governments. The WTO works with a one-country-one-vote principle and hence one can argue that all members have meaningful influence in the voting procedure. However, it is clear that realistically a country's influence depends on other factors such as the size of the market, its financial means and its expertise (Capling & Trommer, 2017, p. 128). Further, if no member actively disagrees with a decision, there is a higher probability that new markets open to give everyone a stake in the package deal.

The second value is *non-discrimination* which aims at the non-discrimination of, on the one hand, its different trading partners, and on the other hand, foreign or national goods and services. Non-discrimination in the WTO is reflected in the contradictory term MFN—Most-favoured-nation—implying that all WTO members should be treated the same and that no special treatments are allowed, under reservation of exceptions.

The third value is *less trade barriers* between members. Lowering trade barriers is one of the easiest and most obvious ways to encourage trade and development which, consequently, contributes to global economic growth. In the past, the largest focus was placed on less barriers at-the-border or tariff barriers, while now the WTO recognises, they should balance their focus between at-the-border barriers and behind-the-border measures or non-tariff barriers. Yet, this has proven to be difficult as the WTO increasingly deals with heterogenous groups of countries who have diverging interests and capabilities (Mavroidis & Sapir, 2019, p. 3) and countries implementing unilateral tariffs outside the WTO.

The final value is creating *predictability* through binding commitments and transparency. Those two factors are incremental to the confidence of businesses and subsequently, increases investment and creates more employment opportunities. Most WTO agreements require countries to publish their practices and policies widely. Moreover, the WTO's Trade Policy Review Mechanism, which aims at the dissemination of information and the evaluation of compliance, further improves transparency both on the national and multilateral level (WTO, n.d.c).

1.3. Challenges Impeding the WTO's Effectiveness

Over the years, the WTO increasingly had and still has to deal with several challenges, which subsequently impedes the WTO's working. This section will highlight and analyse some of the main pressures the WTO currently faces: (1) the failure of the Doha Round, (2) the DSB under President Trump, (3) the new Sino-American reality and (4) the COVID-19 pandemic.

1.3.1. Failure of the Doha Round

The Uruguay Round, the predecessor of the Doha Round, already had to deal with an increasing difficulty in trade talks due to several factors such as the rise of importance of developing countries and shifts in interests (Baldwin, 2016, p. 106). Other important aspects complicating the Doha Round include the increase in issues dealt with such as Intellectual Property Rights (IPRs) and simply the large amount of member states. The significance of those factors only increased on the path leading towards the Doha Round and hence, gave a negative perspective on the eventual outcome of the trade talks. This has been proven as the Doha Round commenced in 2001 and has no specific outcome until today.

The road to Doha started unsteadily and as some would say, doomed to fail. It is important to set the agenda in negotiations as it is a crucial step and that can make or break a deal. The rise in diverging interests between states and the rise of fast-growing economies complicated the agenda-setting process. For example, the EU aimed at including new issues such as competition policy, investment, trade facilitation and government procurement (known as the Singapore Issues) while the United States thrived for a focus on industrial goods and protectionist domestic policies and finally the developing countries emphasised that the inequalities arising from the Uruguay Round should be eliminated first (Capling & Trommer, 2017, p. 134). After two years of negotiating, an agreement was found for the agenda. The agenda largely consisted out of implementation issues, agriculture, the Singapore Issues, services and IPRs (WTO, n.d.d).

It was clear from the start that concessions would have to be made but no state was capable or willing to make the amount of concessions needed to reach an agreement. Over the years, the packages and agenda shifted a little, however, the main stumble block, agriculture, remained the same (Capling & Trommer, 2017, p. 134). Moreover, the consensus voting principle muddled the process. This was the case because the original major players—the EU, the United States, Canada and Japan, known as the "Quad"—did not automatically have the upper hand anymore as the BRIC countries (Brazil, Russia, India and China) gained significance. Besides, smaller nations and LDCs started to engage in coalitional diplomacy as a negotiation strategy to increase their level of importance (Capling & Trommer, 2017, p. 136). Coalitional diplomacy is a strong strategy in international political economy and happens between several like-minded groups of developed and developing countries, for example, the Cairns Group. Higgot and Cooper (1990) emphasise the importance of issue-oriented coalition and their importance in securing cooperation between an eventual hegemon and other players (p. 631). For example, in 2019, India created a coalition of nine countries to thrive for "placing special provisions for developing countries and high farm subsidies in advanced nations that harm African states at the forefront of global trade talks", according to Kirtika Suneja (2019). They aim at eliminating the asymmetries between developing and developed countries (Suneja, 2019).

The several shifts in the agenda and concessions did not lead to the key of success and after almost 20 years of negotiating a concrete package deal has still not been reached. This result is not beneficial and might imply that the limits of multilateralism within the WTO are reached and that new ways of operating effectively must be established which will be discussed later in this chapter.

1.3.2. The Dispute Settlement Body and President Trump

A current big threat to the existence of the WTO is the blockage of the Appellate Body, part of the DSB by President Trump as settling disputes between states is one of the WTO's core functions. Johns and Pelc (2018) argue that "countries challenge protectionist policies as soon as they appear" (p. 873). The DSB is a two-tier mechanism consisting of, on the one hand, the Dispute Settlement Understanding (DSU) panels and on the other hand, the Appellate Body. Their purpose is to "maintain surveillance of implementation of rulings and recommendations and authorise the suspension of obligations under the covered agreement" (WTO, n.d.e). A DSU panel is an internal organ established when states do not come to a dispute settlement in the consultation stage, the first stage in the dispute settlement process. They make a judgment on the case and prepare a final report which mostly consists of countermeasures such as the implementation of righteous, similar tariffs. Yet, it happens that the defendant in the case addresses the safeguard clause to counter a decision. Textbox 4.1 represents a simple example to clarify the safeguard clause.

This so-called safeguard clause creates the opportunity for states that are opposed to the final decision made by the DSU panel, to appeal against the decision and address the Appellate Body. The Appellate Body is an external organ, consisting of seven judges, mostly commercial law professors, who have a renewable mandate of four years. The Appellate Body can "uphold, modify or reverse the panel's legal findings and conclusions" (WTO, n.d.d).

TEXT BOX 4.1.   SCENARIO WHEN SAFEGUARD CLAUSE CAN BE USED.

(Simplified) Scenario: The United States imposes tariffs on Chinese steel

The DSU panel judges that the United States is not allowed to impose tariffs on Chinese steel. Consequently, the United States counters this verdict by arguing that the high amount of import of Chinese steel causes too high unemployment rates in the U.S. steel industry and thus highly negatively impacts the American economy. Theoretically, this is allowed under the safeguard clause.

The former tier, the DSU panel, works ordinarily. Now it is the latter tier, the Appellate Body, which currently puts the WTO in danger. Since December 2019, the Appellate Body is blocked as President Trump vetoes the appointment and reappointment of judges. Initially, the impact of this blockage was not detrimental towards the working of the WTO, as there were still enough judges. However, in December 2019, two out of the last three judges retired and thus, only one judge is remaining which makes the Appellate Body insignificant as a weighted decision cannot be taken (Clifford Chance, 2019). The main reason Washington blocks the appointment of new judges finds its roots in the safeguard clause and the United States' strong will to completely reform the DSB (Johnson, 2019; Schott & Jung, 2019). Though, according to Schott and Jung, U.S. officials refuse to negotiate reforms and thus the negotiations to solve this crisis finds itself in a deadlock (2019, p. 1). The likelihood that the blockage will be lifted under the Trump administration is low and hence an alternative solution must be found. The EU took the initiative to form a parallel DSB in the form of a multiparty agreement, which will be extensively discussed later (EC, 2020a; Moens, 2020).

1.3.3. A New Reality for the WTO: Sino-American Tensions

The accession of China to the WTO in 2001 started to change the playing field of the WTO. It was the first time in the WTO's history that a non-democratic and large country joined the organisation. Previously, non-democratic countries from Eastern Europe joined the WTO, but their contribution in terms of world trade was rather negligible. The accession of China posed significant threats to the functioning of the WTO. First of all, the shift of power from the old, homogenous Quad (the US, Canada, the EU and Japan) to the new, heterogenous Quad (the EU, the United States, India, Brazil and later China) complicated the working due to diverging interests. Second, the failure of the Doha Round led to a weaker WTO, which remained too static for a dynamic organisation. Lastly, the nature of China's economic system, called socialist market economy by the Communist Party and state capitalism by the rest of the world, posed problems as it contains heavy state involvement (Mavroidis & Sapir, 2019, pp. 2–3). The accession of China has indeed shown to be challenging at times. There have always been two diametrically opposed views on how to act upon the accession of China. The first view from the United States suggests that China must accept a regime change while the second view states that China must stay robust in not becoming westernised and that the WTO should be able to handle diversified countries (Mavroidis & Sapir, 2019, p. 6).

Shortly after the election of President Trump in 2016, the growing competition between China and the United States created a new reality for the

WTO and its members. The two powerful members both have a populistic leader but their nations are fundamentally different: the difference in regime determines a lot on the WTO's playing field. On the one hand, Xi Jingping does not need approval from others when he wants to reach a specific goal, while on the other hand, Donald Trump needs approval from Congress to attain objectives. Over the years, China and its make-economy created a new role for themselves on the global level which means that they behave differently than the way in which they used to. Consequently, China is able to decide on a lot of rules as the WTO uses implicit language such as "the liberal understanding of law and economy" which is rather vague and open to interpretation (Mavroidis & Sapir, 2019, p. 36). As Craig VanGrasstek (2013) put it based on Gao (2012): "China is increasingly more active in the WTO, with its role in the system having progressed since accession from a rule taker that passively accepts existing rules imposed by other countries to a rule shaker that tries to exploit the existing rules to its advantage, and then to a rule maker that is making new rules that reflects its own interests" (p. 560). According to a diplomat permanently representing his country at the WTO, the Chinese behave assertively and do not take other parties' needs and wants into consideration, as long as they fulfil their own hidden agenda (interview with diplomat, April 2020).

The United States and China are involved in a series of unilateral duties since 2018 and moreover, President Jinping and President Trump constantly engage in a "who-is-the-smartest" game which is detrimental to the effective functioning of the WTO.

1.3.4. The WTO in the midst of the COVID-19 Pandemic

The COVID-19 pandemic that is shaking up the world since the end of 2019–beginning of 2020 has shown to have a considerable impact on all sectors worldwide. Moreover, it will take a long time until the world crawls out of the recession and trade is at its pre-pandemic levels. One of the main characteristics of a global economy is the interdependence of states and their hyper integration, depicted by the value chain, the process to reach a valuable final product with respect to customer value and the supply chain. One of the biggest immediate consequences for international trade is the interruption of the value and supply chain worldwide as many companies and businesses had to shut down due to severe governmental restrictions. Consequently, products cannot be assembled, delivery times are delayed, products cannot be shipped due to closed borders, the decrease in oil production and so forth (WTO, 2020a).

Whilst still in the middle of the crisis, top WTO economists have made estimations on the contraction of world trade (WTO, 2020a). The estimated relapse lies between 13% and 32% while the real value will probably lay in the range between 15% and 20% (WTO, 2020a). As countries are slowly easing their restrictions, businesses and factories can restart their activities, yet, not at full capacity, to start minimising the consequences. The WTO can help in the process to stimulate a coherent, quick decision-making plan of action by the members in order to attempt reducing the disruption in the value chain as soon as possible. It is important to follow the evolution of the pandemic closely and have an action plan ready. Furthermore, the creation of a vaccine and its potential matching patent might also cause a hurdle for the WTO. It is impossible to measure the impact of the pandemic just yet, but an attempt on how to deal with the consequences will be made in the next section.

2. THE FUTURE OF THE WTO: HOW TO TACKLE ITS CHALLENGES?

The WTO's current challenges discussed in the previous section have clearly shown the WTO is facing a crisis. It is of utmost importance that the WTO finds ways to reposition itself as a strong international organisation and thus reshapes its way of functioning. Hence, this section will provide a potential outlook of the WTO in the future based on the challenges addressed previously.

2.1. The Necessary(?) Shift from Multilateral towards Plurilateral Agreements

The Doha Round has indicated that multilateralism in the WTO has attained its limits. Multilateralism in the WTO can be seen as a stricter form of multilateralism due to the consensus principle and that thus all 164 members need to be on the same page in order to reach an agreement. It becomes harder and harder for the WTO to get all 164 members on the same line and current globalisation only complicates the process even more as developed and developing countries have diverging priorities. The WTO is a dynamic organisation and the failure on efficiently anticipating global trends might be detrimental to its future. Therefore, it is time to find alternatives on the multilateral agreements, core to the WTO's mission. Countries, individually and collectively, already started looking for substitutes. First of all, there is an increase in interest for bilateral agreements between states, which are happening outside the WTO. For example, the EU is currently negotiating several bilateral agreements "to improve market access for European food and drinks", with several groups of countries outside the EU (EC, 2020b). Yet, as this activity does not support the WTO's core value of trade liberalisation, it is not the best option for the survival of the WTO.

Second, the WTO has started exploring the potential for plurilateral agreements instead of multilateral ones. Plurilateral agreements are defined by the WTO as "agreements with a narrower group of signatories" (WTO, n.d.f). Proponents see plurilateral agreements as a valuable complement to multilateralism, according to Craig VanGrasstek (2013, p. 552). During the Ministerial Conference in Buenos Aires (Argentina) in 2017, the WTO members started focusing more on this path, with an emphasis on sectoral agreements. The ultimate goal of the Ministerial Conference was to find an outcome on illegal fishing and e-commerce, which failed for the most part (WTO, 2018; EC, 2017). Instead, according to a diplomat permanently representing his country at the WTO, there was an increasing interest in sectoral accords in the field of facilitating investment, the liberalisation of rules in services, best practices for micro, small and medium enterprises (MSME). The initiatives have received positive signals and since, the sectoral agreements have attracted a considerable amount of members. The current developments in this area are beneficial and the agreements made will certainly expand in the future. The main advantage of plurilateral agreements is their range for expansion. Certain states might initially not show interest in signing a specific agreement and change their mind later on and still be able to participate. Subsequently, countries have less pressure, which is favourable, definitely for developing countries which generally operate at a slower pace. Redesigning the WTO with a focus on plurilateral, sectoral agreements instead of huge, multilateral package deals might be a valuable solution for the WTO.

2.2. An Alternative Arrangement for the Appellate Body: The MPIA, a Parallel Appellate Body

The likelihood that the DSB will be reinstalled under President Trump is very small, so there are two options for the other members: hoping for a change in the Trump administration or proactively seeking a solution. The latter is the path the EU and other like-minded countries opted for by creating an alternative. It is noteworthy that the EU chose this path as it might generate resentment towards them by the United States (Moens, 2020). The EU established a parallel DSB called the "Multi-party interim appeal arbitration arrangement" (MPIA) and convinced 15 other like-minded countries so far to take part in the project as they attach importance to a fully working two-tier DSB. The second tier is essential to guarantee an independent and impartial judgement as the Appellate Body is an external organ (EC, 2020a). Important players already engaged in the alternative body include China, Canada and Brazil. States can participate in this alternative organ on a voluntary basis. According to EU Trade Commissioner Phil Hogan, the alternative arrangement "remains a contingency measure needed because of the paralysis of the

WTO Appellate Body" and that the EU "will continue our efforts to seek a lasting solution to the Appellate Body impasse, including through necessary reforms and improvements" (Moens, 2020). Moreover, Director-General (DG) of the WTO Roberto Azêvedo outlined the importance of finding a permanent solution for this impasse and stated that "a well-functioning, impartial and binding dispute settlement system is a core pillar of the WTO system" (WTO, 2019).

The MPIA is an effective temporary alternative as it operates in the same way as the initial body and, in this way, the least knowledge and expertise evaporates. This is an important element as the probability that the initial Appellate Body will be reinstalled once the Trump administration is out of office, according to a diplomat permanently representing his country at the WTO (interview with diplomat, April 2020). Therefore, it could be interesting if more countries join the parallel body as it will subsequently facilitate the reimplementation of the initial Appellate Body once its time has come. In the meantime, efforts are made to find a durable solution suitable for all members as not only the U.S. claims reforms are needed. In 2018, the EU already formally proposed a plan for reform in name of several WTO members, which so far has not been accepted (Johnson, 2019). The probability that the negotiations on reform will take a long time is high as the United States is thriving for fundamental reforms as they claim that there are essential misunderstandings in the foundations of the Appellate Body (Johnson, 2019).

Moreover, the DSU is advocating the particular situation of developing countries and asks for comprehension from developed states. The DSU wants to complement the Special and Differential Treatment (SDT) that developing countries and LDCs get that are already in place such as flexible time frames, legal assistance and so on and come up with more initiatives (WTO secretariat, 2017, p. 176). These initiatives taken to support developing countries and LDCs will be fully outlined later on. It is clear that the DSB which is one of the WTO's main assets needs improvement in order to be fully operational. The concepts explored in this chapter are a temporary solution and can be used as a basis for the long-term solution.

2.3. The Impact and Consequences of the New Sino-American Reality

The rise in tensions between China and the United States has clearly shaped a new reality within the WTO, which has an impact on all WTO members. Thus, it is now time to find an appropriate way on how to deal with this reality to minimise the detrimental consequences for the WTO and its members, as they find themselves in the middle of Sino-American tit-for-tat strategies. The tit-for-tat retaliation commenced right after the election of President

Trump in 2016, operating on an "America First" platform (Colback, 2020; Sapir, 2017, p. 58). Jeffrey Sachs, special advisor of several UN Secretary-Generals, argues that the "America First" platform has now translated itself in a raw and vulgar variant, and warns that the frantic attempts of the United States to form an anti-Chinese front bear a big threat towards multilateralism (De Deken, 2020).

Currently, the WTO tries to manage the opposition, in the form of tit-for-tat strategies and lack of cooperation, of the major players in order to facilitate its functioning; however, it seems to be complicated to align their diverging interests. Hence, a real solution on how to deal with this remarkable situation has not been found yet as a trade deal has not been achieved. The most obvious solution is stronger enforcement of their actions, but one can be sure that this will receive strong resistance. The non-participation of the United States in the Appellate Body also further complicates the enforcement. It is clear that all WTO members must carry the impact the Sino-American relations bring along and that the need for a harmonious middle ground is highly needed.

Moreover, once the spread of the COVID-19 pandemic is further stabilised, it will also have tremendous consequences on the future of the Sino-American combative trade relations. The following section will discuss the consequences of the COVID-19 pandemic on the future of the WTO.

2.4. The WTO in a Post-COVID-19 Era

The COVID-19 pandemic is still expanding further negatively impacting everyone's daily life. It is thus impossible to already measure the tangible consequences the pandemic caused on contraction of international trade. Yet, the prospects are not rosy as the impact is likely to exceed the impact of the 2007–2008 financial crisis. The WTO aims at a recovery in 2021, but this will depend on different factors and circumstances and the further spread of the virus (WTO, 2020a). Deputy Director-General (DDG) of the WTO Alan Wolff addressed the need for more intense international cooperation to tackle the global crisis: "the time now is for action rather than reflection". According to DDG Wolff, this includes "addressing measures to deal with the global health emergency, cooperation to support the needed economic recovery, and assuring the system is more resilient and effective in underwriting future global economic growth" (WTO, 2020a).

A plan of the direction that can be taken to minimise the consequences can be outlined, by now. However, an official plan has not been announced yet. Earlier in the chapter, the importance of the value chain and supply chain has been underlined, and will thus be one of the main points that one should focus on in the aftermath of the pandemic. The WTO needs to establish measures for states so that they can support businesses, manufacturers and so on for their restart, in order to fix the disrupted value chain. Yet, the pandemic will leave significant marks in the long run as many business need to file for bankruptcy or at least lay off part of their workers. Furthermore, businesses will adapt their strategies in order to avoid negative effects of this scale in the future. According to Bart Haeck (2020), businesses will rethink about the locations of their factories in order to minimise the disruption of the value and supply chain in the future. It is possible that companies will locate their manufactories closer by the headquarters or final consumers to have less impact on a value or supply chain disruption (Haeck, 2020).

As a consequence of the interruptions in value and supply chain due to the COVID-19 pandemic both supply and demand fell worldwide (WTO, 2020a). This will also need a considerable time span to recover. Yet, one winner of the pandemic is e-commerce (Haeck, 2020; WTO, 2020b). Subsequently, the WTO could potentially explore this globalisation trend more deeply and expand the rules concerning e-commerce as it definitely brings challenges along. A recently published report by the WTO secretariat argues that "experiences and lessons emerging from the Covid-19 crisis could be a further incentive for global cooperation in the area of e-commerce, which could help to facilitate cross-border movement of goods and services, narrow the digital divide and level the playing field for small businesses"(WTO, 2020b).

Moreover, national governments already started implementing protectionist and nationalistic policies and will definitely continue to do so. These measures are reflected in trade-restrictive measures, export restrictions on medical goods and food, and trade-facilitating measures, the suspension of tariffs and internal taxes on imports (WTO, 2020a). The increase in protectionist policies clearly stands in the way of the multilateral trading system and is potentially detrimental in the long run.

2.5. The Need for Empowerment of LDCs

This section will discuss one last aspect that the WTO should focus on to regain its name of a strong international organisation: the empowerment of LDCs. The significance of developing countries and LDCs has increased tremendously over the years, as 117 of the 164 members are developing countries (or separate customs territories) and 36 members are LDCs (WTO, n.d.a; WTO, n.d.g). During the Doha WTO Ministerial in 2001, there was a lot of focus on the efforts made, in terms of market access and technical assistance in order to improve the condition of the LDCs (WTO, n.d.g). Even though the WTO and its members have established several initiatives, such as the consensus and single undertaking principle and the SDT, to support LDCs, their influence is still minimal. According to a practitioner, LDCs are able to negotiate with major players and can achieve agreements on some points of their agenda; however, due to their lack of power, their achievements can be identified as a footnote in the final outcome (interview with diplomat, April 2020). This is exactly where reform is needed: LDCs need a stronger voice in order to reach a global, inclusive economy where not only the major players have the upper hand.

Further initiatives can potentially be built on the strategies that have been used to empower developing countries. A first positive sign is that Gonzalez and Jung (2020) claim that developing countries could help restore the WTO's Dispute Settlement System. They further argue that no other state or nation needs a working dispute settlement mechanism more than fast-growing economies (Gonzalez & Jung, 2020, p. 1). Their growing economies have raised the life standard of millions of citizens and are thus a good example for LDCs.

The most prosperous solution is to help the LDCs to get rid of their status and bring them beyond their LDC status. A structural approach to support LDCs is to expand the projects the UN established in order to "pursue structural economic progress towards and beyond graduation" (UN, 2018). It would be a great opportunity for the WTO and its members to collaborate with the UN to expand these initiatives to a wider range of LDCs. However, giving more concessions to LDCs will potentially put significant pressures on the "developed" world and thus decrease their incentive to help.

Yet, according to Jeffrey Sachs, the possible exponential spread of the COVID-19 in developing countries and LDCs will have detrimental economic and geopolitical consequences. Consequently, it will lead to more hunger, diseases, unemployment and conflicts. Hence, the approach of developing countries and LDCs in handling the COVID-19 pandemic will affect the survival of the multilateral system, due to the lack of global leadership (De Deken, 2020).

3. CONCLUSION

This chapter has extensively analysed the current status of the WTO and the challenges it faces. What is clear is that the WTO is in an existential crisis and reforms are needed for its survival. First, the chapter has explored the impact of the failure of the Doha Round, due to the widening and deepening of the agenda, and how this led to an increase in plurilateral agreements at the expense of multilateral agreements. Slowly this will most likely become the new normal within the WTO. Second, it analysed one of the main functions of the WTO: the DSB that can be considered the biggest threat to the multilateral nature of the WTO. The blockage of the reappointment of judges in the Appellate Body by President Trump increased tensions and are far from being solved. Yet, the EU created an alternative Appellate Body for the time being as negotiations on the reforms needed are stuck. Next, a big part of the chapter dealt with is the new reality the WTO operates in. This new reality is shaped both by the rise of populistic leaders acting in self-interest and the combative trade relations between the United States and China. The emergence of new actors might have strengthened the legitimacy of the organisation but perhaps at the expense of its effectiveness. Currently, the WTO is struggling to align the rising diverging interests between members and is finding a middle ground in which it can function acceptably. Fourthly, an important part focused on the (at the time of writing) topical COVID-19 pandemic, which shook the whole world late 2019–2020. The consequences cannot be measured yet; however, it is clear that the impact on world trade is enormous and that it will take a considerable amount of time to re-establish the disrupted value and supply chain. Moreover, more governments implement nationalist policies in order to protect their own business and factories which destructs the multilateral trading system. Finally, the future of LDCs and the further need for their empowerment has been addressed to raise awareness for the initiatives of the UN.

A prosperous future for the WTO is currently hard to imagine as it currently finds itself in a static momentum instead of in a dynamic process. As Hoekman (2012) stated: "The WTO is often likened to a 'bicycle' that needs to keep moving if it is not to fall over" (p. 745). This downturn in multilateralism is likely to continue in the foreseeable future; however, hopefully COVID-19 and other trends will foster cooperation between all states.

NOTE

1. The IMF/World Bank will be extensively discussed in the next chapter by Nicolas Verbeek.

REFERENCES

Baldwin, R. (2016). The World Trade Organization and the Future of Multilateralism. *Journal of Economic Perspectives, 30*(1), 95–116. doi: 10.1257/jep.30.1.95

Capling, Ann & Trommer, Silke. (2017). The Evolution of Global Trade Regime. In Ravenhill, John (ed.), *Global Political Economy* (pp. 111–140). Oxford: Oxford University Press

Clifford Chance. (2019). The WTO appellate body crisis—A way forward? *Clifford Chance*. Retrieved from https://www.cliffordchance.com/content/dam/clifford chance/briefings/2019/11/the-wto-appellate-body-crisis-a-way-forward.pdf

Colback, Lucy. (2020). How to Navigate the US-China Trade War. *The Financial Times*. Retrieved from https://www.ft.com/content/6124beb8-5724-11ea-abe5-8e03987b7b20

De Deken, Jan. (2020). "De VS zijn incompetent en Europa is zwak". *Knack, 50*(19), 36–39.

European Commission. (2017). WTO meeting in Buenos Aires: A missed opportunity. Retrieved from https://trade.ec.europa.eu/doclib/press/index.cfm?id=1772

European Commission. (2020a). EU and 15 World Trade Organization members establish contingency appeal arrangement for trade disputes. Retrieved from https://trade.ec.europa.eu/doclib/press/index.cfm?id=2127

European Commission. (2020b). Internal market, industry, entrepreneurship and SMEs. Retrieved from https://ec.europa.eu/growth/sectors/food/processed-agricultural-products/trade-agreements_en

Finlayson, J., & Zacher, M. (1981). The GATT and the Regulation of Trade Barriers: Regime Dynamics and Functions. *International Organization, 35*(4), 561–602.

Gao, H. (2012). The Shifting Stars: The Rise of China, Emerging Economies and the Future of World Trade Governance. In Ricardo Meléndez-Ortiz (ed.), *The future and the WTO: Confronting the challenges* (pp. 74–79). Geneva: International Centre for Trade and Sustainable Development.

Gonzalez, A., & Jung, E. (2020*)*. Developing countries can help restore the WTO's dispute settlement system (20-1*)*. *Peterson Institute for International Economics*. Retrieved from https://www.piie.com/sites/default/files/documents/pb20-1.pdf

Haeck, B. (2020). Wie moeten we redden? *De Tijd*. Retrieved from https://www.tijd.be/ondernemen/algemeen/wie-moeten-we-redden/10227531.html.

Hoekman, B. (2012). Proposals for WTO Reform: A Synthesis and Assessment. In Martin Daunton, Amrita Narlikar, and Robert M. Stern (eds.), *The Oxford Handbook on the World Trade Organization* (pp. 743–775). Oxford: Oxford University Press.

Higgott, R., & Cooper, A. (1990). Middle power leadership and coalition building: Australia, the Cairns Group, and the Uruguay Round of trade negotiations. *International Organization, 44*(4), 589–632. doi:10.1017/S0020818300035414

Johns, L., & Pelc, K. J. (2018). Free Riding on Enforcement in the World Trade Organization. *The Journal of Politics*, *80*(3), 873–889. doi: 10.1086/697463

Johnson, Keith. (2019). How Trump may finally kill the WTO. *Foreign Policy*. Retrieved from https://foreignpolicy.com/2019/12/09/trump-may-kill-wto-finally-appellate-body-world-trade-organization/

Kolb, M. (2018). What is globalization? *Peterson Institute for International Economics*. Retrieved from https://www.piie.com/microsites/globalization/what-is-globalization

Low, P. (2011). WTO decision-making for the future. *WTO*. Retrieved from https://www.wto.org/english/res_e/reser_e/ersd201105_e.pdf

Mavroidis, P., & André, S. (2019). *China and the World Trade Organization: Towards a better fit*. Working Paper 2019/06, Bruegel.

Moens, B. (2020). EU sets up WTO court with group of countries without US. *Politico*. Retrieved from https://www.politico.eu/article/eu-sets-up-wto-court-with-group-of-countries-without-us/

Sapir, Andre. (2017). La grande Transformation. In Telo Mario (ed.), *La place de l'Europe dans lemonde du 21ᵉ siècle* (pp. 41–60). Brussels: Académie Royale de Belgique.

Schott, J. J., & Jung, E. (2019). The WTO's Existential Crisis: How to Salvage Its Ability to Settle Trade Disputes (19-19). *Peterson Institute for International*

Economics. Retrieved from https://www.piie.com/sites/default/files/documents/pb19-19.pdf

Suneja, K. (2019). India sews coalition of 9 nations to push development at WTO. *The Economic Times*. Retrieved from https://economictimes.indiatimes.com/news/economy/foreign-trade/india-sews-coalition-of-9-nations-to-push-development-at-wto/articleshow/70321343.cms?from=mdr

United Nations. (2018). Helping least developed countries (LDCs) pursue structural economic progress toward and beyond graduation. Retrieved from https://www.un.org/development/desa/capacity-development/projects/project/helping-least-developed-countries-achieve-structural-economic-progress-toward-graduation/

VanGrasstek, C. (2013). The history and future of the World Trade Organization, WTO, Geneva. Retrieved from https://doi.org/10.30875/14b6987e-en.

World Trade Organization. (2018). Spotlight: Buenos Aires Ministerial Conference—Annual Report. *WTO*. Retrieved from https://www.wto.org/english/res_e/booksp_e/09_anrep18_spotlight_e.pdf

World Trade Organization. (2019). DG Azevêdo to launch intensive consultations on resolving appellate body impasse. Retrieved from https://www.wto.org/english/news_e/news19_e/gc_09dec19_e.htm

World Trade Organization. (2020a). DDG Wolff: "The time now is for action rather than reflection". *WTO*. Retrieved from https://www.wto.org/english/news_e/archive_e/covid_arc_e.htm

World Trade Organization. (2020b). WTO report looks at role of e-commerce during the COVID-19 pandemic. *WTO*. Retrieved from https://www.wto.org/english/news_e/news20_e/rese_04may20_e.htm

World Trade Organization. (n.d.a). WTO in brief. *WTO*. Retrieved from https://www.wto.org/english/thewto_e/whatis_e/inbrief_e/inbr_e.htm

World Trade Organization. (n.d.b). Overview of the WTO secretariat. *WTO*. Retrieved from https://www.wto.org/english/thewto_e/secre_e/intro_e.htm

World Trade Organization. (n.d.c). What we stand for. *WTO*. Retrieved from https://www.wto.org/english/thewto_e/whatis_e/what_stand_for_e.htm

World Trade Organization. (n.d.d). Doha Round: What are they negotiation. *WTO*. Retrieved from https://www.wto.org/english/tratop_e/dda_e/update_e.htm

World Trade Organization. (n.d.e). Understanding the WTO: A unique contribution. *WTO*. Retrieved from https://www.wto.org/english/thewto_e/whatis_e/tif_e/disp1_e.htm#appeals

World Trade Organization. (n.d.f). Eleventh WTO Ministerial Conference. *WTO*. Retrieved from https://www.wto.org/english/thewto_e/minist_e/mc11_e/mc11_e.htm

World Trade Organization. (n.d.g). Towards free market access for least-developed countries. *WTO*. Retrieved from https://www.wto.org/english/thewto_e/minist_e/min01_e/brief_e/brief03_e.htm

World Trade Organization Secretariat. (2017). Developing Countries in the WTO Dispute Settlement System. In *A Handbook on the WTO Dispute Settlement System* (pp. 176–182). Cambridge: Cambridge University Press doi:10.1017/9781108265423.010

Chapter 5

The Future of IMF and World Bank: New Dynamics in Times of COVID-19 Crisis, 2020

Nicolas Verbeek

1. INTRODUCTION

The IMF and the WB are essential pillars of the American-dominated post–World War II global economic order. Due to enormous economic power shifts from North to South in the past few decades, the Bretton Woods institutions are now facing a considerably more challenging strategic environment in which they must overcome challenges of legitimacy loss, philosophy contestation and competition. There is an institutional deadlock in which the dichotomy of interests between the Western states (United States and European states) and the BRICS states (Brazil, Russia, India, China and South Africa) as well as other developing countries is preventing far-reaching coherent reforms to address the challenges (Wade & Vestergaard, 2015). A new dynamic is needed to initiate a reformation process in response to the existing deadlock. The global COVID-19 pandemic that flared up at the beginning of 2020 represents such a new dynamic, which will have enormous implications for the global economic order and thus also for the IMF and the WB. This chapter discusses the potential impact of COVID-19 as a new dynamic for a possible future reform process in IMF and WB, that is, as a new dynamic for a future of these multilateral organizations.

This chapter offers (1) a brief literature review of the existing strategic environment of the IMF and WB in times of global power shifts; and (2) a discussion of the potential impact of the COVID-19 crisis as a new dynamic in the ongoing process of relative power loss of the Bretton Woods institutions.

The chapter discusses the likely impact of COVID-19 on the IMF and the WB in three different dimensions: (1) the short-term renewed increase in relevance of the IMF and WB as crisis firefighters and the implications of this rise in relevance for the overarching process of relative institutional decline; (2) the medium-term potential of COVID-19 as a driver of change in the philosophy of lending conditionalities; and (3) the long-term economic consequences of COVID-19 for China and the United States and the related implications for the Bretton Woods institutions in terms of leadership, reform and relevance

2. IMF AND WORLD BANK IN A DIFFICULT STRATEGIC ENVIRONMENT: A BRIEF OVERVIEW

The increasing contestation of the existing liberal economic world order is often described in the literature. In this context, this liberal economic order is characterized as a product of the American hegemonic position after World War II, especially in the unipolar American position after the end of the Cold War (Wade, 2011; Schwarzer, 2017; Stephen, 2017; Layne, 2018). The BRICS states (Brazil, Russia, India, China and South Africa) are identified as the formative force of this contest, with the incomparable economic rise of China playing a particularly important role. The global economic power shift from North to South and its implications for the global economy are enormous. While the BRICS share of global GDP was 11% in 1990, by 2014, it had risen to just under 30% and the IMF estimates that the BRICS countries will provide 50% of global GDP by 2030 (Devonshire-Ellis, 2019). The immense economic power shift puts the three institutional pillars of the liberal world financial system—the WTO, the WB and the IMF—under enormous pressure to reform, as the BRICS countries, above all China, demand an adjusted representation in the economic institutions. In fact, however, the United States and the European states have been able to maintain their historically determined structural overrepresentation as founding states of the Bretton Woods institutions to a large extent (Wade & Vestergaard, 2015). Despite the final implementation of an IMF quota reform of 2010 (14th review of quotas) on 26 January 2016, in which the BRICS states gained 6% of the vote shares, the long ratification process and a another quota reform, which is already delayed again within the framework of the 15th review of quotas (end of 2019) (IMF, 2020a), testify to the blocking attitude of the United States and European states and their unwillingness to admit their loss of economic influence at the institutional level. With 16.51% of the vote shares, the United States fears for its sole veto power, which requires 15% of the vote shares. There is currently a deadlock situation in the Bretton Woods institutions, which (1) undermines their legitimacy; and (2) has led China to directly contest the existing IMF and WB by creating alternative international development organizations, such as the Asian Infrastructure Investment Bank (AIIB) (2015) or the Chiang Mai Initiative (2010) on multilateral currency exchange with the aim of minimizing the risk of foreign currency debt. On the future of the AIIB, Taylor Garrett offers a comprehensive analysis elsewhere in this book. Although the complementary character of various regional banks of the BRICS countries to the existing IMF and WB is often emphasized (Henning, 2011), the establishment of the AIIB can be seen both as a direct extension of China's role in the management of international economy and development as well as a signal of China's seriousness in its demand for a larger vote share in IMF and WB (Layne, 2018, p. 103). The AIIB and other regional banks of the BRICS countries (see: Ray & Kamal, 2019) represent a direct challenge to the existing American-dominated financial order, whereby especially the so-called Washington Consensus, as the core philosophy of the lending and conditionality practice of IMF and WB, is actively challenged by the BRICS countries.

The Washington Consensus outlines the philosophy behind the content of conditionality in the granting of condition-based loans by the IMF and the WB to borrower states. The policy set includes trade liberalization, privatiza-tion, deregulation, rule of law, fiscal discipline, development of democracy and human rights, labour standards and other policies aimed at liberalizing and opening up national markets (Chow, 2016, p. 16f.). The scope of these policy prescriptions is so far-reaching that they may be regarded as economic policy instruments for pushing through the economic agenda of the United States and its close Western allies.

The Washington Consensus is strongly criticized and increasingly rejected by developing countries as borrowers of IMF/WB funds on the basis of three factors. (1) The policy conditionalities are interpreted as a significant interfer-ence with state sovereignty, placing the borrower states in humiliating posi-tions where they must decide between money and surrender of sovereignty in emergency situations. In the case of unstable, more corrupt regimes in devel-oping countries, Washington Consensus reforms can potentially even trigger regime change (Crotty & Lee, 2008). (2) From a historical perspective, the policy conditionalities of the IMF and the WB have in a number of cases in Africa and South America proved to be detrimental to sustainable growth of national economies, as liberalization massively undermined the protection of population and environment while benefiting above all global corporations (Kentikelenis et al., 2016, 566). (3) The enormous economic boom of the BRICS states in the past decades, especially in Asia, which pursue a much more state-controlled interventionist economic policy, clearly challenges the "best practices" of the Washington Consensus. China explicitly rejects the Washington Consensus, as it officially views conditionality as illegitimate interference in the sovereign rights of the borrower states over their internal affairs. It promotes an alternative doctrine of non-interference in the IMF and WB, as well as the China-dominated AIIB, which holds that the internal political characteristics of a borrower state do not concern anyone but the nation itself (Aidoo & Hess, 2015, p. 111).

In response to these criticisms, there has been an ongoing reform of the IMF/WB conditionalities (post-Washington Consensus) since 2005 under the slogan of borrower ownership, whereby more emphasis was placed on sustainable social and environmental development (Best, 2007, p. 477f.). At the operational level, an increasing focus on benchmarks and triggers, that is, outcome conditionality, has sought to provide policy space for national governments to individually achieve set goals in order to minimize interference with state sovereignty (Cormier & Manger, 2019, p. 32f.). Despite the adjustment process, there is still considerable criticism of the BRICS countries, as aspects such as privatization and the promotion of democracy and human rights still reveal the ideological dichotomy between Western liberal countries and the frequently more authoritarian BRICS and other developing countries. Thus, the Bretton Woods institutions find themselves in a relative deadlock situation with regard to philosophy development and representation, in which increasing loss of legitimacy and outside competition is to be expected. While the impact of AIIB will not be truly evident until the next decade, the fact that all major states (UK, Germany, France etc.) except Japan and the United States have joined the AIIB despite explicit American opposition to its creation already points to the relatively increasing influence of the AIIB (Layne, 2018, p. 102). In the light of the transition to a multipolar world, that is, in an age of choice in which borrowers are no longer necessarily dependent on the lending of IMF and WB, far-reaching and coherent reforms of the IMF and WB are essential to escape an uncertain future. In addition, the increasingly populist-conservative aversion in leading advanced polities to multilateral organizations is another factor that contributes to the uncertain future of the IMF and WB (Linn, 2018, p. 99).

However, the current deadlock situation renders comprehensive reforms unlikely, which means that a new dynamic is required. According to Güven, a new institutionalized settlement in international economy/development can only be achieved by an additional dynamic that undermines the political and economic rationale of rising multipolarity and deficient multilateralism, such as China's economic implosion or transformative political uprisings in the North, which overcome the intense scepticism towards global economic cooperation (Güven, 2017, p. 1166). With the rapid spread of the COVID-19 pandemic since early 2020, a new dynamic has emerged on the stage of global cooperation, which has huge implications for the world economic system and thus potentially also for the IMF and the WB.

Setting up the stage for a general understanding of the current state of affairs, the chapter mainly discusses the potential implications of COVID-19 for the Bretton Woods institutions (IMF and WB) in their current deadlock situation.

3. INTRODUCING COVID-19 AS A NEW DYNAMIC: STRATEGIC IMPLICATIONS FOR THE FUTURE OF IMF AND WORLD BANK

3.1. Times of Crisis—Decisive Dynamics

Crises have the habit of clarifying trends. The COVID-19 crisis, as other crises before, does not fundamentally change the strategic constellations and rivalries, but rather intensifies and accelerates them (Gabriel, 2020), that is, it clarifies existing trends. Given the trend towards increasing multipolarity, the COVID-19 crisis offers lessons about existing competitive advantages of IMF and WB in a more competitive market and about acute opportunities for further institutional adaptation to a changed operational environment. Third, as an accelerating and clarifying dynamic, COVID-19 offers the opportunity for speculation on a long-term role of the old U.S.-backed Bretton Woods institutions.

3.1.1. *Short Term: The New Relevance of IMF/WB—Operational Capacities and Know-How as Competition Advantage*

Like the eurozone crisis, the COVID-19 crisis reveals the still prominent position of the IMF and WB for the global financing and safety net, which is relatively untouched at the operational level despite global power shifts. The institutions are currently experiencing a renewed surge in relevance and their complex structure/function of lending facility, policy advisor, steering committee and coordinator of international institutions reveals the decisive competitive advantage, especially in times of crisis. The Bretton Woods institutions are the multilateral hub for global crisis management in 2020 for four main reasons:

First, the IMF offers its 189 member states directly available $1 trillion in lending via crisis-adapted credit lines (RCF/ RFI/ CCRT (Catastrophe Containment and Relief Trust) financing), while the WB can provide an additional $160 billion in project-based financing over the next 15 months (IMF, 2020b; WB, 2020a). By comparison, in the face of the crisis, AIIB has doubled its mainly infrastructure-related funding to $10 billion (AIIB, 2020a). According to IMF estimates, there is a global crisis financing need of around $100 billion (IMF, 2020c), that is, IMF/WB are the only multilateral institutions capable of meeting global demand. Not only the lending volume but also the financing conditions are benign: relatively few conditions, 0% interest rates and the offer of technical assistance (IMF, 2020d). The IMF is flanked by the WB's highly concessional public health–related lending projects, which use WB expertise to initiate sustainable, highly specialized health reforms in countries where this expertise would otherwise be absent.

As of April 2017, emergency requests for funding from 102 countries (more than 50% of all existing states) are submitted to the IMF and, as of 1 May, WB is offering assistance (funding and expertise) in COVID-related health projects through its fast-track facility credit line to 93 countries, with another 18 countries about to join (WB 2020b). These figures are likely to further increase during the next weeks.

Second, the obvious strength of the IMF and especially the WB in the very complex COVID-19 crisis is the combination of financial resources with leading expertise in providing public health goods. The WB currently offers highly specialized lending projects in well over 100 projects, coupled with technical assistance along the entire COVID-19 problem complex: social protection, poverty alleviation, medical supplies, disease surveillance, research collaboration and building of medical facilities and equipment (WB, 2020c). The IMF not only offers states well-known surveillance and advice on regional, national and global economic issues and capacity development, but it has also established a policy tracker of national economic measures (economic measures to supplement social safety nets and insurance) on COVID-19 since the end of March 2020. Thus, it offers policymakers further support by sharing best practices (IMF, 2020e). Clearly, the non-lending activities of IMF and WB go far beyond the simple services of normal banks and regional development banks. A high number of countries, especially in the South, are critically dependent on the policy expertise of the institutions, as these countries cannot provide such a high level of expertise themselves.

Third, the IMF (with the support of WB) has once again proven itself as the central steering committee of the global response of the world's leading states to global crisis. The informal institutional link between the various G formats (G7; G20) and the Bretton Woods institutions is well known. In the age of summit diplomacy, the G7/G20 formats often act as informal decision-making bodies for IMF/WB (Stone, 2013, p. 134). Conversely, IMF/WB serve as bureaucratic initiators of policy ideas in the decision-making bodies of multilateral politics. The Bretton Woods institutions thus possess an extremely high degree of institutional embeddedness in global multilateral governance. When the IMF and the WB called on the G20 leaders in a joint statement on 25 March 2020 to provide temporary debt relief from all official bilateral creditors to IDA countries (the poorest countries in the world) with highly unsustainable debt situations in order to enable immediate financial liquidity for the fight against COVID-19 (IMF, 2020f), their call was quickly heard. Following the approval of the policy advice in the spring meetings of the finance ministers of the lending states, debt repayment was temporarily suspended as of 1 May in a coherent action by the G20 (WB, 2020d). The arrangement presented a gesture of solidarity in a time of increasing inequality. This anecdote is just one among many, yet it illustrates the base-line that the IMF/WB stands out from other competing banks through its weight as a policy advisor in key multilateral decision bodies.

Fourth, the IMF and the WB assume a node-like coordinating role not only in intergovernmental cooperation but also in the inter-institutional cooperation of multilateral organizations. On 30 April, numerous heads of regional Multilateral Development Banks (MDBs), David Malpass (Head of World Bank Group) and IMF Managing Director Kristalina Georgieva met for a virtual discussion of joint initiatives to support the fight against COVID-19 (ibid.). There is a strong inter-institutional coordination of different regional MDBs with IMF and WB (WB, 2005). The spring meetings of national finance ministers, which are held in Washington at the IMF and WB buildings, can traditionally be seen as important meetings for the coordination of regional MDBs. For example, the joint initiative of numerous MDBs to establish a platform for coordination of the support for economic migration and forced displacement originates from the spring meetings (WB, 2018). The WB and IMF are surrounded by an extensive network of multilateral regional banks (e.g. African Development Bank [ADB], Asian Development Bank [ADB], European Investment Bank [EIB] and Inter-American Development Bank [IADB]) in which WB/IMF exerts significant (American-European) influence. Against this backdrop, the creation of the regional MDBs AIIB and New Development Bank (NDB) by China and the BRICS countries are often understood as a counter-draft to the formal/informal U.S./EU dominance in the existing MDB cooperation network. AIIB and NDB also cooperate as part of the global network of regional MDBs, but they focus primarily on the needs of emerging economies for infrastructure financing and seek to break the dominance of Western states in the financing and implementation of large infrastructure projects (above all for middle-income countries [MICs]) by developing and offering technical expertise in this area (AIIB, 2020b; NDB, 2020).

The COVID-19 crisis highlights once again the prominent role of the Bretton Woods institutions as global crisis managers and pillars of international financial cooperation. The institutions are socialized into the organizational environment of multilateral organizations to an extent that cannot easily be substituted. However, a glance at the list of countries that receive IMF/WB support in the fight against COVID-19 suggests that large MICs continue to strategically avoid cooperation, in particular, with the IMF. In the challenging situation of COVID-19, however, some MICs are forced to turn to the IMF despite their reluctance. Turkey, for example, is currently still struggling to cooperate with the IMF to finance the management of the COVID-19 crisis, although in the absence of other options, an immediate opening of IMF negotiations appears almost inevitable (Pitel, 2020). In light of the disastrous crisis, South Africa has approved an IMF stimulus package for the first time in its history (Cotterill, 2020). It seems that developing economies that do not have any outside opportunities, that is, sufficient financial reserves or private financing, continue to rely on the IMF as lender of last resort. The first months of the COVID-19 crisis reveal the various assets of IMF/WB, which cannot simply be compensated by another competitive bank. Yet, it is equally evident that large MICs are strongly opposed to the offer of the IMF and WB, as they seek to escape the influence of Western donor states for strategic reasons. While the creation of regional MDBs led by China and the BRCIS states cannot operationally match the performance of the overall portfolio of the Bretton Woods institutions in the foreseeable future, it does lead to direct competition in the main area of need of developing economies—infrastructure financing—which has been highly lucrative for the IMF and WB in the past. MICs pursue a strategy of national financial security measures (building up financial reserves), bilateral insurance agreements (swap-lines) and use of newly created MDBs to escape the potential need for IMF programmes. This situation is problematic for the IMF, as large MICs have historically been an important source of income in lending. The WB faces the same challenges in a markedly weaker form, as its conditionality is already more flexible and its financing less dependent on the contributions of powerful Western donor states. Despite ad-hoc adaptation mechanisms (especially operations expansion to Africa), a long-term return of large MICs to being borrower states seems possible only through reform of conditionality and the quota share system. Potential findings of the COVID-19 crisis for the medium-term philosophy development of IMF/WB conditionality could represent a first step towards reform.

3.1.2. Mid-Term: Gaining Experience and Learning Lessons— An Opportunity for Philosophy Development

The IMF and the WB are in a unique position to lead the globally coordinated response to COVID-19 due to their special position in the global financial architecture. While the EU is combating the domestic economic consequences of COVID-19 through the No-Limit Buying of sovereign and corporate debt, and the United States through a $2 trillion stimulus bill, the G20 has chosen IMF and WB as the central crisis firefighters for those countries that will bear most of the burden: LICs and MICs. As described in section 4.1, IMF/WB have initiated a number of actions to address the financing needs of the COVID-19 crisis. However, many experts agree that the measures taken will not be enough for a globally coordinated initiative to ensure global health security. While the steps taken by IMF/WB testify to their currently unrivalled position in the international financial architecture, the COVID-19 crisis might present an important crossroads. IMF/WB could either become a truly

global actor and regain confidence in LICs and especially in the operationally critical MICs, or the BRICS countries and other MICs could find their
negative stance confirmed, that is, a continuation and even acceleration of the
path of relative decline. The COVID-19 crisis provides the opportunity for a
pronounced step away from a purely market-fundamentalist logic towards the
provision of public goods. This is a decisive philosophy development for the
future competitive viability of the Bretton Woods institutions.

For the following reasons, the current IMF/WB initiatives are insufficient and,
in some cases, even detrimental to the global provision of public health goods:

1. Unsustainable debt assessment practice in times of uncertainty
    The IMF is addressing the challenge of the COVID-19 crisis through
a fast-track processing of emergency requests from indebted countries. In
their Public Debt Sustainability Analysis (DSA), they risk prematurely
classifying existing national debt as sustainable, even though the high
degree of uncertainty of the current situation does not permit this statement. The DSA only allows binary results (sustainable/ non-sustainable),
which means that there is an incentive to be too hastily optimistic about
the debt analysis in order to provide countries with short-term assistance in
combating COVID-19. This state of affairs potentially damages the long-
term integrity of the IMF's economic forecast and analysis. Moreover, it
could ultimately make the debt of many countries less sustainable, delay
necessary action and increase the risk of even more destabilizing restructuring in the future. This problematic pattern indicates that the normal
assessment practice as part of IMF conditionality, which proposes structural adjustments to make debt sustainable, is not appropriate at a time
when countries are gearing their fiscal instruments to immediate crisis
response (Rediker & Rediker, 2020).

2. Existing debt moratorium to little
    The debt relief negotiated so far by IMF and G20 (in use from 1 May)
is only a temporary postponement of payment obligations. This is likely to
be too little. Money borrowed by indebted states through the conventional
lending instruments of IMF and WB means additional debt repayments,
while the money is urgently needed to combat COVID-19. The IMF has
already used its CCRT bond to pay itself back money that is owed to it by
borrower states. The WB is reluctant to defer debt repayments because it
has no comparable fund to repay itself. Reality suggests that debt repayments are most likely unavoidable (Chhibber, 2020).

3. Detrimental structural conditionality for public health
    The huge share of the $1 trillion fund provided by the IMF and WB is dis-
tributed to crisis-ridden countries through conventional lending instruments,

that is, despite supposedly minimal conditionality, they remain subject to structural conditionalities that have potentially adverse effects on public health through poorly designed policy measures such as budget cuts, reducing wages of workers, weakening of social protection and privatization. David Malpass has announced that the WB's lending practice in the COVID-19 crisis will depend on the adoption of structural adjustment policies by the borrower states. There is a long track record of these institutions for the negative impact of IMF/WB conditionality on national health systems (Kentikelenis et al., 2020).

4. Controversial public-private partnerships in health

Much ($8 billion) of the WB's initially announced $14 billion fast-track assistance package will be channelled through the IFC, the WB's private sector financing arm, rather than through the Health, Nutrition, and Population Division, which has strong expertise in health. IFC has no expertise in building public health systems, and at the same time, the track record of public-private partnerships in health is extremely poor. The remainder of the first fast-track assistance package ($6 billion) is earmarked for direct support of health care, although it is not yet clear whether this will support shaky public health systems or finance private health services that are pulling staff out of the public sector. According to Kentikelenis et al. (2020), the second option is more likely, since IFC loans include direct financing of private companies in the health care sector and the WB has emphasized the need for structural adjustment policies (deregulation, liberalization, privatization, etc.) in crisis lending.

Based on the aforementioned points, there is considerable potential for improvement for the IMF and the WB in their role as global crisis firefighters. The following section presents a non-exhaustive list of proposals for solutions that have been developed by various experts:

1. Invest in universal public health

Certainly, the economic consequences of the COVID-19 crisis are of enormous impact, yet a pandemic is first of all health-related. A current ratio of 6:1000 ($6 billion of WB for direct purchase of medical supplies vs. $1 trillion total lending volume of IMF and WB) does not primarily meet the critical goal of financing public health systems. There must be a significant increase in specific unconditional procurement programmes for medical supplies to explicitly strengthen public health. (Kentikelenis et al., 2020).

2. Pandemic funds with no conditionality/flexible conditionality practice

The creation of non-conditional pandemic funds with a focus on real economic activities and health and social protection. Unconditional emergency pandemic aid will act as a lifeline for many LICs/MICs as they do not have the reserves to fight COVID-19, prevent bankruptcies and compensate for economic damage in the long run. A flexible debt sustainability assessment, which does not make lending dependent on a binary code (sustainable/non-sustainable debt), would provide private and public investors, policymakers and financial markets with a more realistic assessment, allowing them to play a more constructive role without nasty surprises. It would also avoid situations such as an IMF request for debt restructuring to lenders while the borrower countries were initially considered sustainable. No structural conditionality and a flexible debt assessment increase the risk of default for the lending countries, but the increased risk benefits the public good (Kentikelenis et al., 2020; Rediker & Rediker, 2020).

3. New debt-moratorium/Debt restructuring

   The existing deal for the temporary postponement of debt-related payment obligations is not sufficient. A substantial relief in sovereign debt must be provided for LICs and MICs, which can only be achieved through a joint initiative for debt relief. In this way, already existing public money that had been earmarked for the repayment of debts can be directly invested in the fight against the repercussions of COVID-19 (Ghosh & Kasumovic, 2020; Chhibber, 2020).

4. Carbon consumption taxes (administered by WB)

   One way to temporarily finance the developing countries' fight against COVID-19 could be to levy a small tax on global oil and gas consumption (carbon tax). The revenues would then be collected in a fund and made available to states in trouble. Even though the proposal seems difficult to implement, Chibber proposes a viable plan: A fund could be run by the WB because (1) it has the necessary infrastructure for the task and (2) rich countries can keep control through controlling vetoes. According to Chibber's calculations, the minor taxation of oil, coal and natural gas could generate around 200 billion dollars annually (Chhibber, 2020).

5. SDR issuance

   Another way to relieve the burden on LICs/MICs would be a massive issuance of special drawing rights (SDRs), the IMF/WB reserve assets, to countries without conditionality and according to their quotas (maximum amount countries are eligible to borrow is determined by their vote quota in the institutions). The existing IMF/WB financial quota pot of $1 trillion must be borrowed under IMF/WB arrangements, but many MICs are afraid to approach the IMF due to the poor track record of past IMF stand-by agreements. According to Ghosh, the short-term increase in money supply must not lead to global inflation if the unlocked resources go towards preventing supply bottlenecks that occurred during the lockdown situation. Experts disagree on the exact amount of money supply. According to Chhibber, $650 billion may be sufficient to cover the initial demand, while Ghosh considers at least $1.4–2.7 trillion realistic (Ghosh & Kasumovic, 2020; Chhibber, 2020).

6. Capital controls

The IMF, as coordinator of the global financial architecture, could help developing countries to establish tighter capital controls to prevent financial markets from further exacerbating COVID-19 fallout in emerging markets. Capital controls mean restrictions on the free movement of capital, that is, a protective measure against rapid withdrawal of money from emerging markets (Ghosh & Kasumovic, 2020).

The current provision of global health security and economic stimulus by IMF/WB offers much room for improvement. The implementation of some proposed solutions could mean a pronounced step away from a hierarchical— market fundamentalist approach, which is categorically rejected by MICs, towards a global provision of public goods. The COVID-19 crisis thus offers a potential momentum for a decisive institutional philosophical development towards a reinforced global position of the Bretton Woods institutions—this time, not as an instrument of a global hegemony, but as a truly global actor. Within the framework of the proposed solutions, there is an opportunity to resolve operational goal conflicts (public goods versus market liberalism) and regain the trust of LICs/MICs. IMF and WB can redeem themselves and thereby cement their global position in a turbulent period of power shifts. The long-term future of the Bretton Woods institutions after the COVID-19 crisis contains many unknown variables, but it depends on the conditions and decisions made today. In the following section of the chapter, two possible scenarios will be briefly discussed, which potentially arise (1) from global power shifts and conflicts currently observed and (2) from the institutional responses that IMF and WB may take towards these trends.

3.1.3. *Long Term: COVID-19 as Trend Accelerator, Aggravator and Clarifier—Possible Future Scenarios for IMF/WB*

3.1.3.1. Assumptions about Geopolitical Implications of COVID-19

The geopolitical implications of COVID-19 encompass many uncertain variables. However, the following can be said for now. The first weeks of the COVID-19 pandemic have demonstrated that U.S.-China relations have hit a new bottom during the crisis. While the United States and China attempted to end two years of trade tensions through the "Phase One" trade deal just before the crisis (Gertz, 2020), the COVID-19 crisis has reignited old tensions. The two countries are playing a blame game armed with misinformation campaigns to shift responsibility for the magnitude of the global COVID-19 pandemic (Liang, 2020). The two major powers have so far proven that they are not able to coordinate the global fight against COVID-19. The crisis accelerates the process of decoupling, which started after a series of escalatory U.S. moves in 2019, that is, China and the United States are trying to decouple the dependencies caused by their joint economic linkages (supply chains) in order to become strategically independent. Ian Bremmer, head of the Eurasia Group, cites this process as the most important geopolitical development since the fall of the Soviet Union (Bremmer & Kupchan, 2020, p. 6). As part of this process, China is expected to continue to intensify its efforts to reshape international technology, trade and financial architecture to pursue its interests in an increasingly multipolar world with two main poles. So far, the COVID-19 crisis has thus aggravated and accelerated U.S.-China rivalry and provided clarity about the mutual containment strategies of the two major powers. A post-COVID-19 world is likely to be more multipolar, less globalized and more nationalist. This means that there will be more clearly defined spheres of influence between the United States and China. Despite the early stage, a sort of new Cold War between two, even after the crisis, potent poles (United States and China) and other powerful players in-between (EU and BRICS) can be expected. A time of more uncertainty, more diverging interests, and more ad-hoc strategic alignment between states. The magnitude of emerging economic nationalism and the actions and adjustment processes of the IMF and WB will determine the future role of the Bretton Woods institutions. Two possible scenarios should be briefly considered. It is worth to think of these two scenarios along a number of variables, whereby the presented cases form poles of a continuum, therefore other shades of grey are possible in-between:

3.1.3.2. Scenario 1: No Decoupling and Adaptive Reform

In scenario 1, the United States and China reach a timely joint solution to their rivalry, that is, they stop the decoupling process and acknowledge that the United States and China are so closely linked by their global supply chains and supplemental demand structure that comprehensive decoupling is extremely counterproductive for economic growth and the global position of both states. China and the United States each have competitive advantages that cannot be easily reproduced by other countries. In fact, a diversification of production sites would be a much more effective measure to deal with supply chain disruption (Liang, 2020). Second, a quota governance reform

is being carried out in the IMF and the WB, which means that at least the
vote shares of the BRICS states will be adjusted to their real global economic
weight. This requires agreement on a new formula to determine the global
economic weight of each country (Wade & Vestergaard, 2015, p. 1). The consequence of a quota reform is, with China's increasing economic power, the
loss of American veto power and the associated clear decline of American-
European influence in the institutions. On the other hand, a quota reform may
help the Bretton Woods institutions to regain legitimacy as a global financial
actor and to regain trust from LICs/MICs. A gain in trust will be linked to philosophy development towards non-structural conditionality and less focus on
social reform, human rights and democracy building. These are all norms that
are of secondary importance in the BRICS countries compared to economic
upswings and their enforcement as part of conditionality is seen as intrusive
into domestic affairs.

3.1.3.3. Scenario 2: Decoupling and Fragmentation

In Scenario 2, the institutional deadlock in IMF and WB will continue in a
post-COVID-19 world, since the West cannot allow IMF/WB money-lending
without conditions such as market opening, democracy development, or
human rights, as it represents an indispensable instrument of Western (value-
based) foreign policy. A veto against a quota reform in IMF/WB is thus an
essential part of a Western containment strategy vis-à-vis the BRICS states.
The decoupling process is continuing. Although the relapse into economic
nationalism is connected with enormous costs, China and the United States
will increasingly and persistently try to decouple economic dependencies for
strategic reasons against the background of growing rivalry. One aspect of the
decoupling process is the continuation and strengthening of the fragmentation of international development aid and financing. While a strong U.S./EU
influence will continue to exist in the IMF and WB, the BRICS states will further develop the rival AIIB and NDB and probably increasingly expand them
by adding new areas of competence. While IMF/WB, as shown in 3.1.1/3.1.2,
has clear competitive advantages in the short/medium term, the newly created competing organizations concentrate on sub-areas such as infrastructure
financing where the developing countries have the greatest current need.
These organizations could then gradually build up a parallel financing structure in which, building on their rival philosophy (no interfering conditionality, no promotion of human rights, liberalization, etc.), competencies in other
areas of financing, technical assistance, expertise and international and inter-
organizational cooperation and influence are progressively built up. A long-
term extreme might be parallel financial structures, but a medium variant in

the sense of clear spheres of influence and an age of choice is likely to be more viable for the first time. In scenario 2, the IMF and WB will potentially loose more clients. How many and which clients IMF and WB can retain in their portfolios depends also significantly on the institutional decisions in the COVID-19 crisis. If a post-COVID-19 world were to remember the IMF and the WB as successful and truly global crisis managers, the shift from MICs away from IMF/WB could be more fragmented and, despite the ongoing U.S.-China rivalry, more MICs and LICs could be inclined to stay with IMF/WB. This calls for determined leadership from IMF/WB and a philosophy development away from a fundamentally market-oriented and mainly donor-friendly philosophy towards a real provision of public goods. This philosophy development is reflected in the acute corona measures presented in 3.1.2. A poor post-COVID-19 memory of the role of the IMF and the WB by developing countries will further encourage increasing fragmentation.

3.1.3.4. Why Scenario 2 Is Far More Likely

The two scenarios presented can be seen as poles between which the future of the IMF and WB will fall in the face of various uncertain variables. However, a future of IMF and WB that is close to scenario 2 seems much more likely. For the following reasons:

(1) Trump's foreign policy, as well as the foreign policy vision of his Democratic challenger in 2020, Joe Biden, clearly point towards a continuation of containment (Toosi, 2020). Without containment, Xi Jinping's long-term strategy of "change through trade" would work, not along the Western hoped-for way of democratization, but through China's economic overtaking of America. China would thus have used the double advantages of a liberal world trade system and an authoritarian regime for economic growth. It is impossible for the United States to stand by and watch this happen.

(2) China's president has also proclaimed a "new long march", which means a technological-economic decoupling in anticipation of increasing tensions in economic matters (Nakazawa, 2019). The costly establishment of the AIIB is an inherent indication of the low Chinese expectation of quota reforms in IMF/WB.

(3) Empirical evidence points out that throughout world history hegemons have always sought to leverage their still superior resources in transition phases (power shifts due to underlying power shifts) to defend their existing power position (Allison, 2017).

4. CONCLUSION

In this chapter, the future of the Bretton Woods institutions IMF and WB was examined with special attention to the current COVID-19 crisis.

First, the chapter described how the institutions are experiencing a more challenging strategic environment in a world of increasing power shifts (2), in which they face loss of legitimacy, philosophy contestations and increasing competition.

Against this background, the COVID-19 crisis with its far-reaching economic, social and political consequences was introduced as a new dynamic in the strategic environment of IMF and WB and discussed in its short-term, medium-term and long-term implications for the position of IMF and WB (3). The analysis concluded that the COVID-19 crisis has demonstrated that the Bretton Woods institutions still have unique capabilities in the international financial architecture (3.1). Due to their superior capabilities as lending facility, policy advisor, steering committee and coordinator of international institutions, IMF/WB enjoys clear comparative advantages in an increasingly competitive environment in the short to medium term (3.1). The crisis offers a distinct opportunity for IMF and WB to develop their philosophy further towards becoming a global provider of public goods (3.2). In 3.2, various opportunities for improvement in IMF and WB support for developing countries were presented. By implementing these proposals, the institutions could use the COVID-19 crisis to take a pronounced step away from a purely market-fundamentalist logic towards becoming a truly global actor, thus regaining essential trust among MICs.

Which decisions IMF and WB—and thus also the powerful donor states—make to support LICs/MICs in the fight against COVID-19 and the subsequent economic reconstruction, as well as the explicit features of the U.S.-China rivalry (degree of decoupling, economic consequences of COVID-19, Corona Diplomacy), will determine the future of the Bretton Woods institutions in the long run in an most likely increasingly fragmented system of international financing (3.3).

REFERENCES

Aidoo, R., & Hess, S. (2015). Non-interference 2.0: China's evolving foreign policy towards a changing Africa. *Journal of Current Chinese Affairs*, *44*(1), 107–39.

AIIB. (2020, April 17). AIIB Doubles COVID-19 Crisis Response to USD10 Billion—News. Retrieved 23 May 2020 from https://www.aiib.org/en/news-events/news/2020/AIIB-Doubles-COVID-19-Crisis-Response-to-USD10-Billion.html.

AIIB. (n.d.). Our Work. Retrieved 23 May 2020 from https://www.aiib.org/en/about-aiib/who-we-are/our-work/index.html.

Allison, G. T. (2017). *Destined for war: Can America and China escape Thucydides trap?* Melbourne: Scribe.

Best, J. (2007). Legitimacy dilemmas: The IMFs pursuit of country ownership. *Third World Quarterly, 28*(3), 469–88.

Bremmer, I., & Kupchan, C. (2020). *Top Risks 2020*. New York, NY: Eurasia Group.

Chhibber, A. (2020, April 22). Global Solutions to Global Bads: 2 Practical Proposals to Help Developing Countries Deal with the COVID-19 Pandemic. Retrieved 23 May 2020 from https://www.brookings.edu/blog/future-development/2020/04/22/global-solutions-to-global-bads-2-practical-proposals-to-help-developing-countries-deal-with-the-covid-19-pandemic/.

Chow, D. (2016). Why China Established the Asia Infrastructure Investment Bank. *Vanderbilt Journal of Transnational Law*, Forthcoming; Ohio State Public Law Working Paper No. 333. Retrieved from https://ssrn.com/abstract=2737888.

Cormier, B., & Manger, M. (2019). *The Evolution of World Bank Conditionality: A Quantitative Text Analysis.* Paper for presentation at the 2019 Pacific International Politics Conference (PIPC) Academia Sinica, Taipei.

Cotterill, J. (2020, April 21). South Africa Unveils $26bn Stimulus and Taps IMF for First Time. Retrieved 23 May 2020 from https://www.ft.com/content/e07b70bd-71ae-4b8a-9855-09665330fed9.

Crotty, J., & Lee, K.-K. (2008). Was IMF-Imposed Economic Regime Change in Korea Justified? The Political Economy of IMF Intervention. *Review of Radical Political Economics, 41*(2), 149–69.

Devonshire-Ellis, C. (2019). The BRICS Nations Are Headed for 50% of Global GDP By 2030. This Is What It Could Mean for Developing Global Supply Chains & Emerging Consumer Markets. Retrieved 23 May 202 from https://www.silkroadbriefing.com/news/2019/11/21/brics-nations-headed-50-global-gdp-2030-mean-developing-global-supply-chains-emerging-consumer-markets/.

Gabriel, S. (2020, May 3). Mehr als eine Seuche. Retrieved 23 May 2020 from https://www.zeit.de/politik/ausland/2020-05/corona-folgen-konjunktur-ungleichheit-globalisierung-sigmar-gabriel.

Gertz, G. (2020, March 11). Phase One China Trade Deal Tests the Limits of US Power. Retrieved 23 May 2020 from https://www.brookings.edu/opinions/phase-one-china-trade-deal-tests-the-limits-of-us-power/.

Ghosh, J., & Kasumovich, M. (2020, April 9). COVID-19 ist die Chance des IWF auf Wiedergutmachung by Jayati Ghosh. Retrieved 23 May 2020 from https://www.project-syndicate.org/commentary/how-imf-can-lead-global-covid19-response-by-jayati-ghosh-2020–04/german.

Güven, A. B. (2017). Defending supremacy: How the IMF and the World Bank navigate the challenge of rising powers. *International Affairs, 93*(5), 1149–66.

Henning, C. R. (2011). Coordinating regional and multilateral financial institutions. *SSRN Electronic Journal*. Peterson Institute for International Economics Working Paper No. 11–9. Retrieved 14 April 2021 from https://ssrn.com/abstract=1793242.

IMF. (2020a). *Fifteenth and Sixteenth General Reviews of Quotas—Report of the Executive Board to the Board of Governors.* Washington, DC: International Monetary Fund.

IMF. (2020b). Questions and Answers: The IMF's Response to COVID-19. Retrieved 24 May 2020 from https://www.imf.org/en/About/FAQ/imf-response-to-covid-19.

IMF. (2020c). Confronting the Crisis: Priorities for the Global Economy. Retrieved May 24, 2020 from https://www.imf.org/en/News/Articles/2020/04/07/sp040 920-SMs2020-Curtain-Raiser.

IMF. (2020d). *Enhancing the Emergency Financing Toolkit—Responding To The Covid-19 Pandemic.* Washington, DC: International Monetary Fund.

IMF. (2020e). IMF Is Launching a Tracker of Policies Governments Are Taking in Response to COVID-19. Retrieved 24 May 2020 from https://www.imf.org/en/ News/Articles/2020/03/25/pr20106-imf-is-launching-a-tracker-of-policies-govern ments-are-taking-in-response-to-covid-19.

IMF. (2020f). Factsheet—Debt Relief under the Heavily Indebted Poor Countries (HIPC) Initiative. Retrieved 24 May 2020 from https://www.imf.org/en/About/ Factsheets/Sheets/2016/08/01/16/11/Debt-Relief-Under-the-Heavily-Indebted-Poor-Countries-Initiative.

Kentikelenis, A., Gabor, D., Ortiz, I., Stubbs, T., Mckee, M., & Stuckler, D. (2020). Softening the blow of the pandemic: Will the International Monetary Fund and World Bank make things worse? *The Lancet Global Health, 8*(6), 1–2.

Kentikelenis, A. E., Stubbs, T. H., & King, L. P. (2016). IMF conditionality and development policy space, 1985–2014. *Review of International Political Economy, 23*(4), 543–82.

Layne, C. (2018). The US-Chinese power shift and the end of the Pax Americana. *International Affairs, 94*(1), 89–111.

Liang, Y. (2020). The US, China, and the Perils of Post-COVID Decoupling. Retrieved 24 May 2020 from https://thediplomat.com/2020/05/the-us-china-and-the-perils-of-post-covid-decoupling/.

Linn, J. (2017). Recent Threats to Multilateralism. *Global Journal of Emerging Market Economies, 9*(1–3), 86–113.

Nakazawa, Katsuji (2019). The New Long March—Xi's 15-Year Battle Plan with the US. Retrieved 24 May 2020 from https://asia.nikkei.com/Editor-s-Picks/ China-up-close/The-new-Long-March-Xi-s-15-year-battle-plan-with-the-US.

Pitel, L. (2020, April 12). Turkey Rejects any Suggestion of IMF Help. Retrieved 23 May 2020 from https://www.ft.com/content/7c9d9851-58cf-4561-9e8e-24dca0 e6866e.

Ray, R., & Kamal, R. (2019). Can South-South cooperation compete? The Development Bank of Latin America and the Islamic Development Bank. *Development and Change, 50*(1), 191–220.

Rediker, D. A., & Crebo-Rediker, H. (2020, April 15). COVID-19 Uncertainty and the IMF. Retrieved 24 May 2020 from https://www.brookings.edu/blog/ future-development/2020/04/14/covid-19-uncertainty-and-the-imf/.

Schwarzer, D. (2017). Europe, the End of the West and Global Power Shifts. *Global Policy, 8*, 18–26.

Stephen, M. D. (2017). Emerging powers and emerging trends in global governance. *Global Governance: A Review of Multilateralism and International Organizations, 23*(3), 483–502.

Stone, R. W. (2013). Informal governance in international organizations: Introduction to the special issue. *The Review of International Organizations, 8*(2), 121–36.

Toosi, N. (2020, April 23). Biden ad exposes a rift over China on the left. Retrieved 24 May 2020 from https://www.politico.com/news/2020/04/23/biden-ad-exposes-left-rift-china-202241.

Véron, N. (2016). The IMFs Role in the Euro-Area Crisis: Financial Sector Aspects. Retrieved 24 May 2020 from https://www.bruegel.org/2016/08/the-imfs-role-in-the-euro-area-crisis-financial-sector-aspects/.

Wade, R. H. (2011). Emerging world order? From multipolarity to multilateralism in the G20, the World Bank, and the IMF. *Politics & Society, 39*(3), 347–78.

Wade, R. H., & Vestergaard, J. (2015). Why is the IMF at an impasse, and what can be done about it? *Global Policy, 6*(3), 290–96.

WB. (2005). *Update on Cooperation among Multilateral Development Banks.* World Bank.

WB. (2018, April 20). MDBs Launch New Platform to Coordinate Support for Economic Migration and Forced Displacement. Retrieved 24 May 2020 from https://www.worldbank.org/en/news/press-release/2018/04/20/mdbs-launch-new-platform-to-coordinate-support-for-economic-migration-and-forced-displacement.

WB. (2020a). The World Bank Group Moves Quickly to Help Countries Respond to COVID-19. Retrieved 24 May 2020 from https://www.worldbank.org/en/news/feature/2020/04/02/the-world-bank-group-moves-quickly-to-help-countries-respond-to-covid-19.

WB. (2020b). World Bank Group: 100 Countries Get Support in Response to COVID-19 (Coronavirus). Retrieved May 24, 2020 from https://www.worldbank.org/en/news/press-release/2020/05/19/world-bank-group-100-countries-get-support-in-response-to-covid-19-coronavirus.

WB. (2020c). How the World Bank Group Is Helping Countries with COVID-19 (coronavirus). Retrieved 24 May 2020 from https://www.worldbank.org/en/news/factsheet/2020/02/11/how-the-world-bank-group-is-helping-countries-with-covid-19-coronavirus.

WB. (2020d). May 1, 2020 End of Week Update: Debt Relief for the World's Poorest Countries. Retrieved 24 May 2020 from https://blogs.worldbank.org/voices/may-1-2020-end-week-update-debt-relief-worlds-poorest-countries.

Part II

REGIONAL ORGANIZATIONS
AND INSTITUTIONS

Chapter 6

The African Union
and Multilateralism

Nandi Makubalo

1. THE HISTORICAL CONTEXT ON
CONTEMPORARY MULTILATERALISM

The foundations of many of the current multilateral organisations including the UN, WTO, the WB and the IMF, as well as GATT that later became the WTO, were laid in the aftermath of the Second World War. The United States was especially pushing for a new world order based on peace, democratic values and prosperity through an economy adhering to free market principles (Møller, 2005). Nevertheless, the differences in views between capitalist states and the communist states were a source of tension during the forty-year Cold War. With the downfall of communism in the late eighties and early nineties in the Soviet bloc, one would have expected that multilateralism and peace would become the new norm (EU Institute for Security Studies, 2016). Now, three decades after the end of the Cold War, we must recognise that the United States, once the leading proponent of multilateralism and winner of the Cold War, has impeded many of the steps taken in enhancing multilateralism. For instance, the disdain for a multilateral world order by Russia and North Korea is not new. The United States illustrated this clearly with the invasion of Iraq despite opposition from NATO allies and the UN. The fact that the United States is now trying to undermine the international institutions that it helped to create is astonishing. We should look at the causes of these evolutions and reflect upon the consequences of these decisions for the AU.

At the Paris Peace Forum in 2018, the UN Secretary-General António Guterres stated that the UN's position on multilateralism, particularly cooperation and institution-building, was invaluable in creating a post-war order marked by peace and prosperity. The Secretary-General's statements went on further to explain that multilateralism has become a necessity in the fight against poverty, deadly diseases and conflict.

Africa simultaneously faces all of these challenges. African multilateralism dates back to 1963 when the Organisation for African Unity (OAU) was formed to help African countries attain their independence and to end Apartheid in South Africa (Murithi, 2005, pp. 1–5). Along with the OAU of 1963–2001 and the subsequent formation of its successor the AU in 2002, African multilateralism has evolved in its scope and efficiency. This is particularly true as the organisation has evolved from solely focusing on the attainment of independence to more complex programme such as economic prosperity, conflict resolution, disaster management, good governance, the creation of a free trade area and possibly a single monetary union. During the Cold War, there was a huge struggle for influence by many states in the developing world. The USSR certainly tried to pull African states in its favour as did the United States. African countries were also slowly decolonising which amongst other factors might explain why multilateralism was never really successful in Africa during the 1960s. The internal preconditions (strong and independent states) and external preconditions (recognition and sovereignty) were not in place to support multilateralism. However, along with other strategies in achieving its goals and ambitions, to some extent, the AU has depended on multilateralism. The AU is currently more than ever an active participant in regional, continental and global multilateralism. The purpose of this chapter is to address the AU as an active but often overlooked player in the world's multilateral system. This chapter will share an overview of the AU's multilateralism at an international level, outlining the AU's institutional relations with the UN and other multilateral organisations. On a continental level, the chapter focuses on AU's internal development and its relations with its member states. The chapter then proceeds to discuss some of the current threats to the AU as a multilateral body. Finally, the chapter ends with a short reflection on the importance of multilateralism for the AU. In doing so, it sheds light on the AU as an active but often overlooked player in the world's multilateral system.

2. THE AFRICAN UNION'S INTERACTION WITH THE UNITED NATIONS AND THE IMPLICATION OF THESE INTERACTIONS

Ruggie (1993) defines multilateralism as cooperation that centres on diplomatic strategies used by states in order to coordinate policy among three or more actors. Under this definition, multilateralism is designed in such a way that all those engaging in multilateralism can benefit from it. Ruggie (1993) further explains weaker economies that do not attract extensive bilateral cooperation can benefit from multilateral cooperation (Touval & Zartman, 2010). As countries and organisations face varying challenges and opportunities, it is beneficial to engage in multilateralism in order to lessen challenges and strengthen opportunities for all. Multilateralism is particularly important because it gives rise to the creation of institutions and policies which make cooperation easier. For instance, in multilateral trade, transaction costs might be reduced or removed.

Relations between regional organisations and the UN all have their foundation in Chapter VIII of the UN Charter (UN Charter, Article 52). However, relations between the AU and the UN were officially discussed in 1992 in then Secretary-General Boutros Ghali's Agenda for peace. The Agenda for peace promoted greater cooperation and delegation to regional organisations, encouraging them to help alleviate the burden on the Security Council (in the sense that regional affairs could be better addressed by a regional organisation).

In 2006, the declaration between the UN and AU on cooperation was signed, reinforcing the continuation of the UN-AU partnership forged in 1992. An update of the 2006 cooperation, 'Joint United Nations-African Union Framework for Enhanced Partnership in Peace and Security', was signed in 2016.

The 2016 partnership focuses mainly on collaborative efforts on issues of peace and security in Africa, additional focus is placed on development (S/RES/2320, 2016). Along with the Joint Framework, the creation of the United Nations Office to the African Union (UNOAU) is another notable example of UN-AU multilateral engagement. Other multilateral engagements include groupings such as the Group of African States, the G77 and China and the Non-Aligned Movement (NAM). All three groups are represented in the United Nations General Assembly (UNGA).

For instance, the AU-G77-NAM alliance is key in resolutions relating to contemporary development issues such as the environment, agricultural technology and trade (Zang, 2018). The fact that most African states are members of two or more of these groups influences their voting patterns in the UNGA where member states all have one vote per state (Zang, 2018; Laatikainen & Smith, 2020). More often than not, these groups meet and agree on topics that would later be discussed and voted upon in the UNGA. Being that Africa has more states than any other continent in the UNGA, the coordination and cooperation patterns of African states matter in the selection of discussions and in decision making.

2.1. The Joint UN-AU Framework for Enhanced Partnership in Peace and Security

The aforementioned Security Council Resolution 2320 highlights a strengthened partnership between the UN and AU, focused on peace and security, in particular conflict prevention, conflict management, conflict resolution and peace building (S/RES/2320, 2016). Under the auspices of Resolution 2320, the UN and AU agreed to the implementation of both organisations' agendas—for the AU, *Agenda 2063* and the UN's *Sustainable Development Goals (SDGs)*. Under this enhanced partnership, the UN and the AU meet biannually to review their commitment towards their partnership. It cannot be stressed enough that the joint UN-AU framework works beyond mere collaboration on peace missions but rather ensures a holistic approach that pledges commitment to the implementation of both UN-AU agendas, thus strengthening their collaboration on an array of programmes and action points.

2.2. United Nations Office to the African Union

In 2010, the UN General Assembly adopted Resolution 64/288 for the creation of a UNOAU. The UNOAU was specifically created to tackle issues pertaining to the relationship between the UN and AU, and the office is financed by the UN.

'The three main mandates of the UNOAU are centred on enhancing its partnership with the UN in the area of peace and security, the provision of coordinated and consistent UN advice to the AU on long-term capacity-building and short-term operational support matters, and streamlining of UN presence in Addis Ababa to make it cost-effective and efficient in delivering UN assistance to the AU' (UNOAU Bulletin, 2018).

UNOAU's deliberate efforts in cooperating on UN-AU peace missions include the planning for and the management of peace missions (analysis, mediation, conflict prevention and elections), organising an annual meeting between the UN Security Council and the AU Peace and Security Council, and supporting the AU Commission in its efforts to enhance its institutional capacity.[1] The creation of this office explicates UN-AU cooperation on peace missions in that the key areas of a peace mission which consist of planning, execution and management are covered and catered for under the auspices of this office.

3. THE AFRICAN UNION AND MULTILATERALISM ON THE AFRICAN CONTINENT

Despite Africa's immense cultural and political variability, the desire for peace and security coupled with economic development remains constant unifying factor that holds the AU together.

In 2013, Agenda 2063[2] and its flagship initiatives were adopted to lead social and economic development from 2013 to 2063. Agenda 2063 focuses on a strategic framework for the socio-economic transformation of the

African continent over a 50-year period by accelerating the implementation of past and existing national, regional and continental initiatives to ensure growth and sustainable development. Silencing the Guns by 2020 which is perhaps the most prominent flagship initiative provides a precise method of developing and concretising a roadmap towards realising a peaceful and secure Africa free from conflict. In addition to the AU's commitment to Agenda 2063 and Silencing the Guns by 2020, the AU is also committed to achieving the Sustainable Development Goals (SDGs)[3] and some of the ways by which it does this is by partnering with the UN, international regional organisations and African regional bodies such as the Southern African Development Community (SADC) and the Economic Community of West African States (ECOWAS).

The African Union Development Agency (AUDA, also formerly NEPAD) is the technical arm for development within the AU. The AUDA plans and implements AU development projects. The AUDA also serves as the continent's interface with development stakeholders and partners at bilateral and multilateral levels. In order to attain development, it is necessary to have a specialised agency like the AUDA taking the lead on issues such as the governance of natural resources, industrialisation, technology and innovation.

With regards to integration, the AU has clearly indicated the need for stronger economic, social and cultural integration. The desire for economic integration was first expressed by the founder of the AU and late Libyan president Muammar Al-Gaddafi in 1986. Gaddafi profoundly spoke of an economic union encompassing a free trading area, a borderless continent and a single currency when he became the AU Chairperson in 2009.

Ten years later, the signing of the African Continental Free Trade Area (AfCFTA) agreement, entered into force in 2019, is to date the most viable evidence of AU economic integration. The AfCFTA agreement is expected to be a large continental single market with a collective GDP of US$2.5 trillion (World Economic Forum, 2017) but these estimates are only applicable if the agreement is implemented successfully. The free trade agreement is expected to enhance continental and economic integration through the free movement of goods and services; empower citizens; lead to improved business acumen through an increase of entrepreneurial courses throughout the continent; enhance investments in the private sector; and increase public-private partnerships, industrialisation and South-South cooperation.

Møller (2005) argues that regional trade in Africa normally produces few benefits because of the low level of intra-African trade even within regional economic organisations such as ECOWAS and SADC. On the other hand, the AfCFTA is expected to reduce the cost of doing business in Africa, especially for Africans, by the reduction of taxes, the removal of some of the formalities that are required in setting up a business in a different country and a better legal framework for operating transnational businesses. The AfCFTA is also expected to improve African multilateralism by forming economically stable and stronger multilateral development partnerships within and outside the continent.

In the future, it will be interesting to observe how trade and development will be operated under the AfCFTA, when African countries depend more on each other rather than the current global system where African countries are the main suppliers of raw materials and main importers of finished products. It will be important to observe whether the AfCFTA will bring about a positive shift for Africa's current position in global supply chains.

4. CHALLENGES TO THE AFRICAN UNION'S MULTILATERALISM

Some of the biggest blows to modern-day multilateralism even within the AU have been dealt by the United States during the presidency of Donald Trump, and include the following:

- Withdrawal from the Paris Agreement
- Withdrawal from the deal about nuclear development in Iran
- The announcement to cut funding to the WHO
- The refusal to appoint experts in the WTO appeal panel ruling
- The withdrawal from further nuclear disarmament
- The start of trade wars in spite of an international agreement and a conflict management system in the WTO that has been set up under strong pressure by the United States itself
- Refusal to sign the concluding text of a G7 summit in 2018
- Open support for countries that shun multilateralism

These actions have clearly left an impact on the AU which is trying to build and strengthen constructive relations with multilateral organisations such as WHO and WTO, which are currently being weakened as a result of some of the decisions of the United States. Mainly the decisions listed earlier.

Some of the main challenges to the AU's multilateralism and African development are climate change, ongoing African conflicts and economic and political challenges. Political challenges, such as unconstitutional presidential terms, government censorship of independent media, manipulation of constitutions in order to stay in power and electoral violence, have been detrimental to multilateralism both within and outside the AU.

These types of undemocratic practices by the heads of AU member states tarnish the reputation of the AU within and outside the continent, with some members of the international community calling the AU complacent and irresponsive to threats against democracy for not strongly rebuking the undemocratic practices of its member states (Wiesbuch, 2019). Sometimes this has also resulted in fewer multilateral engagements and the cancellation of multilateral development projects. On an economic level, high inflation rates and currency instability, the wide income inequality gap between the rich and the poor, high unemployment rates and deadly epidemics and pandemics, including HIV/AIDS and currently, the novel COVID-19, all pose challenges to the AU's multilateralism and its functioning.

There is a great deal of challenges to attend to but funds and personnel are never enough. Paradoxically, the aforementioned challenges can also be used to advance multilateralism, if it is seen as a solution. Numerous countries have formed institutions, agreements, alliances and policies for tackling such challenges. This has been the case with agreements such as the Paris Agreement, Global Compact for Safe, Orderly and Regular Migration (GCM) and multilateral organisations including the WTO, WB and IMF which have become viable multilateral development partners to the AU and AU member states. For instance, the WB offers loans intended for development projects to countries, while the IMF oversees currency stability. These multilateral organisations are useful for African development and its economic growth.

4.1. Climate Change

Climate change is a result of increasing concentrations of greenhouse gases in the atmosphere. It alters weather patterns, such as in instances of very hot temperatures, droughts and violent rains. All these have negative effects on the environment.

The effects of climate change are and can be detrimental to agricultural productivity, the management of ecosystems and biodiversity. All of these effects have continued to severely set Africa aback by hindering its agricultural development. Locally, people have less to eat. Economically, there are less agricultural products to sell and internationally, it positions countries at a disadvantage when it comes to exports and trade in general.

This is even more severe for African countries as the agricultural sector is the largest form of African employment, with more than 70 percent of the people in rural areas employed in agriculture. The EU Institute for Security Studies (2017) explains that the 2017 drought played a huge role in causing famine in South Sudan; this is because the majority of Africa is dependent on subsistence and rain-fed agriculture.

In 2015, the G-7 countries, through their 'New Climate for Peace Report', outlined seven global climate risks—local resource competition, livelihood insecurity and migration, weather events and disasters, volatile food prices and provision, trans-boundary water management, sea-level rise and coastal degradation—unintended effects of climate change (EU institute for security studies, 2017). Climate change and its effects have placed tension on multilateralism to the extent that some countries might be unable to rise to the occasion, in terms of following through on initial agreements. For instance, the United States has withdrawn from the Paris Agreement and has rolled back policies designed to reduce emissions. This has negative implications on the AU's multilateral relations within the Paris Agreement because African countries are impacted by this agreement due to their vulnerability caused by the effects of climate change—hunger, loss of livelihoods and poverty. The neglect of multilateral institutions and agreements sends an unwavering message of self-interest and disdain for multilateralism.

4.2. Conflicts

Ruggie (1993), Job (1997) and Touval and Zartman (2010) all make the argument that multilateralism takes a variety of different institutional forms in international relations, specifically in the area of global conflict management. This can clearly be seen in the different multilateral engagements that have been formed in the fight against conflicts—UN-AU engagements, UN-EU-AU engagements and the EU-AU engagement.

Since October 2019, conflicts were still prevalent in DR Congo, Somalia, South Sudan, Nigeria, Central African Republic, Mali and Libya. This is a clear indication as to why the promotion of peace is at the top of the AU's agenda. As a result of persisting violent conflicts in Africa, most of the AU's resources are targeted towards ending conflicts and promoting peace and security. The AU is currently taking the lead on peace operations on the continent. Some examples of these include African Union Mission in Sudan (AMIS) and the African Union Mission in Somalia (AMISOM).

By virtue of being the key implementing organs of peace missions, the UNSC and AU's Peace and Security Council work in tandem on African peace missions. The AU Peace and Security Council is responsible for the AU Peace and Security Architecture (APSA). APSA was created and adopted in 2004 with the intention of providing a technical framework that would frame the structure of peace missions, particularly peacekeeping and peace enforcement. APSA lays down the procedural and strategic mechanism for missions before they officially begin (African Union Commission Peace and Security Department, 2015). Despite aiming for sustainable self-reliance, which would mean APSA's own ability to finance its operations, APSA through the AU Peace and Security Council has received technical, financial and logistical support from the UN Security Council. The support from the UN Security Council has helped to strengthen the AU and APSA's capacity to respond to conflicts. As a way of strengthening APSA, the joint UN-AU framework for enhanced partnership in peace and security pledged to support the APSA roadmap. This is evident as, the UN and the AU have jointly undertaken collaborative field missions in Sudan (UNAMID) 2007, South Sudan (UNMISS) 2011, DR Congo (MONUC)1999, Sierra Leone (UNAM-SIL)1999 and Liberia (UNMIL) 2003 (Makubalo et al., 2020). The UNOAU supports operations in Somalia, Mali, Central African Republic and operations of the Regional Cooperation Initiative for the elimination of the LRA (RCI-LRA). The difficulty the AU faces with these missions is the ability to successfully channel its resources and efforts towards peace and security, leaving fewer resources for its other development projects.

4.3. Political Challenges

African states are democratic states, which has led to the AU's establishment of special mechanisms and charters such as the *African Peer-Review Mechanism* (APRM) and the *African Charter on Democracy, Elections and Governance* (ACDEG). Despite being democratic, politics and governance on the African continent leaves much to be desired. This assertion can be made because presidential and parliamentary elections are hardly ever free and fair. For instance, in Nigeria, the contestation of the 2011 election results turned into attacks on minorities across the country in which more than 800 people died (Mentan, 2014). After the 2007 presidential election in Kenya, independent observers stated that the counting of votes was extremely flawed to the extent that it was impossible to tell which candidate had won the presidential election, and as a result of the confusion in Kenya, violence erupted, killing 1,000 people (Mentan, 2014). These are just two instances, but in reality, there are many incidences of this nature that occur during and after elections.

The APRM is a specialised agency of the AU. The APRM was established in 2003 and it serves as a specialised tool for monitoring and strengthening democracy and political, economic and corporate governance within its member states. The APRM conducts its work through peer learning, problem identification and country reviews. Membership to the APRM is voluntary and currently, its membership stands at 38 countries.[4] On a multilateral scale, the APRM works with partners such as UNDP Regional Bureau for Africa, United Nations Economic Commission for Africa (UNECA) and ADB, among others. According to Mangu (2014), the mandate of the APRM is to ensure that policies and practices of participating states conform to the agreed political, economic and corporate governance values, codes and standards. Mangu (2014) further argues that the APRM has not had an all-encompassing success story because it is underfunded and its member states do not comply to the set values and standards. Additionally, the fact that membership to the

APRM is voluntarily almost undermines how essential the APRM is as a tool that enhances democracy and democratic practices within states.

The ACDEG was adopted in 2007 as the AU's main normative instrument that would set the standards for improved governance on the African continent. The ACDEG works towards its goal by combining the key elements of democracy, human rights and governance. Forty-six member states have signed the charter (Wiebusch, 2019). Unlike the APRM, the ACDEG is legally binding, unfortunately though, the ratification of the treaties to be entered into force is very long and tedious. Although it was not initially in the AU's agenda to intervene in the political affairs of its member states due to its non-interference in the internal affairs of states (Møller, 2005, p. 17), the AU through instruments such as the ACDEG now participates in political negotiations involving government transitions and mediation efforts (Mangu, 2014). For instance, the AU, in collaboration with ECOWAS, intervened in the Gambian political crisis that occurred in 2016 as a result of the Gambian President Yahya Jammeh's refusal to leave office after losing the presidential election to his opponent Adama Barrow. The result of this intervention saw the instating of Adama Barrow as the president of the Gambia.

Also, through its instruments such as the ACDEG, the AU has found itself in the process of helping to establish stability and promote a peaceful transition of government after a coup d'état/unconstitutional change of government, as was the case in Egypt in 2011 and Zimbabwe in 2017 (Wiebusch, 2019).

One way by which political challenges could be fought on the continent is by states holding themselves and other states accountable by commitment to the pre-existent governance mechanisms and charters.

Some of the main challenges the AU could possibly face in the coming years are political dispute solving before, during and after presidential elections in its member states. For instance, for 2020, the AU has already prioritised its resources and programme of work to deterring the possible violence that might arise from presidential elections in Ethiopia, Somalia, Burkina Faso, Cote d'Ivoire and Guinea. These countries are all scheduled to have their presidential elections towards the end of 2020. The AU also faces the responsibility and challenge of deterring its member states from amending constitutional rules in order to have leaders staying in government longer. Currently, the AU is working to deter the manipulation of the constitutions in Cote d'Ivoire and Guinea, so that both countries' 2020 election results are not flawed.

4.4. COVID-19

'Never waste a good crisis' is an important saying amidst the health and economic crisis the world is facing with the COVID-19 pandemic. It is also attributed to Winston Churchill who led the UK through the Second World War.[5] The COVID-19 pandemic could push countries to improve their health sectors, by improving their infrastructure, hiring more health experts and increasing their supply of medicines. Economically, countries could improve their ways of doing business by including the online delivery of goods and services.

There has been a rapid increase in the number of confirmed cases of COVID-19 revealed following improved testing. Although Africa (and particularly the AU) has the advantage of examining outcomes for possible case scenarios, responses and policy-making surrounding COVID-19 against Asian and European countries (as they experienced COVID-19 earlier than African nations), the African context and vulnerabilities have inhibited its responses and policing (Economic Commission for Africa, 2020).

The nationalistic reactions taken in wake of the COVID-19 pandemic in maintaining and managing migration[6] are rather severe as states avoid surrendering their sovereignty to regional and supra-national organisations in migration related issues (Economic Commission for Africa, 2020). States are afraid and hesitant to weaken their state security and national interests by allowing the movement of people and goods. So far, the virus has hindered aspirations for unity as states prioritise the security and health of their citizens. With the exception of ECOWAS member states, African states have made little tangible progress to implement a free movement regime. Throughout the COVID-19 crisis, ECOWAS has kept its borders open within its (15) member states. The AfCFTA Secretary-General Wamkele Mene added that as long as the pandemic continues, it would test the aspirations for a borderless continent in the midst of economic uncertainty.

Another challenge COVID-19 poses to the AU is the postponement in the implementation of the AfCFTA. Wamkele Mene has stated that a global recession has begun, with severe consequences for Africa's economies as the continent may see its GDP growth fall from 3.2% to about 2% (Economic Commission for Africa, 2020). The financial challenges ahead mainly due to COVID-19 might also see a reduction in the amount of money set aside for development projects.

On a multilateral scale, the AU's response to COVID-19 has seen the formation of five regional task forces representing the five regions of the continent (North, East, South, West and Central Africa). The task forces are headed by national ministers of health. In addition, the Africa COVID-19 Response Fund which is also known as the Solidarity Fund has been created. The Solidarity Fund is working with the Africa Centres for Disease Control and Prevention (Africa CDC) and helping countries in greatest need. As of March 2020, the South African president and AU Chairperson Cyril Ramaphosa reported that $17 million were raised to combat COVID-19 through the

Solidarity Fund.[7] This money would be used to further support the procurement of diagnostics and other medical commodities by Africa CDC for distribution to the 55 member states, and to support the deployment of community healthcare workers to support contact tracing.

5. CONCLUSION

The United States' withdrawal from multilateralism is not an ideal setting for multilateralism worldwide, and for the AU which is impacted by international decisions and policies. Reflecting back on the words of the UN Secretary-General, António Guterres, multilateralism is not a luxury but rather a necessity in today's world, when states and regions work together their efforts produce positive results. This chapter on the AU and multilateralism shared an overview of the AU's multilateralism by discussing how it engages in multilateralism with the UN and also the AU's position as an active but often overlooked player in the world's multilateral system. Contemporary challenges and opportunities to multilateralism were also discussed in the chapter. Currently, the novel COVID-19 pandemic has shocked both Africa and the world, and challenged regional integration and multilateralism to the extent that the future could either go in one of two directions for states and multilateral systems: the reliance on stronger integration and stronger multilateralism, or a turn towards nationalism and isolation. For a young and growing continent like Africa and its member states, the turn towards nationalism and isolation could hurt its economic and political potential, as states relay on each other for their comparative strengths. For Africa in general and the AU in particular, 'there is strength in numbers'; this is because the AU needs the active participation of its member states in order to engage in effective multilateralism. The AU needs multilateralism in order to seek leverage for desired outcomes on issues pertinent to the future of its member states and their people, issues such as climate change, conflicts, deadly epidemics and pandemics and the consequential economic challenges caused by these issues.

NOTES

1. https://unoau.unmissions.org
2. Agenda 2063: The Africa We Want
3. sustainabledevelopment.un.org A/RES/70/1
4. https://aprm-au.org
5. European Union Institute for Security Studies (2017) after the EU Global Strategy: Building Resilience

6. Some migrants had to return to their home countries either by choice or forced return at the onset of the COVID-19 pandemic.

7. https://africacdc.org/

REFERENCES

African Peer Review Mechanism (ARPM): Base Document. Assembly of Heads of State and Government, Thirty-Eighth Ordinary Session of the Organization of African Unity, document presented on 8 July 2002, South Africa: Durban. *https.// aprm-au.org*

African Union. (2013a). *Agenda 2063: The Africa We Want*. Addis Ababa: African Union.

African Union. (2013b). Strategic Plan 2014–2017 for the African Union Commission. 21st Ordinary Session of the African Union, Addis Ababa, 26–27 May 2013. Addis Ababa: African Union.

African Union Commission, Peace and Security Department. (2015). 'African Peace and Security Architecture: Roadmap 2016–2020', Addis Ababa: African Union Commission.

European Union Institute for Security Studies. (2017). *After the EU Global Strategy: Building Resilience*. Luxembourg: Imprimerie Centrale.

Laatikainen, Katie V., & Smith, Karen E. (2020). *Group Politics in UN Multilateralism*. Leiden: Koninklijke Brill.

Makubalo, Nandi, Hosli, Madeleine O., & Lantmeeters, Michael. (2020), The African Union in the United Nations. In Laatikainen, Katie V., & Smith, Karen E., (eds.), *Group Politics in UN Multilateralism*. Leiden: Koninklijke Brill. 76–96.

Mangu, Mbata André. (2014). The African Union and the promotion of democracy and good political governance under the African Peer-Review Mechanism: 10 years on. *Africa Review*, 6:1, 59–72, DOI: 10.1080/09744053.2014.883757

Mentan, Tatah. (2014). *Africa: Facing Human Security Challenges in the 21st Century*. Mankon, Bamenda: Langaa Research and Publishing Common Initiative Group.

Møller, Bjørn. (2005). The pros and cons of subsidiarity: The role of African regional and sub-regional organisations in ensuring peace and security in Africa, DIIS Working Paper, No. 2005:4. Copenhagen: Danish Institute for International Studies (DIIS). ISBN: 8776-050-63-7.

Murithi, Timothy. (2005). *The African Union: Pan-Africanism, Peacebuilding and Development*. Farnham: Ashgate Publishing.

Touval, Saaid, & Zartman, William I. (2010). *International Cooperation: The Extents and Limits of Multilateralism*. Cambridge: Cambridge University Press.

United Nations-African Union. (2017). 'Joint UN-AU Framework for Enhanced Partnerships in Peace and Security', paper presented at the United Nations-African Union Annual Conference, New York, unpublished.

United Nations Economic Commission for Africa. 2020. *COVID-19 in Africa: Protecting Lives and Economies 2020*. Addis Ababa: Economic Commission for Africa.

United Nations Office to the African Union, UNOAU Bulletin, A publication from the United Nations Office to the African Union. March–May, 2018. https://unoau.unmissions.org/sites/default/files/unoau_bulletin_march_to_may_2018_asg_bintou_keita_at_au_headquarters.pdf

United Nations Security Council Resolution 2320, UN Doc. S/RES/2320, November 2016. https://www.securitycouncilreport.org/un-documents/document/sres2320.php

United Nations Office to the African Union https://unoau.unmissions.org

Wiesbuch, Micha. (2019). Introduction: The African Charter on Democracy Elections and Governance at 10. In *Journal of African Law*. Special supplementary issue: *The African Charter on Democracy, Elections and Governance at 10*. London: Cambridge University Press for SOAS University of London, 63: S1, 3–7, DOI: 10.1017/S0021855319000068

World Economic Forum. (2017). The Africa Competitiveness Report 2017. Geneva. https://www.weforum.org/reports/africa-competitiveness-report-2017

Zang, Laurent. (1998). The contribution of African Diplomacy to the Non-Aligned Movement and the Group of 77. *African Journal of International Affairs*, 1, 1: 1–16.

Chapter 7

European External Action and Multilateralism

Sonja Niedecken

INTRODUCTION

The system of multilateralism and the organisations that spring from it have influenced the lives of billions of people around the globe. This book seeks to provide a glance at what might be ahead for the political system that has defined our world in the past decades. The European Union (EU) is the most comprehensive and encompassing regional multilateral organisation ever conceived. It has become an important player in many sectors and has a unique position in the multilateral system. As stated by Spence EU member states "have delegated extensive responsibilities for foreign policy, trade policy, development and humanitarian aid, and even the international aspects of almost every domestic policy area" (2015, p. 2). Trade agreements are negotiated by the EU and not by single member states. The EU also has either shared or full competence in all policy sectors relating to EU external matters. Thus, even though its member states are not always fond of this fact, EU foreign policy is hugely important for Europe and the multilateral system.

This chapter discusses European Union External Policy and the EU organisations most involved in this policy area. The chapter begins with a general overview of how EU External Policy works in regard to the main EU institutions. The following section highlights current challenges, with a focus on how the COVID-19 pandemic is affecting EU foreign relations. The chapter then introduces and explains the different EU bodies involved in External Policy, hereby a focus is put on administrative bodies because they "play a central role in virtually everything that EU institutions do", especially regarding the implementation of external policies (Gatti, 2016, p. 2). The bodies examined are the European External Actions Service (EEAS) and the Directorate General for International Cooperation and Development (DG

DEVCO), for Trade (DG Trade), for Neighbourhood and Enlargement (DG NEAR) and for European Civil Protection and Humanitarian Aid Operations (DG ECHO). The bodies were selected because they are congruent with the make-up of the current European Commission group for *A Stronger Europe in the World* (European Commission, 2019a). Of course, there are other policy areas, such as energy, climate and migration that are important for EU External Relations and they are touched upon in the third part of this chapter. The third part contains sections on the relationship of the EU with the United States and China, on the future of relations with Russia and the EU eastern and south-eastern periphery and on the future relationship of the EU with several other multilateral organisations such as the UN, the WTO and the WHO.

1. EU EXTERNAL POLICY AND THE INSTITUTIONS

The framework of European Union foreign policy as it is today was set in the Lisbon Treaty. The Lisbon Treaty was also the founding treaty of the EEAS and moulded the position of the High Representative into what it is today (Hill et al., 2017). All major EU institutions have important roles in the making of EU Foreign Policy. The European Council functions similar to a

> board of directors: setting the overall framework and discussing and taking broad decisions on major and contested issues, but leaving the operationalisation of the outcomes of its meetings to management which in the European Council's case means a mixture of the European Council President, the Commission, the Council, and the EEAS. (Nugent, 2017, p. 194)

The Council of the European Union (hereafter referred to as the Council) is the main decision-maker in foreign policy matters (Hill et al., 2017, p. 111). The Foreign Affairs Council, meeting about once a month, will decide matters of the Common Foreign and Security Policy, the Common Commercial Policy and matters related to other parts of External policy (Nugent, 2017, pp. 405–406). Other than relating to budgetary measures or agreements where consent is required, the European Parliament has little power in foreign policy issues; but its resolutions are relevant contributions to the debate. According to Nugent "the EP is largely confined to advisory, monitoring, and holding-to account roles on foreign policy" (Nugent, 2017, p. 410). The European Commission has a variety of functions in EU foreign policy making. The High Representative of the Union for Foreign Affairs and Security Policy, also a vice president of the Commission, "is charged with the coordination of all EU external policies" (Nugent, 2017, p. 410). Furthermore, the Commission has the right of initiative in areas like trade, aid and economic sanctions. Lastly, the Commission houses many experts on the different areas of external policy as well as some of the bodies implementing the EU Foreign Policy such as the DGs examined in section two.

1.1. Current Challenges to EU Foreign Policy and COVID-19

Beginning in the Bush presidency, there has been a steady decline in the transatlantic relationship. Under the Trump administration, this decline has increased rapidly. The United States and the EU are divided on many issues and this divide has only been exacerbated by the COVID-19 pandemic (Brattberg, 2020). The trade politics of the current U.S. administration are greatly consternating to EU leaders and the withdrawal of the United States from many important multilateral agreements has left the EU questioning the integrity and accountability of its long-time partner (Brattberg, 2020). In the beginning of the pandemic, the White House issued a travel ban for Europeans without any prior communication with constituencies abroad or with their European allies, completely surprising EU leaders. Then President Trump tried to shift blame towards the EU for the rising COVID-19 cases in the United States, as well as attempting to lure away a German vaccine manufacturer. The actions and policies of the Trump administration have pushed the transatlantic relationship into an increasingly deeper crisis and the EU has to adjust to the loss of its most powerful partner to a certain degree (Ischinger, 2020).

The EU response to the coronavirus crisis in China was cordial, although questions were raised in relation to the humanity of Chinese containment measures and a lack of communication in the beginning of the outbreak. However, as COVID-19 cases rose in the EU, so did the level of Chinese disinformation efforts regarding their image in the crisis (Rudd, 2020). Culminating in a scandal when Chinese officials allegedly tried to pressure EEAS officials into altering the content of a report on the outbreak (Cerulus & Herszenhorn, 2020). Here it is important to mention that in 2019 the European Commission released a paper in which China was identified as a "systematic rival" to the EU (European Commission, 2019b, p. 1). Regarding other parts of the world, the EU is currently mobilising aid efforts as well as promising that a vaccine would be made available to all globally (European Commission, 2020). However, in the Eastern Neighbourhood and the Balkans, the EU has a competitor in China regarding the delivery of aid to countries with weaker healthcare systems. Another point to mention is the constant threat of digital attacks from Russia, as recently news has broken about a hacking attack on the German government—a matter which must be contended with on top of the health crisis (Burchard, 2020). Another aspect that the crisis has highlighted is the EU's dependency on trade with China in a number of sectors such as pharmaceuticals, but the EU has made efforts to rectify the situation by diversifying supply chains (Mullin, 2020, Brattberg, 2020). Of course, a great challenge already looming from the pandemic is the expected financial crisis, due to the economic paralysis provoked by lockdown policies. This issue is further analysed in the next chapter by Carolina D'Ambrosio. The current pandemic is one of the most difficult crises the EU has faced since its inception. In the next part, different bodies of EU Foreign policy are introduced to explain how EU Foreign Policy is made and what is currently being done in each policy field. Furthermore, the section also addresses the implications of the pandemic for each of the bodies presented.

2. THE "MINISTRIES" OF THE EU FOREIGN POLICY

2.1. European External Relations and the EEAS

The person responsible for foreign policy within the highest ranks of EU officials is the High Representative. The High Representative has a position in the Commission, the Council and the EEAS. In addition to the Commissioner role he or "she chairs the Foreign Affairs Council, other than when trade items are on the agenda; and she is the head of the EEAS" (Nugent, 2017, p. 408).

One of the most important organisations when talking about European Foreign Policy and EU External Relations is naturally the EEAS. "All in all, from the perspective of administrative autonomy, the EEAS appears as a 'hybrid' organ, part service and part institution" (Gatti, 2016, p. 139). It has a function similar to that of a foreign ministry. The EEAS does a great deal in terms of foreign policy-making having also taken over the programming stage of the policy cycle from other DG's (Hill et al., 2017, p. 108). Its role is to be the general oversight and coordinator for all foreign policy action, also regarding other DGs, to ensure coherence in the EU Foreign Policy (Gatti, 2016, p. 3). Sometimes it functions as a mediator between different actors in EU foreign policy (Gatti, 2016, p. 190). Moreover, the EEAS is the organisation which houses the EU diplomatic service and the military personnel for EU missions (Nugent, 2017, pp. 409–410). The EEAS has diplomatic delegations in many countries, as well as at the UN where it coordinates the member states' actions within the UN General Assembly and other UN bodies (Jin & Hosli, 2013). The EEAS is not in charge of trade, development, humanitarian, enlargement, or energy policy, as these policy areas are covered by Commission DGs, some of which are introduced further. However, the EEAS is often consulted by the DGs and vice versa.

The EEAS has its headquarters with around 1,500 staff in Brussels, its "operational work is undertaken by the delegations and offices the EEAS is responsible for running throughout the world" (Nugent, 2017, pp. 409–410).

2.1.1. Challenges

A great recent challenge for the EEAS is Brexit. Many experienced staffers and diplomats within the EEAS were British citizens and the EEAS must now replace them. Furthermore, the UK was a great contributor of staff to the EU military missions, many of these vacated posts were covered by France (Barigazzi, 2019). Another constant issue is competition between EU delegations and member states diplomatic services. Due to this issue, many EU delegations are underutilised and the EU is underrepresented abroad. Additionally, the EU often has difficulty in funding its missions as well as in finding qualified staff. Furthermore, as already mentioned in the previous section, in May 2020, the EEAS was involved in a scandal about claims that it had succumbed to pressure by Chinese officials on altering the contents of a report about the responsibilities for the COVID-19 outbreak (Cerulus & Herszenhorn, 2020). This scandal illustrates how the EEAS just like national diplomatic services has to walk the difficult path of appeasing both their public but also not angering powerful rival countries. The EEAS-led missions around the world are currently engaged in aiding with the pandemic by "supporting civilian authorities and our citizens with medical, logistic and security resources", while being coordinated by an EEAS task force in Brussels (Borrell, 2020). Looking towards the future, the current High Representative has announced the ambition to make missions and operations more flexible and to bolster digital defence capabilities (Borrell, 2020). He has also reaffirmed the commitment of the EU and the EEAS to work with partners such as NATO and the UN (Borrell, 2020).

2.2. European Development Policy and DG DEVCO

Development policy is an important part of EU External Action. It is a shared competence thus the member states retain the right to have their own aid policies and agencies, giving the EU the role of coordinator as well as implementer (Hill et al., 2017, p. 106). The EU together with its member states provides the largest amount of Official Development Assistance (ODA) worldwide (Nugent, 2017, p. 411). The primary objective of EU development policy is the eradication of poverty, as laid out in Article 21 (2) (d) Treaty of the European Union (TEU, 2012). Article 4 (4) Treaty on the Functioning of the European Union (TFEU) and Articles 208 to 211 TFEU regulate the coordination of development aid between the EU and the member states as well as the EU institutions and the EIB (TFEU, 2012). Other focuses are to "foster sustainable growth, defend human rights and democracy, promote gender equality, and tackle environmental and climate challenges" (Treviño, 2019). Many EU organisations are involved in the making of EU Development Policy, such as the Foreign Affairs Council, the Commissioner for Development, DG DEVCO and the EP Committee on Development. In EU development policy, the Council is the most powerful decision maker and the Commission the initiator because in many aspects of development policy, the European Parliament only has the power of consent or an advisory role due to the legislative procedures applicable (Nugent, 2017, p. 413; Hill et al., 2017, p. 107). The most important implementer and designer of EU Development Policy is DG DEVCO. In this work, it is aided by the EEAS and its missions and diplomatic delegations abroad (Admin_DEVCO, 2016). DG DEVCO is the organisation that puts development policy into action as well as coordinates and cooperates with member states aid agencies. Relations with recipient states and regional organisations, for example, the AU, ASEAN and the ACP countries are governed by cooperation and association agreements, the most notable one being the Cotonou partnership (Hill et al., 2017, p. 105). Furthermore, DG DEVCO collaborates with international organisations such as the UN and its agencies as well as international NGOs either through these organisations' Brussels offices or it engages with them though the different EU delegations in the field (Medinilla, Veron & Mazzara, 2019, p. 11).

The structure of DG DEVCO as shown in figure 7.1 serves as an example of how a European Commission Directorate-General is usually set up. The DG is organised into more than 40 units divided into nine directorates attached to the DDGs and the Director-General, who heads the DG. The Commissioner for International Partnerships is the commissioner responsible for this DG.

2.2.1. Challenges

Naturally, the work of DG DEVCO is not devoid of challenges. Development and aid policy are a shared competence, so the DG always needs to coordinate with member states however sometimes policies clash and overlap. Furthermore, the EU is a gigantic policy project so DG DEVCO needs to make sure that other policy sectors do not hinder or rollback development policy efforts. Due to this, the EU has introduced the concept of policy coherence for development (PCD) which aims at making sure that EU development concerns and the Sustainable Development Goals (SDGs) are respected in each policy sector (Admin_DEVCO, 2019, Krätke, 2013). This effort is still a struggle, especially when not all member states recognise PCD as a priority, preferring economic gains over development (Carbone, 2008, p. 328). Other challenges are the continued disregard of the 0.7% GNI target spending for

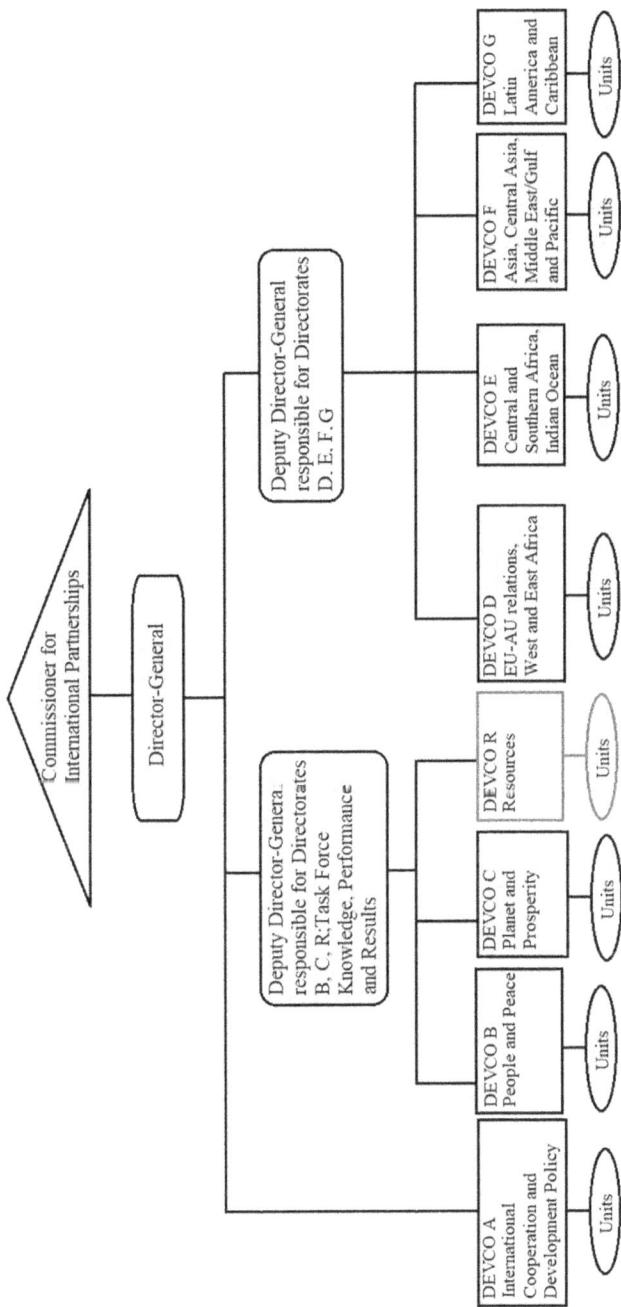

Figure 7.1. Simplified structure of DG DEVCO. *Source:* **Sonja Niedecken, 2020.**

development set by the OECD, which only a small number of member states have reached (OECD, 2017). This struggle will most likely be exacerbated by the COVID-19 pandemic as in the long-term, member states will spend more money to aid their own populace and will have less budget to spare for matters abroad in the form of ODA. Furthermore, DG DEVCO and the Commissioner for International Cooperation and Development are working on providing aid to partners in direct response to the health crisis especially for African countries, so far, the Commission and member states have mobilised around €20 billion towards these goals (Riegert, 2020).

2.3. External Trade Policy and DG Trade

Trade policy is one of the policy areas on which the member states are most united. Trade is for the most part an exclusive competence of the EU, conferring the role of negotiator within the multilateral trade system onto the EU and its institution (TFEU, 2012, Article 207). During trade negotiations, the Commission is responsible for negotiation and the Council is the decision maker, while the parliament receives regular reports on the negotiation. Both Council and Parliament have to consent to the signing of an agreement. The EU has a great number of signed free-trade agreements with countries around the world like Japan, Canada, Vietnam and many others. These agreements are largely negotiated, managed and maintained by DG Trade, although other DGs are involved as necessitated by their areas of responsibility (Nugent, 2017, p. 392). During negotiations, DG Trade has great leverage because first, it has very experienced negotiators and second, a very strong mandate due to the nature of EU decision making (if a consensus has been reached within the EU, it is very firm so that the negotiators have certainty in the positions they represent) (De Bièvre, 2018, p. 72). One of the largest recently negotiated trade agreements is with the Latin American regional organisation MERCOSUR (also mentioned in chapter 10 by Amber Scheele in this manuscript). DG Trade is also largely responsible for the WTO relations and negotiations within the EU as observed in figure 7.2.

The structure of DG Trade is shown in figure 7.2. The Commissioner for International Partnerships is the commissioner responsible for this DG. The DG is under the authority of the European Commissioner for Trade. DG Trade consists of 28 units divided into 8 directorates attached to the DDGs and the Director-General who heads the DG.

2.3.1. Challenges

A novel position is the DDG Chief Trade Enforcement Officer. The position was created to "monitor and enforce environmental and labour protection

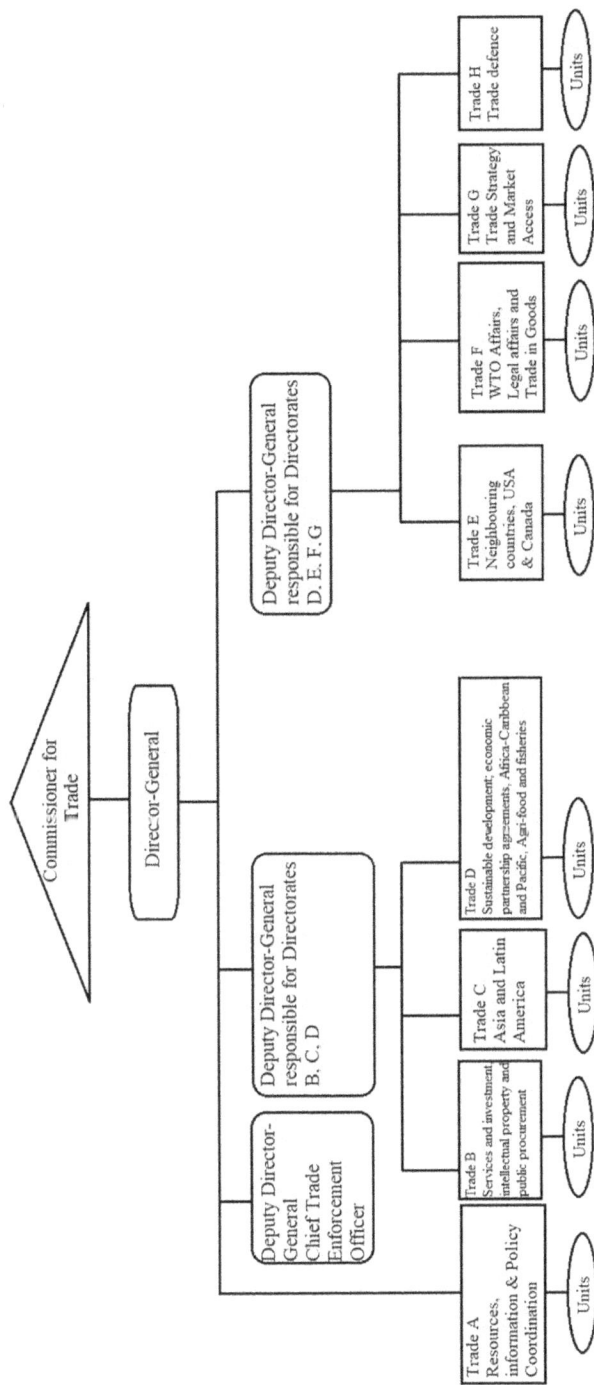

Figure 7.2. Simplified structure of DG Trade. *Source:* Sonja Niedecken, 2020.

obligations of EU trade agreements with third countries" and the DDG will "have authority to confront countries that are found to be in breach of the WTO Agreement and EU free trade agreements" (Kim, 2020).

Thus, one of the challenges DG Trade will face in the next years is to truly define this new position and build the institutional structure, such as units and directorates, that it will require. Moreover, it is rather unclear how exactly the new DDG is expected to enforce the responsibilities and authority given to him by the Commission vis-à-vis other countries. In regard to human right clauses, Donno and Neureiter (2018) have shown that it is not always easy to enforce more normative trade agreement clauses and the chance is high that the same will hold true for environmental and labour clauses. Another great challenge after years of stagnation DG Trade and the EU face in the coming years is the previously declared intention to reform the WTO (DG Trade, 2018). (For further information on the current struggles of the WTO, see chapter 4 by Morgane De Clercq in this manuscript.) Moreover, in their Trade Agreement with Canada, the Comprehensive Economic and Trade Agreement, the EU has decided on the creation of a multilateral court for investment disputes (De Bièvre, 2018, p. 79). The Court of Justice of the European Union (CJEU) has decided that such an endeavour is within EU law and thus the Commission and DG Trade have been tasked with negotiating a multilateral court for investment disputes (Bungenberg & Reinisch, 2020, p. v). The United States thus far has been against such a solution so it remains to be seen if the EU will be successful (Nielsen, 2015). During the COVID-19 pandemic, DG Trade is tasked with delivering speedy analyses about the ramifications of the pandemic on trade currently and in the years to come (DG Trade, 2020).

2.4. The European Neighbourhood and Enlargement Policy and DG NEAR

The European Neighbourhood and Enlargement Policy is targeted at the countries and regions neighbouring the European Union such as the Western Balkans, Turkey, North Africa, the Middle East and the Eastern Partnership countries. The aim of this policy field is to foster special relations and European Union values such as human rights and democracy but also to ensure resilience and stability in the European Neighbourhood (Tocci, 2020b). Furthermore, the policy aims to eventually integrate some of the countries directly neighbouring EU borders into the Union. Decisions related to enlargement policy usually require unanimity in the Council as well as the consent of both Commission and Parliament.

DG NEAR is the directorate responsible for managing and monitoring this policy sector in close cooperation with the EEAS and other DGs concerned. DG NEAR's mission "is to take forward the EU's neighbourhood and enlargement policies, as well as coordinating relations with EEA-EFTA countries insofar as Commission policies are concerned" (DG NEAR, 2019). DG NEAR manages the Stabilisation and Association Agreements (SAA) and "the bulk of the Union's financial and technical assistance to the neighbourhood and enlargement countries" (DG NEAR, 2019). Therefore, this DG monitors and assists candidate countries on their way towards EU accession.

2.4.1. Challenges

A constant challenge to the EU and for DG NEAR is migration and refugees. DG NEAR is responsible for aiding the Neighbourhood countries in their efforts to host refugees. COVID-19 exacerbates this challenge to a great degree, since the health systems in the host countries were already insufficient prior to the outbreak and the situation within refugee camps and settlements is dismal. Another factor related to COVID-19 that DG NEAR, the EEAS and the main institutions are currently working on is providing assistance and funding to the Balkans and the Eastern partnership countries. The pandemic might also lead to new health standards becoming a part of the accession criteria and DG NEAR will be in charge of overseeing their implementation (Tocci, 2020a). Additionally, some of the accession candidate countries have adopted highly restrictive measures to combat the pandemic and DG NEAR will have to make sure these measures are rolled back once the danger of the pandemic has passed (Tocci, 2020a). Furthermore, in regard to the Balkans, the Commission has announced a new investment plan—although this is tied to conditionalities relating to rule of law, democracy and similar matters (European Council, 2020)

2.5. European Humanitarian Aid and DG ECHO

The EU is one of the most important actors in humanitarian aid globally. According to Hill et al., the EU and its member states provide around two thirds of humanitarian aid worldwide (2017, p. 105). Like development, humanitarian aid policy is a shared competence. Thus, the policy processes and institutional roles, responsibilities and powers are similar to the ones described earlier. Albeit in the area of humanitarian aid, the EU provides more funds itself than in the area of development (Nugent, 2017, p. 411). EU humanitarian aid is grounded in the principles of international humanitarian law, namely humanity, neutrality, impartiality and independence (DG, 2020). Furthermore, EU humanitarian action is grounded in the principle of solidarity, which states that the EU will provide assistance, relief and protection for victims of natural and man-made disasters and encourage cooperation between member states to this aim (TFEU, 2012, Articles 196 and 214). The primary function of DG ECHO "is to preserve lives, prevent and alleviate human suffering and safeguard the integrity and dignity of populations affected by natural disasters and man-made crises" (DG ECHO, 2019). DG ECHO, through its Emergency Response Coordination Centre (ERCC), is in charge of coordinating the European Union Civil Protection mechanism which is activated in case of major emergency (EEC, 2020). Another focus of the DG is to also address and deliver aid to countries and regions in forgotten crises, meaning crisis that do not receive much public attention and as a result often do not receive sufficient aid, for example, the conflict in Sudan (DG ECHO, 2019; Hill et al., 2017, p. 177).

A very important addition to the Brussels headquarters of DG ECHO is its network of 7 regional and over 40 country field offices around the world (DG ECHO, 2019b). The offices are vital for helping DG ECHO to gather information about humanitarian needs around the world, while also ensuring a timely delivery of humanitarian aid (DG ECHO, 2019b). The allocation of field offices may change over time as allocation rests on a needs-based approach (DG ECHO, 2019, September 26). Moreover, DG ECHO is in charge of cooperation with UN humanitarian agencies and humanitarian NGOs (Medinilla, Veron & Mazzara, 2019, p. 11). A great amount of EU humanitarian aid is channelled through the aforementioned organisations, making the EU and DG ECHO a very important partner to the UN in the humanitarian aid sector.

2.5.1. Challenges

Long-term challenges for DG ECHO, similarly to DG DEVCO, revolve around the fragmentation and uncertainty of funding. There have been attempts to overhaul the system of aid instruments and funds, yet so far, they have not been successful. Another challenge that DG ECHO is constantly working on is humanitarian aid for refugees around the globe. The COVID-19 pandemic has exacerbated this challenge and DG ECHO has been striving to provide aid funds for refugee camps. Moreover, COVID-19 has triggered the Civil Protection Mechanism which DG ECHO is coordinating to respond to many countries' calls for aid around the globe. In the long-term, the pandemic could have negative effects on the availability of funding for humanitarian aid due to the economic crisis expected in its wake as the same happened after the Global financial crisis ten years ago (DARA, 2010, p. 163). At the same time, many of the poorer and less developed countries in the world will have an increased need for aid, both for their health care systems and overall economic and financial support.

3. THE FUTURE OF EU EXTERNAL RELATIONS AND THE EU ROLE IN MULTILATERALISM

3.1. The EU, Other Great Powers and Regional Cooperation

After a more technical insight into the working of the EU Foreign Policy and the institutions and bodies involved, this section attempts to draw out some scenarios of the future of EU foreign policy in relation to multilateralism. It is becoming clear that the next decades of our century will be very much defined by the conflict of power between China and the United States (Esteban et al., 2020; Rudd, 2020). The likelihood of China and the United States going to all-out war is very low due to both countries' nuclear capabilities which prescribe mutually ensured destruction in case of a hot war. However, a U.S.-China trade war is already well under way and the power struggle will continue in this vein, but also along other political, social and cultural avenues (Esteban et al., 2020, p. 185). This struggle will impact every international organisation and very likely every country in the world because of the intertwined nature of our global economy and society. The EU is already drawn into different directions. Within the Union, some are calling for a clear committal towards the long-standing close partnership with the United States, others are favouring a close partnership with China due to new economic opportunities (Döpfner, 2020; Münchau, 2020). However, both options are not necessarily attractive. The United States is openly criticising EU relations with China and the Chinese government is clamouring for more access and improved trade relations (Münchau, 2020). The United States, since the election of Donald Trump, has become a difficult and uncomfortable partner for the EU on many issues (Brattberg, 2020). At the time of writing, it was impossible to predict the outcome of the U.S. presidential elections in November 2020. If Democrat Joe Biden is elected president, it will be much more likely that the EU chooses to closely align with the United States as it would signify a dramatic political shift in the country. But even if Joe Biden wins the U.S. presidential elections, the past years under the Trump administration have badly shaken the EU-U.S. relationship (Ischinger, 2020). The United States withdrew from the Paris Agreement to address global warming and the Joint Comprehensive Plan of Action to institute international oversight of Iran's controversial nuclear programme. Both agreements were particularly important to the EU and its institutions as the EU has a significant part in the agreements making and they align with EU foreign policy strategy. Now in May 2020, President Trump has decided to cut funding and threatened the WHO, actions immediately criticised by EU leaders (Gill, 2020). Trust and confidence have been compromised on many levels and the citizens of the EU currently have an extremely negative picture of the U.S. presidency and even the country in general (Brattberg, 2020). How can the EU trust there will not be another Trump after Biden? Suffice to say, the EU has reason to doubt the stability of a future close EU-US partnership in terms that are compatible with EU norms and principles. In the case, the EU chooses to align with China, a host of new problems would present themselves. Firstly, the United States would likely withdraw from a lot of its formal partnerships and alliances with the EU and it is doubtful whether China would be able and willing to replace them, especially in regard to defence. Additionally, aligning with China would betray the EU's own principles of democracy and human rights and would negatively affect the EU's global standing. The EU would lose a great deal of its normative power. However, there is a third option: the EU will not choose a side and rather hold onto its current position as a non-partisan player and periodic mediator. In this case, the EU might be able to manage its relationship with the United States and retain many of its beneficial agreements with both powers. It is questionable that in this case, NATO in its current form would persevere. Therefore, if the EU decides on this option, further defence integration as well as defence development will be inevitable. The EU would have to spend a considerable amount to build up its defence and coordination capabilities and France might have to widen and stretch its nuclear umbrella over other member states to ensure the safety of the Baltics. Moreover, if the EU decides to stay independent, it is vital to consolidate its partnerships and cooperation with other regions and nations. The EU seems capable of doing this from an external policy standpoint, but often internal quarrels and disagreements impede external developments. These will have to be overcome so the EU can build upon its trade, cooperation and association agreements to establish stable and deep relationships and alliances, especially with important economic players such as Canada, Japan, South Korea and India, as well as regional organisations such as MERCOSUR, ASEAN, the AU and ECOWAS (for more information on the AU, see chapter 6). Furthermore, as the EU right now is already regarded as the guardian of multilateralism, it could use the UN and other international organisations to consolidate its leadership positions in the area of development and humanitarian aid. However, for this to be successful, the EU needs to reform its development and humanitarian aid policy and financial framework towards a more consolidated and integrated approach. This does not mean that the member states need to close their aid agencies, but it would be beneficial if the EU and especially the Commission had the power to direct them, so there is less fragmentation and overlap. Such an initiative can help strengthen the EU relationship with African countries and regional organisations. In the next decades especially, the African continent will see a rise in population and hopefully gains in development. For the future success of the EU, it is vital that EU foreign policy manages to closely align the two continents and that the EU supports the regional organisations and countries striving to better their economic situation and the lives of their citizens. Currently, China is very involved in many African countries, funding infrastructure and facilitating investment (Ursu & van den Berg, 2018). (This topic is further explored in chapter 11 by Taylor Garrett.) Within the aid sector, the EU is strongly focused on social and humanitarian aspects of development, funding education, health and anti-poverty programmes which are also vitally important. However, due to the preferences of the EU regarding aid spending and conditionalities, China had the opportunity to present itself as a partner for the other areas of development. The Chinese have few normative and humanitarian conditionalities making them easier partners than the EU for some governments on the continent. (This topic is further explored by Taylor Garrett in chapter 11.)

The EU and in particular the policymakers in the EEAS and the relevant DGs need to find a way to stay competitive amidst Chinese investment in this area of development, to keep being the main partner in Africa. One of the new approaches that could be considered in regard to African regional organisations such as the AU and ECOWAS is moving towards self-sufficiency in terms of food and other basic necessities. The current pandemic has shown how important regional self-sufficiency is and the EU with its Common Agricultural Policy is an expert in such measures. Considering the threat of further pandemic and the expected population growth in many African countries, establishing self-sufficiency, especially in terms of food crops, is a sensible approach. Even though this might impact imports for some EU member states, stability and development on the African continent would create many benefits for the EU in the long-term.

3.2. The EU, Russia and the EU Eastern and South-Eastern Periphery

Another challenge the EU has been and is still facing, regardless of its alliances with the major powers, is its relation with Russia. Russia manages to be a constant cause of disruption within the EU, the Balkans and in the Eastern neighbourhood, for example, cyber-attacks and disinformation campaigns (Zweers, 2018). Current circumstances suggest that the current Russian administration has no intention of ceasing these actions in the future (Zweers, 2018; Limnell, 2018). The EU has taken important strides in finally starting the official road to enlargement for North Macedonia and Albania. It needs to show continued strong commitment in the Balkan region because both Russia and China are competing for influence in the region as well (Tocci, 2020a). The next enlargement will not be a quick process, as all current candidates still have a long list of accession requirements to complete and the EU cannot let them join for solely political reasons (Tocci, 2020a). However, the EU institutions, the member states and DG NEAR will have to ensure that their presence and aid is sufficient and visible enough to ensure progress and pro-EU sentiment in the Balkan region. Aside from competition in the Balkans, Russia has managed a continuous stream of digital and alleged physical attacks within the Union. The 'Macron leaks' in France in 2017 and the assassination of a former Chechen separatist commander in Berlin in 2019 are recent examples (Vilmer, 2018, p. 75; Eddy & Bennhold, 2019; Zweers, 2018). The EU member states need to collaborate more on intelligence matters, although important strides have been taken in recent years. Brexit poses a challenge to this as the UK has crucial intelligence capabilities but recently the UK government agreed to continue the sharing of criminal suspects data with EU member states (Gallardo, 2020). This agreement could be interpreted as an indicator that the UK would be willing to cooperate on intelligence in the future. Furthermore, the EU needs to fundamentally strengthen its digital capabilities to thwart the new kind of interference that has surfaced with the rise of the internet (Fiott, 2020). The relationship with Russia has always been complicated (Zweers, 2018). Neither does the EU want a powerful and adverse Russia, interfering in its affairs, nor would the Union want an unstable and crumbling Russia, posing major problems especially in light of its big nuclear arsenal. Therefore, to ensure stability and prosperity in the region, the EU has not cut off all cooperation and trade with Russia. Furthermore, some member states are quite dependent on Russia for energy resources and the EU has a strategic interest in a stable Russian energy sector (Zweers, 2018). However, this might change in light of the Union's ambitious environmental protection plans and an oversupply of oil and gas that has manifested in recent times. There is much unused potential for renewable energy in many EU countries, and at some point, the energy lobby might have to resign itself to a complete shift towards non-fossil energy supplies.

3.3. The EU and Multilateral Organisations

The EU is a regional multilateral organisation itself and has historically been an ardent supporter of multilateralism. In many areas, this will not change in the next decades, as the current High Representative and others have confirmed EU support for multilateralism repeatedly (Guillot, 2020). The EU is committed to international cooperation under the umbrella of the UN and has managed to become increasingly more coherent as a unit in the UN General Assembly (Jin & Hosli, 2013). Furthermore, the EU is very supportive and participative in the UN reforms currently taking place (Medinilla, Veron & Mazzara, 2019). Additionally, the EU has a long-standing and good working relationship with the UN and its programmes such as the UNDP in the area of development and humanitarian aid. The EU has committed to the UN and humanitarian law principles as well as the SDGs not only in its aid policy but also in its other policy sectors. This is unlikely to change as the EU and its member states actively contributed to the design of the SDGs, and the SDGs are widely recognised and supported in the EU populace (OECD DevCom, 2017). A problem stemming from Brexit is the loss of one EU member states seat in the UN Security Council, this should, and in all likelihood will, lead to a demand by the EU to reform the UN Security Council (Pindják, 2020). China and Russia are very reluctant to accept such a reform (Pindják, 2020). Thus, it is highly probable to take some time until a reform is realised. The most likely member states to join the UN Security Council with a permanent seat would be Germany due to its size, international standing and capabilities (Pindják, 2020). Regarding the currently very important WHO, the EU and its members have made their support clear (Brattberg, 2020, pp. 3–4). The EU has often successfully collaborated with the WHO and it is unlikely to follow the lead of President Trump in blaming and threatening the WHO over the COVID-19 pandemic. The relationship between the WTO and the EU is further described in chapter 4 of this book written by Morgane De Clercq. As elaborated in chapter 5, difficulties in the WTO are likely to continue. The EU might make further attempts at reform, but has shown that it has the ability to form far reaching and beneficial trade agreements with both single countries and regional organisations like Mercosur. Therefore, although in favour of a multilateral approach to trade, the EU is far from dependent on it. In addition to the current multilateral trade system, the EU has proposed a new international investment court. As of today, the character this new court will take and when it will be established is unclear, but this is certainly a multilateral project which the EU will work on in the next years. All in all, the EU has demonstrated and also specifically stated many times that it is a supporter of multilateralism. Currently, all indicators point towards this position remaining firm in the near future as the EU perceives multilateralism as beneficial to its goal and ideals.

4. CONCLUSION

In some policy sectors such as trade, development and humanitarian aid, the EU is quite successful in its cohesion, even setting international standards such as the initiative for a multilateral investment court and policy coherence for development. However, in light of the current crisis and the recent protectionist tendencies throughout the global economy, it is questionable how far the EU will get with the endeavours it has planned. Internally the EU has many difficulties in reaching a common ground on a variety of policy areas, an example of this is fiscal and monetary policy which is discussed at length by Carolina D'Ambrosio in the following chapter. These internal issues already impact EU external policy and relations and they might also hinder the more successful external policy sectors such as trade and development policy in the future. Another growing concern that will surely impact EU external policy is the growing tension between China and the United States. Increasingly calls are made for the EU to choose a side internally and externally. However, member states do not seem to be in agreement about whether they even want to choose a side and if so, which side they should choose. In this chapter, a proposal is made for the EU to retain its independence and neutrality in the dispute and strengthen its own position alongside multilateralism and multilateral institutions. The European Union itself is a multilateral organisation and it can thrive in a multilateral system. However, with the two great powers of the century in conflict, the EU will need to act intelligently and united internally and externally to weather the fallouts of the conflict and continue prospering. The EU will have to cultivate its relationships with other countries, regions and international organisations on all levels of governance to ensure that multilateralism stays intact. As Professor Heinz Gärtner from the University of Vienna said in a recent virtual seminar, "The European Union is the only one that can really save multilateralism in a post Corona world" (Spui25, 2020, 52:02). It remains to be seen whether the EU will find itself capable and willing to do so.

REFERENCES

Admin_DEVCO. (2016, June 10). About international cooperation and development—DG DEVCO. Retrieved 14 June 2019, from https://ec.europa.eu/europeaid/general_en

Barigazzi, J. (2019, April 5). EU warns of no-deal Brexit impact on peacekeeping mission in Bosnia. *Politico Europe*. Retrieved 17 May 2020 from https://www.politico.eu/article/eu-warns-of-brexit-implications-on-peacekeeping-mission-in-bosnia/

Borrell, J. (2020, May 14). European defence: Fighting COVID-19, preparing for the future [Blog post]. Retrieved 17 May 2020 from https://eeas.europa.eu/headquarters/headquarters-homepage/79305/european-defence-fighting-covid-19-preparing-future_en

Brattberg, E. (2020, April 29). The pandemic is making transatlantic relations more toxic. Retrieved 17 May 2020 from https://carnegieendowment.org/2020/04/29/pandemic-is-making-transatlantic-relations-more-toxic-pub-81675

Bungenberg, M., & Reinisch, A. (2020). *From Bilateral Arbitral Tribunals and Investment Courts to a Multilateral Investment Court Options Regarding the Institutionalization of Investor-State Dispute Settlement* (2nd ed. 2020. ed., Special Issue).

Burchard, H. von der. (2020, May 13). Merkel blames Russia for "outrageous" cyberattack on German parliament. *Politico Europe*. Retrieved 6 June 2020 from https://www.politico.eu/article/merkel-blames-russia-for-outrageous-cyber-attack-on-german-parliament/

Carbone, M. (2008). Mission impossible: The European Union and policy coherence for development. *Journal of European Integration, 30*(3), 323–342, DOI: 10.1080/07036330802144992

Consolidated version of the Treaty on the European Union (TEU). (2012). OJ C326/13–47.

Consolidated version of the Treaty on the Functioning of the European Union (TFEU). (2012). OJ C326/47–390.

Cerulus, L., & Herszenhorn, D. M. (2020, April 30). Parliament hammers Borrell over China disinformation report. *Politico Europe*. Retrieved from https://www.politico.eu/article/parliament-grills-borrell-over-handling-of-china-disinformation-report/

De Bièvre, D. (2018). The paradox of weakness in European trade policy: Contestation and resilience in CETA and TTIP negotiations. *The International Spectator, 53*(3), 70–85. doi:10.1080/03932729.2018.1499849

Development Assistance Research Associates. (DARA). (2010). *Humanitarian Response Index (Hri) 2009: Whose Crisis? Clarifying Donor's Priorities*. Palgrave Macmillan UK.

DG ECHO. (2019, March 19). Needs assessment. Retrieved 16 May 2020 from https://ec.europa.eu/echo/what/humanitarian-aid/needs-assessments_en

DG ECHO. (2019, September 26). Field network. Retrieved 16 May 2020 from https://ec.europa.eu/echo/who/about-echo/field-network_en

DG ECHO. (2020, January 21). About European Civil Protection and Humanitarian Aid Operations. Retrieved 17 May 2020 from https://ec.europa.eu/echo/who/about-echo_en

DG NEAR. (2019, November 28). The Directorate-General. Retrieved 17 May 2020 from https://ec.europa.eu/neighbourhood-enlargement/about/directorate-general_en

DG Trade. (2018, June 29). EU Concept Paper on WTO reform. Retrieved 17 May 2020 from https://ec.europa.eu/trade/policy/eu-and-wto/

DG Trade. (2020, May 29). Commission publishes second report on impact of coronavirus on EU trade. [Press release]. Retrieved 6 June 2020 from https://trade.ec.europa.eu/doclib/press/index.cfm?id=2150

Döpfner, M. (2020, May 3). The coronavirus pandemic makes it clear: Europe must decide between the US and China. *Business Insider*. Retrieved 16 May 2020 from https://www.businessinsider.com/coronavirus-pandemic-crisis-clear-europe-must-choose-us-china-2020-5

Donno, D., & Neureiter, M. (2018). Can human rights conditionality reduce repression? Examining the European Union's economic agreements. *The Review of International Organizations, 13*(3), 335–357.

Eddy, M., & Bennhold, K. (2019, December 04). Germany says Russia is suspected in Berlin assassination. *New York Times*. Retrieved 6 June 2020 from https://www.nytimes.com/2019/12/04/world/europe/germany-assassination-russia.html

Environmental Emergencies Centre (EEC). (2020). The European Union Civil Protection Mechanism. Retrieved 22 May 2020 from https://www.eecentre.org/partners/the-european-union-civil-protection-mechanism/

Esteban, M. A., Otero-Iglesias, M. A., Bērziņa-Čerenkova, U. A., Ekman, A. A., Poggetti, L. A., Jerdén, B. A., . . . Szczudlik, J. A. (Eds.). (2020, January). Europe in the Face of US-China Rivalry. *Report by the European Think-tank Network on China (ETNC)*. Retrieved 17 May 2020 from https://www.clingendael.org/sites/default/files/2020-01/Report_ETNC_Europe_US_China_Rivalry_ETNC_January_2020.pdf

European Commission. (2019a). The commissioners. Retrieved 25 May 2020 from https://ec.europa.eu/commission/commissioners/2019-2024_en#bootstrap-fieldgroup-nav-item-commissioners-group-2

European Commission. (2019b). EU-China—A strategic outlook. Joint communication to the European Parliament, the European Council and the Council. March 12. Retrieved 25 May 2020 from https://ec.europa.eu/commission/sites/beta-political/files/communication-eu-china-a-strategic-outlook.pdf

European Council. (2020, May 6). Zagreb Declaration, 6 May 2020. Retrieved 15 May 2020 from https://www.consilium.europa.eu/en/press/press-releases/2020/05/06/zagreb-declaration-6-may-2020/

European Commission. (2020, May 28). Coronavirus global response: Kick off of new campaign with support of global citizen. [Press release]. Retrieved 6 June 2020 from https://ec.europa.eu/commission/presscorner/detail/en/ip_20_952

Fiott, D. (2020, March 11). DIGITALISING DEFENCE Protecting Europe in the age of quantum computing and the cloud (ISS Policy brief 4). Retrieved from https://www.iss.europa.eu/content/digitalising-defence

Gatti, M. (2016). *European external action service: Promoting coherence through autonomy and coordination* (Ser. Studies in EU external relations, volume 11). Brill Nijhoff.

Gallardo, C. (2020, June 15). UK caves in to EU demand to share criminal suspects' data. Retrieved 26 June 2020 from https://www.politico.eu/article/criminal-suspects-data-sharing-uk-eu-brexit/

Gill, J. (2020, April 15). EU slams Donald Trump's decision to suspend WHO funding. Retrieved 17 May 2020 from https://www.euronews.com/2020/04/15/eu-slams-donald-trump-s-decision-to-suspend-who-funding

Guillot, L. (2020, May 4). Europe has been "naive" about China, says Josep Borrell. *Politico Europe*. Retrieved from https://www.politico.eu/article/europe-has-been-naive-about-china-josep-borrell/

Hill, C., Smith, M., & Vanhoonacker, S. (Eds.). (2017). *International relations and the European Union* (Third ed., The new European union series). Oxford: Oxford University Press.

Ischinger, W. (2020, May 18). *NATO remains key to security, Ischinger tells Kathimerini*. (Interview by Alexis Papachelas for Kathimerini). Retrieved 20 May 2020 from https://www.ekathimerini.com/252788/article/ekathimerini/comment/nato-remains-key-to-security-ischinger-tells-kathimerini

Jin, X., & Hosli, M. (2013). Pre- and Post-Lisbon: European Union voting in the United Nations General Assembly. *West European Politics: Decision-Making in the EU before and after the Lisbon Treaty, 36*(6), 1274–1291.

Kim, J. W. (2020, March 2). Shedding light on the role of the EU's chief trade enforcement officer: Dispute over labor commitments under EU-Korea FTA and EU Enforcement Regulation [Blog post]. Retrieved from https://europeanlawblog.eu/2020/03/02/shedding-light-on-the-role-of-the-eus-chief-trade-enforcement-officer-dispute-over-labor-commitments-under-eu-korea-fta-and-eu-enforcement-regulation/

Krätke, F. (2013, November 11). Policy coherence: A sensible idea lost in translation? Retrieved 10 June 2019 from https://www.theguardian.com/global-development-professionals-network/2013/nov/11/policy-coherence-global-development-zero-sum-game

Limnell, J., (2018). *Hacks, leaks and disruptions Russian cyber strategies* (Chaillot Paper N° 148) (N. Popescu & S. Secrieru, Eds.). Paris: European Union Institute for Security Studies.

Medinilla, A., Veron, P., & Mazzara, V. (2019). EU-UN cooperation: Confronting change in the multilateral system. (ecdpm Discussion Paper No. 260). Retrieved from https://ecdpm.org/publications/eu-un-cooperation-confronting-change-in-the-multilateral-system/

Mullin, R. (2020, April 27). COVID-19 is reshaping the pharmaceutical supply chain. *Chemical and Engineering News.* Retrieved from https://cen.acs.org/business/outsourcing/COVID-19-reshaping-pharmaceutical-supply/98/i16

Münchau, W. (2020, May 24). China is pitting EU countries against each other. *Financial Times.* Retrieved 24 May 2020 from https://www.ft.com/content/4ca9 aafe-9c37-11ea-adb1-529f96d8a00b

Nielsen, N. (2015, September 16). EU proposes new trade court with US. Retrieved 16 December 2018 from https://euobserver.com/economic/130297

Nugent, N. (2017). *The government and politics of the European Union* (8th ed., European Union series.) Palgrave Macmillan Education.

OECD. (2017). The 0.7% ODA/GNI target—a history. Retrieved 10 June 2019 from https://www.oecd.org/dac/stats/the07odagnitarget-ahistory.htm

OECD DevCom. (2017, November). What people know and think about the sustainable . . . Retrieved 16 May 2020 from http://www.oecd.org/development/pgd/International_Survey_Data_DevCom_June 2017.pdf

Pindják, P. (2020, March 9). Time for the European Union to reassert itself in the UN Security Council. Retrieved 15 May 2020 from https://www.atlanticcouncil.org/blogs/new-atlanticist/time-for-the-european-union-to-reassert-itself-in-the-un-security-council/

Riegert, B. (2020, April 21). Coronavirus: Debt relief key to helping Africa, says EU Commissioner. *Deutsche Welle.* Retrieved from https://www.dw.com/en/coronavirus-debt-relief-key-to-helping-africa-says-eu-commissioner/a-53201524

Rudd, K. (2020, June 4). The coming Post-COVID anarchy. *Foreign Policy.* Retrieved 6 June 2020 from https://www.foreignaffairs.com/articles/united-states/2020-05-06/coming-post-covid-anarchy

Spence, D. (Ed.). (2015). *The European external action service: European diplomacy post-Westphalia* (Ser. The European Union in international affairs). Palgrave Macmillan.

Spui25. (2020, May 20). *Virtual Visions of Europe #4 | Changing geopolitical orders.* [Video file]. Retrieved 6 June 2020 from https://www.youtube.com/watch?v=qDxA5Sw_b98

Tocci, N. (2020a, May 6). The Western Balkans belong with Europe. *Politico Europe*. Retrieved from https://www.politico.eu/article/the-western-balkans-croatia-serbia-kosovo-belong-with-europe-european-union/

Tocci, N. (2020b). Resilience and the role of the European Union in the world. *Contemporary Security Policy: Resilience in EU and International Institutions, 41*(2), 176–194.

Ursu, A., & van den Berg, W. (2018, April). China and the EU in the Horn of Africa. [Clingendael Policy Brief]. Retrieved 19 May 2020 from https://www.clingendael.org/publication/china-and-eu-horn-africa

Vilmer, J. J. (2018). *Hacks, leaks and disruptions Russian cyber strategies*. (Chaillot Paper N° 148) (N. Popescu & S. Secrieru, Eds.). Paris: European Union Institute for Security Studies.

Zweers, W. (2018). The State of EU relations with Russia and the Eastern Neighbourhood in Clingendael State of the Union 2018 towards better European integration. Retrieved 17 March 17 2020 from https://www.clingendael.org/pub/2018/clingendael-state-of-the-union-2018/

Chapter 8

The European Union and the Challenges to Internal Multilateralism: A Perspective on European Macroeconomic Governance and the COVID-19 Crisis

Carolina Alice D'Ambrosio

1. INTRODUCTION

In a context of raising global uncertainty due to the COVID-19 crisis, international cooperation between states seems to be facing some important challenges. A global pandemic-induced chaos is pushing nations to close their borders in the desperate attempt to save as many human lives as possible. But when the lockdown phase will cease, its consequences will be knocking on the door of the governing elites, who are now refraining from engaging in a collective, global effort to face this new threat. An economic recession is on its way, and urges multilateral institutions to find a common and compact front to face it. Will the European Union, the greatest multilateral experiment of the contemporary world (Keohane, 1990, p. 731), be able to find a common stance in facing the consequences of a new economic recession?

In the first section, this chapter will critically analyse how the structure of European macroeconomic governance impacts and hinders the internal multilateral relationship between member states, due to its differentiated integration character. It will then assess how the changes undertaken at both the fiscal and monetary levels by the European institutions at times of economic crises further deepened the frictions between member states, especially between large-sized and small-sized economies. In the light of these analyses, the networked structure of the internal multilateral relationship between member states over fiscal and economic matters will be briefly assessed, revealing the patterns of association between states in this policy area and paving the way to the subsequent analysis of multilateralism during the COVID-19 economic response.

Indeed, the second section will address the economic and fiscal response to the recession induced by the COVID-19 crisis. Particularly, it will try to assess how the COVID-19 crisis and its economic consequences will affect EU's internal multilateralism. The Eurogroup has found itself divided in the debate about the way forward: Southern European states, importantly Italy and Spain, backed up by France, asked for the emission of common debt titles in order to face the crisis, the so-called Eurobonds. On the other hand, the "Frugal Four" economies—Denmark, Sweden, Netherlands and Austria, supported by Germany—found themselves opposing this measure, as it would be too costly for their more developed and fiscally healthy economies. This debate could eventually lead to a breaking point after years of clashes between these two blocs for what concerns the harmonization of the fiscal and economic policies of the EU. How will economic choices impact the future of multilateralism in the EU?

As a way forward, the chapter finally envisages fiscal federalism as a solution to the appeasing of internal multilateral clashes between member states, since it would create a more inclusive and coordinated system of economic governance.

2. THE EUROPEAN UNION: THE GREATEST MULTILATERAL EXPERIMENT

The international system is ruled by evolving structures, represented by international institutions and organizations, which endured the test of time by constantly adapting to external challenges to the system itself. In the era of globalization, multilateralism constitutes the main paradigm of conduct entertain relationships between countries. In this context, the European Union (EU) has been defined as "the contemporary world's most extensive and ambitious multilateral institution" (Keohane, Macedo, & Moravcsik, 2009, p. 3). The values it embodies resonate with the values of globalization, as the EU grounds its foundation in the belief that, through cooperation and pooling of sovereignty, state entities are able to achieve policy goals which would be impossible to achieve through unilateral conduct only (2009, p. 4). Free economic exchange and multilateral cooperation lie at the basis of its functioning, which is coordinated and supervised by the balancing power of institutions such as the European Commission and the European Court of Justice (ECJ), which discourage any hegemonic push by bigger member states. Furthermore, as pointed out by political scientist Henry Farrell, the EU "is most comfortable when the outside world mirrors its traditional internal principles of organization" (2020, p. 2). In fact, the existence of the EU in the globalized world created a "feedback loop between European integration and global markets" (Farrell, 2020, p. 6). The European Union and the globalized system are mutually interconnected, since the ideals of globalization stimulated further integration reform for the European framework, while global markets were reciprocally influenced in the light of the increasing success of the European project.

Despite this long-term, profitable relationship between the European reality and globalism, the global order seems to be undergoing multiple challenges, which are pushing the actors of the multilateral system to refrain from further integration in a united, globalized community. Financial crises, humanitarian emergencies such as the migratory crisis and the trade war between China and the United States constitute the warning signs of a globalized world under threat. The most recent outbreak of the COVID-19 pandemic shed the light on some changes which were slowly occurring beneath the surface, and possibly enhanced them as the dividing forces of a future "deglobalisation" (Irwin, 2020, p. 1). In this new order, driven by geopolitical assertiveness, the EU risks losing perspective on its founding principles under the growing populistic tension perpetrated by some member states. The greatest threat to its multilateral identity would be to give in and be driven back to the old, divisive reasoning of self-interest over solidarity. This dynamic has partly been mirrored in the ardours labour of cooperation over the economic response to COVID-19, in which member states showed timid willingness to find a compromise over the necessity of financing the emergency necessities of gravely affected states such as Italy and Spain (Herszenhorn & Wheaton, 2020, p. 1). Indeed, the harmonization between member states over economic and fiscal policy still constitutes a policy area which raises several issues and barriers to internal multilateralism (Rankin, 2020). Internal dynamics are obstructed by the clashes between different clusters of member states on policy matters. For this reason, the following section will undergo a concise analysis of the dynamics of EU's internal multilateralism, with a specific focus over the divide between Northern and Southern member states on economic and fiscal policy matters, by pointing out the past and current status of European economic governance.

2.1. European Economic Governance

The debate over fiscal and economic policy in the European arena continuously raises frictions between member states. This section will disentangle the unique and peculiar structure of European economic governance, in order to illustrate the dynamics of power-sharing and the patterns of hegemony which concur as factors that trouble the relationship between member states.

Economic integration was always at the very core of the European project, which started off in 1951 with the European Coal and Steal Community (ECSC), leading to 1957's European Economic Community (EEC), to finally develop into the well-oiled multilateral machine that today brings together 27 national economies into one Single Market (Nugent, 2010, p. 22). Since the Treaty of Rome and the establishment of the "four freedoms"—the free movement of goods, services, capital and labour—(Bublitz, 2018, p. 338), European economic integration began to take shape through various layers of Treaty law and institutions, aiming at achieving a fundamental role in the free market economy and mutual economic gains and growth for the member states. This progressive process of integration brought about the contemporary outlook of European macro-economic governance, characterized by several layers with "fuzzy boundaries, comprising hybrid patterns of unitary and differentiated integration" (Dyson, 2010, p. 215). A lot of factors brought about this internally varied structure. First and foremost, the fact that the Economic Union and the Monetary Union were developed at different historical times, through different instruments, causing discrepancies in the coordination between national- and European-level responsibilities for member states (Dyson, 2010, p. 215). Indeed, market integration enjoys a much more unified and integrated status than the European Monetary Union (EMU), which still considerably lacks delegation of sovereignty from member states to European financial institutions. In the context of the EMU, the European Commission still lacks powers of "representation, initiation and execution in relation to EU economic governance" (Chang, 2013, p. 258). Consequently, the differentiated integration of the EMU—which provided for the gradual introduction of a single currency, without, however, putting in place an efficient system of governance of economic policies or envisaging any form of fiscal integration (Chang, 2013, p. 259)—became a structural cause of dispute between member states, hampering further harmonization of national fiscal regimes. Therefore, member states' multilateral relations have been endangered by persistent disagreements over employment policies and business tax harmonization, due to the clashes deriving from the different approaches of 27 national policies over these matters, as well as due to a differentiated system which inevitably creates net contributors and net beneficiaries.

The impulses towards deeper economic integration, translated into Germany's call for compliance to the standards of the Stability and Growth Pact (SGP), are further prevented by the fact that being an outsider of the Euro Area is perceived as a net gain (Dyson, 2010, p. 218). In fact, strong economies such as Denmark and Sweden enjoy the benefits of a special regime on exchange rates to interact with the members of the Euro Area, while being free to adjust their interest rates as they believe fit in case of asymmetric shocks (Dyson, 2010, p. 217). Their privileged access contrast sharply with the situation of smaller insider economies, such as the Greek or the Irish one, which in times of exogenous shocks must sum up the shortcomings of the crisis to the responsibility of complying with the costly standards of the

SGP—the most historically opposed among them being the deficit rule of 3% GDP limit (Hopkin, 2020, p. 177). The resulting reality pictures disincentives to commit to deeper economic integration, especially because of the high political costs national politicians face when forced to perform costly cuts in wages and non-wage costs under the European directives (Dyson, 2010, p. 217).

The incomplete integration of monetary and fiscal policy contrasts deeply with the unitary principle embodied in the economic union, through the Lisbon agenda of economic reform (Dyson, 2010, p. 216), and also successively embodied in the efforts of the Euro Plus Pact of 2011 (Eurofound, 2014). Particularly, the establishment of the Euro Plus Pact constituted a formal commitment towards more integrated and coordinated economic governance between member states (Eurofound, 2014). The way forward envisaged by the pact importantly tackles the harmonization of national policies in the fields of employment policy, labour market and tax reform (Eurofound, 2014). Nonetheless, the Euro Plus Pact does not state the final destination of this harmonization process. Fiscal federalism, which will be envisaged as a possible solution to the frictions populating European internal multilateralism later in this chapter, would constitute the final product of such process of European macroeconomic harmonization.

In the process of establishing a wider economic integration, nonetheless, the issues deriving from the discrepancies at the national and European policy levels are even more enhanced when economic crises hit the Euro Area and the globalized, free market economy. The next section will be devoted to give a brief overview of the multilateral relationships between member states in times of fiscal and economic recessions.

2.2. Internal Divisions over Fiscal and Economic Policy: A Perspective on Past Crises

The great power of crises lies in their capacity to bring to the surface neglected issues, and to be a force for change that hopefully leads to improvements to the status quo. In the history of the Euro Area, economic crises such as the global recession of 2008 and the consequent Eurozone crisis enabled the European political élite to uncover the limitations of EU's "soft" institutional mechanisms (Dyson, 2010, p. 222) in terms of fiscal policy, even though unfortunately this revelation did not lead to immediate structural reforms. This lack of reactiveness is still evident in the current COVID-19 response, as will be uncovered in section 2.

The main issues with past crises and the current health emergency are uncovering concerns about the networked structure of European integration. As explained by Josef Janning, the core of EU decision making, embodied by

Qualified Majority Voting (QMV), is characterized by the continuous contrast between the defence of national self-interest of member states and cohesive European behaviour (2005, p. 822). This underlying dichotomy inevitably pushes member states to caucus, and creates smaller bilateral or multilateral networks based on their policy affinity. These blocs tend to vary by different policy areas and are usually identified by geographical and cultural affinities, such as the Franco-German or the Mediterranean one (Heywood & McLaren, 2010, p. 170). The process of integration, especially the economic one, is therefore based on these forms of compromise-building to create joint positions on EU issues (Janning, 2005, p. 826), which over the years resulted in a polarization of the policy instruments created and verted inevitably towards the position of the majority, due to the structure of the system being based on QMV. In the case of the Lisbon agenda on economic integration, for example, the prevailing position of Germany and of other net contributor member states prevailed over the preferences of the smaller, minority economies of the Southern states, a situation which led to numerous frictions which eventually exacerbated in times of economic crisis (Janning, 2005, p. 826). The contrasts arising between member states, then, deepened the mechanism of network layers creation at the expense of a harmonized and balanced integration (Janning, 2005, p. 827). In order to improve internal multilateralism in this economic context and overcome the creation of a networked multilateralism, the diversity in the socio-economic level of member states ought to be acknowledged, overcoming the majoritarian perspectives on the matter.

In times of crisis and critical junctures, the divide between small and large-sized member states usually has been proven to shift in favour of "continental welfare states" (Janning, 2005, p. 832), represented by Franco-German Europe and their regulatory drive. The "founders' coalition" (Janning, 2005, p. 829) has been defined through a history of collaboration in the very making of the *acquis* and of the corpus of institutions that constitute the EU, such as in the creation of the European Council and of the European Monetary System (EMS) in the 1970s (Cole, 2010, p. 157). France and Germany always collaborated with close bilateral ties on most important decisions regarding the process of European integration, most importantly the creation of the Single Market and of the EMU, even if some disagreements in the implementation form of economic integration were latent. These disagreements resulted in the formation of alternative networks for these two historically tied parties: during the COVID-19 crisis, most notably, France aligned with Italy and Spain over the issuing of Eurobonds to face the looming economic crisis, clashing with Germany which, instead, caucused with the Northern economies who prefer economic intervention in the form of loans (Rankin, 2020, p. 1).

Nonetheless, in the case of EMU, Germany's leadership role in agenda-setting—backed up by British, Dutch and Danish governments and central banks—influenced fiscal policy towards economic convergence but also towards the implementation of the Monetary Union according to German rules, resulting in the current spectrum of differentiated integration (Cole, 2010, p. 160). During the economic crisis of 2008 and in the subsequent Eurozone crisis, the tough criteria of the SGP—aimed at controlling the compliance of weaker economies such as Italy and Greece—brought about severe economic consequences for the labour markets of the economies of the Mediterranean states, highlighting that "core European strategies are not only divisive, but also difficult to implement" (Cole, 2010, p. 168).

The alignment of the "Mediterranean Europe", on the other hand, largely groups Cyprus, Greece, Italy, Malta, Portugal and Spain as a cohesive strand inside the European network of member states (Heywood & McLaren, 2010, p. 171). Even though these countries do not converge in terms of voting patterns—or at least not always—they experienced both positive and deteriorating effects on their national economies, either from entering the Eurozone or from complying with Community directives in times of economic crisis (Heywood & McLaren, 2010, p. 175). The benefits of joining the EU and EMU for Mediterranean countries are multiple, and can notably be found in the overall expansion of their trade relations, market liberalization and increased competition, which enabled them to upgrade their mostly local economies and their administrative apparatus, to join the common benefits of the Single Market (Heywood & McLaren, 2010, p. 173). But the downsides of their accession and compliance processes eventually caused an increase in unemployment and in painful cuts to their welfare systems—especially the pension system—which resulted from the highly demanding EU budgetary constraints (Ladi & Graziano, 2010, p. 118). Indeed, the budget requirements have not been tailored to the smaller sizes of their economies and to the precarious situation of their social provision and employment systems.

The multilateral relationship between the countries of these two blocs, in the context of the process of economic integration of the Mediterranean states, was exacerbated during the European debt crisis. The pressure between Germany, the European Central Bank (ECB) and the most affected countries took the unprecedented form of an exit memorandum procedure set up for Greece and a warning letter sent to Italy by the ECB (Ladi & Graziano, 2010, p. 109). Mediterranean countries, which were already in the process of adjusting to the institutional and financial reforms required by the EU, were further targeted with cost containment requirements in a moment in which budget deficit was needed to face the crisis (Ladi & Graziano, 2010, p. 110).

European institutions, nonetheless, employed a series of policy instruments to face the grievous effects of recession on the socio-economic issue of national societies, most importantly the Europe 2020 strategy (European Commission, 2010), the European Stability Mechanism (ESM) and the fiscal compact treaty.[1] These instruments, despite aimed at relieving damaged economies (in the case of the ESM also through the concession of credit lines), reiterated compliance with Community budget constraints. The fiscal compact treaty, in particular, established that the budget for the 25 signatory member states had to be in either balance or surplus (Ladi & Graziano, 2010, p. 115), a measure which was hard to comply with during economic recession, and that had strong implications for the Greek and Italian economies. Most importantly, the relationship between Greece and EU's economic and financial institutions was increasingly eroded by the issuing of two memoranda by the "troika"—EC, ECB and IMF—(Ladi & Graziano, 2010, p. 117) (Commission of the European Communities, 2010c; 2010d). While the conditionality of the credit lines was necessary to ensure Greek compliance of the "hard Europeanization" principles, it also proved detrimental to the spirit of solidarity and trust which underlies the European project.

These budgetary provisions triggered welfare state policy cuts for the countries with the higher public debt/GDP ratio, notably Greece and Italy (Ladi & Graziano, 2010, p. 115). The approach on "flexicurity" envisaged by the fiscal compact and, more broadly, by the European employment agenda ended up favouring policies of flexibility—such as reduction of severance pay, simplified lay-off programmes and lower labour costs—over policies of security—such as basic income schemes—to induce compliance (Ladi & Graziano, 2010, p. 118). The social repercussions have been multiple, and are still cause of disagreement and overall slowing of the economic alignment process at present. By making compliance prevail over solidarity, and by delaying the completion of EMU with specific macroeconomic instruments of governance or fiscal integration mechanisms, the laws governing the Euro Area created a dangerous grey area of ambiguity and differentiation, which will be at the very heart of the economic recession of the COVID-19 crisis, analysed in the next section of this chapter.

3. COVID-19 AND GLOBAL ECONOMIC RECESSION: PERSPECTIVES FROM THE EU

The WHO on 11 March 2020 characterized the outbreak of COVID-19 as global pandemic (World Health Organization, 2020). Since 11 January, when the first confirmed cases were reported according to the official data of the WHO, 138,688,383[2] people have been tested positive for COVID-19, with 2,978,935[3] deaths globally registered. Europe has been confirmed as one of the territories most hardly hit by the pandemic, with 46,521,544[4] cases and 999,410[5] deaths ravaging its territories. The reaction to such a widespread, global crisis was difficult to implement, whereby multilateralism and global cooperation are the key to arrange an effective coordinated response. Nevertheless, because of the considerable lack of information about this new virus and the level of danger it entails, the global response was slow and proceeded with progressive trial and error measures to tampon the spread of COVID-19. Europe was the second in order, after China, to be called to deal with this unfortunate event. When the first Italian towns went into total lockdown, the EU started to comprehend that serious response measures were necessary, even if in the initial phase of the epidemic, the virulence and speed of contagion has been highly underestimated. Soon, COVID-19 would have reached the entirety of EU's member states, calling for a prompt and coordinated response, which was characterized by slow reactive times and a scattered nature.

The lockdown of member states territories already provoked serious economic consequences, leading EU countries into a first recession phase derived from the social distancing measures, that were necessary to flatten the curve of the pandemic. The path towards the consolidation of the perception that COVID-19 was not just "China's problem" or successively "Italy's problem" was progressive, but finally triggered evolving policy reactions from the European institutions. The great European multilateral debate about how to deal with the economic consequences of social distancing is nevertheless taking to the surface ancient disagreements between member states over fiscal and economic policy approaches, limiting the capability of EU institutions in creating an overarching Communitarian mechanism to flatten the economic recession curve. This divide in the debate concerning the way forward sees deployed Southern European States on one side—importantly Italy and Spain, backed up by France—asking for the emission of common debt titles in order to face the crisis, the so-called Eurobonds. On the other hand, Northern European States—the most vocal represented by the "Frugal Four" group, composed of Austria, Netherlands, Sweden and Denmark (Kurz, 2020, p. 1)—found themselves opposing this measure, as it would be too costly for their more developed and fiscally healthy economies. Multilateralism has been put under considerable pressure due to the incumbent debate between these two blocs, and their opposing economic visions. A common agreement is underway, necessary as it is to create and finance appropriate instruments that are able to tackle the economic recession which will hit every European country, without discrimination. The next section will analyse the instruments adopted so far in the light of the current debate, and envisage their effectiveness for the future.

3.1. Fiscal and Monetary Reactions: An Overview

The challenge we face is how to act with sufficient strength and speed to prevent the recession from morphing into a prolonged depression, made deeper by a plethora of defaults leaving irreversible damage.—Mario Draghi

These words, written by former president of the ECB Mario Draghi for the Financial Times (Draghi, 2020), encapsulate the priorities for a European counter-action, in the name of fiscal and monetary coordination. A clear-cut plan on how to overcome the economic shutdown is still under consideration, but the speed of deployment of funds could largely be improved, and it is being delayed by the constant debates between "frugal" northern economies and southern economies, which demand financial aid to be delivered without conditionality, in the form of grants (Barigazzi, 2020, p. 1).

As a first instance of collective reaction, on the 15th of April, the presidents of the European Council and of the Commission presented the Joint European Roadmap, briefly describing the recovery plan that will be undertaken to relaunch member states' economies (European Council; Council of the EU, 2020, p. 2). It is important to highlight that the joint document emphasizes the need for the values of solidarity, cohesion and convergence to be the drive behind the joint efforts for recovery (European Council; Council of the EU, 2020, p. 2), an important realization which takes an even more valuable char-acter in times of crisis. A breakeven point seems to have been reached, since the document highlights that the shock provoked by the COVID-19 has been largely symmetric amid member states, and it is imperative for EU institutions to avoid the recovery becoming asymmetric (European Council; Council of the EU, 2020, p. 2). The document as well highlighted that the financial effort undertaken will be inclusive and co-owned by all member states involved in the spirit of a team effort (p. 2). This new awareness constitutes a positive sign that the EU might be able to set up an undifferentiated, collective response mecha-nism, and finally overcome the frictions and obstacles to its internal multilater-alism in the field of macroeconomic governance, which have been previously discussed in this chapter. The following sections will briefly describe the char-acter which this symmetric response took up so far, in the form of the policy instruments currently envisaged or already put into action by EU institutions.

3.1.1. Recovery Fund/Next Generation EU

On the 23rd of April 2020, EU leaders in the European Council agreed to sustain the economic recession through the creation of a recovery fund, targeted at the countries and economic sectors, which most suffered from the dreadful effects of COVID-19 (European Council, 2020). The European Commission is currently working on a specific proposal, but the Franco-German axis proposed the amount of the fund to reach €500 billion in the form of grants (Bayer, Von Der Burchard, & Smith-Meyer, 2020), an unprecedented effort in the history of the Union. Chancellor Merkel and President Macron proposed this amount to be borrowed on financial markets of behalf of the EU and to be delivered to the member states which may need it from EU budget expenditure, waiving any eventual conditionality linked to the loan model—the mostly adopted manner of investment employed so far by EU institutions. Of course, the recovery fund is aimed specifically at financing COVID-19 related issues, and mostly to sustain the efforts of national economies to strengthen competitiveness and support green and digital transitions (Bundesregierung, 2020).

On the 27th of May, the European Commission further enlarged the firepower of the recovery fund, proposing to increase the initial €500 billion to €750 billion, renaming the recovery plan "Next Generation EU" (European Commission, 2020, p. 1). The funds will be directed at supporting "public investment and key structural reforms in the member states, concentrated where the crisis impact and resilience needs are greatest" (European Commission, 2020, p. 2). Nonetheless, it is still unclear whether and how this money will have to be paid back, since the budgetary expenditure is linked to EU's Multiannual Financial Framework (MFF), which ends in 2027, and the amount of the fund to be issued in the form of grants or loans is to be determined upon agreement of all 27 member states (Lee, 2020). Furthermore, the "Frugal Four" are manifesting doubts and considerable resistance to this proposal (Khan, 2020).

3.1.2. SURE

The temporary support package of the EU also comprises other measures, following the willingness to employ an unprecedented investment effort to fight this unprecedented type of crisis. SURE (Support to mitigate Unemployment Risks in an Emergency) is a temporary employment scheme created to support workers which have mostly been hit by the COVID-19 crisis. Unlike the recovery fund, SURE will be delivered in the form of loans under favourable terms to member states, providing up to €100 billion and part of the three "safety nets" for jobs and workers to be operational by the 1st of June 2020 (Council of the EU, 2020). The scheme is aimed at helping European citizens to keep their jobs and to limit as much as possible bankruptcy for the businesses most hardly hit by the public health crisis. Nonetheless, it contains some justified restrictions as to who are going to be the recipients of these funds. The decision of who to grant the loans to will be the responsibility of the Council of the EU upon proposal by the European Commission, as the hardest-hit economies are given precedence over this matter. The instrument has a shorter jurisdiction than the aforementioned recovery fund, since it tackles short-run initial employment cuts until the 31st of December 2022 (Council of the EU, 2020). The loans envisaged by this temporary employment plan are totally worth €540 billion, and include two other safety nets: a pan-European guarantee fund directed at businesses—specifically small and medium-sized enterprises (SMEs)—with loans of up to €200 billion; as well as an improved credit line, the Pandemic Crisis Support, which envisages loans to all Euro Area member states up to 2% of their GDP (up to €240 billion).

The loan capacity made available is incredibly extensive and for sure unprecedented. The only downside it presents, nevertheless, it doesn't completely match the requests of those member states which have been most hardly hit by the COVID-19—such as Italy, Spain and (partially) France—to receive financial aid in the form of grants, and not loans. The refund terms are a matter of incredible distress for "Southern States", fearful as they are of a repetition of ancient patterns of memoranda and disciplinary measures as for the experience of Greece. It will be of utmost importance to avoid the worsening of multilateral relations and the disaggregation of the Euro Area, and to finally confront this crisis as a collective issue, with equal sacrifices and equal sharing of burdens, and with a substantial dose of solidarity.

3.1.3. Suspension of the Stability and Growth Pact

In order to protect the collapse of the economy, the first step undertaken by EU institutions was to suspend the obligation to fulfil the requirements of the Stability and Growth Pact (SGP) and of the state aid regime, in order to provide national governments with the adequate flexibility to save private businesses from bankruptcy and protect citizens' livelihoods (European Council; Council of the EU, 2020, p. 3). The suspension of the SGP is a step of exceptional importance and a signal of a change in perspective, of a newly reinforced willingness to address the crisis as a collective problem, with no discrimination between sizes of national economies. Compliance with the principles of the Treaty of Maastricht and the SGP have been used as a powerful tool to induce national reform towards convergence and deep European integration, and have indeed sparked considerable structural change in economic policy within member states (Coman & Crespy, 2014, p. 57). But when the debt crisis struck, sticking with the requirements of the SGP for southern European countries meant having to withstand its semi-coercive mechanisms through the application of harsh austerity programmes. The negative impact of such policies on multilateral relations between member states ought to be avoided with this new crisis, as demonstrated by the suspension of its requirements.

3.1.4. Monetary Policy: The ECB and Eurobonds

A first instance of federalization of European economic policy has been under consideration for several years: the possibility of issuing the so-called Eurobonds. The common issuance of bonds has been discussed for a long time now, in order to address liquidity constraints (Zerhdoud, 2013, p. 173) and promote growth inside the Euro Area. The argument on the issuing of Eurobonds was historically sustained by Jean-Claude Juncker and Giulio Tremonti in 2012, who envisaged the creation of "European sovereign bonds" to stabilize the economy and send a strong signal of the consolidation of EMU to financial markets (Zerhdoud, 2013, p. 172). Despite being supported by a large portion of European leaders, the measure was always strongly opposed by Germany, which does not support debt mutualization in the light of the presence of countries who still struggle to abide to the rules of fiscal responsibility (Zerhdoud, 2013, p. 173). German economist Michael Hüther defined Eurobonds as a negative reward incentive for Southern European countries, and historically opposed giving up national fiscal policy at the times of the Eurozone crisis (Chazan, 2020).

Nonetheless, since the outbreak of the pandemic, a group of prominent German economists—among which Hüther—radically changed perspective, and asked the Eurozone governments to issue €1 trillion in joint "European crisis bonds" in order to help the countries which had been worst affected by the pandemic (Chazan, 2020). Despite the measure being vehemently requested by most European leaders—especially by southern European states—the frugal northern economies' governments still highly oppose this measure, and call for other, less costly, instruments to be employed to face the crisis (Khan, 2020).

In the middle of this intense debate, the ECB activated a Pandemic Emergency Purchase Program (PEPP) worth €750 trillion, to be conducted until the end of 2020 and directed at both private and public sector securities (European Central Bank, 2020). This measure represents the banner of ECB's strong independence, and constitutes a significant sign of EU's institutions willingness to support this new economic challenge by learning from the mistakes of the past. Notably, the ECB granted a waiver of the eligibility requirements for securities issued by the Greek government (2020), in line with Mario Draghi's "whatever it takes" fashion. Also notably, Germany's constitutional court ruled against ECB's bond-buying programme, asking for it to be scrutinized by the European Court of Justice (ECJ) (Arnold, Chazan, & Fleming, 2020). The high polarization over this issue comes as proof that the way towards higher macroeconomic harmonization is paved with a big multilateral confrontation to be experienced.

4. FUTURE PROSPECTS

The Marshall-Plan like investment effort envisaged so far and to be further developed by European institutions is an incredibly hopeful sign of their renewed capacity to hear out the necessities of member states and deliver on them. Not only the institutions could temporarily deviate from the rigorist approach by suspending the requirements of the Growth and Stability

Pact (GSP), they also could implement considerable and adequate financial aid—and promise to also increase it in the future—for this new collective issue. While these measures still need to be further refined and charged with credit, they constitute a great starting point, which shows a real and concrete change in perspective. In the document that presents the cardinal principles of the Roadmap for Recovery initiative, it is clearly stated that "a functioning system of governance is a key requisite for overcoming the crisis and ensuring recovery" (European Council; Council of the EU, 2020, p. 5). This constitutes an important awareness, and stands for a lesson learnt from the past experiences with Greece and Italy. Multilateral cooperation within member states and among member states and European institutions is the key feature that the system so far struggled to implement in a symmetric way, and future prospects at least acknowledge this necessity, hopefully being able to make it a concrete achievement. The magnitude of the crisis seems to be functional in making the Union reflect on its own rules, as well as in creating the momentum to finally take the leap and create a more inclusive and coordinated system of economic governance, which is the missing piece in achieving a non-differentiated Europeanization in economic terms. But how exactly this new system of governance could look like? Fiscal federalism might be the answer to this pending question.

4.1. Fiscal Federalism

At present, the EU cannot be described as a federalist system. More appropriately, the union has been identified throughout literature as a case of "multilevel" governance, characterized by "several levels of governing with overlapping consequences", by intense interaction at the political, public-private and private-private levels among the different layers of governance constituting its networked structure (Fossum, 2017, p. 363). Even if the Union presents some clear federal features, it presents the substantive lack of an agreed-upon federal constitution. As previously analysed in this chapter, the exogenous shocks which hit the EU in the past two decades highlighted the necessity for EMU to address structural inequalities between different Euro Area economies, as well as to improve the current macroeconomic structure to better counteract asymmetric shocks (Hinarejos, 2013, p. 1621). These challenges might be correctly addressed by a regime of fiscal federalism.

Fiscal federalism has been defined as an economic theory which "aims to find a normative framework for the assignment of functions and fiscal instruments to different levels of government" (Hinarejos, 2013, p. 1636). Currently, the EU enjoys a decentralized federalist system, characterized by the fact that national sovereignty is preserved by the member states, who have the prerogative of raising revenue through taxes and allocate it on their own policy terms (Hinarejos, 2013, p. 1634). The decentralized model, nonetheless, has proved to be inefficient when asymmetric shocks hit the economic system, because of the macroeconomic disparities it entails. The lack of an overarching fiscal structure has proven to be among the causes of increased inequalities among Euro Area economies, which under the compliance of the "Golden Rule"—the requirement that European budgets are in balance—were hit differently by the austerity reforms put into place after the Eurozone crisis (Heywood & McLaren, 2010, p. 118).

The recession induced by social distancing measures under the COVID-19 response could finally be a pivotal moment towards the creation of a "European federal budget", or a new measure of central spending power devoted to counteracting measures in times of asymmetric shocks. When fiscal federalism is contemplated, two alterative models are usually envisaged: the surveillance model and the classic fiscal federalist model (Hinarejos, 2013, p. 1635). The surveillance model is a "softer" transitional model to pursue further macroeconomic integration between member states, as well as to preserve their sovereignty prerogatives. Indeed, member states are entitled full fiscal competence over their territories, and they maintain their right of dictating economic policy accordingly, yet the EU would act as a discipline enforcer though budgetary surveillance and new discipline rules, which are to be settled by agreement between member states (Hinarejos, 2013, p. 1634). What could be achieved by this model is the eventual creation of a mechanism of debt mutualization such as the Eurobonds, a measure which has already been called for by national governments over the COVID-19 crisis. The classic fiscal federalist model, on the other hand, is a model focused on the centralization of fiscal surveillance, through the creation of a new central authority which raises revenue and allocates it through the delegation of sovereignty (Hinarejos, 2013, p. 1635). Even though this model might be more functional in addressing the structural inequalities and the exogenous shocks which are currently hindering multilateralism, its viability is impeded by democratic legitimacy concerns of member states.

As Hinarejos correctly points out, the creation of a centralized European tax authority "requires identifying, first, the public good for whose provision it is responsible" (2013, p. 1636). Since the space for this change in perspective is provided by the COVID-19-induced economic crisis, the EU could perhaps create a new tax authority devoted at providing a structural fund to finance member states' economies in times of economic and fiscal shocks, and to work towards an impairment of their inequalities at the budgetary expenditure level. Ordinary taxes would still be raised by single member states, and an independent European budget would be created through the collection of a specific tax. The revenues obtained through this semi-centralized system of fiscal federalism could finally properly address the long-needed harmonization of macroeconomic governance, that is so accentuated at times of economic recession.

5. CONCLUSION

The sovereign debt crisis revealed a big contradiction of the Europeanization process: macroeconomic integration became more necessary, yet harder to achieve (Coman & Crespy, 2014, p. 58). The resentment nurtured after years of austerity policies and inflation in the European countries most affected by the Eurozone crisis led to a politicization of European integration with a negative connotation, further inflamed by the rise of populist leaders and of new unilateral tendencies by international actors. The main problem which saw the light during the exogenous shock of 2008 and the following sovereign debt crisis of 2010 was that the process of creation of EMU and the basis of the Maastricht Treaty represented an "unfinished" form of monetary integration (Coman & Crespy, 2014, p. 58). The asymmetric nature of this integration processes needed to be supported through adequate and deeper macroeconomic and fiscal integration in member states national economies, but especially at the European level, to achieve deeper harmonization. At the same time, the reform campaigns initiated in the Mediterranean states to align their economies with the standards of the SGP launched an incomplete process of economic integration, by raising interdependence between member states de facto (Coman & Crespy, 2014, p. 58).

The COVID-19 crisis could finally be the critical juncture needed to fill this gap in harmonization policies, and solve the current inequalities that are hampering European internal multilateralism. The risk of renationalization is real, after Brexit set a dangerous precedent in the history of the Union. If the instrumental value of this crisis will be neglected, the differences between member states could become too deep to be healed, and the incredible multilateral experiment that is the EU could suffer unsustainable losses.

A deep structural change is needed. The economic and fiscal response given by the European institutions during the COVID-19 crisis seems to have acknowledged that, by taking important steps towards a more coherent harmonization of European macroeconomic policy. Furthermore, in the instance of the COVID-19 pandemic, these steps seem to be characterized by an underlying sense of solidarity, rather then through requests of compliance. This chapter started to envisage a solution based on a semi-centralized fiscal federalism system, which seems to be the compromise that the EU is on its way to find between sovereignty concerns and a deeper coordination in times of economic need. While the Eurozone crisis lacked this reformatory power, given the fact that the recession had a differentiated effect over a restricted cluster of member states, the recession induced by the COVID-19 crisis put every member states on the same level of risk without discriminations. It could be the pivotal critical juncture to provide the momentum to bridge differences among member states, and save multilateralism inside the European

Union. It will be up to future leaders to start the shaping process of a Union which stands united in front of difficulties, and overcomes them as the true global player it always aspired to be.

NOTES

1. Treaty on Stability, Coordination and Governance in the Economic and Monetary Union (TSCG).
2. Data as of 16 April 2021 from WHO online global barometer https://covid19.who.int.
3. Idem Supra note 2.
4. Data as of 15 April 2021 from the European Centre for Disease Prevention and Control https://www.ecdc.europa.eu/en/geographical-distribution-2019-ncov-cases.
5. Idem Supra note 4.

REFERENCES

Arnold, M., Chazan, G., & Fleming, S. (2020, May 12th). *How can Europe solve the crisis created by Germany's highest court?* Retrieved from Financial Times: https://www.ft.com/content/2d4a6959-8bdc-4d74-b617-873bba839807

Barigazzi, J. (2020, April 22nd). *Conte's Gamble.* Retrieved from POLITICO: https://www.politico.eu/article/giuseppe-conte-gamble-coronavirus-european-union-leaders/

Bayer, L., Von Der Burchard, H., & Smith-Meyer, B. (2020, May 18th). *France, Germany propose €500B EU recovery fund.* Retrieved from POLITICO: https://www.politico.eu/article/france-germany-propose-e500b-eu-recovery-fund/

Bublitz, E. (2018). The European Single Market at 25. *Intereconomics, 53*(6), 337–342.

Bundesregierung. (2020, May 18th). A French-German Initiative for the European Recovery from the Coronavirus Crisis. *Pressemitteilung (173/20).* Berlin.

Chang, M. (2013, April). Fiscal Policy Coordination and the Future of the Community Method. *European Integration, 35*(3), 255–270.

Chazan, G. (2020, April 6th). *Coronavirus crisis prompts German rethink on eurobonds.* Retrieved from Financial Times: https://www.ft.com/content/8da39299-b257-4e8f-9b83-a84a8930f1c1

Cole, A. (2010). Franco-German Europe. In K. S. Dyson, *Which Europe?: The politics of differentiated integration (Palgrave Studies in European Union Politics)* (pp. 156–169). New York: Palgrave Macmillan.

Coman, R., & Crespy, A. (2014). Still in Search of Europeanization: From Limited to Structural Change? In R. Coman, T. Kostera, & L. Tomini, *Europeanization and European Integration: From Incremental to Structural Change (Palgrave Studies in European Union Politics)* (pp. 50–70). London: Palgrave Mcmillan UK.

Council of the EU. (2020, May 19th). *Press release. COVID-19: Council adopts temporary support to mitigate unemployment risks in an emergency (SURE).* Retrieved from www.consilium.europa.eu: https://www.consilium.europa.eu/en/press/press-releases/2020/05/19/covid-19-council-reaches-political-agreement-on-temporary-support-to-mitigate-unemployment-risks-in-an-emergency-sure/

Draghi, M. (2020, March 25th). *Draghi: We face a war against coronavirus and must mobilise accordingly*. Retrieved from Financial Times: https://www.ft.com/content/c6d2de3a-6ec5-11ea-89df-41bea055720b

Dyson, K. (2010). "Euro" Europe: "Fuzzy" Boundaries and "Constrained" Differentiation in Macro-Economic Governance. In K. Dyson, & A. Sepos, *Which Europe? The politics of differentiated integration* (pp. 215–232). Palgrave Mcmillan.

Eurofound. (2014, April 09th). *Euro Plus Pact*. Retrieved from www.eurofound.europa.eu: https://www.eurofound.europa.eu/observatories/eurwork/industrial-relations-dictionary/euro-plus-pact

European Central Bank. (2020, March 18th). *Press Release: ECB announces €750 billion Pandemic Emergency Purchase Programme (PEPP)*. Retrieved from https://www.ecb.europa.eu/press/pr/date/2020/html/ecb.pr200318_1~3949d6f266.en.html

European Commission. (2010). *Europe 2020. A Strategy for Smart, Sustainable and Inclusive Growth*. Brussels.

European Commission. (2020, May 27th). *The EU Budget Powering the Recovery Plan for Europe*. Retrieved from https://ec.europa.eu/info/sites/info/files/factsheet_1_en.pdf

European Council; Council of the EU. (2020, April 15th). *A Roadmap for Recovery. Towards a more resilient, sustainable and fair Europe*. Retrieved from consilium.europa.eu: https://www.consilium.europa.eu/media/43384/roadmap-for-recovery-final-21-04-2020.pdf

European Council. (2020, April 23rd). *Conclusions of the President of the European Council following the video conference of the members of the European Council, 23 April 2020*. Retrieved from https://www.consilium.europa.eu/en/press/press-releases/2020/04/23/conclusions-by-president-charles-michel-following-the-video-conference-with-members-of-the-european-council-on-23-april-2020/

Farrell, H. (2020). *A Most Lonely Union: The EU is a creature of multilateralism. Can it survive in a deglobalized world?* Retrieved from Foreign Policy: https://foreignpolicy.com/2020/04/03/brexit-european-union-deglobalization/

Fossum, J. E. (2017). European federalism: Pitfalls and possibilities. *European Law Journal, 23*(5), 361–379.

Herszenhorn, D. M., & Wheaton, S. (2020, April 7th). *How Europe failed the coronavirus test*. Retrieved from POLITICO: https://www.politico.eu/article/coronavirus-europe-failed-the-test/

Heywood, P. M., & McLaren, L. (2010). Mediterranean Europe. In K. S. Dyson, *Which Europe?: The politics of differentiated integration (Palgrave Studies in European Union Politics)* (pp. 170–183). New York: Palgrave Macmillan.

Hinarejos, A. (2013). Fiscal Federalism in the European Union: Evolution and Future Choices for EMU. *Common Market Law Review, 50*, 1621–1642.

Hopkin, J. (2020). *Anti-system politics: The crisis of market liberalism in rich democracies*. New York: Oxford University Press.

Irwin, D. (2020, May 5th). *The pandemic adds momentum to the deglobalisation trend.* Retrieved from voxeu.org: https://voxeu.org/article/pandemic-adds-momentum-deglobalisation-trend

Janning, J. (2005). Leadership Coalitions and Change: The Role of States in the European Union. *International Affairs (Royal Institute of International Affairs 1944), 81*(4), 821–833.

Keohane, R. O. (1990). Multilateralism: An Agenda for Research. *International Journal (Toronto), 45*(4), 731–764.

Keohane, R., Macedo, S., & Moravcsik, A. (2009). Democracy-Enhancing Multilateralism. *International Organization, 63*(1), 1–31.

Khan, M. (2020, June 7th). *Europe's capitals take aim at €750bn recovery plan.* Retrieved from Financial Times: https://www.ft.com/content/f31722d0-b875-46a9-82e6-4449758bf366

Kurz, S. (2020, February 16th). *The "frugal four" advocate a responsible EU budget.* Retrieved from Financial Times: https://www.ft.com/content/7faae690-4e65-11ea-95a0-43d18ec715f5

Ladi, S., & Graziano, P. R. (2010). "Fast Forward" Europeanization: Welfare State Reform in Light of the Eurozone Crisis. In K. S. Dyson, *Which Europe?: The politics of differentiated integration (Palgrave Studies in European Union Politics)* (pp. 108–126). New York: Palgrave Mcmillan.

Lee, G. (2020, May 27th). *Coronavirus: Von der Leyen calls €750bn recovery fund "Europe's moment".* Retrieved from BBC news: https://www.bbc.com/news/world-europe-52819126

Nugent, N. (2010). *The government and politics of the European Union* (7th ed. ed.). London: Palgrave Macmillan.

Rankin, J. (2020, April 23rd). *EU leaders clash over trillion-euro Covid-19 aid in online meeting.* Retrieved from The Guardian: https://www.theguardian.com/world/2020/apr/23/clashes-predicted-over-trillion-euro-covid-19-aid-as-eu-meets-online

World Health Organization. (2020, March 11th). *WHO Director-General's opening remarks at the media briefing on COVID-19-11 March 2020.* Retrieved from: https://www.who.int/dg/speeches/detail/who-director-general-s-opening-remarks-at-the-media-briefing-on-covid-19-11-march-2020

Zerhdoud, B. (2013). The European Sovereign Debt Crisis—the Call for a Consistent Federal Economic Policy of Europe as a Response to Financial Turmoil. *Transnational Law and Contemporary Problems, 22*(1), 153–180.

Chapter 9

ASEAN and the Challenges to Its Legitimacy

Rizwan Togoo

1. INTRODUCTION

The Association of Southeast Asian Nations (ASEAN) was founded in 1967 and remains the primary intergovernmental organization in Southeast Asia. It comprises 10 member states from the region. The organization was formed when Southeast Asia consisted of nations that were newly independent and were still in their infancy. This was in the post–World War II bipolar world that was dominated by two main rival superpowers, that is, the United States and the Soviet Union. During this era, countries were actively forming alliances such as the Northern Atlantic Treaty Organization (NATO) and the Warsaw Treaty of Friendship that defined their ideological leaning to either the democratic or socialist power.

After their independence in the 1950s and 1960s, the young post-colonial nations in Southeast Asia were going through a period of political instability, lacked political and ethnic unity and most importantly did not have a strong regional defence and security alliance to protect their sovereignty (Keling, Md.Som, Saludin, Shuib, & Ajis, 2011). To address these weaknesses, several countries in the region signed a number of multilateral agreements such as the Southeast Asia Friendship and Economic Treaty (SEAFET), and the now-defunct Association of Southeast Asia (ASA) and MAPHILINDO which comprised Malaysia, the Philippines and Indonesia. This eventually paved the way for the Bangkok Declaration signed by Indonesia, Malaysia, the Philippines, Thailand and Singapore. This Declaration became the founding document of ASEAN. The Declaration stipulates as foremost aims of this intergovernmental organization: the acceleration of economic growth, to promote regional peace and stability, social progress and cultural development in the region, and to maintain close and beneficial cooperation with existing international and regional organizations (ASEAN, 2020a).

Brunei joined the ASEAN in 1984, and after the end of the Cold War in 1991 which saw the end of the civil war in Cambodia and normalization of Vietnamese-American relations that bought relative peace in Southeast Asia, the membership of the organization increased with Vietnam becoming the seventh member in 1995; and Myanmar and Cambodia joining in 1997 and Laos in 1999.

Pursuant to Article 2 of the 1976 Treaty of Amity and Cooperation in Southeast Asia (TAC), the core principles of ASEAN multilateralism are

(1) mutual respect for the independence, sovereignty, equality, territorial integrity and national identity of all nations,
(2) the right of every state to lead its national existence free from external interference, subversion or coercion,
(3) non-interference in the internal affairs of one another,
(4) settlement of differences or disputes by peaceful manner,
(5) renunciation of the threat or use of force, and
(6) effective cooperation among themselves (ASEAN, 2020b).

Over the years, ASEAN has earned a reputation of one of the most economically successful regional groupings. The organization has managed to maintain peaceful relations between the member states. A notable achievement of the organization is that ever since its inception, none of the member states has ever engaged in an armed conflict with another member (Nischalke, 2000). However, it continues to face various challenges both domestically and internationally, such as questions on the doubts about its commitment towards human rights and its role in the Asia-pacific region that raises questions about the legitimacy of the organization in international affairs. Among the biggest issues, ASEAN faces, which undermines its legitimacy in the international community, is the Rohingya humanitarian crisis, and the international community has persistently criticized ASEAN for its role in the crisis.

Hence, this chapter focuses on the challenges to the legitimacy of ASEAN in the international community that prevents the organization from playing a more proactive role in international relations. This chapter argues that a lack of proper international coordination hampers ASEAN to pursue a unified approach to many issues in regional affairs. The structure of this chapter is as follows: The next section provides a brief overview of the foreign policy of ASEAN and discusses the decision-making process of the organization, specifically focusing on ASEAN's external relations. The section also analyses how often the member states have a common consensus and similar priorities on many core issues. The third section discusses the ASEAN response to the

Rohingya humanitarian crisis that emerged as a major challenge to the legitimacy of the organization. It details how ASEAN has failed to come up with a strong and united response to the crisis. The fourth section examines how ASEAN deals with the threat of losing its influence in the Asia Pacific region and its reputation as the major player in the Asian continent. The section particularly studies factors that contribute to ASEAN's diminishing position in international affairs and it also suggests a number of steps that could help ASEAN to better respond to humanitarian crises and preserve its influence in the Asia-Pacific region. Next, based on the examples of the Rohingya crisis and developments in the Asia-Pacific region, it discusses future challenges to ASEAN multilateralism and possible solutions. The final section provides some concluding remarks.

2. THE ASEAN DECISION-MAKING PROCESS AND ITS EXTERNAL RELATIONS

Ever since its founding in 1967, ASEAN has strived to maintain sustainable peace and stability in Southeast Asia with greater regional integration and has constantly engaged in conflict management among member states to solve any internal dispute that exists within the organization. This is reflected in the ASEAN Declaration of 1967, which states that while the organization does not encourage interference in intrastate conflicts, but as far as interstate conflict is concerned, ASEAN adopts a method of conflict prevention (Soomro, 2017).

This kind of strategy is extremely crucial for an organization like ASEAN that inherits a long history of conflict and disputes among member states prior to its inception. In fact, the period when ASEAN came into existence was when the regional situation in Southeast Asia deeply fractured in many ways, to name a few: Indonesia had just emerged from a violent conflict with Malaysia (better known as *Konfrontasi*), Singapore and Malaysia had gone through a bitter separation based on political and economic differences, and the Philippines and Malaysia were engaged in conflict over Sabah, which meant that Southeast Asian countries were in a struggle for survival in a post–Cold War situation (ASEAN, 2001).

As a consequence of the bitter past many of the ASEAN member states have had with each other prior to the Bangkok declaration, it would be logical to assume that many times on many critical issues member states would be on the opposite end of the spectrum, and this creates a major challenge for ASEAN to ensure a fair decision-making process where no member states feels left out or treated unfairly.

According to Feraru (2015), ASEAN has adopted a mechanism that has so far prevented any intra-regional conflicts into escalating into a major armed conflict and has built confidence among its member states. However, its sovereignty centred decision-making process acts as a deterrence to greater regional integration. The founding reason of ASEAN was to neutralize any prospects of intra-regional or outside meddling in any of the member states with the aim to secure internal political stability. On the other hand, leaders in the region also desired to foster greater integration and cooperation among the member states to prevent any power intervention in the region (Feraru, 2015, p. 28). This combination of sovereignty and regional cooperation among the member states helps display an image of harmony and strong ties among the member states which is extremely crucial to achieve the required legitimacy in the international community so as to play a significant role in diplomatic issues concerning the region and also deter any foreign intervention in the conflicts in the region.

The ASEAN member states share the similar approach to sovereignty and regional cooperation which they believe will act as a deterrence towards intrastate conflicts and fend off any threats of foreign intervention in the region. To be able to achieve regional cooperation and protection of sovereignty, confidence-building measures between the member states are extremely necessary (Ba, 2009). In case of ASEAN, to develop such confidence between members meant that the power of decision making remained firmly under the control of member governments and the key to ensure mutual agreement among member states on many critical issues lied in "informality" in the decision-making process and fostering of personal relations among governing elite in the body (Collins, 2007, p. 213).

The decision-making process in any international or multilateral organization is extremely important to ensure cooperation among its member states. According to Severino (2006), in an organization where the member states have diverse interests and priorities along with political and territorial disputes, cooperation can only progress "at a pace comfortable to all", whereby in the end all the members reach a common consensus. This creates a dilemma for many organizations like ASEAN, where controversial issues are needed to be discussed and managed to avoid any further escalation, but on the other hand, governments of member states are also depending on the reaction of their local constituencies.

This approach of ASEAN, where decisions are made on the basis on mutual agreement and consensus among all the member states, is often termed as the "ASEAN way". It specifically upholds one core principle, that is, the principle of non-interference that gives the power to individual member states to veto any motion which they deem as against their interests.

The decision-making process in ASEAN involves informal consultations between member states prior to a motion being passed for approval by all the member states. Authors like Jong and Ping (2011) draw parallels between the ASEAN decision-making process and the historical significance of dialogue in the form of consensus and consultation in Southeast Asian history. In the ASEAN region, a commonality among participants and the preference of "we" opposed to "the others" is integral to the dialogue process among the member states prior to the approval of any motion (Jong & Ping, 2011, p. 957).

When analysing the decision-making process and policies of ASEAN, it is visible that there is a clear prioritization to protect the existing power structure, but, at the same time regional as well as international cooperation is sought. The decision-making process of ASEAN, like many other regional and international originations (EU, UN, etc.), is founded on idealism or liberal theory, which is reflected in the "ASEAN Way" of reaching consensus on the basis of equality (Tekunan, 2014). The ASEAN principle of non-interference, which is one of the core founding principles of the organization, is one the most contested and debated issues by scholars when analysing its impact on regional and international peace and cooperation especially after the Rohingya humanitarian crisis in Myanmar (discussed in the next chapter).

Susy Tekunan states that the principle of non-interference makes sure that countries preserve their sovereignty even if there is erratic behaviour from one member of the government (Tekunan, 2014). She also states that human rights violations such as trafficking of people in a particular country are domestic affairs, and involvement from others can only be justified if it has a direct effect on the other country. Tekunan also states that while ASEAN may not be the only organization to adopt the principle of non-interference in their charter, it is definitely the only organization that has taken it at face value.

Corthay links the principle of non-interference to many of the domestic security concerns that are racial, religious, or cultural in nature. These concerns are further complicated since the state structures are weak in nature, and regimes lack legitimacy and stability. This poses a danger to the national security of the member states, and this is where he believes the principle of non-interference comes into play since it thwarts any attempt to worsening domestic conflicts by foreign agents (Corthay, 2016).

Critics of this principle believe that it acts as an obstacle towards reforms as well as towards taking steps to tackle many critical human rights issues such as statelessness, human trafficking, racial and religious discrimination, and protection of asylum seekers and refugees. Amitav Acharya states that the emphasis on national security that is used as a justification for the principle of non-interference is in contradiction to the spirit of regionalism. The manner in which the ASEAN bureaucracy interprets the principle of non-interference supports "refraining from criticizing the actions of a member government towards its own people, including violations of human rights" (Acharya, 2001).

The external relations policy of ASEAN does not include any supranational ambitions like other multilateral organizations, such as the European Union

(EU), where the external affairs policies are an extension of the policies they adopt domestically. The external relations policy of ASEAN is crucial in the sense that: (1) The ASEAN position of open regionalism does not sufficiently distinguish between members and non-members; (2) the close relations and dialogue between ASEAN and other partners in the international community have allowed ASEAN to enhance their reputation as a regional power; and (3) the lack of proper institutional structure in important fields like security in other Asian regions has allowed ASEAN to project itself as a central player on the continent (Portela, 2013).

The UN identifies ASEAN as an important partner in the international community when it comes to maintaining international peace and battling issues such as terrorism and climate change. In the words of the ASEAN Secretary-General Lim Jock Hoi:

> *South-East Asia was able to evolve away from being described as "the Balkans of the region" to a community that provides opportunities for all despite diverse political, economic and social systems. This transformation was achieved through the ASEAN Way, by which member States have committed to peaceful relationships with each other, guided by mutual respect and peaceful dispute settlement.* (United Nations, 2020)

3. ASEAN LEGITIMACY AND THE ROHINGYA HUMANITARIAN CRISIS

Legitimacy in multilateralism refers to the justification and political authority of an organization in international affairs, where a legitimate organization has the right to govern and rule while an organization deemed as illegitimate does not have this authority (Bodansky, 2012). In the case of multilateral organizations, it is the regional stability that such organizations provide, which ensures their legitimacy among their people and also in the international community. ASEAN was similarly founded with the stated objective of promoting regional peace and stability through their socio-economic goals (Narine, 2008, p. 414). The economic achievements of ASEAN member states may have been attained independently of ASEAN but were made possible only with the regional stability that was provided by the organization.

In a democratic system, legitimacy in the eyes of citizens and governments determines the long-term capacity of an organization to deliver upon its promises (Tallberg & Zürn, 2019). According to Morse and Keohane (2014), in multilateralism, where states, international organizations, and civil society actors may oppose each other's policies, it is the legitimacy that helps gather support for their policies and fend off opponents. A suitable example would be that of the Arab League, which has increasingly been facing criticism for failing to protect the sovereignty and human rights of the citizens of its member states particularly the Palestinian people and has also been unable to mediate between many of its conflicting member states. As a consequence of this failure, the leadership of these countries has tried to look for assistance elsewhere in other international and multilateral forums.

According to Junne (2001), analysing the legitimacy of bodies such as ASEAN, which interacts with a multi-level audience, is more complicated in comparison to governments of nation-states. As a consequence of increased globalization, international organizations are at a potential risk of losing their legitimacy and being weakened, the reason being that as more societal actors interact with each other in a more organized manner, the role of the traditional international actors such as multilateral organizations is reduced (Junne, 2001).

ASEAN has historically faced various challenges in the past like the Asian financial crisis and the conflict in the South China Sea that challenged its reputation as the supreme intergovernmental organization in the region but in the years to come the organization faces unprecedented challenges to its legitimacy particularly with respect to the protection of its citizens and human rights (which has been a part of the ASEAN Charter). The ASEAN Intergovernmental Commission on Human Rights (AICHR) was held in 2009 during the 15th ASEAN Summit in Cha-Am Hua Hin, Thailand, with the aim to strengthen regional cooperation among the member states on human rights and was touted to be an integral part of the organizational structure of ASEAN (AICHR, 2020).

According to Poole (2015), the traditional core principles of ASEAN which include the principle of non-interference and sovereignty come across as a hindrance towards the implementation of the stated objectives of the AICHR since these principles mean that domestic governance issues such as the human rights records of states towards its own people are topics that will not be able to make it at the top of the agenda of ASEAN during its annual summits. It also discourages member governments from publicly condemning their fellow member governments for any atrocities and human rights violations. She further points out that the main driving force behind the formation of the AICHR was the "external regional legitimacy", that is, the perceptions of legitimacy held by countries, international and intergovernmental organizations and civil society groups that are based outside Southeast Asia. In fact, the perception that countries outside the region, other international and multilateral organizations, and NGOs had, were linked directly to the credibility and international standing of ASEAN during the drafting process of the human rights body (Poole, 2015).

The Rohingya, who are a stateless ethnic group in Myanmar, have been facing a humanitarian crisis since the controversial 1982 citizenship law that was imposed by the military government in Myanmar that refused to recognize them as one of the ethnic groups of the country. The conflict reached its peak in the past four years and has evolved into a major humanitarian and refugee crisis in the Asia-Pacific region. It has gained attention at a global scale, with tens of thousands of Rohingya fleeing persecution from Myanmar state and armed forces to Cox Bazars in neighbouring Bangladesh and undertaking boat journeys to ASEAN member states such as Indonesia, Malaysia and Thailand. ASEAN faces a critical challenge due to the humanitarian crisis, which raises several questions on its institutions and its lack of a legal or political framework to deal with migrant refugee groups such as Rohingyas and pressure member states like Myanmar.

Vo Xuan Vinh states that ASEAN has refrained from following the steps of other international and regional organizations such as the UN and the EU on outrightly condemning Myanmar for human rights violations (which would require them to go against the ASEAN principle of non-interference) and has instead adopted an approach of "flexible engagement" with Myanmar (Vinh, 2014). The most suitable way to understand ASEAN's reaction to the Rohingya humanitarian crisis is to view their approach towards Myanmar as a whole (Vinh, 2014). The "flexible engagement" policy employed by ASEAN towards Myanmar after the country joined ASEAN in 1997 aimed to include Myanmar in forums and cooperation mechanisms in the region and avoided to mention issues concerning Myanmar in its statements and press releases to varying degrees (Vinh, 2014). In conclusion, the author states that the perception that the events in Myanmar may not pose any major challenges to ASEAN in the short term. This encourages the organization to include Myanmar in the ASEAN community building, and the issues concerning the Rohingya are viewed as a challenge that will take an extended period of time to get resolved (Vinh, 2014).

Ever since the crackdown on the Rohingya community by the Myanmar armed forces, ASEAN has been under constant watch from international organizations and human rights groups who have repeatedly called upon ASEAN to not turn a blind eye to the grievances of the Rohingya and take concrete steps to pressure the Myanmar government. Brad Adams, director (for Asia) of the Human Rights Watch has claimed that: "ASEAN seems intent on discussing the future of the Rohingya without condemning—or even acknowledging—the Myanmar military's ethnic cleansing campaign against them" (Human Rights Watch, 2019).

According to (Ducci, 2018), the ASEAN response to the Rohingya humanitarian crisis shows a complete disregard for the applicability for the responsibility to protect (R2P). ASEAN has traditionally downplayed the treatment of the Rohingyas as an internal issue of Myanmar despite the numerous reports and independent fact-finding missions such as the United Nations Office of the United Nations High Commissioner of Human Rights (OHCHR) report that claims the threat of genocide of the Rohingya people and the conditions that led to "killings, rapes and gang rapes, torture, forced displacement, and other grave rights violations" by the country's military that prompted some 700,000 Rohingya to flee to neighbouring Bangladesh are still present (United Nations News, 2019).

ASEAN has also refrained from using the term "Rohingya" in many of its statements and documents, which appears as an acknowledgment of Myanmar's controversial citizenship law of 1982 Myanmar, which does not formally recognize the Rohingya as one of the country's ethnic groups and stripped them off their Burmese citizenship. This group of people has constantly been referred to as "Bengali" and "foreign aliens" by the Myanmar government and military officials. ASEAN has also shown a negative reaction when granting refugee protection and asylum to the tens of thousands of Rohingyas who were expelled from Myanmar and many of those who had to flee persecution at the hands of the military and referred to them as "illegal migrants" (Ducci, 2018).

The Rohingya humanitarian crisis has been recognized by the international community as perhaps the largest refugee crisis ever in Southeast Asia. In the event of any major humanitarian crisis like that of the Rohingya, it is a responsibility of regional and multilateral organizations to actively participate in relief efforts and share the burden of applying international humanitarian principles such as the R2P as well as mediate conflicts and send peacekeeping troops.

The response of ASEAN towards the Rohingya humanitarian crisis goes against the traditional role multilateral organizations have played in such conflicts. ASEAN has not even termed the crackdown on the Rohingya community as "potential genocide" but has instead on numerous occasions acted as a protector of the Myanmar government from any kind of international sanctions and criticism.

In 2019 the NGO Médecins Sans Frontières (MSF) called upon ASEAN to "show compassion" for the Rohingya community and push Myanmar's government to put an end to the persecution of the Rohingya. They also called upon ASEAN to have a broader conversation with Myanmar and place the exclusion and discrimination of the Rohingya at the centre of their discussions (Médecins Sans Frontières, 2019).

When considering the potential role ASEAN can play in finding a solution to this crisis within the framework of the ASEAN Charter, it can be clearly observed that the two main hindrances for ASEAN to play a more proactive role is (1) the ASEAN principle of non-interference, and (2) the complications of applying Article 20(1) of the ASEAN Charter to the Rohingya humanitarian crisis. When adhering to the ASEAN principle of non-interference, the

Rohingya humanitarian crisis would be considered as an internal issue of Myanmar, yet, the application of Article 20(1) of the ASEAN Charter would require the top decision-making body of ASEAN, the ASEAN summit to take a decision by consensus.

The Rohingya humanitarian crisis has raised several concerns on the future legitimacy of ASEAN in the region. Principle Two of the ASEAN Human Rights Declaration stipulates that every person is entitled to the rights and freedoms, without distinction of any kind, such as race, gender, age, language, religion, political or other opinions, national or social origin, economic status, birth, disability, or other status (ASEAN, 2020c). ASEAN and its member states collectively have been unable to take any concrete steps to even recognize the crackdown on the Rohingya as an atrocity and human rights violation committed by the state on its own people, let alone find any permanent solution to the conflict. The AICHR itself has faced criticism as being a body that is not independent in its assessment, but instead is an organization where members are nominated through their government. Therefore, its role in human rights is limited to education and awareness-building (Chachavalpongpun, 2018). This response from ASEAN might even affect the public opinion of other minorities in many other ASEAN member states, for example, the Hindu and Buddhist minorities in Malaysia, the Christian minority in Indonesia and the Muslim minority in the Philippines, who have also allegedly faced discrimination and inequality in their countries. This can lead to civil society groups and other NGOs to directly approach international organizations like the UN and EU instead of presenting their protests to the AICHR.

This failure and lack of initiative on the part of ASEAN to be a more people-centred organization and find a sustainable solution to the Rohingya conflict may lead to a crucial loss in the legitimacy of the organization (The Singapore Institute of International Affairs, 2020). While the role of the governments of member states like Malaysia and Indonesia is also very important in finding a solution to this crisis, there still is a sense of discontent among these countries that despite their numerous attempts ASEAN has not been able to develop the required framework to confront the Myanmar government. Therefore, they choose to directly engage with the government of Bangladesh and other multilateral bodies such as the UN and the Organization of Islamic Cooperation (OIC). According to Tobing (2018), ASEAN has always been frozen when dealing with sensitive issues of member states such as the Rohingya crisis. The ASEAN approach of "constructive engagement" with Myanmar, where ASEAN is in consultation with Myanmar without criticizing them in public, has not yielded any significant changes with respect to Myanmar's treatment of the Rohingyas.

In order to keep their legitimacy intact and continue to be recognized as the principal multilateral organization in the region, ASEAN must come to terms with the fact that the existing policy of non-interference—refraining from outrightly condemning and taking strong actions against its member states towards many critical issues in the region like the Rohingya crisis—is something that is not possible to continue with, especially in the era of globalization where multilateralism is touted as the key to strengthening economic and social progress. The Rohingya crisis is a disturbing example of how a domestic issue of religious and racial discrimination can evolve into a transnational refugee and humanitarian conflict (The Singapore Institute of International Affairs, 2020).

4. THE ROLE OF ASEAN IN THE ASIA-PACIFIC REGION AND THREATS OF CONCEDING INFLUENCE

ASEAN has, over the years, positioned itself as a multilateral organization that plays a key role in shaping the regional security and social order of not only in Southeast Asia but throughout the Asia-Pacific region.

According to Yates (2016), the role that ASEAN has played in the Asia-Pacific region can be described as that of a "primary manager", where it has taken up the diplomatic responsibility of working on intra-regional relations and establishing the normative framework of governing relations on the core principle of non-interference. Yates furtherer states that the reason ASEAN has been able to maintain this role of a "primary manager" is due to its ability to reclaim , refine and renegotiate its evolving role in the region.

Fenna Egberink and Frans-Paul van der Putten state that the lack of internal coordination and differences between the member states impair ASEAN's role as a multilateral organization in the region and limit its progress (Egberink & Putten, 2011). This can be seen in the case of the ASEAN security forum, which was founded in 1994 with the purpose of filling in the void for a body to manage relations among countries in the region after the end of the Cold War, but has failed a develop a proper binding framework.

China, due to its increasing economic footprint in the Asia-Pacific region, can be singled out as a significant threat to ASEAN's legitimacy as an influential player in the region. The ongoing conflict in the South China Sea is one of many areas where intrusions by China within the region and directly into the ASEAN member states governments have undermined the perception of ASEAN as the principal guardian of the sovereignty and interests of its member states and partners in the region.

Evelyn Goh concludes that the ASEAN led multilateralism in the region requires a major revaluation. The reasons are the regional maritime conflicts in the South China Sea where China has been asserting its dominance and presence over the United States and its transpacific allies like Japan. This increasing assertiveness of China puts ASEAN in a tight spot where it is facing complications with its relations with China with regard to the maritime disputes and at the same time tries to preserve its partnership with the United States, which has been increasing its security footprint in East Asia. Goh states that such a status quo suggests that ASEAN-led multilateralism in the region is more instrumental and less effective in mediating conflicts, leaving room for the big powers to play kingmakers in the region (Goh, 2014).

Yanmei Xie suggests that the rising economic footprint of China in the Asia-Pacific region, which includes many of the ASEAN member states, gives China the opportunity to keep tight control over Southeast Asia, which has been easier due to internal differences among the member states. By succumbing to Chinese pressure, ASEAN's unity is being undermined, which might even lead to the dismantling of the organization (Xie, 2016).

Another major challenge for ASEAN is the mechanisms of its security policy. Ever since its inception in 1967, ASEAN has been perceived as an organization whose security policy is more aligned towards the anti-communist western superpowers, it was only after 1975 that global economics and politics compelled them to develop much friendlier relations with China (Ganesan, 2000, p. 260). Instead, ASEAN needs to follow the EU and adopt policies where it can design and built its own security independent of any foreign influence. According to Ho (2020), ASEAN must formally institutionalize defence cooperation like the EU has done in the form of the Permanent Structured Cooperation (PESCO) and the European Defence Fund (EDF), ensure common threat perceptions among all of its member states and ensure greater collaboration in security and defence at an intergovernmental level. Also, to make sure that in the future, ASEAN reaches a stage where it can have one central command over its security forces and function in a supranatural manner, it is necessary to reduce rivalries and strengthen relations among member states.

5. FUTURE CHALLENGES AND POSSIBLE SOLUTIONS

As discussed in the previous chapter, the role ASEAN has played in the Rohingya humanitarian crisis, and its diminishing role in the Asia-Pacific region are two major challenges to its legitimacy in the international community. Based on the nature of the challenges identified in the previous section, we will discuss potential solutions to the challenges with respect to ASEAN's future ambitions in multilateralism.

As far as the Rohingya crisis is concerned, it can be clearly observed that ASEAN is facing a dilemma between its commitment to human rights under the framework of the AICHR and its principle of non-interference that is a part of its charter. The existing mandate of the AICHR is not sufficient to make a significant difference to the status quo since it merely endorses the concept of human rights without addressing the exact problems such as that of the Rohingya. A potential solution to the Rohingya humanitarian crisis can be making amendments to the AICHR. Arendshorst (2009) proposes the setting up of an unbiased judicial body like an ASEAN human rights court which will hold the authority to issue binding judgments. Such a move would validate ASEAN's commitment to the international standards of human rights and would send out a message that ASEAN is not turning a blind eye to the atrocities committed by Myanmar on the Rohingya people. John Arendshorst cites the European Court of Human Rights and Inter-American Commission on Human Rights as bodies that an ASEAN human rights court could model itself on.

Another solution to the conflict, keeping in mind the principle of non-interference of the ASEAN charter, is the setting up of an ASEAN-led coordinating body that appears as less intrusive in nature. According to Thuzar and Rieffel (2018), ASEAN can set up a coordinating body that can take up the responsibility to negotiate and coordinate the ongoing Rohingya crisis in Myanmar. Myanmar State Counsellor Aung San Suu Kyi has already pledged to keep her ASEAN counterparts updated on the situation concerning the Rohingya and allow access to ASEAN humanitarian aid (Bangkok Post, 2019), which means that ASEAN is in a position to hold discussions without any unnecessary politicization of this humanitarian conflict. The creation of such a body will send out the message in the international community that ASEAN is serious in finding a sustainable solution to the conflict.

The step that may be viewed as most appropriate and legitimate to the international community would be ASEAN imposing sanctions on Myanmar. According to Arendshorst (2009), ASEAN can sanction Myanmar outside the mechanisms of human rights. Myanmar, in its treatment of the Rohingya minority, has not only violated the AICHR, but other ASEAN principles such as (1) the commitment of all the member states to promote human rights, fundamental freedoms and social justice, and (2) to uphold the UN charter and other forms of international law, which includes the international humanitarian law (ASEAN, 2020c). The ASEAN charter, which was sanctioned by Myanmar, requires all its member states to follow the rules of the charter as a condition of membership. In case ASEAN takes this step, it will send out a clear message in the international community that the organization upholds human rights and security of all of its people, including stateless people such as the Rohingya.

While this move might give ASEAN legitimate respect in the international community, it also risks that China gains a greater foothold in Myanmar and fills in the void that would be created by ASEAN. Such a move would also not guarantee any improvement in the human rights situation of the Rohingya since China has stated that the conflict involving the Rohingya in the Rakhine state is not a problem of human rights but that of unemployment and under-development in the Rakhine state (Anadolu Agency, 2019).

The manner in which ASEAN dealt with the entire Rohingya humanitarian crisis has compelled two of their member states, that is, Malaysia and Indone-sia, who have been among the rare voices in ASEAN that have been critical of Myanmar's treatment of the Rohingya people to engage with governments and other multilateral bodies independently rather than look for a solution within ASEAN. In 2016, in a rare and unprecedented move, voices within the Malaysian government called for a review of Myanmar's ASEAN member-ship in view of the "large-scale ethnic cleansing" of the country's Rohingya Muslim minority (Radio Free Asia, 2016). A few months later the then Malaysian Prime Minister Najib Razak, after joining a rally to the embassy of Myanmar, was quoted on Twitter saying that: "it was not my intention to interfere in Myanmar's internal affairs but that the cruelty against Rohingya had gone too far" (Myanmar Times, 2016). In 2017 after failing to see suf-ficient condemnation from ASEAN, Malaysia in a violation of the ASEAN principle of non-interference called an emergency meeting of the Organiza-tion of Islamic Cooperation (OIC) in Kuala Lumpur that attended delegates from 57 countries, where they called upon Myanmar to end violence against the Rohingya (Wahari, 2017). In 2020 during the ASEAN Foreign Ministers Retreat in Vietnam, the then Malaysian Foreign Minister Saifuddin Abdul-lah called upon ASEAN to find a long-term solution to the Rohingya crisis and demanded that those responsible for the genocide against the Rohingya should be brought to justice (The Daily Star, 2020). Indonesia has similarly condemned the violence perpetrated upon the Rohingya's and called for the humanitarian crisis to be resolved and not merely by making statements of condemnation (Channel News Asia, 2017). Indonesian Foreign Minister Retno Marsudi paid a visit to Myanmar in 2017, where she urged the Myan-mar government to end the violence against the Rohingya (Reuters, 2017).

In order to address the challenges to the diminishing role of ASEAN in the Asia-Pacific region, it is important to understand the manner in which member states in ASEAN have decided to engage with China on issues that concern them directly.

After the outbreak of the coronavirus (COVID-19) pandemic, which originated in Wuhan, China, the first country to report a death outside China was the Philippines. The close geographical proximity and travel and supply chain links to China meant that the ASEAN member states were among the first countries to be at the receiving end of the outbreak. The socio-economic impact of COVID-19 was very heavy, due to the dependence on tourism from China, which constitutes 17% of all the tourists in the region (ASEAN, 2020d).

The effect of the outbreak in China also had a major impact on the supply chains in the ASEAN countries, with China being the biggest trade partner and exporter to countries in the region. In 2018 alone, 17.1% of Southeast Asians total trade came from China with constituted 6.5% of the total foreign direct investment in the region (ASEAN, 2018).

The manner in which ASEAN has responded to the COVID-19 pandemic does not come across as helpful in order to protect its reputation and influence in the region. Ever since the outbreak of the pandemic, ASEAN has taken a very cautious approach in dealing with China, which is reflected in many of their actions and statements. The actions and statements of ASEAN when it comes to reacting to the pandemic are based upon the anticipated reaction of China and governments in ASEAN readjust their behaviour accordingly (Rocher, 2020). A suitable example would be the joint statement that was released after the teleconference between the foreign ministers of ASEAN member states and the U.S. Secretary of State Mike Pompeo which clearly suggested that ASEAN refrained from following the American line and condemning China's role in the outbreak of the pandemic (US Department of State, 2020). According to (Chongkittavorn, 2020), it took three days of work by the coordinator of ASEAN-US relations, that is, Laos, to come up with a joint statement. This was because ASEAN did not want to endorse the strong anti-Chinese sentiments expressed by Pompeo during the virtual meeting.

The manner in which China has conducted its diplomacy post the COVID-19 pandemic reflects that in a bid to keep its prestige intact, they have begun to categorize countries which they consider as friends and enemies. The foreign ministry of China listed 21 countries that offered "friendly understanding and helped"; this list included three ASEAN member states, that is, Thailand, Indonesia and Malaysia (Ministry of Foreign Affairs the People's Republic of China, 2020). Later, the Communist Party of China-controlled media outlet *Global Times* went on to confirm that the list is a signal to states as to where they stand after the open spat between the United States and China over the blame game regarding the COVID-19 (Kim, 2020).

The manner in which Southeast Asian countries responded to the outbreak of the COVID-19 pandemic and refrained from joining the U.S.-led condemnation of China as the country responsible shows a de facto acceptance of the standards and practices of China in the region, and follows a standard rule of not displeasing China, especially when it is facing a critical period (Rocher, 2020). This approach was clearly visible when Cambodian Prime Minister Samdech Techo Hun Sen paid a symbolic visit to China at a critical moment during the pandemic. Chinese President Xi Jinping hailed this support at a critical juncture and described the visit as "A friend in need is a friend indeed" (CGTN, 2020). Similarly, in a letter to the Chinese premier, the prime minister and president of Singapore praised the Chinese government for "swift, decisive and comprehensive measures to contain the Covid-19 outbreak and safeguard the health of their people" (Koh, 2020).

This response of ASEAN member states to the COVID-19 pandemic suggests that economic dependence on China, particularly in terms of tourism and supply chains, compels them to refrain from taking a position that is in complete alignment with their Western allies. There seems to be a sense of apprehension among the ASEAN countries that in case they take any position that does not suit the narrative of Beijing, the Chinese government may use their influence in the Asia-Pacific region to seek economic retribution.

In order for ASEAN to make their policies in the Asia-Pacific region, without the fear of economic and diplomatic repercussion, it is important for its member states to take steps to further strengthen the economic integration among their member states. To achieve this, they need to work on their cross-border policies and develop their domestic industrial transformations so as to encourage foreign investments from other countries (Das, 2017) ASEAN also needs to strengthen the multilateral dialogues with other advanced economies around the world. The ASEAN +3, the East Asia Summit, and ASEAN-EU Dialogue Relations established in 1977 are the examples that show that there is an intent on the part of the governments to cultivate cooperation with other economies, but these relations must be further advanced and further institutionalized (Das, 2017).

6. CONCLUSION

In this chapter, the future challenges to the legitimacy of ASEAN in the international community were outlined, with their response to the Rohingya humanitarian crisis and their diminishing role in the Asia-Pacific region highlighted as two major obstacles.

The Rohingya humanitarian crisis was identified as a major challenge to the legitimacy of ASEAN as an organization that is committed to human rights as guaranteed by the AICHR. The ASEAN principle of non-interference was identified as the major hindrance to properly implement the stated objectives of the AICHR, especially in the context of a major humanitarian crisis like that of the Rohingya. The inability of ASEAN to take any action or condemn Myanmar for the atrocities they have committed upon the Rohingya has compelled member states like Malaysia and Indonesia to engage with Myanmar government and other intergovernmental bodies like the OIC directly in order to bypass the ASEAN channels.

The weakening role of ASEAN in the Asia-Pacific region can be primarily blamed on the rise of China and the economic dependence of ASEAN member states on it. The ASEAN response to the COVID-19 pandemic, where they refused to toe the line of their Western allies, shows that the organization is not willing to risk economic retribution from China. In order to end this phenomenon of economic dependence on China, ASEAN needs to not only further strengthen economic integration between its member states and make reforms in border laws but also institutionalize the annual dialogues they have with other economies like the United States, the EU and Canada.

REFERENCES

Acharya, A. (2001). Constructing a security community in Southeast Asia: ASEAN and the problem of regional. *Contemporary Southeast Asia, 23*. Retrieved from http://www.amitavacharya.com/sites/default/files/Contemporary%20South east%20Asia.pdf

AICHR. (2020). *About AICHR: Structure, Work and History of the AICHR.* Retrieved from ASEAN Intergovernmental Commission on Human Rights (AICHR): https://aichr.org/about-aichr/

Anadolu Agency. (2019, May 9). *Regional development can resolve Rohingya issue: China.* Retrieved from Anadolu Agency: https://www.aa.com.tr/en/asia-pacific/regional-development-can-resolve-rohingya-issue-china/1474035

Arendshorst, J. (2009). The dilemma of non-interference: Myanmar, human rights, and the ASEAN Charter. *Northwestern Law Journal of Human Rights.* Retrieved from https://scholarlycommons.law.northwestern.edu/cgi/viewcontent.cgi?article=1095&context=njihr

ASEAN. (2001). *ASEAN: Building the peace in Southeast Asia.* Retrieved from ASEAN: https://asean.org/?static_post=asean-building-the-peace-in-southeast-asia-2

ASEAN. (2018). *ASEAN Investment Report 2018: Foreign Direct Investment and the Digital Economy in ASEAN.* Jakarta: The ASEAN Secretariat; United Nations Conference on Trade and Development. Retrieved from https://asean.org/storage/2018/11/ASEAN-Investment-Report-2018-for-Website.pdf

ASEAN. (2020a). *About ASEAN.* Retrieved from Treaty of Amity and Cooperation in Southeast Asia Indonesia, 24 February 1976: https://asean.org/treaty-amity-cooperation-southeast-asia-indonesia-24-february-1976/

ASEAN. (2020b). *The ASEAN declaration (Bangkok declaration) Bangkok, 8 August 1967.* Retrieved from ASEAN: https://asean.org/the-asean-declaration-bangkok-declaration-bangkok-8-august-1967/

ASEAN. (2020c). *ASEAN Human Rights Declaration.* Retrieved from ASEAN: https://asean.org/asean-human-rights-declaration/

ASEAN. (2020d). *Tourism Statistics.* Retrieved from ASEAN: https://asean.org/?static_post=tourism-statistics

Ba, A. D. (2009). *Renegotiating East and Southeast Asia: Region, regionalism and the association of Southeast Asian Nations.* Stanford University Press.

Bangkok Post. (2019, Feburary 19). *Asean Rakhine approach: Slow but sure.* Retrieved from Bangkok Post: https://www.bangkokpost.com/opinion/opinion/1631302/asean-rakhine-approach-slow-but-sure

Bodansky, D. (2012). Legitimacy in International Law and International Relations. (J. L. Dunoff, & M. A. Pollack Eds.) *Interdisciplinary Perspectives on International Law and International Relations: The State of the Art*. Cambridge University Press, 321–342.

CGTN. (2020, Feburary 6). *"A friend in need is a friend indeed": Chinese President Xi Jinping hails Cambodia's support*. Retrieved from CGTN News: https://news.cgtn.com/news/2020-02-05/-A-friend-in-need-is-a-friend-indeed-Xi-hails-Cambodia-s-support-NQaqqZUjzG/index.html

Chachavalpongpun, P. (2018, January 19). *Is promoting human rights in ASEAN an impossible task?* Retrieved from The Diplomat: https://thediplomat.com/2018/01/is-promoting-human-rights-in-asean-an-impossible-task/

Channel News Asia. (2017, September 4). *Indonesian President Jokowi deplores violence against Rohingya*. Retrieved from Channel News Asia: https://www.channelnewsasia.com/news/asia/indonesian-president-jokowi-deplores-violence-against-rohingya-9182930

Chongkittavorn, K. (2020, May 5). *Asean link in China-US COVID-19 fight*. Retrieved from Bangkok Post: https://www.bangkokpost.com/opinion/opinion/1912712/asean-link-in-china-us-covid-19-fight

Collins, A. (2007). Forming a security community: lessons from ASEAN. *International Relations of the Asia-Pacific, 7*(2), 213.

Corthay, E. (2016). The ASEAN Doctrine of Non-Interference in Light of the Fundamental Principle of Non-Intervention. *Asian-Pacific Law & Policy Journal, 17*(2). Retrieved from http://blog.hawaii.edu/aplpj/files/2016/09/APLPJ_17.2_Corthay_Final.pdf

The Daily Star. (2020, Janauary 18). *Rohingya Crisis in Rakhine: Asean should push for long-term fix*. Retrieved from The Daily Star: https://www.thedailystar.net/backpage/news/rohingya-genocide-rakhine-asean-should-push-long-term-fix-1855555

Das, S. B. (2017, November 3). *Southeast Asia worries over growing economic dependence*. Retrieved from ISEAS-Yusof Ishak Institute: https://www.iseas.edu.sg/images/pdf/ISEAS_Perspective_2017_81.pdf

Ducci, C. (2018). *ASEAN's Norm Contestation over the Responsibility to Protect: A Comparative Study of the Humanitarian Crises of Cyclone Nargis and the Rohingyas in Myanmar*. Retrieved from Leiden University: https://openaccess.leidenuniv.nl/bitstream/handle/1887/63969/Ducci%2C%20Cecilia-s2097508-MA%20Thesis%20POWE-2018.pdf?sequence=1

Egberink, F., & Putten, F.-P. v. (2011). ASEAN, China's rise and geopolictical stability in Asia. *Netherlends Institute of International Relations "Clingendael"*. Retrieved from https://www.clingendael.org/sites/default/files/pdfs/ASEAN,%20China's%20rise%20and%20geopolitical%20stability%20in%20Asia.pdf

Feraru, A. (2015). ASEAN decision-making process: Before and after the ASEAN charter. *Asian Development Policy Review, 4*(1), 28.

Ganesan, N. (2000). ASEAN's relations with major external powers. *Contemporary Southeast Asia, 22*(2), 260.

Goh, E. (2014). ASEAN-led multilateralism and regional order: The great power bargain deficit. *The ASAN Forum, 8*(3). Retrieved from http://www.theasanforum. org/asean-led-multilateralism-and-regional-order-the-great-power-bargain-deficit/

Ho, S. (2020, March 8). *Areas for improvement in ASEAN multilateralism.* Retrieved from The ASEAN Post: https://theaseanpost.com/article/areas-improvement-asean-multilateralism

Human Rights Watch. (2019, June 19). *ASEAN: Don't Whitewash Atrocities against Rohingya.* Retrieved from Human Rights Watch: https://www.hrw.org/ news/2019/06/19/asean-dont-whitewash-atrocities-against-rohingya

Jong, K. H., & Ping, L. P. (2011). The Changing Role of Dialogue in the International Relations of Southeast Asia. *Asian Survey, 51*(5), 957.

Junne, G. C. (2001). International organizations in aperiod of globalization: New(problems of) legitimacy. In J.-M. Coicaud, & V. A. Heiskanen (eds.), *The Legitimacy of International Organizations.* Tokoyo; New York: United Nations University Press.

Keling, M. F., Md.Som, H., Saludin, M. N., Shuib, M. S., & Ajis, M. N. (2011, July). The Development of ASEAN from Historical Approach. *Asian Social Science, 7*(7). Retrieved from https://core.ac.uk/download/pdf/12122063.pdf

Kim, J. (2020, May 2). *Friends and Enemies: China Is Grading the World's Coronavirus Reactions.* Retrieved from The Diplomat: https://thediplomat.com/2020/03/ friends-and-enemies-china-is-grading-the-worlds-coronavirus-reactions/

Koh, F. (2020, Feburary 24). *Coronavirus: President Halimah, PM Lee reaffirm Singapore's support for China's efforts to combat outbreak.* Retrieved from The Straits Times: https://www.straitstimes.com/singapore/president-halimah-pm-lee-send-letters-to-xi-jinping-affirming-singapores-support-for

Kudo, T. (2012, October). *China's Policy toward Myanmar: Challenges and Prospects.* Retrieved from Institute of Developing Economies—Japan External Tiade Organiation: https://www.ide.go.jp/library/English/Research/Region/Asia/ pdf/201209_kudo.pdf

Médecins Sans Frontières (MSF). (2019, September 13). *ASEAN should show true leadership on Rohingya, Myanmar.* Retrieved from Médecins Sans Frontières (MSF): https://www.msf.org/general-assembly-asean-should-show-true-leadership-rohingya

Ministry of Foreign Affairs the People's Republic of China. (2020, Feburary 5). *Foreign Ministry Spokesperson Hua Chunying's Daily Briefing Online on February 5, 2020.* Retrieved from Ministry of Foreign Affairs the People's Republic of China: https://www.fmprc.gov.cn/mfa_eng/xwfw_665399/s2510_665401/2511_665403/ t1740929.shtml

Morse, J.C., & Keohane, R. O. (2014). Contested multilateralism. *The Review of International Organizations, 9*(4).

Myanmar Times. (2016, December 6). *President, military chiefs meet to smooth Myanmar-Malaysia ties.* Retrieved from Myanmar Times: https://www.mmtimes. com/national-news/nay-pyi-taw/24063-president-military-chiefs-meet-to-smooth-myanmar-malaysia-ties.html

Narine, S. (2008). Forty years of ASEAN: A historical review. *The Pacific Review: Special Issue—Towards ASEAN's Fifth Decade: Performance, Perspectives and Lessons for Change, 21*(4), 414.

Nischalke, T.I. (2000). Insights from ASEAN's foreign policy co-operation: The "ASEAN way", a real spirit or phantom? *Contemporary Southeast Asia, 22*(1).

Poole, A. (2015). "The World Is Outraged": Legitimacy in the making of the ASEAN Human Rights Body. *Contemporary Southeast Asia, 37*(3). Retrieved from https://search.proquest.com/openview/bb1407398dc289c16cb7d77efac3641c/1?pq-origsite=gscholar&cbl=30302

Portela, C. (2013). The External Relations of ASEAN are of critical importance to the future expansion and legitimacy of the organization. *Research Collection School of Social*. Retrieved from https://ink.library.smu.edu.sg/cgi/viewcontent.cgi?article=2946&context=soss_research

Radio Free Asia. (2016, November 30). *Malaysia Calls on ASEAN to Review Myanmar's Membership over Rohingya Crisis*. Retrieved from Radio Free Asia: https://www.rfa.org/english/news/myanmar/malaysia-calls-on-asean-to-review-myanmars-membership-over-rohingya-crisis-11302016160013.html

Reuters. (2017, September 24). *Indonesia foreign minister flies to Bangladesh after Myanmar visit on Rohingya*. Retrieved from Reuters: https://www.reuters.com/article/uk-myanmar-rohingya-indonesia-bangladesh/indonesia-foreign-minister-flies-to-bangladesh-after-myanmar-visit-on-rohingya-idUSKCN1BF252

Rocher, S. B. (2020, April 8). *What COVID-19 Reveals about China-Southeast Asia Relations*. Retrieved from The Diplomat: https://thediplomat.com/2020/04/what-covid-19-reveals-about-china-southeast-asia-relations/

Severino, R. (2006). *Southeast Asia in Search of an ASEAN Community: Insights from the Former ASEAN Secretary-General*. Singapore: Institute of Southeast Asian Studies.

The Singapore Institute of International Affairs. (2020). *The Rohingya Crisis—A catalyst for change in ASEAN*. Retrieved from the Singapore Institute of International Affairs: http://www.siiaonline.org/the-rohingya-crisis-a-catalyst-for-change-in-asean/

Soomro, N. N. (2017). *ASEAN's Role in Conflict Management: Active and Effective?* Retrieved from Asia Research Institute: https://theasiadialogue.com/2017/11/14/aseans-role-in-conflict-management-active-and-effective/

Tallberg, J., & Zürn, M. (2019). The legitimacy and legitimation of international organizations: introduction and framework. *The Review of International Organizations, 14*. Retrieved from: https://link.springer.com/content/pdf/10.1007/s11558-018-9330-7.pdf

Tekunan, S. (2014). The Asean way: The way to regional peace? *Jurnal Hubungan Internasional*.

Thuzar, M., & Rieffel, L. (2018). ASEAN's Myanmar Dilemma. *The ISEAS—Yusof Ishak Institute*. Retrieved from https://www.iseas.edu.sg/images/pdf/ISEAS_Perspective_2018_3@50.pdf

Tobing, D. H. (2018). The limits and possibilities of the ASEAN way: The case of Rohingya as humanitarian issue in Southeast Asia. *The 1st International Conference on South East Asia Studies, 2016*. Retrieved from

https://pdfs.semanticscholar.org/0442/1c38780be8fe7842d70d97185d07b8f6c1a9.
pdf?_ga=2.136817203.2024971692.1591596754-717807462.1591596754

United Nations. (2020, Janauary 30). *United Nations Cooperation with South-East Asian Nations Association Vital for Fight against Climate Change, Terrorism, Organizations' Chiefs Tells Security Council.* Retrieved from United Nations: https://www.un.org/press/en/2020/sc14093.doc.htm

United Nations News. (2019, September 16). *United Nations News.* Retrieved from Genocide Threat for Myanmar's Rohingya Greater than Ever, Investigators Warn Human Rights Council: https://news.un.org/en/story/2019/09/1046442

U.S. Department of State. (2020, April 22). *The United States and ASEAN Are Partnering To Defeat COVID-19, Build Long-Term Resilience, and Support Economic Recovery.* Retrieved from U.S. Department of State: https://www.state.gov/the-united-states-and-asean-are-partnering-to-defeat-covid-19-build-long-term-resilience-and-support-economic-recovery/

Vinh, V. X. (2014). ASEAN's Approach to Myanmar. *Himalayan and Central Asian Studies, 18.* Retrieved from http://www.himalayanresearch.org/pdf/Vol18%20 Nos1-2,%20January-June%202014.pdf

Wahari, H. (2017, Janauary 19). *Muslim Countries Call on Myanmar to Cease Anti-Rohingya Violence.* Retrieved from Benar News: https://www.benarnews.org/english/news/malaysian/oic-request-01192017145129.html

Xie, Y. (2016, July 8). *The South China Sea needs ASEAN more than ever.* Retrieved from International Crisis Group: https://www.crisisgroup.org/asia/south-east-asia/south-china-sea-needs-asean-more-ever

Yates, R. (2016). ASEAN as the "regional conductor": Understanding ASEAN's role in Asia-Pacific order. *Pacific Review.* Retrieved from https://pure.royalholloway. ac.uk/portal/files/25576318/Robert_Yates_ASEAN_as_the_Regional_Conductor_ understanding_ASEAN_s_role_in_East Asian_regional_order_.pdf

Chapter 10

Mercosur: Breaking the Stalemate in a Post-COVID-19 World

Amber Scheele

1. INTRODUCTION

As the world becomes ever more globalized and interconnected, multilateral organizations are simultaneously on the rise to meet the subsequent challenges that these inexorable global forces pose. The resulting renaissance of multilateral organizations has been underlined by the fact that "economic globalization has the potential to ring increased prosperity to all" (Jackson & Sørensen, 2016, p. 199). Even as the world's economy is being ravaged by the COVID-19 pandemic, causing countries to look inward rather than outward, the global forces continue to function. In Latin America, a continent characterized by unique issues deriving from its diverse indigenous and colonial histories and the stark differentials in terms of land size and levels of development between nations, the case of multilateralism entails its own unique problems and shortcomings.

Mercado Común del Sur, or Mercosur, was founded with the Treaty of Asunción, or Tratado de Asunción in Spanish, on the 26th of March 1991 (Nogués & Quintanilla, 1993, p. 294) by Argentina, Brazil, Paraguay and Uruguay, and came into effect in December 1994. This regionally based organization was designed "to promote a common space that generates business and investment opportunities through the competitive integration of national economies into the international market" ("MERCOSUR in brief—MERCOSUR", n.d.) through the facilitation of free trade and the uninhibited movement of goods and people. Headquartered out of Montevideo, Uruguay, Mercosur takes the form of a customs union with a common market (ISEAS, 2018, p. 38), similar to the European Union, which also focuses on trade and economic profitability at its core (Brummer, 2007, p. 1356). As of 2019, the state parties of Mercosur contained a combined GDP of $3.4 trillion (Felter,

Renwick, Chatzky, & Labrador, 2019) making Mercosur the largest regional integration arrangement in South America, the fifth-largest economy in the world ("MERCOSUR—Official website", n.d.).

The founding document of Mercosur is the Treaty of Asunción of 1991, supplemented by the Protocol of Ouro Preto in 1994 and the Agenda de Buenos Aires of 2000. The founding countries of Mercosur are officially known as the state parties. The state parties are in full power and constitute all the organs within the organization. Additional state parties can be added to Mercosur, although they must first be a member of the Latin American Integration Association as in accord with Article 20 of the Treaty of Asunción (Argentina, 1992, p. 6). Beyond full membership or state party status, a country can still become an associated member of Mercosur (ISEAS, 2018, p. 101); however, associated states must have an established trade agreement with the state parties of Mercosur. Associated states can actively participate in the formal meetings and activities of Mercosur ("MERCOSUR in brief—MERCOSUR", n.d.). The currently associated states are Chile, Peru, Guyana, Colombia, Ecuador and Suriname with Bolivia still currently in the accession process. Additionally, New Zealand and Mexico hold observer state status.

The advent of Mercosur is considered to be part of the regionalism wave of the 1990s when new regional organizations were created around the world with the focus of enhancing globalization by employing trade liberalization and democracy (Van der Vleuten & Hoffman, 2010, p. 737), that is, New Regionalism. In general, Latin America's (new) regionalism has been dominated by the political economy over the past few decades resulting in commercial, social and political integration projects, such as the aforementioned Mercosur (Riggirozzi & Tussie, 2012, p. 11). Since its origin, Mercosur has struggled with its internal integration and cohesion, especially concerning the foundations of its customs union. This chapter has five sections in which it will explore an alternate leadership structure which has the potential to overcome these issues of internal multilateralism. Section two explains the case of Mercosur, with the help of several concepts and theories. Subsequently, section three outlines the rising challenges of Mercosur including the pressures towards regionalism, outlined in order to grasp the surroundings and struggles Mercosur is facing daily. Section four outlines the Venezuelan ascension and subsequent suspension from Mercosur to demonstrate how the organization is responding to regional challenges. Section five jumps to a current discussion of Mercosur today in the context of the recent dramatic and still ongoing COVID-19 crisis. Finally, this chapter introduces a possible solution for Mercosur's organizational challenges by advocating for two policy changes in regard to the presidency of the Council of the Common Market (CCM), the highest organ of Mercosur.

2. UNDERSTANDING THE CASE

Generally speaking, Mercosur can be considered a product of neoliberalism due to its focus on democracy, domestic economy (Cammack, 2002, pp. 63, 64), and its strong foundation in regionalism. In this section, five concepts are addressed: regionalism, multilateralism, customs unions, sub-imperialism and macroeconomic policies.

The first concept, regionalism, is defined as "policies and practices of state-based permanent organizations with membership confined to a limited geographical area" (Fawcett, 2012, p. 3). The regionalism wave of the 1990s, which Mercosur was a part of, was heavily influenced by the independence of many South American countries in the 1900s. As a reaction to colonialism and fuelled by the relatively newfound independence, Latin America came together to form a regionally based bloc. In this context, the conceptualiza-tion of regionalism was derived from anti-colonialism independent South American states (Fawcett, 2012, pp. 2, 8). In an ever more globalizing world, multilateralism is an important vector, however, regionalism has expanded over the past two decades influencing the foundations of regional organiza-tions (Brummer, 2007, p. 1355). The concept itself strongly involves "policy coordination through formal institutions, often—although by no means always—this coordination occurs among states located in close geographic proximity" (Mansfield & Solingen, 2010, p. 146). This is a new type of regionalism, and it was adopted in neoliberal economic policies in the 1950s as New Regionalism. New Regionalism combines neoliberal development strategies and regionalism. In general, regionalism emerged as a policy choice for developing countries. This choice emerged to focus on cooperation in the global economy, on cooperation with countries of different develop-ment stages. Meanwhile investing through foreign direct investment (Bowles, 2000, pp. 433–439), and focussing on transnationalization, the phenomenon of global interconnectivity (Bøas et al., 1999; Hettne, 1999:7 as cited in Rig-girozzi & Tussie, 2012, p. 7).

The second concept, multilateralism, is defined in the introduction by Mad-eleine Hosli. Multilateralism incorporates a cooperation mechanism of the regional and international level, focussing on the indivisibility and "diffused reciprocity" (Ruggie, 1992, p. 565), while incorporating a social construction of management, based on solidarity (Keohane, 1990, p. 731; Ruggie, 1992, p. 565). Chapter 8 "The European Union and the Challenges to Internal Mul-tilateralism: A Perspective on European Macroeconomic Governance and the COVID-19 Crisis" by Carolina D'Ambrosio focuses on internal multilateral-ism within the European Union. This chapter similarly incorporates internal multilateralism within Mercosur, as the regional organization struggles with its internal cohesion.

The third concept to be defined is a customs union. Which in its simplest form is a trade bloc with a common external tariff (Gavin & De Lombaerde, 2005, p. 69). Mercosur functions as a customs union and as such only allows internal trade between states, with external trade governed by the customs union. For example, the United States cannot trade with Brazil specifically, alternatively, they trade with Mercosur. This is outlined in Resolution 32 of the reintegration programme Agenda of 2000, which reads that the state parties cannot negotiate trade or economics individually with other countries or organizations (Brummer, 2007, pp. 1369, 1370). Which is in accord with Mercosur official documents: "El establecimiento de un arancel externo común y la adopción de una política comercial común con relación a terceros Estados o agrupaciones de Estados y la coordinación de posiciones en foros económicos-comerciales regionales e internacionales" ("Objetivos del MER-COSUR", n.d.). Explicitly stating that third parties will be held accountable towards any external tariffs. However, in terms of investments, Mercosur does not inhibit foreign direct investment between individual member states internally or externally, it only governs physical trade.

The fourth concept, sub-imperialism, is defined as "intermediaries in the relations between centre and periphery when they are simultaneously both dominant and dominated units; more dominated than dominant" (Väyrynen & Herrera, 1975, pp. 165, 167). Sub-imperialism is a form of super-imperialism which is part of the "Marxist Dependency theory school of thought" (Luce, 2015, p. 27), or "ultra-imperialismus" in German, coined by Kautsky in 1914 (Kautsky, 1914, p. 13). In other words, sub-imperialism refers to the fact that a more powerful state exerts great power over weaker or rival states. Sub-imperialism in Mercosur is exerted by Argentina and Brazil, the dominant actors or "sub-imperialistic agents", towards Uruguay and Paraguay, which are the weaker actors or "periphery countries" within this theory. A periphery country is a country farther away from the core markets and generally has a lower GDP per capita than the other parties within the regional integration scheme (Gavin & De Lombaerde, 2005, p. 75). In sub-imperialism, the dominant actors exert their power over the periphery countries with "economic exploitation" (Väyrynen & Herrera, 1975, p. 170). Sub-imperialism occurs in Mercosur, since Uruguay and Paraguay rely on intra-regional trade, whereas Brazil constitutes most of the intra-regional trade while focusing on international trade (Arestis, Ferrari-Filho, De Paula, & Sawyer, 2003, p. 242; Meissner, 2016, p. 151). Thus, sub-imperialism is present in Mercosur since one actor controls the actions of the other actor by exploiting them on economic terms, which in itself will increase the control of the one actor to the other actor, constituting the hierarchic dependence system (Väyrynen & Herrera, 1975, p. 176). As this issue has been present since the origins of Mercosur, sub-imperialism is an explanation of why the foundations of Mercosur are not functioning properly and why a change is needed.

3. PREFERENTIAL TRADE AGREEMENTS

Mercosur is a customs union with Preferential Trade Agreements (PTAs) quite similar to the European Union. Unfortunately, a customs union and PTAs are often undermined in Mercosur as is regionalism itself. A custom union implies that all participating countries of Mercosur have internally free trade and a common external tariff for those not belonging to the regional organization (Gavin & De Lombaerde, 2005, p. 69). A PTA is in its essence a policy which creates an "institution that provides each member-state with preferential access to the other participants" (Mansfield & Solingen, 2010, p. 147). Therefore, a PTA is a form of regionalism and customs union is a form of a PTA. Generally speaking, PTAs are easier to establish when states are similar in their domestic institutions and economic policies (Mansfield & Solingen, 2010, p. 150). A lack of similarity domestic institutions can negatively influence conflict between member states as it can damage the PTAs and in this case Mercosur itself. Thus, the greater the benefit for a state, the greater the vulnerability if there are internal issues or disruptions (Mansfield & Solingen, 2010, pp. 150, 152). Now having defined PTAs and customs union, this section moves to elaborate two extraordinary issues of Mercosur within these agreements.

3.1. PTA Issues

When a PTA is formed between smaller and bigger economic states, the resulting factor tends to be that the smaller states generally have greater economic gains than the bigger state parties; however, this has not occurred in the case of Paraguay and Uruguay (ISEAS, 2018, p. 123). Nonetheless, Uruguay has been acquiring immense economic gains in recent years. Uruguay's GDP per capita is now the highest amongst Mercosur (The World Bank, n.d.), and Uruguay is considered to be democratic in its government (Boix, Miller, & Rosato, 2013). In accord with several scholars, such as Gilpin (1987) and Krasner (1976), a PTA is likely to fail when there is no hegemonic state present in the combined economic region. Therefore, PTAs are formed to ensure the stability of trade with "key economic partners" (as cited in Mansfield & Solingen, 2010, p. 151). Brazil has proven to be unsuitable as a hegemonic leader due to its historical Mercosur track record. Brazil's behaviour has been dominated by a focus on domestic policies, a sentiment which was made even more apparent during the 1999 economic crisis. The crisis originated in Brazil due to its internally domestic-focused economic policies which eventually backfired and severely impacted their neighbouring states (Meissner, 2016, p. 160). Fuelling the irregular dis-cohesion of the internal multilateralism within Mercosur, which is presented in constant disagreements and several disputes between the state parties, such as Argentina versus Brazil in 2002. These disputes are handled within Mercosurs dispute settlement system (Leathley Wilmer, 2002, pp. 11, 12).

A second challenge is expressed in the state party's usage of Resolution 32, this resolution ensures that each state party cannot negotiate a trade deal with another country or organization on its own (Brummer, 2007, pp. 1369, 1370). Even though this resolution exists, it has been breached frequently, for example, trade deals are made individually, such as the trade agreement between Uruguay and the United States of America in 2007 (ISEAS, 2018, pp. 115, 116). The apparent reasoning for the frequent disregard of this resolution is a lack of willingness by the member states to supersede part of their sovereignty in the pursuit of trade integration. This unwillingness has further implications, as Mercosur does not contain a supranational power needed to steer Mercosur, resulting in national policies often ignoring Mercosur policies (ISEAS, 2018, p. 128). Mercosur has continuously disregarded its regional foundations, which, in turn, has normalized this practice of undermining its foundations; Mercosur is at a stalemate. Argentina has expressed that if state parties continue with trade agreements individually with others, then Argentina might focus more and more on leaving Mercosur (MercoPress, 2020).

A possible reason for the normalization of undermining Resolution 32 can be identified by analysing the history of Mercosur and in particular, how the member states have operated in the space of intra-regional trade. Moreover, it is this type of trading and its dependency on "the size and structure of regional economies" (Meissner, 2016, p. 150), which led to the normalization of this problematic behaviour. The 1990s was a flourishing time for Mercosur, relying on extra-regional trade instead of economic interdependence, the latter being a primary aim of Mercosur, as such a base of normative power within Mercosur can be found. The asymmetry was fuelled by the fact that Brazil constituted most of the intra-regional trade, whereas Uruguay and Paraguay did not, even though they both relied heavily on it (Meissner, 2016, p. 151). This asymmetry re-emphasizes the sub-imperialistic issue within Mercosur, as the "weaker parties" continue to be "weak", whereas the "stronger parties" continue to dominate non-cohesively in Mercosur which, in turn, perpetuates the internal multilateral issues within Mercosur, like sub-imperialism.

In summary, sub-imperialism explains the internal multilateral issues due to self-preoccupation and undermining objectives of the regional organization. A possible solution to these internal issues should be to focus on the internal cohesion of Mercosur if international cohesion can be achieved then the regional bloc will act as one in international trade, which, in turn, is beneficial for all member states. While this lingers, it recognizes that even though two out of the four state parties are regional hegemons, the support of Uruguay and Paraguay is essential for the sustainability of Mercosur (Adler-Nissen, 2014, p. 111). The following section explains challenges to regionalism, such as the Venezuelan accession process into Mercosur because it is crucial in understanding Mercosur's challenges.

4. REGIONALISM CHALLENGES TO MERCOSUR

As Mercosur grew into existence, the founding members, known as state parties, and whom today are the member states within Mercosur, joined the organization for several reasons. Uruguay and Paraguay joined Mercosur seeking visibility on global markets, with their accession to Mercosur, they were able to boost their internal liberal trade investments. Argentina and Brazil's focus in Mercosur are on a stable region via regional integration and through the normalization of "liberal economic policies" (Meissner, 2016, p. 152). However, the larger multilateral ideals that defined the creation of Mercosur have been undermined by internal pressure from state parties prioritizing regional and even national interests. An example of the internal instability of Mercosur is Venezuela's transition and suspension of member states status. The COVID-19 pandemic has only highlighted and propelled many of these pre-existing issues.

Argentina and Brazil have had a longstanding rivalry within Mercosur mostly in part due to their competition for regional hegemonic power. This rivalry influences internal multilateralism negatively. The first economic quarrel between Brazil and Argentina occurred four months after Mercosur came into effect in April 1995. This was promptly followed by a second trade dispute two years later between Brazil and Argentina (IRELA, 1997, p. 7). These internal disputes can be generally explained by the openly stated position of Brazil: the order will occur when "the interest[s] of a dominant state" are followed (Riggirozzi & Tussie, 2012, p. 13). There was an internal issue due to a difference in perception of powers of the member states, and Brazil's ambitions counter-intuitively added a new layer of conflict to the lacking cohesiveness of Mercosur's member states. Brazil's position later developed into a strategic goal of becoming the regional leader in Latin America and Mercosur; however, this was never achieved (Malamud, 2011, p. 2; Riggirozzi & Tussie, 2012, p. 4). Due to its stronger economic influence in Latin America, Brazil's behaviour transformed from collaborative to self-preoccupation in Mercosur during the 1990s (Meissner, 2016, pp. 147, 148). After the first two trade disputes in Mercosur, an intense crisis between Brazil and Argentina broke out, which lasted from 1999 to 2001. This was caused by the devaluation of export tariffs of Brazil which directly caused a larger economic crisis throughout Latin America. Argentina's economy was particularly devastated by the devaluation; a fact that further deteriorated the Brazil-Argentina relations. Unfortunately, both countries had lost sight of their original intentions behind the creation of Mercosur's intentions, based on creating regional stability and growth via multilateral integration. With the reintegration programme of 2000, launched via the Agenda de Buenos Aires (Bouzas, Veiga, & Torrent, 2002, p. 18), Brazilian-Argentinean relations were stable again due to reassurance of their intentions for Mercosur. Even though several crises have originated from the contention Brazil-Argentina relationship, their interest in Mercosur remains strong. Nevertheless, both actors remain self-preoccupied (Pastore & Henry, 2016, p. 206). Accordingly, Mercosur is not functioning as presented in its foundational purposes and goals, owing to the fact that regional integration is being blocked by member states' inabilities to resolve the internal multilateral issues.

Following this constant struggle, member states of Mercosur are unable to focus on the internal cohesion within Mercosur. At best this failing is expressed in the example of upholding Resolution 32. Trade deals with Mercosur can only be made with all of its state parties, as Mercosur is a mission that requires collaboration including a general external tariff. Instead of trading as Mercosur—in line with Resolution 32—state parties of Mercosur still agree on "solo" trade deals, such as Uruguay with the United States of America in 2007 (Adler-Nissen, 2014, p. 111). These actions completely disregard the cohesive mission, Resolution 32, and with it, the foundations of Mercosur (ISEAS, 2018, pp. 106, 109), furthering the internal multilateral issues.

4.1. The Accession Process of Venezuela

A prime example of how Mercosur deals with existential crises can be seen in the events that surrounded the accession and later suspension of Venezuela from Mercosur. Venezuela was not a founding country, however, so far it is the only country that has been an accessional state party within Mercosur. The accession process of Venezuela started in 2006 and was approved in 2012, making Venezuela a state party (Brummer, 2007, p. 1356). Later in 2016, Venezuela was suspended from Mercosur membership over issues surrounding Venezuela's democratic differences from Mercosur's core democratic values. In essence, the presence of Venezuela in Mercosur severely questioned the democratic values that were fundamental to Mercosur which had been undoubtedly a point of consideration by foreign bodies when establishing Mercosur's already-existing international relations and agreements. The entire process of the Venezuelan accession was "extremely controversial" (Meissner, 2016, p. 168). A core value of Mercosur is to promote "democracy in their member states" (Van der Vleuten & Hoffman, 2010,

p. 738). Mercosur had shown to honour this aim as it intervened twice in Paraguay after a military coup, via suspending their voting rights and suspension of the Mercosur bodies (Jatobá & Luciano, 2018, pp. 2, 3), as such a base of normative power regarding democracy in Mercosur can be found. Yet, Venezuela undermined the democratic values of Mercosur, as the Venezuelan government became increasingly more socialistic with the new President in April 2013, Nicolás Maduro (BBC, 2019).

Even though the accession of Venezuela started in 2006, the ratification of their accession did not occur until 2012. Argentina and Brazil were in favour of the Venezuelan accession; however, Paraguay and Uruguay did not agree. Paraguay had blocked the Venezuelan accession, but in June 2012 when President Lugo of Paraguay was impeached due to domestic issues between the Police and the public, Paraguay was temporarily suspended from Mercosur and Venezuela was promptly voted in (Meissner, 2016, p. 168). Once accepted into Mercosur, Venezuela aligned with Uruguay and Paraguay, due to the negative sentiments towards Argentina and Brazil for their treatment of the three smaller state parties. Uruguay and Paraguay had cried out against the sub-imperialism exerted by Argentina and Brazil. Venezuela aligned with Uruguay and Paraguay on this mistreatment (Brummer, 2007, p. 1387). On the 2nd of December 2016, Venezuela was officially suspended from Mercosur as they had "failed to ratify certain agreements" before the imposed deadline (Dreier, 2016; Gaudín, 2017, p. 2). These agreements were designed to bring Venezuela in line with the established norms of Mercosur on the basis of politics and democracy (Dreier, 2016). In short, ratifying Mercosur's resolutions is a standard part of becoming a member states of Mercosur, and this did not occur under the socialist government of President Nicolas Maduro, due to which Venezuela was suspended from Mercosur (Dreier, 2016).

Latin America is a very diversified region, diverse in its "language, culture, politics and level of economic development" (Pastore & Henry, 2016, p. 206), yet Mercosur already exists since 1991. However, as the Venezuelan case illustrated, there is little cohesiveness in Mercosur as there are intense internal multilateral issues. The next section focuses on Mercosur today and the possible implications of the global pandemic COVID-19.

5. MERCOSUR TODAY AND COVID-19 IMPLICATIONS

Mercosur today is in a stalemate, fuelled by the ongoing COVID-19 crisis. Uruguay and Brazil expressed its willingness to reform the organization, Argentina desires to leave Mercosur if there are no changes made (MercoPress, 2020). Mercosur's most challenging issues are predominantly related to internal multilateralism. Such as the continuous struggle between

Brazil and Argentina for power, and Uruguay and Paraguay crying out while trying to lessen the control of the "local hegemons".

In 2021, we are living in a pandemic caused by coronavirus. Officially known as COVID-19, this virus has been spreading rapidly through the entire world since the first couple of months of 2020, starting at the end of 2019. At first, the Latin American hemisphere was spared up until the 25th of February of 2020, when the first case of COVID-19 was confirmed by the Brazilian government (Rodriguez-Morales et al., 2020, p. 1). As per May 2020, Brazil was third in regard to the number of contamination cases of COVID-19, right behind the United States and Russia (Reuters, 2020). In April 2021 Brazil has immense high death rates related to the Corona virus, only second to the USA, who has the highest death toll (BBC, 2021). In general, the health care of this region is quite fragile and has known other fast-spreading global diseases too, there are protocols in place on how to handle this. Still, the situation is a "complex epidemiological scenario" and can have immense consequences, economically and socially (Rodriguez-Morales et al., 2020, p. 2; Baldwin & Tomiura, 2020, p. 59). Most countries have responded immediately with non-pharmaceutical interventions to COVID-19, such as social distancing and the wearing of face masks due to a current lack of a vaccine. Non-pharmaceutical interventions have a direct and indirect effect on the economy (Hevia & Neumeyer, 2020, p. 5), as for now it is to see what those effects are, but not all sectors will be affected the same (Craven, Liu, Mysore, & Wilson, 2020, p. 2). Mercosur reacted immediately to the COVID-19 crisis with an emergency fund, in April 2020, a fund of $16 million was founded to "combat the virus" via doing research, purchasing supplies and implementing biotechnology (Kalinina, 2020; Sabatini, 2020). Besides, the "Declaration of the Presidents of the member states of Mercosur of March 2018" (Arredondo, 2020) was adopted, focusing on the continuance of the Mercosur bodies in times of this crisis. With this, a legal framework in regard to videoconferences was created in April to "streamline the operation of the organization" (Arredondo, 2020).

Meanwhile, Mercosur is in the process of negotiating trade deals with the Caribbean Community, the Gulf Cooperation Council, the Andean Community and the European Union. As of the 28th of June 2019, the EU-Mercosur trade agreement was signed, after a negotiation period of 25 years, on the topics of tariffs, rules of origin, intellectual property and more (European Commission, 2020; Ghiotto & Echaide, 2019, p. 8).

After a crisis, the focus of Mercosur reinstates neoliberalism and regionalism (Bowles, 2000, p. 450), showcased in the 1999 recessions of Brazil and Argentina. After this recession, the reintegration programme in 2000 was founded to boost Mercosur. As a response to the upcoming financial crisis (Gurría, 2020, p. 1), Mercosur should focus more on regionalism, especially since regional groupings are more attractive for foreign direct investment (Bowles, 2000, p. 438).

6. A SOLUTION

Mercosur consists of six institutional organs: The CCM, the Common Market Group, the Mercosur Trade Commission, the Joint Parliamentary Commission, the Economic-Social Consultative Forum and the Mercosur Administrative Secretariat, as is established in Article 1 of the Protocol de Ouro Preto. This Protocol constitutes the Treaty of Asunción regarding the institutional structures of Mercosur (Protocol of Ouro Preto, 1994). The CCM is the highest ruling organ within Mercosur, the leader of Mercosur, and is constituted by the Ministers of Foreign Affairs and Economics of each state party (Protocol of Ouro Preto, Article 4, 1994). This structure is quite similar to that of the Council of the European Union. However, the CCM differs from the Council of the European Union in that all decisions made by the CCM are binding for all member states (Protocol of Ouro Preto, Article 9, 1994). The presidency of CCM rotates every six months and meets "whenever it deems appropriate", in accord to Article 6 (Protocol of Ouro Preto, 1994). These elements of the CCM, although created with the intention of facilitating the core functions of Mercosur, have resulted in the problematic cohesive nature of Mercosur. Internal multilateralism is still challenged, especially via sub-imperialism tendencies, even in this presidency system.

In 2002, voices arose out of Uruguay and Paraguay against the sub-imperialistic behaviour of Argentina and Brazil (Mario Osava, 2002). These voices kept increasing, and even Venezuela sided with Uruguay and Paraguay; however, this has yet to result in any substantial change. Nonetheless, Uruguay is increasingly moving away from its position as a periphery country, as they are focusing more and more on trade agreements, such as the Trade and Investement Framework Agreement (TIFA) of 2007, which reinstates their importance in the region. In order to tackle the problematic sub-imperialism nature of Mercosur, more focus on the bureaucratic structure of the organization needs to be taken as bureaucracy creates the behaviour of an international organization (Barnett & Finnemore, 1999, p. 700). A primary focus should be on democratization within the bureaucracy of Mercosur and institution-building through structural bureaucratic policy reform. At the moment, the presidency of the CCM and the bureaucratic structure of Mercosur that allows it to function is not operating cohesively.

6.1. Policy Changes

A solution to the cohesion issues within Mercosur and the region should focus on bureaucratic policy changes in general, and, in particular, the presidential powers in the CCM need to be reformed. Both Mercosur and the European Union are a customs union, with several organs constituting the organization. The Council of the European Union's structure is quite similar to the CCM, as both are constituted by the ministers of member states and rotate the presidency every six months. Yet, the powers of the presidency are not established in CCM, only Article 5 of the Protocol of Ouro Preto focuses on the powers, solely outlining the fact that there is a rotation every six months in alphabetical order (Protocol of Ouro Preto, 1994). Contrary to the presidency of the Council of the EU, which has established powers, the president chairs the meetings, sets the agenda, sets the work programme and facilitates dialogue with other European institutions (Ambroziak, 2012). Therefore, it is rather apparent that the lack of presidential powers has led to the lack of cohesion in the CCM. As such a reform of the power structures in the CCM particularly to the abilities of the president is needed.

The president of the CCM, for a period of six months, should attain the ability to set the agenda to a similar manner as in the Council of the European Union. Agenda-setting power is incredibly influential in legislation (Andres & Griffin, 2006, p. 106). This would allow for the presidents to choose which topics are to be discussed and for how long they will be a focus within the CCM, and since the president rotates every six months, all state parties will be able to insert their interest and values into Mercosur. Everyone would get an equal voice, while all decisions still require unanimity before being passed. This would increase the internal cohesiveness, as every state party is heard and listened too. Furthermore, there would be an established agenda of which the other state parties and associated states will know what the meeting will be about and based on that assumption they can prepare themselves on the specific topics as addressed by the agenda-setter. However, this structure would require that permanent positions within the CCM are created. The current structure of the CCM is that the heads of the ministries meet when they all deem necessary (Protocol of Ouro Preto, Article 6, 1994); the effectiveness of the CCM is not consistent. Therefore, having each state party elect a representative on the CCM would allow the CCM to operate consistently and would further establish the proposed agenda-setting power of the president. Having this structure would vastly improve the current issues, and further the conversation around the ability to call a CCM meeting, or if they are regularly scheduled, this would potentially eliminate these issues. Currently, the CCM is only required to meet every six months for the change of presidency.

These proposed changes are highly influential and run the potential to be handled poorly. Given the history of conflict between Brazil and Argentina, the possibility of one of these states abusing these new powers over each other is quite high. Of the remaining other states, Paraguay and Uruguay, Paraguay is currently too weak both politically and economically (Gavin & De Lombaerde, 2005, p. 75) to normatively set a strong example of proposed new presidential powers. Therefore, given both Uruguay's economic status and general political neutrality within Mercosur, Uruguay should be the first to harness these proposed Presidential powers.

6.2. Normative Power

To establish the required norms within Mercosur and bring the organization back to its original design, a mentor state should be given the status of mentorship over the organization. This transitionary status and power would help maintain an example that Uruguay would set as the first president of the CCM with the new proposed presidential powers. The transitory mentor country should have the requirement that all agenda items be first discussed with them before being imposed by the new, more powerful president. In doing so this allows for a private critique of these items before they are presented to the rest of Mercosur and the wider public. To this end, Uruguay should be the mentor country, for the same reasons advocated that it should be the first new president and for the more in-depth reasons given further.

Over the past decade, Latin America has experienced significant economic growth, especially Uruguay has experienced a rapid increase. The highest GDP per Capita belongs to Uruguay, as opposed to Argentina, Brazil and Paraguay (The World Bank, n.d.). Furthermore, Uruguay has the lowest Gini coefficient compared to the other founding countries of Mercosur. The Gini coefficient ranks income distribution, to measure the wealth of a nation, which includes its income, health and more socio-economic aspects (Smith, 2020). The outcome of a Gini coefficient can be minimum zero or maximum one, zero being perfectly equal regarding income distribution, whereas one means perfectly unequal income distribution. In the latter inequality between citizens is immense. Additionally, Uruguay is economically stable. Even though Mercosur has experienced some (financial) crises, economic deviations due to the financial crisis were not persistent and soon returned to normal again (Mlachila & Sanya, 2016, p. 584). Looking at the hard numbers, regarding the profitability of asset return for Argentina, Brazil and Paraguay were negative following the crises. Yet, remarkably this was positive for Uruguay (Mlachila & Sanya, 2016, pp. 596, 597). Generally, Uruguay has been economically stable during (most) of the financial crises; underlining the advocating claim made in this chapter that Uruguay should be the mentor of Mercosur. Other actors have noticed the increase of Uruguay's democracy and economics too, illustrated in the example of Uruguay's relationship with the European Union. Uruguay is a very interesting party for the European Union. Moreover, the country's third-biggest trading partner is the European Union, accounting for €3.06 billion of bilateral trade in 2017 ("Uruguay", 2020).

When the democratic wave hit the continent of Latin America after the independence of its residing countries, it still took years for these states to hold democratic elections: Argentina in 1983, Brazil in 1985, Uruguay in 1985 and Paraguay in 1989. According to the study of Van der Vleuten and Hoffman (2010) on the democratic levels of the state parties of Mercosur, Mercosur was deemed to have an "intermediate" form of democratic institutions. From the criteria of this study, regional democracy is assessed via its democratic clauses in Mercosur's founding documents, its mode of intervention in case of undemocratic events and its democratic ratings of all member states are known "to establish the homogeneity of democratic membership" (Van der Vleuten & Hoffman, 2010, p. 740). Of the state parties, Paraguay is ranked the lowest with the label "partly free", while the others are all deemed "freely democratic". Remarkably, it is shown that Uruguay has been established as freely democratic, already since 2002 (Van der Vleuten & Hoffman, 2010, pp. 746, 747). The fact that Uruguay is a democratic country is underlined by their trade agreement with the United States, known as TIFA because trade agreements are formed with those who are politically allied towards each other (Mansfield & Solingen, 2010, p. 152). The research of van der Vleuten and Hoffmann illustrates that a strong common democratic identity can foster a regional organization. As Uruguay has the highest degree of democracy regarding the other state parties, it can be logically considered that Uruguay should be the mentor in the reforms. Moreover, Uruguay is known to have the highest "GDP per Capita vs type of Political regime" (Boix, Miller, & Rosato, 2013). Therefore, as the two most prominent aims of Mercosur are reinstated by Uruguay ("Uruguay", 2020) and exerted in its normative power, Uruguay should be the mentor in the reforms.

Uruguay is becoming more active in the international hemisphere, illustrating that Uruguay is a formidable force within Mercosur, as outlined in the example of a trade agreement with the United States. Due to existing trade asymmetry within Mercosur, Uruguay and Paraguay were forced to solve this trade asymmetry of Mercosur, within their common markets. As a response to this deficit, Uruguay threatened to leave Mercosur in 2006. Even though there were some proposals from Argentina and Brazil to help out, these proposals came with very severe restrictions, and thus Uruguay and Paraguay did not agree. Instead, Uruguay signed TIFA in 2007 with the United States (ISEAS, 2018, pp. 115, 116). Even though this act was not in favour of regional integration, it was a strong sign that the commonly thought as "weaker" countries of Mercosur were not so "weak" after all. Especially since another hegemon, the United States, was willing to sign this trade agreement with Uruguay. This underlines the fact that trade agreements are usually between parties who align in politics and democracy. Both restating the fact that Uruguay is economically and democratically independent, which, in turn, increases its normative power within Mercosur and in its foreign relations.

7. CONCLUSION

At the 55th summit of Mercosur in 2019, President Bolsonaro of Brazil expressed his vital interest in Mercosur "we cannot waste time, we need to carry out the reforms that are making Mercosur more vital, without ideological delays" (Xinhua, 2019). Now is the time to act. Multilateral organizations are rising on the basis of the assumption that economic globalization is prosperous for all (Jackson & Sørensen, 2016, p. 199). Mercado Común del Sur, known as Mercosur, was born with the desire to strengthen the region of Latin America. The birth of this organization happened in the middle of the second regionalism wave, (Fawcett, 2012, p. 3), which had a normative effect on the establishment of its foreign relations. However, since these efforts have been affected by issues of sub-imperialism and regional incoherence, the original Mercosur desires have not yet been actualized. Brazil's early desire to become the local hegemon has proven to be unsuitable due to their behaviour focussing on domestic policies, historically illustrated in their behaviour in the 1999 economic crisis (Malamud, 2011, p. 2; Riggirozzi & Tussie, 2012, p. 4). This crisis was caused as Brazil focussed on internal domestics only, which impacted several neighbouring states severely (Meissner, 2016, p. 160), and further impacted the already contentious cohesive nature of Mercosur. Considering Latin America's history of being dominated by Argentina and Brazil, the local hegemons (Brummer, 2007, p. 1389), the resulting sub-imperialistic issues are apparent and obvious. The weaker states, defined as peripheral countries, Uruguay and Paraguay, rely on intra-regional trade from Brazil and Argentina. The rivalry between the Argentina-Brazil relations is exerted in the several trade disputes in the Mercosur Dispute Settlement (Leathley Wilmer, 2002, p. 11). The case of Venezuela, its accession and suspension process, is outlined as an example of how the internal multilateral cohesiveness is problematic in the functioning of Mercosur. Venezuela became a state party in 2012 and was suspended in 2016 based on not signing Mercosur's resolutions, especially the ones on the basis of democratic values (Jatobá & Luciano, 2018, pp. 2, 3). In 2020, Argentina expresses its desire to leave Mercosur if reforms are not made, and Uruguay and Brazil express their willingness to reform the organization (Mercopress, 2020). The current pandemic has created a unique opportunity for Mercosur to be unified under a common goal, we have already seen what a cohesive body can do; hopefully, this sets the stage for continual improvement for the future. Multilateral organizations reacted immediately to this crisis, mostly with an emergency fund; Mercosur purchased supplies and funded research (Kalinina, 2020; Sabatini, 2020). History illustrates that after a crisis Mercosur focuses on reinstating neoliberal and regional values (Bowles, 2000, p. 450), which would be an extension of the already-expressed desire of many of the state parties to reform Mercosur (MercoPress, 2020). Mercosur is at a stalemate.

A solution is to reform the presidency within the CCM of Mercosur, the highest organ in the regional organization. The powers of the presidency are not established in Mercosur, only that there is a presidency and that this presidency rotates every six months. A possible policy change is to increase the powers of the president via providing agenda-setting power, as this is very influential in legislation (Andres & Griffin, 2006, p. 106). Furthermore, each state party should elect a representative for the CCM because this will increase the cohesiveness within the council as well as improve the conversation and the ability to call a meeting. The first president during these reform changes should be Uruguay to oversee the changes, as Uruguay is in line with the core values of Mercosur of economic interdependence (Meissner, 2016, p. 151) and democracy (Van der Vleuten & Hoffman, 2010, p. 378), ensuring their normative power within the customs union. Adding to the transitional period of reforms is that the mentorship of this period should be overseen by Uruguay, to maintain the establishment of a normative structure that is in line with Mercosur's core values. Only then with strong leadership facilitated by this improved structure, Mercosur will be able to break this stalemate and become the multilateral organization that it was designed to be.

REFERENCES

Adler-Nissen, R. (2014). Symbolic power in European diplomacy: The struggle between national foreign services and the EU's External Action Service. *Review of International Studies, 40*(04), 657–681. https://doi.org/10.1017/S026021051 3000326

Ambroziak, A. A. (2012). The presidency of the Council of the European Union. Managing the process or creating the policy? *Yearbook of Polish European Studies, 15*, 125–153. Retrieved from https://www.researchgate.net/publication/242330214_The_Presidency_of_the_Council_of_the_European_Union_Managing_the_Process_or_Creating_the_Policy

Andres, G., & Griffin, P. (2006). Managing legislative affairs in the twenty-first century. In A. Thurber (Ed.), Rivals for Power: Presidential-congressional Relations. Retrieved from http://libcat.calacademy.org/title/rivals-for-power-presidential-congressional-relations/oclc/875533223

Arestis, P., Ferrari-Filho, F., De Paula, L. F., & Sawyer, M. (2003). The euro and the EMU: Lessons for MERCOSUR. In *Monetary Union in South America: Lessons from EMU: Vol. IX* (pp. 14–36). https://doi.org/10.4337/9781781009642.00011

Argentina, B. and U. *The Treaty of Asuncion—General agreements on Tariffs and Trade.*, Argentina -Uruguay-Brazil, (1992, Chapter 4).

Arredondo, R. (2020, May 2). Mercosur: A New Victim of the Coronavirus?. Retrieved 6 June 2020 from OpinioJuris website: https://opiniojuris.org/2020/05/02/mercosur-a-new-victim-of-the-coronavirus/

Baldwin, R., & Tomiura, E. (2020). Thinking ahead about the trade impact of COVID-19. In R. Baldwin & B. W. di Mauro (Eds.), *Economics in the Time of COVID-19* (pp. 59–71). Retrieved from https://voxeu.org/content/economics-time-covid-19

Barnett, M. N., & Finnemore, M. (1999). The politics, power, and pathologies of international organizations. *International Organization, 53*(4), 699–732.

BBC. (2019, January 28). Venezuela's Nicolás Maduro: Dictator or defender of socialism?—*BBC News*. Retrieved 4 July 2020 from BBC news website: https://www.bbc.com/news/world-latin-america-20664349

BBC (2021, April 7th), Covid: Brazil has more than 4,000 deaths in 24 hours for first time—*BBC News*. Retrieved 16 April 2021 from BBC News website: https://www.bbc.com/news/world-latin-america-56657818

Boix, C., Miller, M., & Rosato, S. (2013). A complete data set of political regimes, 1800–2007. *Comparative Political Studies, 46*(12), 1523–1554. https://doi.org/10.1177/0010414012463905

Bouzas, R., Veiga, P. D. M., & Torrent, R. (2002). *In-depth analysis of Mercosur integration, its prospectives and the effects thereof on the market access of EU goods, services and investment.* Retrieved from https://www.sciencespo.fr/opalc/sites/sciencespo.fr.opalc/files/in-depth%20analysis%20of%20mercosur%20integration.pdf

Bowles, P. (2000). Regionalism and development after (?) the global financial crises. *New Political Economy, 5*(3), 433–455. https://doi.org/10.1080/713687783

Brummer, C. (2007). The ties that bind? Regionalism, commercial treaties, and the future of global economic integration. *Vanderbilt Law Review, 60*, 1349–1408. Retrieved from https://heinonline.org/HOL/Page?handle=hein.journals/vanlr60&id=1361&div=46&collection=journals

Cammack, P. (2002). Mercosur/l and Latin American integration. *Japanese Economy, 29*(4), 54–66. https://doi.org/10.2753/jes1097-203x290454

Craven, M., Liu, L., Mysore, M., & Wilson, M. (2020). *COVID-19: Implications for business*, McKinsey & Company. Retrieved from https://www.aedcr.com/sites/default/files/docs/mckinsey-full_article.pdf.pdf.pdf

European Commission. (2020, May 11). Mercosur-Trade-European Commission. Retrieved 6 June 2020 from European Commission website: https://ec.europa.eu/trade/policy/countries-and-regions/regions/mercosur/

Fawcett, L. (2012). The history and concept of regionalism. In N. Krisch, A. van Aaiken, & M. Prost (Eds.), *European society of international law*: *Vol. 5th Bienni.* Retrieved from http://ssrn.com/abstract=2193746

Felter, C., Renwick, D., Chatzky, A., & Labrador, R. C. (2019, July 10). Mercosur: South America's Fractious Trade Bloc. *Council on Foreign Relations*. Retrieved from https://www.cfr.org/backgrounder/mercosur-south-americas-fractious-trade-bloc

Fischer, S. (1991). Growth, macroeconomics, and development. *NBER Macroeconomics Annual, 6*, 329–364. https://doi.org/10.1086/654175

Gaudín, A. (2017). *MERCOSUR Trade Bloc severs ties with Venezuela recommended citation.* Retrieved from https://digitalrepository.unm.edu/notisur

Gavin, B., & De Lombaerde, P. (2005). Economic theories of regional integration. In *Global Politics of Regionalism* (pp. 69–83). Retrieved from https://www.researchgate.net/publication/281612854_Economic_Theories_of_Regional_Integration

Ghiotto, L., & Echaide, J. (2019). *Analysis of the agreement between the European Union and the Mercosur*. Buenos Aires, Brussels, Berlin: Anna Cavazzini MEP, The Greens/EFA.

Gurría, A. (2020). *Coronavirus (COVID-19): Joint actions to win the war*. Retrieved from https://www.oecd.org/about/secretary-general/Coronavirus-COVID-19-Joint-actions-to-win-the-war.pdf

Hevia, C., & Neumeyer, A. (2020). *A conceptual framework for analyzing the economic impact of COVID-19 and its policy implications*, (1), 1–18. Retrieved from https://www.latinamerica.undp.org/content/rblac/en/home/library/crisis_prevention_and_recovery/a-conceptual-framework-for-analyzing-the-economic-impact-of-covi.html

Holz, E. (2004). MERCOSUR: Lessons from the recent past—The case of the financial services. *Law and Business Review of the Americas*, *10*(2), 299–354. Retrieved from https://heinonline.org/HOL/Page?handle=hein.journals/lbramrca10&id=309&div=19&collection=journals

IRELA. (1997). *MERCOSUR: Prospects for an emerging bloc*. Dossier No 67, Madrid: IRELA.

ISEAS. (2018). MERCOSUR economic integration. In *MERCOSUR Economic Integration* (Vol. 5). https://doi.org/10.1355/9789812309174

Jackson, R. H., & Sørensen, G. (2016). *Introduction to international relations: Theories and approaches* (6th ed.). Oxford University Press.

Jatobá, D., & Luciano, B. T. (2018). The Deposition of Paraguayan President Fernando Lugo and its repercussions in South American regional organizations. *Brazilian Political Science Review*, *12*(1), 12. https://doi.org/10.1590/1981-3821201800010006

Kalinina, A. (2020, March 1). COVID-19: What the world can learn from regional responses. Retrieved 6 June 2020 from World Economic Forum website: https://www.weforum.org/agenda/2020/05/covid-19-what-the-world-can-learn-from-regional-responses/

Kautsky, K. (1914). Der Imperialismus. *Die Neue Zeit*, *32*(11), 908–922. Retrieved from https://www.marxists.org/deutsch/archiv/kautsky/1914/xx/imperialismus.pdf

Keohane, R. O. (1990). Multilateralism: An agenda for research. *International Journal*, *45*(4), 731. https://doi.org/10.2307/40202705

Keohane, R. O. (2012). Twenty years of institutional liberalism. *International Relations*, *26*(2), 125–138.

Krapohl, S. (2015). Financial crises as catalysts for regional cooperation? Chances and obstacles for financial integration in ASEAN+3, MERCOSUR and the eurozone. *Contemporary Politics*, *21*(2), 161–178. https://doi.org/10.1080/13569775.2015.1030171

Leathley, Wilmer, C. (2002). *The Mercosur dispute resolution system*. Chatham House. Retrieved from https://www.chathamhouse.org/sites/default/files/public/Research/Americas/leathley_papevers.pdf.

Lenz, T. (2013). EU normative power and regionalism: Ideational diffusion and its limits. *Cooperation and Conflict, 48*(2), 211–228. https://doi.org/10.1177/0010836713485539

Luce, M. (2015). Sub-imperialism, the hightest stage of dependent capitalism. In P. Bond & A. Garcia (eds.), *BRICS an anti-capitalist critique* (pp. 27–45). Retrieved from https://www.lume.ufrgs.br/bitstream/handle/10183/130439/000979166. pdf?sequence=1

Malamud, A. (2011). A leader without followers? The growing divergence between the regional and global performance of Brazilian foreign policy. *Latin American Politics and Society*, *53*(3), 1–24. https://doi.org/10.1111/j.1548-2456.2011.00123.x

Manners, I. (2002). Normative power Europe: A contradiction in terms? *JCMS: Journal of Common Market Studies*, *40*(2), 235–258. https://doi.org/10.1111/1468-5965.00353

Mansfield, E. D., & Solingen, E. (2010). Regionalism. *Annual Review of Political Science*, *13*(1), 145–163. https://doi.org/10.1146/annurev.polisci.13.050807.161356

Mario Osava. (2002, April 3). Uruguay wil af van Mercosur-dwangbuis. *Mondiaal Nieuws*. Retrieved from https://www.mo.be/artikel/uruguay-wil-af-van-mercosur-dwangbuis

Meissner, K. L. (2016). MERCOSUR the ups and downs of regional integration in South America. In *Regional integration in the Global South* (pp. 147–178). https://doi.org/10.1007/978-3-319-38895-3_6

MercoPress. (2008, September 15). *Uruguay favors more trade accords, with or without Mercosur*. Retrieved 2 June 2020 from bilaterals.org website: https://www.bilaterals.org/?uruguay-favors-more-trade-accords&lang=en

MercoPress. (2020, April 29). Uruguay and Argentina presidents discuss the future of Mercosur—MercoPress. *MercoPress*. Retrieved from https://en.mercopress.com/2020/04/29/uruguay-and-argentina-presidents-discuss-the-future-of-mercosur

"Mercosur latests news". (n.d.). Retrieved 21 April 2020 from https://www.mercosur.int/en/

"Mercosur in brief". (n.d.). Retrieved 21 April from https://www.mercosur.int/en/about-mercosur/mercosur-in-brief/

Mlachila, M., & Sanya, S. (2016). Post-crisis bank behavior: Lessons from Mercosur. *International Journal of Emerging Markets*, *11*(4), 584–606. https://doi.org/10.1108/IJoEM-06-2015-0116

Nogués, J. J., & Quintanilla, R. (1993). Latin America's integration and the multilateral trading system. In J. Melo (de) & A. Panagariya (Eds.), *New Dimensions in Regional Integration* (First, pp. 278–313). Retrieved from https://www.cambridge.org/core/books/new-dimensions-in-regional-integration/latin-americas-integration-and-the-multilateral-trading-system/E206E73011438308F37A8B0A0EC80D9B

"Objetivos del MERCOSUR". (n.d.). Retrieved 11 June 2020 from MERCOSUR website: https://www.mercosur.int/quienes-somos/objetivos-del-mercosur/

Pastore, F., & Henry, G. (2016). Explaining the Crisis of the European Migration and Asylum Regime. *The International Spectator*, *51*(1), 44–57. https://doi.org/10.1080/03932729.2016.1118609

Porrata-Doria, J. R. A. (2004). MERCOSUR: The Common Market of the Twenty-First Century. *Georgia Journal of International and Comparative Law*, *32*(1).

Protocol of Ouro Preto: Additional Protocol to the Treaty of Asunción on the Institutional Structure of MERCOSUR, Argentina-Uruguay-Paraguay-Brazil, (1994). Retrieved from http://www.sice.oas.org/trade/mrcsr/ourop/ourop_e.asp

Protocol of Ouro Preto. (1994). Additional protocol to the treaty of Asunción on the institutional structure of MERCOSUR. Retrieved from http://www.sice.oas.org/trade/mrcsr/ourop/ourop_e.asp

Reuters. (2020, May 20). Recordaantal van meer dan duizend coronadoden op een dag in Brazilië. *Nu.Nl*. Retrieved from https://www.nu.nl/coronavirus/6052465/recordaantal-van-meer-dan-duizend-coronadoden-op-een-dag-in-brazilie.html

Riggirozzi, P., & Tussie, D. (2012). The rise of post-hegemonic regionalism in Latin America. In *The Rise of Post-Hegemonic Regionalism: The Case of Latin America* (pp. 2–16). https://doi.org/10.1007/978-94-007-2694-9_1

Rodriguez-Morales, A. J., Gallego, V., Escalera-Antezana, J. P., Méndez, C. A., Zambrano, L. I., Franco-Paredes, C., . . . Cimerman, S. (2020). COVID-19 in Latin America: The implications of the first confirmed case in Brazil. *Travel Medicine and Infectious Disease*. https://doi.org/10.1016/j.tmaid.2020.101613

Ruggie, J. G. (1992). Multilateralism: The anatomy of an institution. *International Organization*, *46*(3), 561–598. https://doi.org/10.1017/S0020818300027831

Sabatini, C. (2020, April 30). Latin America's COVID-19 Moment: Differences and Solidarity. Retrieved 6 June 2020 from Chatam House website: https://www.chathamhouse.org/expert/comment/latin-america-s-covid-19-moment-differences-and-solidarity

Smith, L. (2020, February 3). The Gini Index: Measuring income distribution. Retrieved 8 June 2020 from Investopedia website: https://www.investopedia.com/articles/economics/08/gini-index.asp

Uruguay. (2020, April 23). Countries and regions Uruguay. Retrieved 2 June 2020 from European Commission website: https://ec.europa.eu/trade/policy/countries-and-regions/countries/uruguay/

Van der Vleuten, A., & Hoffman, A. R. (2010). Explaining the enforcement of democracy by regional organizations: Comparing EU, Mercosur and SADC. *JCMS: Journal of Common Market Studies*, *48*(3), 737–758. https://doi.org/10.1111/j.1468-5965.2010.02071.x

Väyrynen, R., & Herrera, L. (1975). Subimperialism: From dependence to subordination. *Instant Research on Peace and Violence, 5*(3), 165–177. Retreived from https://www.jstor.org/stable/40724778.

The World Bank. (n.d.). GDP per capita (current US$)—Brazil, Uruguay, Argentina, Paraguay | Data. Retrieved 14 May 2020 from https://data.worldbank.org/indicator/NY.GDP.PCAP.CD?end=2018&locations=BR-UY-AR-PY&start=1991&view=chart

Xinhua. (2019). Paraguay takes over rotating presidency of Mercosur—World— Retrieved from https://www.chinadaily.com.cn/a/201912/06/WS5de9c06ea310cf3e3557c65a.html

Chapter 11

China's AIIB in the Post-COVID-19 Era: Challenging the World's Financial Architecture

Taylor A. Garrett

1. INTRODUCTION

With rapid worldwide shifts in the midst of a global pandemic and the United States' increasing withdrawal from its leadership and funding roles in international partnerships like the WTO, the WHO, and the Paris Agreement, this chapter continues to probe the question: How will multilateralism evolve and which global actors will lead its future formation? Multilateral institutions are necessary for dealing with the ever-increasing dilemmas of globalization and the states who lead these collaborative vehicles have a high potential for manifesting their own interests (Hurrell, 2004, p. 34). Of course, a range of actors may step-in to transform the nature of global leadership for their own empowerment; yet, this chapter focuses specifically on the role of China and its regionally based MDB the AIIB.

Only recently entering the field of MDBs in 2016, AIIB is often perceived as a direct challenge to the United States' long-time leading global financial framework conducted mainly by the IMF and the WB (Chow, 2016, p. 7). Contrary to this perspective, AIIB claims its functions complement those of the West's MDBs, respectively because low-income countries (LICs) still have a desperate need for sustainable infrastructure development (Hanlon, 2016, p. 548). For AIIB, multilateral development is not a competition but rather a means of expanding wealth in the region and strengthening states' relationships with their neighbours on the Silk and Maritime Roads (Vanhullebusch, 2017, p. 193). Given China's recent financial success and regional connection to many developing countries, the China-led AIIB has quickly consolidated credibility and leadership in a matter of a few years with 102 approved member states till date (AIIB, 2020g). China itself stands to gain immensely from heading a development bank, a scenario considered in sections two and five. Ultimately, this chapter will answer the question: What is AIIB's future role and ambition as an MDB led by China and which challenges will the bank face as it continues to engage in the multilateral sphere?

To understand AIIB's rising role, this chapter will begin by outlining the bank's unique operations. Subsequently, the second section discusses China's impetus for creating another developmental bank alongside the West's IMF and WB. Section 3 of this chapter brings this discussion into the post-coronavirus era taking a critical look at AIIB's response to COVID-19. Like many other financial institutions in the world, the global pandemic has drastically shifted the bank's focus towards public health infrastructure, sustainable economic development, and supply chain stability. This section goes one step further to examine how the Bank's COVID-19 response will impact its international role. Following, section 4 highlights AIIB's growing future challenges as a burgeoning financial institution. AIIB faces three main challenges: (1) maintaining its commitments to the high transparency and anti-corruption standards; (2) upholding its promises to the Environmental and Social Framework (ESF); and (3) serving member states' evolving needs with accountability. Finally, section 5 reimagines how AIIB's COVID-19 response, that is, its renewed value for supply chain resilience, may have bigger geo-economic implications for multilateral cooperation. Section 6 concludes the chapter.

2. AIIB: FUNCTIONS AND DEMAND FOR ANOTHER DEVELOPMENT BANK

Before diving into AIIB's functions, it is essential to understand the importance of development banks. As Nicolas Verbeek mentions in chapter 5 of this volume, MDBs, which are inherently international financial institutions (IFI), determine the future of development. IFIs are central to the global financial system through their implementation of policy advice, financing for projects and application of financial safety-nets and a "rule based-framework for international economic activity" (Callaghan, 2017). More specifically, financial institutions have a unique role in that they construct and regulate the flows of money to other areas of the world and designate not only global norms, but additionally which actors will have the opportunity to expand under designated norms (Hurrell, 2004, p. 34). Holding high percentages of voting power in IFIs allows powerful contributor states to decide how they use their money and under which conditions they will loan it (Suzuki, 2011, p. 15). Therefore, leading contributors' national value systems directly structure and regulate financial flows on a worldwide scale via IFIs. In turn, leaders of IFI's have the capacity to entrench hierarchies, reflect the interests of powerful states, and determine the global power distribution (Hurrell, 2004, p. 48). Due to the influential capacity of IFIs in the twenty-first century, understanding the dynamics between the leading contributors and other IFI members can uncover and highlight the themes and narratives that guide the distribution of power. This chapter reflects on the potential shifts and new dynamics in multilateral development in relation to AIIB's geo-economic posture and governance structures.

2.1. AIIB Mission

At its foundation, AIIB is a China-led development agency with "a mission to improve social and economic outcomes in Asia" and create greater "regional resilience against potential financial crises" (AIIB, 2015, Article I). It invests in sustainable infrastructure and other productive sectors in Asia and beyond for the purpose of connecting "people, services, and markets" with an ambition to ultimately impact billions of lives and "build a better future" (ibid., Article II). Inherently, AIIB prioritizes its mission as a regionally based bank while designating the possibility for the bank's mission to reach far outside Asia.

Moreover, as a strong supporter of the Paris Agreement, AIIB has the opportunity to play an important role in sustainable development. While infrastructure development is often emission intensive, AIIB seeks to accelerate global climate standards through its cooperation with governments, other financial institutions and private sector investors (Germanwatch, 2019, p. 4). To align with the Paris Agreement's objective of limiting a global temperature rise to 1.5 to 2°C above pre-industrial levels, AIIB would be "required to shift all investments to projects supporting the transition towards greenhouse gas neutrality or have no significant impact on emissions" (ibid., p. 15). While highly ambitious and perhaps costly, AIIB's ability to achieve this task is not impossible, as the discussion of AIIB's alignment with the ESF will show in section 4.

2.2. AIIB Membership and Projects

AIIB is headquartered in Beijing and was officially opened in January 2016 with 57 founding member states. It has a current Authorized Capital Stock of $100 billion with 77% funded by regional member states (Germanwatch, 2019, p. 23). Operating as an expanding regional MDB, AIIB's membership goes far outside of Asia with a total of 102 approved members in 2020 from every inhabited continent. The bank's main shareholders include China (27.4% voting power), India (7.6%), Russia (6.0%), Germany (4.2%), South Korea (3.5%), Australia (3.5%), France (3.2%), Indonesia (3.2%), the United

Kingdom (2.9%), Italy (2.5%) and Spain (1.8%) (AIIB, 2020g). Perhaps surprisingly, many of the top contributors to the Asia-based bank reveal to be Western states, further suggesting a power shift away from the 70-year dominating Western financial framework.

With this background, the bank is becoming more than a regional development bank. In fact, AIIB projects are increasingly proposed and approved for extra-regional members in locations like Egypt, Serbia and Fiji (AIIB, 2020c). After only four years of operation, AIIB has a portfolio of more than US$14 billion and over 70 approved projects (AIIB, 2020h). AIIB's major project sectors include but are not limited to (1) energy (2) transport (3) water, that is, sanitation (4) urban, that is, sustainable cities (5) financial institutions, that is, investing equity and mobilizing private capital infrastructure, and (6) information and communications technology (ICT), that is, digital infrastructure (ibid.). These projects include an expansive array of objectives from upgrading roads to improving sanitation systems to setting up climate bond portfolios. For a newly emerging development bank, AIIB is rapidly developing infrastructure projects at a rate almost comparable to that of the more mature Bretton Woods institutions. While it is true the Bretton Woods institutions focus on poverty alleviation rather than infrastructure development, AIIB's already comparable infrastructure development capacities highlight its fast growing momentum.

2.3. AIIB Non-Interventionist Policy

Apart from AIIB's initial regional scope, its financing intentions—that is, aiding middle- and low-income states to achieve growth and stability—match those of the Bretton Woods institutions to which AIIB assures its own complimentary nature (Hanlon, 2016, p. 546). However, what makes AIIB unique from its Western counterparts is its alternative policy of "non-intervention" (AIIB, 2015, Article 31). While there are many degrees of non-intervention, AIIB's interpretation of the policy holds the bank will not interfere with the domestic political controversies of loaning states (Hanlon, 2016, p. 541). Clearly deviating from the IMF's and WB's *Washington Consensus* policy, outlined in greater depth by Nicolas Verbeek in chapter 5, AIIB is changing the field of international development. Breaking away from Western normative standards, AIIB does not require clients to uphold or perform specific political functions, that is, mandating the adoption of free trade policies, the development of property rights, or the privatization of state-owned enterprises. By allowing loaning states' political scenes to remain separate from borrowing conditions, AIIB is beginning to stage a new global financial framework outside of the Bretton Woods system.

This oppositional policy seeds from AIIB's Chinese roots. Historically, China has been hesitant to fully embrace multilateral institutions, like the UN, for the fear of limiting its own sovereignty. Inherently framed by its view that domestic state control is an internal right, China deeply values state sovereignty on the international level (Vanhullebusch, 2017, p. 200). However, stakeholders need to remain cautious because while AIIB lauds a non-interventionist policy, China itself is not completely innocent of using financial tools to gain geopolitical power. In fact, Beijing's choice to lend large amounts of money to low-income states in Africa and Asia, where the risk of debt forbearance is high, has led to China's acquisition of loaning countries' key national assets upon their failure to repay debt (Schultz, 2017). For example, in 2017, Sri Lanka was unable to repay debts to Chinese state-owned enterprises (SOEs) and as a result signed over a 70% stake to a new, Chinese-built port in Hambantota with a 99-year lease (ibid.). Thus, while a highly contested issue, Chinese non-interventionism in practice may still prescribe geopolitical manipulation, only in a more indirect fashion.

Nevertheless, AIIB formally operates on a non-interventionist policy—a policy which aims to prescribe the opportunity for the global South to rise above the poverty line, a challenge other MDBs have yet to overcome. Moreover, even following non-interventionist practices, a less intrusive policy simultaneously teeters with several challenges including the securitization problem of large foreign investments in regions of intrastate conflict, for example, China's own loss of large investments in Libya and Sudan due to intrastate conflicts and an unfitting non-intervention policy (Hodzi, 2019, p. 5). The gravity of these challenges remains to be seen with future development.

2.4. China's Impetus for Creating AIIB

Outside the Bretton Woods institutions, MDBs are by no means sparse, so what precisely led the Chinese leadership to propose AIIB in 2013? The most obvious reason AIIB President Jin Liqun sums up in three points: (1) "the importance of infrastructure development"; (2) "the lack of funds for financing infrastructure"; and (3) well, for the resolution of these issues, "a bank is needed" (Jin, 2019). Additionally, Jin highlighted that "given China's experience and the experience of . . . so many other Asian countries, [Asia] understands infrastructure development [and how] to pave the path for sustained long-term development" (Jin, 2019). China's own success using economic and infrastructure development processes entitles it to a high degree of credibility in its decision to open an MDB. Yet cautiously regarding Jin's statement, China's development is also an example of the pitfalls of fast infrastructure development, for example, large-scale environmental destruction and the displacement of tens of thousands of people (Dubé, 2016).

While considering China's impetus for creating AIIB, this discussion cannot ignore the role of the United States. Even with the world's second-largest economy, China holds a position greatly disproportionate to its economic weight within the U.S.-dominated WB and IMF despite its frequent advocation for balanced representation (International Division of Ministry of Finance, 2011, pp. 132–133). The U.S. Congress not only repeatedly blocked China's attempts at gaining a greater role in the IM, but also purposely excluded China's involvement in the Trans-Pacific Partnership, a free trade agreement that included most of China's Asian neighbours (Chow, 2016, pp. 3, 12). Taking China's high value for self-reliance and state-sovereignty into account (Vanhullebusch, 2017, p. 202), it is no wonder China decided to create AIIB, which now gives China the representation and influence it has yearned for years.

However, at the same time, United States' fears of China's expanding leadership role are not unfounded. Albeit AIIB is a member-driven institution, China's veto power and AIIB's Beijing headquarters designate China a unique decision-making role (Chow, 2016, p. 22). Heading an MDB prescribes a level of influence and power which allows China to play a large part in writing the bank's rules and promoting its own policy, that is, a policy of non-intervention (Chow, 2016, pp. 27, 42). As noted in the beginning of this section, financial institutions carry the capacity to reframe global norms by flowing money into particular markets and regions at the approval of certain conditions. Presently, AIIB conditions are purely economic due to its non-interventionist policy, though its economic influence alone is enough to tilt the global power distribution. For example, AIIB approved funding for projects under China's Belt and Road Initiative, which aims to intertwine China's economy within economies all over Asia, Africa and now Eastern Europe. Thus, there are exponential benefits to founding an MDB and China's gains from doing so are only in the initial stages.

3. REFOCUSING THE BANK'S GLOBAL ROLE: AIIB'S RESPONSE TO COVID-19

The year 2020 brought one of the most disruptive global crises since World War II. In late 2019, the virus SARS-CoV-2 first spread in Wuhan, China, and created a new form of disease, COVID-19. By the time of writing this chapter, the source of the virus was unknown (Zhou et al., 2020). Subsequently, the world's interconnectedness paved the way for the virus's spread from China and other Asian countries to Europe and the United States as well as

Latin America. At the same time, the pandemic exposed global and national governing institutions' severe unpreparedness for responding to such a crisis. Consequently, the 2020 pandemic produced precisely what Rosenthal et al. outline: "a serious threat to the basic structures or the fundamental values and norms of a social system" (1989, p. 10). In the face of such uncertainty, the world's fundamental values revealed to be emphatically more misaligned than they appeared in the pre COVID-19 global landscape.

Moreover, following the outbreak of the pandemic, global economic activity hit a stammering decline diving the world not only into an even greater health emergency but also into severe financial uncertainty. Governments' inabilities to weather economic disruptions—including rapidly rising unemployment, the breakdown of supply chains and the fallout of countless small and large enterprises—increasingly pressed on multilateral banks to play a critical role in supporting countries to address their escalating needs (AIIB, 2020b). Thus, as the world's labs searched for a vaccination, MDBs, like AIIB, were affronted with the challenges of countering the growing global adversities.

3.1. AIIB's Pandemic Response

Similar to many other development banks, AIIB operationally shifted to respond to the needs of governments and vulnerable populations. Through both actions and rhetoric, AIIB stepped into a bigger investment arena by committing US$10 billion to its COVID-19 Crisis Recovery Facility. More specifically, AIIB promised to put the $10 billion towards "both public and private entities experiencing serious adverse impacts as a result of COVID-19" (AIIB, 2020d). From the perspective of AIIB President Jin Liqun, the AIIB has a "responsibility" to "members who face tremendous pressure to maintain health and safety of their citizens while managing the impact of economic downturn" (AIIB, 2020b). Coming to the table with both empathy and a plan, AIIB revealed to be prepared to respond to the ripples of a global pandemic by taking on a greater role than it previously held. Within the first two months of the global declaration of a pandemic, AIIB approved US$500 million for India to purchase equipment and strengthen its national health system; US$250 million for Indonesia to strengthen hospital readiness, enhance pandemic preparedness and enhance testing; and even US$500 million extra-regionally for Turkey to alleviate working capital shortages and liquidity constraints (AIIB, 2020a).

Furthermore, AIIB's decision to make US$10 billion available was not simply meant to tend to the immediate needs of the crisis. Rather, AIIB's investment considerations additionally proposed a blueprint for long-term sustainability, a solution that would better ensure member states' preparedness for handling future crises regardless of regional or global impact. With deep consideration for the different levels of disruption COVID-19 materialized throughout AIIB member states, the bank released a background document stating its reframed understanding of the impact and needs under the new global circumstances: (1) immediate healthcare, (2), ICT (3) supply chain resilience, and (4) post-crisis infrastructure demands (AIIB, 2020f).

Underscoring the importance of resilient infrastructure, the document denotes AIIB's first focus: tend to member states' immediate healthcare and public health infrastructure needs. By citing the economic vulnerabilities that come with an underdeveloped public health infrastructure, AIIB believes it is crucial to support its developing members in dealing with the current challenges. Given the nature of COVID-19, the aging populations in many Asian countries, like China, Vietnam and Thailand, create a large risk for AIIB member states' populations. Thus, AIIB will prioritize investments to level up the quality of healthcare, that is, affording medical supplies and building sufficient healthcare facilities.

Another essential element for ensuring the states' readiness in responding to the crisis is proper access to real-time information and communication, that is, soft (digital) infrastructure. AIIB's definition of soft infrastructure projects includes: (1) services and applications that allow networks to operate efficiently and sustainably (e.g. building information system and security operated centres), and (2) terminals and devices that optimize infrastructure sectors' efficiency (e.g. smart grids and smart meters) (AIIBe, 2020, p. 2). While robust information can improve healthcare efficiency and epidemic containment, communities first need access to networks which can connect them to the rapidly developing information. Thus, AIIB highlights ICT infrastructure as a second priority in its COVID-19 response. Exemplified by the Ebola crisis in Western Africa, mobile communication and broadband internet have the potential to alter the spread of a virus. Simply texting early warnings and instructional preventative measures to hard-to-reach communities offers the potential to slow or potentially cease a virus's spread to new communities. In addition, ICT can quickly deliver standardized trainings to healthcare workers, as well as other necessary information when transport services are halted. In an unfortunate way, COVID-19 exposed the degree to which many developing states do not have sufficient ICT for proactively responding to crises. In response, AIIB reframed its focus to approve investments for utility infrastructure, which will ultimately permit disconnected communities to gain access to electricity and quality ICT.

One of the not-so-immediate repercussions of COVID-19 was the interruption of supply chains around the world. In fact, the pandemic severely prevented many networks from sending or receiving products and services essential for maintaining individuals' livelihoods. In turn, AIIB classifies its third priority as investments directed towards expanding economic resilience through the strengthening of supply chain networks—a solution to better support sections of populations affected by quarantine or stay-at-home measures. Supply chain resilience includes extending support for public and private entities to diversify production, supplies and markets. To advance supply chain stability one step further, AIIB's COVID-19 response includes funding ICT investments which reduce peoples' vulnerabilities by monitoring critical information and automizing helpful processes. Respectively, in adjunct to AIIB's role in supply chain reformation, the bank's interpretation of how to support member states diversify supply chain networks will be significant, especially amidst China's and the United States' current supply chain decoupling. The importance of supply chain reformation, which guides the nature of geo-economics, will further be discussed in section five.

AIIB's final priority brings retroactive elements of investment action into play: post-crisis infrastructure demand. Although not completely retroactive, AIIB understands the importance of assisting developing economies to invest in adequate infrastructure which will prevent or mitigate the impact of future disruptions. Following the immediate containment of COVID-19, AIIB investments particularly include funding satellites for ICT infrastructure and sustainable cities projects across Asia. Another element of AIIB's post-pandemic plan centres on rebounding the lost time of infrastructure development by increasing AIIB cooperation with various stakeholders to propel the speed of development processes. By 2020 and only four years into its existence, AIIB navigated its first global crisis and reimagined itself alongside its counterparts, the IMF and the WB. While AIIB does not yet have the capacity to engage at the level of the two latter IFIs, it is certainly on track to eventually do so.

3.2. A New Role?

As a multilateral bank driven by a large number of members, AIIB's COVID-19 response reveals how both its modern structure and unified bodies can quickly produce powerful initiatives. Even amidst all the devastation that came with the pandemic, the crisis provided a unique opportunity for AIIB to innovate and test the bank's operational capacity. In turn, AIIB was able to formulate clear, immediate and long-term responses for the prevention and mitigation of outbreaks. For example, only two months after the WHO's declaration of a global pandemic in March 2020, AIIB was already on track to provide direly needed public health infrastructure to communities in Pakistan, Bangladesh, India and Egypt by conducting water sanitation and drainage projects (AIIB, 2020c). Thus, this leaves spectators wondering if AIIB's non-interventionist nature is going to become more status quo.

Crises often pose make-or-break moments for institutions leading social and financial frameworks. When a crisis occurs on a global scale, such as COVID-19, international frameworks' competencies are called into question. The downfall of certain entities will subsequently prescribe a new global landscape which rewards the institutions that best serve the relative needs of the world's populations. Therefore, the post-COVID-19 years will largely determine the nature of global leadership whether it is unipolar, bipolar, or a multipolar stalemate. The future of power distribution is by no means certain because it depends on factors unaccountable for in the short-term, but several of the major players are clear. On one hand, although facing its own challenges of accountability and transparency, AIIB is certainly responding to regional, and even extra-regional, needs which is evidenced by its increasingly more expansive global role. On the other hand, dominant Western-led MDBs like the IMF and WB are still incredibly vital in developing countries, but they have some crucial reformations to make in order to ensure their continued relevance and legitimacy while serving their member states in the post-COVID-19 era (discussed in details in chapter 5). What is apparent is that there is more space in the international community for new leaders to form social and financial frameworks largely because the United States is boldly withdrawing from its hegemonic position. China has taken strides to gain greater levels of influence by establishing AIIB, yet AIIB has confronted its own challenges by stepping into such an ambitious mission. To uncover some of these issues, section 4 will dive into AIIB's future challenges as an expanding MDB.

4. FUTURE CHALLENGES TO AIIB'S AMBITIOUS MISSION

The overarching topic of this edited volume is the consideration of the future challenges to multilateralism based on the discussion of several institutions. Therefore, this section assesses several hurdles AIIB will likely face in the post-COVID-19 era by drawing attention to the bank's capacity to implement projects. Gaining momentum in the MDB arena where highly experienced institutions dominate and lead international social and financial standards is not an easy feat. The globalized landscape, shaped by the United States, demands MDBs follow a certain standard of practice while states' developmental needs continue to increase. Compiling a robust inquiry into AIIB's current institutional record and published documents, research reveals AIIB's most pressing challenges for becoming a reputable MDB in the twenty-first century will be (1) maintaining commitments to high IFI transparency standards; (2) upholding AIIB's ESF; and (3) responding to member states' needs with accountability.

4.1. Meeting High Transparency Standards

Multilateral cooperation needs to be founded on a high degree of trust to function optimally and create a desired impact (Rathbun, 2012, p. 2). As a new bank, AIIB comes to the field with a Chinese background and no history of rapport. Consequently, many states question the legitimacy and credibility of China's new bank, a bank that folds Western standards into an Eastern-born mission. Indeed, one of the United States' biggest arguments against a Chinese IFI in the early stages of the Bank's establishment was the question of whether it would uphold the best standards of practice (Chow, 2016, p. 14). In fact, AIIB rhetoric raises the highest value for transparency and anti-corruption. Therefore, the bank's implementational capacity regarding these values warrants closer attention.

In 2019, a study found growing inconsistencies between AIIB's rhetoric and its action (Horta, 2019). AIIB commits to uphold the Western notion of transparency, that is, the measure to which outside sources can obtain timely and accurate information about the activities of a government or private organization (Johnston, 2014). As a "lean" institution with only 300 staff and one physical location in Beijing, AIIB has widely rationalized its lack of transparency by drawing attention to its priority for organizational efficiency.

Yet, promising to uphold the best international standards while cutting certain practices for efficiency is not entirely viable. In 2018, AIIB adopted the Policy on Public Information (PPI), an extensible policy which outlines a "principle-based" premise for disclosing public information but lacks precise operational rules (Horta, 2019, p. 20). In that, PPI's ambiguous transparency intentions entail several implementational issues such as In section 4, the document stipulates the "Bank shall have due regard to the operational efficiency and financial resources of the Bank when implementing this Policy" (AIIB, 2018b). This clause essentially permits AIIB free rein in designating PPI's applicability and scope within AIIB's transparent practice. By relying on this provision, the AIIB can sideline transparency as long as it can cite efficiency as a reason for withholding information.

Additionally, PPI prescribes another crucial issue regarding transparency through its ambiguous leniency towards time-bound public releases of critically important information. Whereas the WB amongst other MDBs classifies explicit time-lines for releasing public information, AIIB bypasses this formality in the PPI by referring to paragraphs 57 and 58 in another document, the ESF, published in February 2016. In reference to the ESF, it does indeed indicate information disclosure requirements by calling for the "timely" release of documents, yet there is little clarity as to what "timely" means (AIIB, 2016, pp. 20–21). Being somewhat more descriptive, the paragraphs indicate sovereign-backed loans must release information prior to appraisal, whereas other loans (i.e. private sector loans) should disclose information as early as possible during appraisal—these timelines are hardly more specific than "timely". At the same time, paragraph 8 in the PPI further permits AIIB to withhold information if it would compromise "the Bank's credit worthiness or access to capital markets at prices the Bank deems reasonable" (PPI, 2018, p. 4). Remarkably, this leaves spectators wondering where AIIB's accountability comes in. This will be further examined in subsection 3.

At first glance, AIIB documents showcase a rather satisfying commitment to transparency and anti-corruption. Unfortunately, when it comes to the implementation of these standards, AIIB seems to choose not to uphold the best practices for international standards because of its prioritization of efficiency and access to finances. Looking to the future, it will need to transform its transparency standards in order to continue growing trust with its shareholders and in recipient countries.

4.2. Upholding the ESF

Not only has AIIB verbally pledged its commitment to the Paris Agreement, but AIIB published its own environmental and social standards in the ESF (AIIB, 2016). Moreover, being a large infrastructure developer comes with high environmental and social risks—to which AIIB's ESF deems to prevent. Although on the contrary, several studies exhibit that AIIB does not yet meet the criteria of the Paris Agreement (Germanwatch, 2019), not to mention its own ESF (Horta, 2019). Therefore, as the salience of sustainable development and human rights grows on global agendas, one of AIIB's most pressing future challenges will be its ability to adhere to its own ESF commitments.

Exclusively considering AIIB's alignment with Paris Agreement standards, AIIB operations provide a mixed picture. On the one hand, the Bank's lip service gives priority to "clean" and "green" strategies. On the other hand, AIIB strategies do not grant a clear reference to energy sector–related priorities and rather leave a high degree of ambiguity insufficient for effectively monitoring AIIB projects' correspondence to Paris Agreement goals (Germanwatch, 2019, p. 28). Even further, AIIB's recent approval of a US$1 billion loan for coal-fired plants in Indonesia exposes an apparent violation of Paris Agreement obligations to make financial flows "consistent with a pathway towards low greenhouse gas emissions" development (Paris Agreement, 2016, Article 2(1)(c)), not to mention its own ESF (Chow, 2019, p. 25). Thus, if AIIB procedures permit sizable coal-energy projects, that leaves stakeholders to question the quality of standards regulating the bank's approval process.

Again, a closer look at AIIB procedures divulges how efficiency precedes adherence to AIIB's other commitments. In fact, the ESF holds that projects "at the time of approval are not required to meet specific standards, since important aspects may not be known" (Horta, 2019, p. 25). Rather, the "mandatory" project prep-work purposed with uncovering environmental and social risks is malleable to arguments averring unknown circumstances. As a result, after project financing is approved and construction plans are advancing, a project sponsor has little reason to resolve previously unknown ESF risks. This leaves another accountability issue within AIIB and has dire repercussions for environmental and human rights interests. Hence, AIIB does not uphold the standards set out by the Paris Agreement nor its own ESF, a framework that does not impose concise rules for AIIB to follow.

Looking to the future, AIIB will have to face the discrepancies between its words and actions. If AIIB continues to laud "lean, clean, and green" as its core values, it must reorient the operational and regulatory structures of the bank to properly reflect environmental and social considerations. To do so, AIIB must ultimately apply a degree of conditionality based on its rhetoric of sustainability in its pre-assessment of prospective projects' environmental and social risks. Reassuringly, the application of conditionalities based on the ESF strictly departs from the *Washington Consensus*'s structural adjustment policies, for example, the IMF's liberalization and privatization conditions, and allows AIIB to honour its non-interventionist policy while respecting climate and social interests. Meanwhile, staying accountable to any reorientations is another matter.

4.3. Responding to Member States' Needs with Accountability

By 2020, AIIB was implementing projects from Asia to Africa to Eastern Europe. At the same time, the bank's expeditious growth heads a downside. One of AIIB's greatest challenges to credibility and legitimacy is its own ability to remain accountable to transparency, environmental and social commitments. AIIB's MDB model presents a peculiar one because while it strives to constantly increase its project profile and membership, it also claims to be "lean", staffing only around 300 people. Yet, as mentioned earlier, efficiency has consistently led AIIB management to reconcile with loss of accountability. This is largely due to AIIB's lack of credible monitoring mechanisms beyond project approval stages (Beniflah et al., 2017, p. 50). Without proper monitoring and evaluation, AIIB's ambitious goals may pressure it to accept riskier projects so as to reach fiscal targets (ibid., p. 49). In turn, AIIB is more likely to rely on efficiency for financing projects rather than upholding international best practices.

However, AIIB's official documents do contain an "Accountability Framework". This framework formally demarcates the division of decision-making responsibilities for project financing between the president and the board of directors (AIIB, 2018a, p. 1). What is misleading about the "Accountability framework" is that unlike most MDBs, which link accountability mechanisms to independent entities within the institution to monitor practices, AIIB's version assumes the power to approve projects completely to the president without the board of director's involvement (Horta, 2019, p. 17). The framework divides responsibilities with vague consideration for oversight and prescribes the board of directors will primarily perform strategy-making roles (AIIB, 2018a, p. 1). Within the entire document, there is also no clear indication of an external accountability mechanism which inherently misleads the quality of accountability, a hallmark of international best practices (Horta, 2019, p. 18).

Additionally, the bank's governance structure exhibits another peculiar quality. Unlike the weekly meetings, the board of governors conduct in the IMF and WB, the member states representatives in AIIB's board of governors meet only annually or at the request of the board of directors or the board of governors (Lichtenstein, 2018, p. 128). AIIB's board of directors, which is composed of representatives of groups of member states, meets slightly more frequently on a quarterly basis (ibid., p. 127). In turn, the members of both bodies, who are non-residents of the bank, do not have constant physical oversight of AIIB operations which inherently prevents greater monitoring by member states. While AIIB may have structured the bank's governance with efficiency in mind, efficiency may again hinder its institutional capacity to honour accountable practices.

When defining AIIB's greatest challenges, the gravity of this issue permeates into every other AIIB commitment and inhibits the bank from joining the ranks of other MDBs as a credible developer. In fact, AIIB's lacking accountability and preference for efficiency directly undermines its own mission to build better social and economic outcomes for communities in Asia and beyond. With AIIB's increasing role, especially after the 2020 pandemic, the bank should look to incorporating independent watchdogs and increasing civil society involvement in its project approval processes (Beniflah et al., 2017, p. 55). Independent monitoring and evaluation will be invaluable in guiding the bank to create relationships backed by trust and confidence rather than exploitation, which will help AIIB establish itself in the long term. Many member states, mostly from European origin, second the Bank's need for greater accountability through both cooperation with civil society organisations (CSOs) (German Federal Ministry of Finance, 2019) and the application of oversight mechanisms (Netherlands Ministry of Finance, 2019). Accountability is crucial for earning continued Western and non-Western support and building a viable project portfolio, to which AIIB currently relies on cooperation with other MDBs to help fill. To say the least, AIIB's unique structure applies more efficient processes; yet, it needs to be careful balancing efficiency with accountability—a tradeoff that can make or break the Bank's future multilateral success.

5. AIIB IMAGINES A NEW MULTILATERAL GEO-ECONOMIC TRAJECTORY

Imagining the future trends of multilateral cooperation, this section brings attention to the powerful geo-economic potential of AIIB's lending efforts. Briefly, geo-economics is most commonly understood as the application of economic tools (i.e. trade policy, economic sanctions, aid, energy and commodities) to advance geopolitical objectives (Petsinger, 2016). While AIIB is a multilateral organization working in collaboration with a multitude of member states, China's personal geostrategic and security interests can be closely linked with Beijing's motivations for creating AIIB (Andornino, 2019, p. 605). Considering China from a national-international paradigm where external entities, such as the Trump administration, threaten China's future development, AIIB can be used as a multilateralized economic-security tool for China's growing global connections and investments (ibid.). Thus, AIIB poses an important opportunity for Chinese leadership to protect and expand its own geostrategic financing and ambitions through multilateral cooperation.

With this background, AIIB's increased prioritization of supply chain resilience can be understood as more than just a reactive measure for aiding vulnerable communities in the post-COVID-19 era. In fact, AIIB's value for supply chain resilience has the potential to reimagine member states' supply chains and inherently shift the global financial architecture. This could either manifest as the redistribution or the complete decoupling of current international producer-consumer relationships via investment in new infrastructure, business and sector development in low- and middle-income states. Given Beijing's "Made in China 2025" plan for moving China up on the global production value chain (i.e. the concept of becoming one of the world's technology innovators rather than the world's textile factory), AIIB's contribution to the redistribution of supply chains could strategically support China in transitioning its own low value industries to low-income member states. In turn, the China-led AIIB would enable China's economy to focus on higher value industries while simultaneously guiding new geo-economic trends throughout the region and beyond. Significantly, AIIB supply chain policy could also act as a counter-strategy to United States, European, South Korean and Japanese intentions to destabilize their dependence on Chinese markets. Yet, if AIIB cannot step up as an accountable, environmentally responsible and transparent MDB, the bank's potential impact on geo-economic trends will substantially decrease because of its inability to cultivate sustainable, constructive relationships.

6. CONCLUSION

AIIB's recent expansion as well as its rapid and concise response to COVID-19 might structurally alter the financing of international collaboration and development. Its actions during the pandemic showcased the bank's ability to act in a crisis and simultaneously tend to its member states' infrastructural needs. With COVID-19 aid projects already underway in India, Indonesia and Turkey, AIIB appears to be a fast-acting and strategic developer with little to no bureaucratic and political constraints that traditional MDBs face. From this perspective, AIIB would naturally be the preferable choice to many borrowers who do not want to develop under the global financial framework which the United States dominates. For these clients, AIIB provides an attractive alternative model which empowers governments to transform their economies.

AIIB's 102 approved members and growing project portfolio are signal to a shifting global power distribution. As the United States steps back from many of its multilateral commitments, the post-COVID-19 era has revealed both China's and AIIB's eagerness to create their own crisis response initiatives as potential leaders in global development and public health. In other words, the pandemic ignited the ultimate opportunity for AIIB to engage in projects that could boost its portfolio, credibility and relevance amongst member states recipient countries while also giving the bank the stage to redirect geo-economic trends.

Contrary to AIIB's "lean, clean, and green" agenda, a closer look at the bank's projects and commitments uncovers that it does not yet operate with the best international standards. In fact, the bank's operational capacity constitutes the biggest threats to its future role in multilateral cooperation. AIIB's emphasis on "leanness" has hindered its ability to deliver on its commitments to transparency, sustainable development and accountability. As long as AIIB's operational logic is to finance large infrastructure projects in LICs to enable these countries to develop their economies and fight poverty, transparency and sustainability will fall secondary to efficiency. Accountability, on the other hand, is truly the most critical challenge for AIIB because as of yet, the bank has had no interest in independent accountability controls. AIIB's approach is often not rule-based, giving it flexibility to revoke informal arrangements approved by the bank's president when key aspects of projects are unknown.

In turn, AIIB's demand-and-response structures need to fundamentally alter to reflect these principles, that is, transparency, environmental and social responsibility and accountability. Otherwise, AIIB's short and mid-term capacity will not honour the best international practices and the bank's rise will most likely be confined to countries that have good bilateral relations with China. No doubt, all MDBs face challenges related to the issues of transparency and accountability. However, AIIB's accountability frameworks are insufficient in comparison.

Unfortunately, the future of multilateralism is at stake if MDBs, like AIIB, cannot evolve to reflect the aforementioned confidence-building measures which also act as checks and balances. Following a changing power distribution in the global economy, new global financial frameworks are likely to emerge. However, the composition of these frameworks is largely informed by dominant discourses and the international community's past experiences. The rise of China certainly gives way to a new discourse based on the country's own geo-economic ambitions, introducing a different range of values in the multilateral arena, such as non-interventionism, an emphasis on state sovereignty and an authoritarian development model. Yet, if multilateral institutions are serious about improving the provision of global public goods, MDBs, like AIIB, have a crucial role to play in balancing efficiency with transparency, sustainability and accountability. Ultimately, in the post-COVID-19 world, AIIB has the potential to play a large role in the recreation of global geo-economic dynamics; yet, the bank's ability to do so lies precisely in its capacity to build trust with other multilateral actors.

REFERENCES

2015 Paris Agreement. (2016). Adoption of the Paris Agreement, Decision 1/CP 21 (FCCC/CP/2015/10/Add.1).

AIIB. (2015). *Articles of Agreement*. Retrieved 29 May 2020 from https://www.aiib. org/en/about-aiib/basic-documents/_download/articles-of-agreement/basic_docu ment_english-bank_articles_of_agreement.pdf.

AIIB. (2016). *Environmental and Social Framework (ESF)*. Retrieved 19 May 2020 from https://www.aiib.org/en/policies-strategies/_download/environment-frame work/Final-ESF-Mar-14-2019-Final-P.pdf.

AIIB. (2018a). *Paper on the Accountability Framework*. Retrieved 20 May 2020 from https://www.aiib.org/en/about-aiib/governance/_common/_download/paper- on-the-accountabilty-framework.pdf.

AIIB. (2018b). *Policy on Public Information*. Retrieved 19 May 2020 from https:// www.aiib.org/en/policies-strategies/public-information/policy/index.html.

AIIB. (2020). *AIIB Doubles COVID-19 Crisis Response to USD10 Billion*. Retrieved 16 May 2020 from https://www.aiib.org/en/news-events/news/2020/AIIB-Dou bles-COVID-19-Crisis-Response-to-USD10-Billion.html.

AIIB. (2020b). *AIIB to Scale Up Public Health Infrastructure in Wake of COVID-19*. Retrieved 28 April 2020 from https://www.aiib.org/en/news-events/news/2020/ AIIB-To-Scale-Up-Public-Health-Infrastructure-in-Wake-of-COVID-19.html.

AIIB. (2020c). *Approved Projects Overview*. Retrieved 12 May 2020 from https:// www.aiib.org/en/projects/approved/index.html.

AIIB. (2020d). *COVID-19 Crisis Recovery Facility—AIIB*. Retrieved 19 May 2020 from https://www.aiib.org/en/policies-strategies/COVID-19-Crisis-Recovery-Facility/index.html.

AIIB. (2020e). *Digital Infrastructure Sector Strategy (Draft)*. Retrieved 23 June 2020 from https://www.aiib.org/en/policies-strategies/operational-policies/digital-infra structure-strategy/.content/_download/AIIB-Draft-Digital-Strategy.pdf.

AIIB. (2020f). *Impact of the Coronavirus (COVID-19) and Its Implications for Infrastructure Priorities*. Retrieved 29 April 2020 from https://www.aiib.org/en/ news-events/news/2020/_download/Background-Impact-of-Covid-19-and-Impli cations-on-Infrastructure-Priorities.pdf.

AIIB. (2020g). *Members of the Bank*. Retrieved 11 May 2020 from https://www.aiib. org/en/about-aiib/governance/members-of-bank/index.html.

AIIB. (2020h). *Project Summary*. Retrieved 12 May 2020 from https://www.aiib.org/ en/projects/summary/index.html.

Andornino, G. (2019). Economic—Security Nexus in the AIIB: China's Quest for Security through Eurasian Connectivity. *Global Policy, 10*(4), 604–613. https:// doi.org/10.1111/1758-5899.12762

Beniflah, M., Kai-Wen, I., Kaplan, A., & Santdasani, A. (2017). *The AIIB and the Future of Multilateral Infrastructure Financing*. Retrieved 29 April 2020 from https://global.upenn.edu/sites/default/files/perry-world-house/AIIBReportFor CampusCopy.pdf.

Callaghan, M. (2017). *The Future Role of International Financial Institutions*. Retrieved 11 May 2020 from https://www.lowyinstitute.org/the-interpreter/ future-role-international-financial-institutions.

Chow, D. (2016). Why China Established the Asian Infrastructure Investment Bank. Public Law and Legal Working Paper Series No. 133. Retrieved 29 April 2020 from https://papers.ssrn.com/sol3/papers.cfm?abstract_id=2737888.

Dubé, F. (2016). Thirty years of development-induced displacement in China. *Forced Migration Review*. Retrieved 23 June 2020 from https://www.fmreview.org/ destination-europe/dube.

German Federal Ministry of Finance. (2019). *Asian Infrastructure Investment Bank achieves major milestones in its first three years*. Retrieved 23 June 2020 from https://www.bundesfinanzmin isterium.de/Content/EN/Standardartikel/Topics/ Financial_markets/Articles/2019-04-03-AIIB-milestones.html.

Germanwatch. (2019). *Aligning the Asian Infrastructure Investment Bank (AIIB) with the Paris Agreement and the SDGs: Challenges and opportunities*. Germanwatch. Retrieved 23 June 2020 from https://www.germanwatch.org/en/16354.

Hodzi, O. (2019). *The End of China's Non-Intervention Policy in Africa*. New York: Springer International Publishing.

Horta, K. (2019). The Asian Infrastructure Investment Bank (AIIB). A multilateral bank where China sets the rules. Heinrich Böll Stiftung, Publication series on democracy (52). https://doi.org/10.25530/03552.6

Hurrell, A. (2004). Power, institutions, and the production of inequality. In *Power in Global Governance* (pp. 33–58). Cambridge: Cambridge University Press. https:// doi.org/10.1017/CBO9780511491207.002

International Division of Ministry of Finance. (2011). Promotion of the reform programs of voting power in the World Bank made the rising power of developing countries. *China State Finance Magazine*, Finance Yearbook of China, 132–133.

Jin, L. (2019). Public Lecture *by Jin Liqun*. Lecture, Lee Kuan Yew School of Public Policy, Singapore.

Johnston, M. (2014). Transparency. *Britannica Encyclopedia*. Retrieved 19 May 2020 from https://www.britannica.com/topic/transparency-government.

Lichtenstein, N. (2018). *A Comparative Guide to the Asian Infrastructure Investment Bank*. Oxford: Oxford University Press.

Netherlands Ministry of Finance. (2019). *Statement Netherlands Annual Meeting 2019 AIIB*. Retrieved from https://www.rijksoverheid.nl/documenten/kamerstukken/2019/09/06/statement-netherlands-annual-meeting-2019-aiib.

Petsinger, M. (2016). *What Is Geoeconomics?* Chatham House. Retrieved 23 June 2020 from https://www.chathamhouse.org/system/files/publications/twt/WiB%20YQA%20Geoeconomics.pdf.

Rathbun, B. (2012). *Trust in International Cooperation: International Security Institutions, Domestic Politics and American Multilateralism*. Cambridge: Cambridge University Press.

Rosenthal, U., Charles, M. T., & 't Hart, P. (1989). *Coping with crises: The management of Disasters, riots, and terrorism*. Springfield: Charles C. Thomas.

Schultz, K. (2017). *Sri Lanka, Struggling With Debt, Hands a Major Port to China*. Retrieved 3 June 2020 from https://www.nytimes.com/2017/12/12/world/asia/sri-lanka-china-port.html.

Suzuki, E. (2011). Global governance and international financial institutions. *Asia Pacific Law Review*, *19*(1), 13–34.

Vanhullebusch, M. (2017). China's Development Banks in Asia: A Human Rights Perspective. *Contemporary Issues in Human Rights Law*, 193–214. doi: 10.1007/978-981-10-6129-5_10.

Zhou, H., Chen, X., Hu, T., Li, J., Song, H., & Liu, Y. et al. (2020). A Novel Bat Coronavirus Closely Related to SARS-CoV-2 Contains Natural Insertions at the S1/S2 Cleavage Site of the Spike Protein. *Current Biology*. https://doi.org/10.1016/j.cub.2020.05.023.

Part III

MULTILATERAL ORGANIZATIONS AND REGIMES

Chapter 12

International Development Cooperation

Gulnara Abbas

1. INTRODUCTION

The development cooperation landscape has significantly changed over the past decade in parallel with shifting paradigms. The international development community is continuously reconceptualising development discourse and re-articulating the cooperation relationship to adapt to the increasingly complex development arena. The traditional aid relationship proves obsolete with the rise of the global South and emerging development partners, as well as non-financial modalities of development assistance. As stated by the OECD-DAC chair "we are no longer a world of donors and recipients; we are a world of partners" (Mawdsley et al., 2014 p. 30). Presently, development cooperation is aiming to move beyond aid by encompassing a broader area of international action including multi-stakeholder partnerships and changing global development rules. Multilateral cooperation is at the heart of the global partnership for development. Apart from being indispensable for capacity building and financial assistance, it guides decision-making and norm-setting in global development.

The COVID-19 pandemic is forcing the world into an unprecedented global development crisis, jeopardising decades of development progress and the advances of the SDG agenda. The crisis has uncovered and intensified vulnerabilities and inequalities both in developing and developed countries. Inequalities in multiple dimensions of wellbeing were on the rise even prior to the pandemic, and failure to address the mutually reinforcing development challenges was undermining the already inadequate gains on the 2030 Agenda (UN Committee for Development Policy, 2020). Thus, effective development cooperation is becoming ever more vital to prevent or mitigate adverse consequences. The pandemic has manifested the depth of global interdependence and henceforth presents an opportunity to move beyond rhetoric and truly embrace an inclusive development cooperation approach.

Multilateral development frameworks need to adapt to the changing global development landscape and to fit into the emerging paradigms and alternative perspectives on development. North-South development cooperation is still dominant, although persistently under pressure to reform. The pressures against multilateralism and the legitimacy crisis of global development governance endanger the achievement of the 2030 Agenda. The 2030 Agenda entails effective development cooperation. At a national level, many governments have incorporated the SDGs by aligning their policies and strategies, but the global response has not been transformative yet. Multi-stakeholder partnerships (MSPs) approach has become the new mantra shaping the UN discourse on global development and cooperation governance. The legitimacy and effectiveness of these partnerships ultimately will rely on a meaningful involvement of all development actors.

This chapter explores the changing dynamics of the international development cooperation system and discusses major multilateral frameworks by assessing their prospects and challenges. The next section gives an overview of the 2030 Agenda and Sustainable Development Goals (SDGs) focusing on its underlying features and challenges to implementation. Section 3 reviews the OECD-DAC-driven aid effectiveness agenda and its more comprehensive successor—development effectiveness, drawing on the principles of Paris Declaration on Aid Effectiveness and Busan Partnership for Effective Development Cooperation. Section 4 explains evolving elements of future development cooperation with a particular focus on beyond aid approaches and emerging development actors. Additionally, the section covers post-pandemic debates. Section 5 concludes on major implications of the chapter.

2. 2030 AGENDA AND SUSTAINABLE DEVELOPMENT GOALS

The 2030 Agenda for Sustainable Development was adopted by the 70th UN General Assembly on 25 September 2015. Its adoption was celebrated as one of the greatest accomplishments of multilateralism in modern history. It is a blueprint pledging to eradicate poverty and achieve sustainable development by 2030. The Agenda aimed to shape global development policy, alongside guiding regional and national development activities. Building on the unfinished agenda of Millennium Development Goals (MDGs),[1] 17 Sustainable Development Goals (SDGs) and 169 targets were introduced. The new development goals underlined the urgency of bold and transformative steps in all three dimensions of sustainable development—economic, social and environmental.

The SDGs are considered more universal and comprehensive. While the MDGs were focused on the challenges of developing countries, the SDGs do not distinguish between developed and developing countries, they recognise today's global challenges transcend borders and therefore require collective action. For example, more than two-thirds of the multidimensionally poor live in middle-income countries (UNDP, 2019). Based on the analysis of 90 MDG-related articles, major limitations of the MDG framework primarily were linked to its formulation process, structure, content and implementation (Fehling et al., 2013). SDGs seek to address the limitations of MDGs that have been subject to significant controversy by launching an inclusive and people-centred development agenda. Additionally, the SDG framework draws attention to cross-cutting issues such as gender equality and environmental sustainability and the inter-linkages of various thematic areas in development.

Besides its universal scope and its notice of wide-ranging structural concerns, the process of defining the new agenda has been more inclusive (Razavi, 2016). The MDGs were devised by a group of experts with a top-down manner, whereas the SDGs have undertaken an extensive consultative process including 70 open working groups, CSOs, thematic sessions, country consultations and the participation of the general public (Kumar et al., 2016).

Yet another input of the Agenda has been the consolidation of global partnership by incorporating meaningful roles for CSOs and the private sector. Partnerships with the private sector adhere to the UN Compact and IMPACT 2030 (Kumar et al., 2016). The formation of partnerships is identified as a fundamental mechanism for the implementation of the SDGs (Haywood et al., 2019). Partnerships are recognised as one of the five areas of critical importance in the preamble to the 2030 Agenda, alongside people, planet, prosperity and peace (UN SDG, 2015). Moreover, SDG 17 aims to "strengthen the means of implementation and revitalise global partnership for sustainable development" (UN, 2017).

In addition to a political declaration, the Agenda included means of implementation and a framework for follow up and review. These mechanisms enable the partners to evaluate their development endeavours. At a multilateral level, the High-Level Political Forum on Sustainable Development (HLPF), also known as SDG summit, provides a central platform for assessment, convening annually under the auspices of the Economic and Social Council (ECOSOC). Voluntary national reviews (VNRs) conducted by member states act as a basis for the regular reviews by HLPF (UN, 2020). The VNRs procedure is intended to promote the sharing of policy experiences, the articulation of challenges and the mobilisation of multi-stakeholder schemes. The Division for Sustainable Development Goals (DSDG) under the UNDESA is responsible for capacity-building for SDGs, advocacy and outreach activities relating to the goals, as well as assessing UN systemwide implementation of the Agenda. In so doing, the DSDG intends to promote broad ownership of the goals and commitment by all stakeholders.

Notwithstanding significant development efforts and the commitment of the international community, the SDG Summit of 2019 expressed concerns on the slow progress in many areas, anticipating that the targets are not likely to be achieved by 2030. At a national level, many governments have incorporated the Agenda by aligning their policies and strategies with the SDGs, although the global response is yet to reach transformative extent. Financing for the goals remains a challenge and will depend on ODA promises, sustainable investments and improving tax systems. The 2030 Agenda is unclear about the roles of bilateral or multilateral ODA, rather encouraging aid agencies to participate in partnerships, ensuring policy coherence and respecting country ownership (Gulrajani, 2016).

Expanding interconnections between local and global development challenges is becoming a crucial aspect of the SDGs. Sachs (2012) underlines the indispensable role of concerted global efforts to accomplish the SDGs, also noting that, three bottom lines of the SDGs—economic development, environmental sustainability and social inclusion—will depend on a fourth condition: good governance at all levels, local, national, regional and global.

The threats against multilateralism with growing nationalist sentiment and legitimacy crisis of global development governance jeopardise the achievement of the 2030 Agenda. The goals are non-binding and member countries are expected to establish their own national plans of implementation. The adoption of the Agenda itself was a triumph for multilateralism, reflecting the largest and most inclusive consultation in UN history. Yet, its successful implementation ultimately relies on the genuine commitment of development governance to the principle of leaving no one behind, thereby asserting its relevance.

The integration of the economic, social and environmental dimensions of sustainable development is at the centre of the SDG agenda. Yet, the existing governance frameworks of UN Development constrain organisation's capacity to meet the integration requirements of the SDGs (Helgason, 2016). In order to address potential conflicts among goals, an integrated approach to the means of implementation that takes into consideration interlinkages among goals is required (Jaiyesimi, 2016). At present, 42 targets relate to the means of implementation, but in a rather scattered manner.

The incompatibility of the SDGs, in particular the contradiction between socio-economic development and environmental sustainability, undermines its realisation (Spaiser et al. 2017; Swain, 2018; Hickel, 2019). Specifically, including economic growth as a goal (SDG8) is an indication of the failure to go beyond GDP. According to Spaiser et al. (2017), the focus on economic growth and consumption triggers the inconsistency. Menton et al. (2020) argue that, sustainable degrowth would generate better conditions for the transformative changes to accomplish the broader aim of the SDGs: to leave no one behind. According to the report by the International Council for Science (ICSU) and International Social Science Council (ISSC), only 29% of the 169 targets beneath the 17 goals are well defined and based on the latest scientific evidence.

Differential commitments on economic growth and sustainability might require significant reframing of the goals. Swain (2018) underlines the policy focus aspect, suggesting developed countries should focus on social inclusion and environmental sustainability policies, while developing countries should stick to economic and social development at least in the short run. In the same way, Hickel (2019) proposes the removal of the requirement for aggregate global growth and presenting quantified objectives for resource use per capita with substantial reductions in high income countries.

Easterly (2015) is highly critical of the SDG framework by identifying three major fallacies of this approach: (i) the answers do not lead to actions; (ii) the ambiguity of the responsible party is to undertake specified actions; (iii) action recommendations are the only way to induce progress. Accordingly, the collective responsibility narrative compromises individual accountability for the outcomes, that is, UN agencies, multilateral and bilateral aid agencies, and a wide range of NGOs, civil society and private sector actors are collectively responsible for all the outcomes.

Measurability of the goals is integral to tracking progress of the Agenda, and it requires comprehensive monitoring and a robust accountability system. However, some of the SDGs are not quantified and the indicators for assessing progress are incomplete (Kumar et al., 2016). There is a need for capacity-building to achieve better comprehension of sustainable development for operationalisation and implementation of the goals. Limited data availability, especially on environmental and social indicators, challenges the quantifying and monitoring of the goals (Swain, 2018). Measurement and monitoring challenges also stem from the broad framing of the goals.

3. FROM AID EFFECTIVENESS TO DEVELOPMENT EFFECTIVENESS

The Organisation for Economic Co-operation and Development (OECD) as a leading donor community coordinates the international efforts for effective distribution of aid via the Development Assistance Committee (DAC). Branded as a *venue and voice* of the world's major bilateral donors (OECD-DAC, 2006, p. 3), DAC is a forum of traditional Western donors to discuss issues around development, aid, poverty reduction in developing countries, to regulate international principles and standards for development cooperation and to monitor the delivery of donor commitments. The Committee also engages with non-DAC donors and other development actors to enhance the relevance and impact of its work.

Alongside key multilateral development actors such as the UN and its funds, programmes and relevant entities and the WB, 200 multilateral agencies participate in the development cooperation system as multilateral donors. Multilateral development finance constitutes almost one-third of total ODA. The increasing share of multilateral ODA—aid distributed through multilateral channels—is a further manifestation of donors' trust and of signalling the significance placed on these organisations for promoting development. Multilateral aid channels are less politicised, less fragmented, more selective, more efficient and more preferred by aid recipients and better suppliers of global public goods compared to bilateral channels (Gulrajani, 2016).

3.1. Aid Effectiveness Agenda

Since the traditional donor-recipient aid relationship proves obsolete, the development community is actively redefining their role within evolving development governance. These endeavours essentially began with the aid effectiveness agenda and culminated at the global partnership for development.

In the mid-1990s, the aid effectiveness discourse began to evolve under the leadership of OECD/DAC. The 2005 Paris Declaration on Aid Effectiveness marked a milestone of this process, recognising that poor institutional quality in recipient countries was not the only culprit, donors needed to alter their practices as well (Brown, 2020). The Paris Declaration was endorsed at the 2nd High Level Forum on Aid Effectiveness with an overall aim to improve the quality of aid and its impact on development. Five fundamental principles are the following:

- Ownership: Developing countries set their own strategies for poverty reduction, improve their institutions and tackle corruption.
- Alignment: Donor countries align behind these objectives and use local systems.
- Harmonisation: Donor countries coordinate, simplify procedures and share information to avoid duplication.
- Results: Developing countries and donors shift focus to development results and results get measured.
- Mutual accountability: Donors and partners are accountable for development results.

The 2008 Accra Agenda for Action (AAA) sought to accelerate the implementation of the Paris Declaration by redefining the relationship between donors and developing countries and recognising the value of cooperation beyond conventional aid arrangements. Three main themes include the following:

- Ownership: Countries determine their own development strategies by playing a more active role in designing development policies, and take a stronger leadership role in coordinating aid. Donors more consequently use existing fiduciary and procurement systems to deliver aid.
- Inclusive partnerships in which all partners—not only DAC donors and developing countries but also new donors, foundations and civil society—participate fully.
- Delivering results that will have real and measurable impact on development.

It should be underlined that, the Paris Declaration (PD) and the following aid effectiveness agreements emerged in the era of the Millennium Development Agenda, when aid provision was considered integral to poverty reduction and donors confronted domestic accountability pressures to prove the significance of ODA. The PD was based on the premise of a shift from a donor-driven to a partner-driven aid paradigm and yielded decisive changes to the norms and guiding principles for delivering development assistance. Despite widespread support for the aid effectiveness norm, *its principles were only slowly and partially put into practice* (Brown, 2020). Brown (2020) argues that broader agenda and expanded participation weakened the aid effectiveness norm. Lundsgaarde and Engberg-Pedersen (2019) highlight three limitations of the agenda: "the lack of consideration for the trade-offs between different dimensions of the agenda; the tension between its global aspirations and acknowledgement of the need for differentiated adaptation to varied contexts of implementation; and the trade-offs related to key approaches to implementation". The lost momentum of the aid effectiveness agenda can also be linked to the rise of non-DAC donors and their reluctance to comply with established principles (also mentioned in chapter 11 by Taylor Garrett). Subsequently, changing global development dynamics shifted the dialogue towards the effectiveness of development.

3.2. Development Effectiveness and GPEDC

The shift from aid effectiveness to development effectiveness happened in Busan. The 4th High Level Forum on Aid Effectiveness (HLF4), convened by the OECD DAC, held in Busan, Republic of Korea, in 2011 resulted in the Busan Partnership for Effective Development Cooperation. The Busan

Partnership document specified the following shared principles for all development actors to achieve common goals: *(a) ownership of development priorities by developing countries; (b) focus on results; (c) inclusive development partnerships; (d) transparency and accountability to each other* (OECD-DAC, 2011, p. 3).

The Busan Partnership agreement led to the establishment of the Global Partnership for Effective Development Cooperation (GPEDC), "a multi-stakeholder platform to advance the effectiveness of development efforts by all actors, to deliver results that are long-lasting and contribute to the achievement of the Sustainable Development Goals" (GPEDC, 2020). Principally, the GPEDC is designed to facilitate accountability for implementation of the Busan commitments and actions at a political level, bringing together 161 countries and 56 international organisations. Since 2012, the UNDP, together with its partners at the OECD, has supported the operational effectiveness of the partnership as its Joint Support Team, given the UNDP's assistance record in national capacity development with respect to the PD and AAA implementation. All types of development stakeholders—governments, bilateral/multilateral institutions, CSOs, the business sector, academia, local governments, regional organisations and representatives from parliaments and trade unions—are expected to participate on the basis of common goals, shared principles and differential commitments.

The 2016 high-level meeting of the GPEDC in Nairobi settled on the Nairobi Outcome Document intended to shape the development partnerships for urgent action to implement the SDGs. In addition to reaffirming effectiveness principles of country ownership, results, inclusiveness and transparency and accountability, the Outcome Document underlined complementary contributions of development stakeholders. The international community expressed differentiated commitments to effective development cooperation based on stakeholder groups, recognising differentiated roles and contributions towards shared effectiveness principles.

That is to say, the changing development landscape, including the rise of non-OECD donors, non-state actors and non-ODA financial flows, changed the international dialogue towards development effectiveness in 2011. According to Brown (2020), aforementioned factors challenged the dominance of the OECD-DAC in development cooperation leading to a diffusion of responsibility towards the multi-stakeholder GPECD.

The emergence of a new development effectiveness model alongside interdependence-driven collaboration sentiments dominates the post-Busan agenda. Busan marked a transition from the traditional donor-recipient relationship to an *equator-less* landscape of multi-stakeholder global partnership (Eyben and Savage, 2013). Key achievements of the Busan forum include shifting discussions from aid effectiveness to development effectiveness, broader engagement with developing country representatives, emphasis on multi-stakeholder partnerships and the launch of the GPEDC as well as the OECD-UN Joint Partnership. The establishment of the GPEDC embodies a rearrangement towards broader and more formal collaboration between organisations in the development system.

4. BEYOND AID—FUTURE DEVELOPMENT COOPERATION

Multilateral development frameworks need to adapt to the changing global development landscape and to fit into the emerging paradigms and alternative perspectives on development. The North-South development cooperation, both on a bilateral and multilateral terms, is still dominant, although persistently under pressure to reform. Re-emerging donors and other developing countries from the global South are increasingly challenging mainstream aid approaches and rearticulating development cooperation relationships. Additionally, non-state actors, including CSOs and the private sector are taking an active part in international development initiatives and contributing with innovative approaches. These dynamics are reconstructing the increasingly complex development arena.

Changing discourse on international development—primarily stemmed from discontent about the concept of development aid and its mixed record—intends to move *beyond aid* by incorporating non-aid instruments and modalities. The premise of this approach is that traditional aid is insufficient to deal with the bottlenecks to growth in multiple developing countries (Lin and Wang, 2016). ODA is expected to remain vital for LICs until 2030, but its role will wane with today's LICs reaching middle-income status (Sachs, 2012).

"Beyond aid" is coined to designate various features of evolving development cooperation. Four dimensions of transformation are identified: *(i) the proliferation of actors; (ii) the diversification of finance; (iii) the changing global rules and policies; and (iv) the knowledge sharing for development* (Janus et al., 2015). The last three correspond to the UN Development Cooperation Forum classification on three main types of contemporary development cooperation—financial (and in-kind) transfer, capacity support and policy change.

The MDGs consisted of a simplistic goal-instrument relationship—OECD DAC donors supporting poverty reduction in developing countries via ODA—without integrating beyond aid instruments. Janus et al. (2015) posits that, reconsidering the interaction between development goals and instruments can lead to development cooperation with specialisation or global cooperation with integration. Accordingly, in case of specialisation, development cooperation policy still concentrates on poverty reduction in developing countries but employs beyond aid instruments. The integration scenario entails redefining goals and establishing strong linkages with other areas of international cooperation embedded within a broader narrative of global challenges. The universal and comprehensive goals of the 2030 Agenda resemble the integration scenario, but also align with development cooperation specialisation, since they are not mutually exclusive. Therefore, an effective implementation of the SDGs relies on a successful utilisation of beyond aid modalities.

4.1. Emerging Development Actors and Multi-Stakeholder Partnerships

Development cooperation architecture is becoming increasingly complex with proliferation of development actors, including emerging and re-emerging donors and non-state stakeholders. South-South and triangular cooperation, multi-stakeholder partnerships, innovative public-private partnerships and other modalities have gained more prominence. It should be underlined that, the North-South cooperation still remains a leading form of development cooperation. Nonetheless emerging modalities are ever more challenging the dominant cooperation frameworks by providing diversity of resources and approaches.

The rise of the Global South has changed the dynamics of traditional development assistance. China, India, Brazil, Russia, South Africa and other emerging donors became significant actors in providing support to developing countries and accomplished successful development outcomes utilising approaches divergent from the DAC model. Chapter 11 by Taylor Garret specifically concentrates on the role of China and its recently established multilateral development bank—the AIIB. There is no consensus whether or not aid from emerging donors undercuts the position of traditional donor community (Chin and Frolic, 2007). Nevertheless, these new development actors and their approaches accelerated the shift from conventional donor-aid relationship towards partnership-oriented development cooperation. Consequently, international development community increasingly attempted to engage with emerging actors in various frameworks seeking to integrate them into existing and potential development cooperation modalities. "The 'mainstream' aid community has moved very rapidly from neglect and oversight of the (re)emerging development partners, to 'outreach' efforts initiated around 2005, to the recognition of the necessity and inevitability of more egalitarian and indeed respectful relationships that call for mutual learning" (Mawdsley et al., 2014, p. 5).

South-South Cooperation is recognised as an increasingly necessary complement to North-South cooperation and is vital to the implementation of SDGs. Branded with an assertion of a shared developing country identity, expertise in development, criticism of hierarchical donor-recipient relations and insistence on mutual opportunity (Mawdsley, 2012), it offers alternative perspectives and approaches to development. However, dominant frameworks constantly underline that South-South cooperation is not a substitute but rather a complement to North-South cooperation. Triangular cooperation is referring to partnerships between two or more developing countries supported by a developed country or multilateral organisation. This modality is important for maintaining development partner relationships during the transition from ODA and beyond, as the country becomes a more established donor its significance may diminish (Calleja and Prizzon, 2019). The underlying premise is to facilitate transformation of developing countries' policies by generating locally owned solutions. The Busan agenda has recognised the complementary role of South-South and triangular cooperation, alongside other modalities on the basis of shared principles and differential commitments.

The challenges posed by proliferation of donors consist of rising fragmentation, transaction costs, management and coordination issues. The Busan forum sought to address these challenges by including objectives on enhancing complementarity and coherence of development cooperation at the partner country and international levels under the Building Block on Managing Diversity and Reducing Fragmentation.

The multi-stakeholder partnerships (MSPs) approach has become the new mantra shaping the UN discourse on global development and cooperation governance. MSPs, emerging as a new form of multilateral cooperation beyond intergovernmental diplomacy, recently have gained increasing prominence in international development initiatives. Fundamentally, MSPs aim to bring together all development actors, including governments, private sector representatives, civil society, multilateral institutions, parliamentarians and academia—to promote a more holistic approach to development and better governance. It seems that the "rule of thumb in international development is that everybody wants to be a partner with everyone else on everything, everywhere" (Fowler, 2000, p. 3 cited in Schaaf, 2015, p. 70).

As a bottom-up transnational initiative, MSPs appear integral to inclusive development cooperation. Growing discontent with IOs and existing multilateral frameworks and the lack of determination and capacity on the part of state actors can be considered as the underlying reasons for the expansion of these partnerships (Martens, 2007). Still, the rise of MSPs in the field of sustainable development has ensued under the auspices of international organisations (Bäckstrand, 2006). Considering their flexible and decentralised characteristics, the MSPs have a distinctive potential to link multilateral development norms with local efforts across sectors via mobilising diverse expertise and resources.

However, recent studies reveal limited evidence for positive performance as partnerships prove incapable of addressing governance gaps through new norms or furthering prevailing intergovernmental regulations (Pattberg and Widerberg, 2016). Additionally, there are concerns over accountability, insufficient representation of formerly marginalised actors as well as consolidating privatisation of global governance by enabling private interests to dictate global affairs.

To a certain extent, the rise of partnerships suggests diffusion of authority from governments and multilateral organisations towards non-state actors. MSP framework encourages bilateral and multilateral donors to reconsider their position and mission with respect to the global development assistance system. On the other hand, developing countries are not entirely confident on the prospects of shifting responsibility and its implications for ODA commitments (Pattberg and Widerberg, 2016).

The launch of the GPEDC as a multi-stakeholder initiative has once again emphasised distinct roles of all stakeholders in supporting development. Moreover, its establishment was a response to changing development architecture, signalling a declining position of the OECD-DAC. The platform enables to uncover potential synergies between South-South cooperation and North-South cooperation. While examining the challenges of operationalising the GPEDC as a truly global partnership, Li et al. (2018) identify the lack of trust and misconceptions from both sides, and according to Rudolph and Holzapfel (2017), the GPEDC does not adequately reflect the diversity of donors. Even though a wide range of international development stakeholders have been engaged with, the general scheme is primarily spearhead by Northern donors. The legitimacy and effectiveness of this partnership ultimately will rely on a meaningful involvement of emerging donors and other development actors.

4.2. Changing Global Rules and New Multilateralism

Policy change at national and international level is not adequately integrated into the development cooperation practices. Development outcomes in partner countries to a larger extent depend on donor policies and multilateral regimes. The future development cooperation regime is likely to integrate various modalities of policy change, especially changing global rules and policy coherence. These approaches need to adapt to the broadening development agenda (from poverty reduction to sustainable development) and diversity of partner countries (Janus et al., 2015).

Development aid and other forms of assistance ought not be considered in isolation from the rules of global development governance which might constrain or hinder effective development cooperation. Development is not an internal issue, thus strengthening global governance or building better enabling rules for global governance for a more equitable distribution of development opportunities and a more efficient provision of global public goods is essential. Development aid basically fails to deliver when global rules constrain government action at a national level, such as denying a developing country an equitable access to international trade or the international finance system. Global policy change examples include exceptions in TRIPS agreements (transition period for LDCs for pharmaceutical products) or trade preferences and reduction of trade duties for LDCs. Challenges persist in asymmetries of access to decision-making processes, asymmetries in process coverage, and consequently asymmetries in outcomes (UN Committee for Development Policy, 2014). Most of the developing countries still lack influence in shaping the rules of global development governance.

Another notable instrument of the post-aid agenda is policy coherence for development (PCD). PCD is also covered by Sonja Niedecken with respect to EU development policy in chapter 7. It emerged from the recognition that actions in other policy sectors (e.g. trade, finance, environment, security and migration) can potentially undermine or disrupt development objectives, so designing comprehensive approaches and evaluating possible trade-offs can moderate disagreements. There are three dimensions to this approach: across national policies, across international regulations and between international and national spheres of policymaking. Despite being increasingly aware of the relevance of PCD, due to its multifaceted nature, aligning non-development policies with development goals and promoting positive synergies have proven rather challenging for governments.

There are also calls for *a new multilateralism* for development that is defined as bringing together governments, the private sector, civil society, multilateral institutions and other development stakeholders to perform together at all levels in inclusive partnerships and initiatives to achieve development objectives. The UN Committee for Development Policy (2020) formulated five principles to support the design of a new multilateralism:

- Global rules should be calibrated towards the overarching goals of social and economic stability, shared prosperity and environmental sustainability and protected against capture by the most powerful players.
- States share common but differentiated responsibilities in a multilateral system built to advance global public goods and protect the global commons.
- The right of States to policy space to pursue national development strategies should be enshrined in global rules.

- Global regulations should be designed both to strengthen a dynamic international division of labour and to prevent destructive unilateral economic actions that prevent other nations from realising common goals.
- Global public institutions must be accountable to their full membership, open to a diversity of viewpoints, cognisant of new voices and have balanced dispute resolution systems.

The new development multilateralism adopts the premise and framework of multi-stakeholder initiatives, in addition to concentrating on the overall dynamics of global governance and regulations. The emergence of this concept is partly an attempt to rearticulate the global partnership for development, but suffers from similar obstacles undermining MSPs partnerships discussed in the previous section.

4.3. POST-PANDEMIC COOPERATION

The COVID-19 pandemic has had devastating effects on developing countries, and its full impact is still unravelling. Economic and social consequences of the crisis may reverse decades of progress in poverty reduction and jeopardise sustainable development efforts. The exports in developing Asia are declining, economic growth in Africa could be halved and more than 30 million people in Latin America could fall into poverty (OECD, 2020). As development challenges aggravate, the demand for international development assistance is pressing.

UNDP has reported that the pandemic could reverse human development for the first time in 30 years. "The world has seen many crises over the past 30 years, including the Global Financial Crisis of 2007–09. Each has hit human development hard but, overall, development gains accrued globally year-on-year", stated UNDP Administrator Achim Steiner. "COVID-19—with its triple hit to health, education, and income—may change this trend" (UNDP, 2020). Additionally, developing countries are likely to encounter higher deterioration in human development.

The Development Initiatives—an international development organisation focusing on the role of data in driving poverty eradication and sustainable development—estimates as much as $25 billion decline in development aid by 2021. Aid has gained a new significance in the context of this crisis and its purpose can be revitalised by bilateral and multilateral donors (Gulrajani, 2020).

During the recent survey conducted by Devex—a media platform for the global development community—more than 560 global development professionals from 156 countries were asked to reflect on the potential long-term consequences of the pandemic. About 53% of respondents selected "backsliding on development gains", and 49% estimated cuts in aid. Similarly, Jorge Moreira da Silva, the director of the OECD Development Cooperation Directorate, articulated his concerns on the backsliding risk.

According to the OECD, international response to the pandemic should follow a new development model contributing to resilience and sustainability. That is to say, the international community including multilateral organisations, international financial organisations, the international private sector and NGOs can bolster cooperation via an inclusive multilateral approach to financing and capacity building and curtail the potential deleterious effects on the hardly won development gains. Da Silva and Moorehead (2020) propose three actions donors can take: (i) protecting exiting ODA commitments; (ii) focusing on health systems and vulnerable people in developing countries; (iii) ensuring coordination of humanitarian and development aid and supporting good governance.

The systemic challenges posed by the pandemic can potentially accelerate the transformation from traditional donor-recipient relationships towards a development cooperation model. As discussed, this transformation has already commenced since Busan. The pandemic also challenges the traditional roles of donors and recipients, as China has stepped in to help Italy in fighting the virus. Government officials increasingly insist on other modalities of cooperation beyond financial aid, such as knowledge sharing and peer learning (Prizzon, 2020). Knowledge sharing will prove essential for a comprehensive understanding of post-pandemic socio-economic challenges and for locating potential solutions.

5. CONCLUSION

The adoption of the 2030 Agenda and SDGs originated with the premise of multilateralism, and its successful implementation relies on multilateral cooperation. In other words, multilateral cooperation is at the heart of the global partnership for development. In order to address existing challenges to development governance, the international community and multilateral cooperation frameworks need to adapt to the shifting global development landscape. The realisation of development objectives ultimately depends on the commitments of all development stakeholders. Development agendas designed and led by dominant donors are no longer in rhythm with the global partnership for development narrative. Therefore, effective development cooperation calls for a more inclusive and comprehensive approach, encompassing developing countries and beyond aid instruments.

The agenda shifting from aid effectiveness towards development effectiveness, a broader engagement with developing country representatives via

South-South and triangular cooperation, an emphasis on multi-stakeholder partnerships and the establishment of Global Partnership for Development marked the past decade. MSP frameworks encourage bilateral and multilateral donors to reconsider their position and mission with respect to the global development assistance system. Nonetheless, challenges persist concerning the design and implementation of these modalities.

Additionally, development aid and other forms of assistance ought not to be considered in isolation from the rules of global development governance which might constrain or hinder effective development cooperation. Therefore, building better enabling rules for global governance for a more equitable distribution of development opportunities and a more efficient provision of global public goods is essential. The pandemic only strengthens the call for more inclusive and equitable development cooperation and renewed commitment to multilateralism. Now is the time to fast-track development cooperation.

NOTE

1. Eight global development goals for 2015, based on United Nations Millennium Declaration, General Assembly resolution 55/2 of 8 September 2000.

REFERENCES

Bäckstrand, K. (2006). Multi-stakeholder partnerships for sustainable development: Rethinking legitimacy, accountability and effectiveness. *European Environment*, *16*(5), 290–306.

Battersby, J. (2017). MDGs to SDGs—new goals, same gaps: The continued absence of urban food security in the post-2015 global development agenda. *African Geographical Review*, *36*(1), 115–129.

Bernstein, S. (2013). Rio+ 20: Sustainable development in a time of multilateral decline. *Global Environmental Politics*, *13*(4), 12–21.

Brown, S. (2020). The rise and fall of the aid effectiveness norm. *The European Journal of Development Research*, 1–19.

Calleja, R., & Prizzon, A. (2019). *Moving away from aid: Lessons from country studies*. ODI report.

Chasek, P. S., & Wagner, L. M. (2016). Breaking the mold: A new type of multilateral sustainable development negotiation. *International Environmental Agreements: Politics, Law and Economics*, *16*(3), 397–413.

Chin, G. T., & Frolic, M. B. (2007). Emerging donors in international development assistance: The China case. Research Report, International Development Research Centre, Canada.

Da Silva, J. M., & Moorehead, S. (2020, March 25). Aid in the time of COVID-19—3 things donors can do now. Retrieved June 21 2020 from https://www.devex.com/news/opinion-aid-in-the-time-of-covid-19-3-things-donors-can-do-now-96848

Easterly, W. (2015). The trouble with the sustainable development goals. *Current History*, *114*(775), 322.

Eyben, R., & Savage, L. (2013). Emerging and submerging powers: Imagined geographies in the new development partnership at the Busan fourth high level forum. *The Journal of Development Studies*, *49*(4), 457–469.

Fehling, M., Nelson, B. D., & Venkatapuram, S. (2013). Limitations of the millennium development goals: A literature review. *Global Public Health*, *8*(10), 1109–1122.

Gulrajani, N. (2016, March). Bilateral versus multilateral aid channels. *Strategic choices for donors*. London: Overseas Development Institute. ODI Report. Retrieved 25 May 2020 from https://cdn.odi.org/media/documents/10492.pdf.

Gulrajani, N. (2020, May 27). How COVID-19 can change incentives for development co-operation. Retrieved 25 June 2020 from https://oecd-development-matters.org/2020/05/27/how-covid-19-can-change-incentives-for-development-co-operation/

Gupta, J., & Vegelin, C. (2016). Sustainable development goals and inclusive development. *International Environmental Agreements: Politics, Law and Economics*, *16*(3), 433–448.

Haywood, L. K., Funke, N., Audouin, M., Musvoto, C., & Nahman, A. (2019). The Sustainable Development Goals in South Africa: Investigating the need for multi-stakeholder partnerships. *Development Southern Africa*, *36*(5), 555–569.

Helgason, K. S. (2016). The 2030 Agenda for Sustainable Development: Recharging multilateral cooperation for the post-2015 era. *Global Policy*, *7*(3), 431–440.

Hickel, J. (2015, September 23). Five reasons to think twice about the UN's Sustainable Development Goals. *Africa at LSE*. Retrieved 26 June 2020 from https://blogs.lse.ac.uk/southasia/2015/09/23/five-reasons-to-think-twice-about-the-uns-sustainable-development-goals/

Hickel, J. (2019). The contradiction of the sustainable development goals: Growth versus ecology on a finite planet. *Sustainable Development*, *27*(5), 873–884.

Independent Group of Scientists appointed by the Secretary-General. (2019). Global Sustainable Development Report 2019: The Future is Now—Science for Achieving Sustainable Development. (United Nations, New York, 2019). Retrieved 29 June 2020 from https://sustainabledevelopment.un.org/content/documents/24797GSDR_report_2019.pdf

Jaiyesimi, R. (2016). The challenge of implementing the sustainable development goals in Africa: The way forward. *African Journal of Reproductive Health*, *20*(3), 13–18.

Janus, H., Klingebiel, S., & Paulo, S. (2015). Beyond aid: A conceptual perspective on the transformation of development cooperation. *Journal of International Development*, *27*(2), 155–169.

Kumar, S., Kumar, N., & Vivekadhish, S. (2016). Millennium development goals (MDGS) to sustainable development goals (SDGS): Addressing unfinished agenda and strengthening sustainable development and partnership. *Indian journal of*

*community medicine: official publication of Indian Association of Preventive &
Social Medicine*, *41*(1), 1.

Lin, J. Y., & Wang, Y. (2016). *Going beyond aid: Development cooperation for
structural transformation*. Cambridge: Cambridge University Press.

Lockhart, C. (2005, January). From aid effectiveness to development effectiveness: Strategy and policy coherence in fragile states. In *Background paper
prepared for the Senior Level Forum on Development Effectiveness in Fragile
States*. London. Retrieved 10 July 2020 from https://gsdrc.org/document-library/
from-aid-effectiveness-to-development-coherence-in-fragile-states/

Lundsgaarde, E., & Engberg-Pedersen, L. (2019). *The aid effectiveness agenda: Past
experiences and future prospects*. Danish Institute for International Studies.

Martens, J. (2007). *Multistakeholder partnerships: future models of multilateralism?*
(Vol. 29). Berlin: Friedrich-Ebert-Stiftung.

Mawdsley, E. (2012). The changing geographies of foreign aid and development
cooperation: Contributions from gift theory. *Transactions of the Institute of British
Geographers*, *37*(2), 256–272.

Menton, M., Larrea, C., Latorre, S., Martinez-Alier, J., Peck, M., Temper, L., & Wal-
ter, M. (2020). Environmental justice and the SDGs: from synergies to gaps and
contradictions. *Sustainability Science*, *15*(6), 1–16.

OECD. (2020). Developing countries and development co-operation: What is at stake?
Retrieved 24 June 2020 from https://read.oecd-ilibrary.org/view/?ref=132_132637-
tfn40fwe1w&title=Developing-countries-and-development-co-operation_What-is-
at-stake

OECD-DAC. (2005). *The Paris Declaration OECD*. Paris: DAC.

OECD-DAC. (2006). *DAC in Dates: The History of OECD's Development Assistance Committee*. Paris: DAC.

OECD-DAC. (2008). *The Accra Agenda for Action OECD*. Paris: DAC.

OECD-DAC. (2011). *Busan Partnership for Effective Development Cooperation
OECD*. Paris: DAC.

Pattberg, P., & Widerberg, O. (2016). Transnational multi-stakeholder partnerships
for sustainable development: Conditions for success. *Ambio*, *45*(1), 42–51.

Prizzon, A. (2020, March 26). How coronavirus is accelerating a new approach to
international cooperation. Retrieved 21 June 2020 from https://www.odi.org/blogs/
16794-how-coronavirus-accelerating-new-approach-international-cooperation

Razavi, S. (2016). The 2030 Agenda: Challenges of implementation to attain gender
equality and women's rights. *Gender & Development*, *24*(1), 25–41.

Sachs, J. D. (2012). From millennium development goals to sustainable development
goals. *The Lancet*, *379*(9832), 2206–2211.

Schaaf, R. (2015). The rhetoric and reality of partnerships for international development. *Geography Compass*, *9*(2), 68–80.

Smith, E. & Chadwick, V. (2020, May 19). Development pros brace for more needs,
less money post-pandemic. Retrieved 21 June 2020 from https://www.devex.com/
news/development-pros-brace-for-more-needs-less-money-post-pandemic-97245

Spaiser, V., Ranganathan, S., Swain, R. B., & Sumpter, D. J. (2017). The sustainable development oxymoron: quantifying and modelling the incompatibility of

sustainable development goals. *International Journal of Sustainable Development & World Ecology, 24*(6), 457–470.

Swain, R. B. (2018). A critical analysis of the sustainable development goals. In *Handbook of Sustainability Science and Research* (pp. 341–355). Cham, Switzerland: Springer.

UN. (2020). Voluntary national reviews database. Retrieved 21 June 2020 from https://sustainabledevelopment.un.org/vnrs/

UN Committee for Development Policy. (2014). Global governance and global rules for development in the post-2015 era*. Retrieved 25 June 2020 from https://www.un.org/development/desa/dpad/wp-content/uploads/sites/45/CDP-excerpt-2014-1.pdf

UN Committee for Development Policy (2020). Development policy and multilateralism after COVID-19. Retrieved 23 June 2020 from https://www.un.org/development/desa/dpad/publication/development-policy-and-multilateralism-after-covid-19/

UNDP. (2016, January 26). UNDP support to the implementation of the 2030 agenda for sustainable development. Retrieved 10 July 2020 from https://www.undp.org/content/oslo-governance-centre/en/home/library/strategy-undp-support-to-the-implementation-of-the-2030-agenda.html

UNDP. (2020, May 20). COVID-19: Human development on course to decline this year for the first time since 1990. Retrieved 23 June 2020 from https://www.undp.org/content/undp/en/home/news-centre/news/2020/COVID19_Human_development_on_course_to_decline_for_the_first_time_since_1990.html

UN SDG (United Nations Sustainability Development Goals). (2015). Transforming our world: The 2030 agenda for sustainable development. *General Assembly 70 session.* A/RES/70/1. Retrieved 25 May 2020 from https://sustainabledevelopment.un.org/post2015/transformingourworld/publication

Chapter 13

Multilateral Cooperation in International Tax Law

Juliana Cubillos, Frederik Heitmüller
and Irma Mosquera Valderrama[1]

1. INTRODUCTION

Cooperation in direct taxation[2] among countries has for a long time been rather limited in scope. Until 2008, this cooperation was mainly based on the use of bilateral tax treaty models to allocate the right to tax income from cross-border transactions among two countries. These treaty models have been developed by the Organisation for Economic Cooperation and Development (OECD) and the UN and used by countries when negotiating their bilateral tax treaties.

Since the 2008 financial crisis, cooperation has become increasingly "multilateralized", as new issues such as tax evasion and aggressive tax planning have gained prominence on the international tax agenda. If one example can illustrate this movement towards multilateralism, it is the setting of international tax standards. These standards relate mainly (i) to exchange of taxpayer information (first on request and thereafter automatic), (ii) tax transparency (ending bank secrecy) and (iii) to prevent harmful tax competition among countries and to tackle base erosion and profit shifting (BEPS) by multinationals.

Developed and developing countries are participating in the implementation of these standards. However, the agenda-setting and decision-making process for these international tax standards have taken place at OECD and G20 level which consist mainly of developed countries.[3] In this multilateral setting, the role of the UN has been reduced. One reason may be the rejection by developed countries in the 2015 Financing for Development Conference to confer the status of intergovernmental body to the UN Tax Committee, despite the call by developing countries and civil society to do so.[4]

Due to the concerns of legitimacy of these international tax standards vis-à-vis developed countries, the OECD and the G20 invited developing countries to participate on equal footing in the implementation of these standards by creating forums such as the Global Transparency Forum (exchange of information and transparency) and the BEPS Inclusive Framework to adopt the BEPS 4 Minimum Standards (aggressive tax planning).[5] At the time of writing, the Global Transparency Forum has 161 tax jurisdictions and the BEPS Inclusive Framework 137 tax jurisdictions.

Within regional blocs, with the prime example being the EU, multilateral cooperation has further deepened mainly by adopting in its Directives the OECD-G20 international tax standards and by introducing the EU Standard of Good Tax Governance for EU and third (non-EU) countries. Other regional blocks have established regional networks for cooperation between tax administrations, such as the African Tax Administration Forum (ATAF) and the Inter-American Centre of Tax Administrations (CIAT).

Notwithstanding the efforts to achieve international cooperation at a multilateral level, the allocation of taxing rights of cross-border transactions between residence (mainly developed) countries and source (mainly developing) countries has not been agreed upon. This allocation is still an important element that is agreed bilaterally (tax treaty) or unilaterally (domestic law) by countries. An example of the allocation of taxing rights problem can be observed in the taxation of highly digitalized businesses. Despite attempts from the OECD and the G20 to come with a global solution, countries are introducing unilateral measures such as the digital service tax (France, Austria, Hungary, Italy, Poland, Turkey and the UK) to tax digital services (online advertising, digital interface among others).[6]

Another example is the proposal to introduce a global anti-base erosion (GLoBE) rule including a minimum tax rate. If adopted, this proposal will call for more international tax cooperation, and also for a single set of rules to prevent harmful tax competition. However, the adoption of both proposals in a multilateral setting is not yet clear. These proposals have been discussed since 2018, and until now, they have not been successful in achieving a consensus among all countries participating in the BEPS Inclusive Framework. Instead, the UN has recently introduced article. 12B to the UN tax treaty model to tax automated digital services, which provides for source taxation (see section 2.3 of this chapter).

Therefore, the landscape of multilateral cooperation that started with the adoption of the global standard of exchange of information and the BEPS 4 Minimum Standards is now uncertain with the new proposals to tax highly digitalized business and the GLoBE. Some reasons are the unilateral approaches to digital tax, and the complexity of the proposals that makes difficult for countries to implement them.[7]

The COVID-19 crisis has also exposed the weakness of governments within the EU and also outside the EU to address collectively the recovery of the economy in a pandemic and post-pandemic era. The OECD, the World Bank (WB), the IMF and the EU have attempted to provide common solutions. However, in practice, countries are introducing their own unilateral measures (e.g. tax incentives, reducing tax exemptions and re-introducing repealed taxes) to provide fiscal stimuli to business and to keep the economy going. The uncoordinated approach might only deepen the breaches between the tax systems that before the pandemic were intended to grow aligned upon general tax standards for international tax cooperation.

This chapter will address these standards with a focus on the interaction between different international and regional (mainly EU) organizations in the process. The first part of the chapter will describe the environment in which international taxation has evolved and explain its foundations. The second part will address multilateral cooperation in tax matters among countries and the role adopted by international organizations in the development of common tax standards. The third part of this chapter will address multilateral tax cooperation at the European Union (EU) level and explain how the EU adopts tax standards to create general principles of conduct for tax matters. The fourth part offers some critical comments regarding the current system of multilateral cooperation as well as some ideas about the future perspectives for multilateral tax cooperation. Finally, this chapter will provide some conclusions.

2. MULTILATERAL COOPERATION IN INTERNATIONAL TAXATION

Taxation has since long been on the agenda of multilateral organizations, from the League of Nations to the UN, the OECD, the EU, the IMF and the WB, among others. However, as pointed out by Ruggie, the fact that physical institutions with large membership work on one issue does automatically mean that Member States (MSs) engage in multilateral cooperation, meaning that their relations are based on general principles of conduct applicable to all of them (Ruggie, 1992). Multilateral institutions are often the fora where such principles are developed, but not necessarily. On the other hand, multilateral institutions might not be able to effectively develop international principles.

We will show in the following sections that during a long time, the activity of multilateral organizations has been confined to developing a model for bilateral conventions, as no agreement on a multilateral convention could be found. However, with the addition of the issues of tax evasion and tax avoidance to the international agenda, multilateral cooperation has deepened over the past two decades. In light of the COVID-19 crisis, however, it remains uncertain whether this deepening trend will continue.

2.1. Bilateralism with a Grain of Multilateralism: Addressing Double Taxation

In essence, taxes are collected not only for the tasks being performed within a country's territory but extended to the earning that such business makes in other jurisdictions, to make sure that the profits earned by the same taxpayer are taxed at least once. Taxation takes place either in the country where the taxpayer conducts the activity (active income—source taxation) or in the country from where the efforts to conduct the activity take place, meaning the residence state of the taxpayer (passive income—residence taxation).

In such a system, however, resident individuals and companies that invest abroad have a disadvantage compared to resident taxpayers that only invest within the country, because their income is likely to be taxed twice: once by the country where they generate income and once by the country where they are resident. Since this prospect of double taxation hampers cross-border investment, countries endeavoured to cooperate to avoid unintended double taxation by allocating the taxing rights between country of residence and country of source. Nevertheless, if both countries want to tax, the struggle is to define which of the two should forego revenue for the sake of the other (Rixen & Rohlfing, 2007).[8]

Different countries have different interests depending on whether they are net capital exporters (mainly developed countries) or net capital importers (mainly developing countries), the former preferring taxation at residence and the latter taxation at source. This conflict is more or less strong depending on how asymmetrical the investment flows between two countries are. Consequently, cooperation has developed principally in a bilateral fashion, with countries negotiating bilateral tax treaties, which allocate taxing rights among two countries.

These bilateral treaties are generally based on model conventions developed by the OECD (1963) and the UN (1980) upon the bilateral convention issued in 1927 by the Fiscal Committee of the League of Nations. Initially, the Fiscal Committee aimed at a collective solution, however, this attempt was rapidly rejected observing that the countries willing to join this multilateral effort were only a few (League of Nations—Fiscal Committee, 1935);[9] and that by virtue of marked differences between tax systems, the convention would encompass provisions "worded in such general terms as to be of no practical value" (League of Nations—Fiscal Committee, 1927). The Committee adopted a solution that despite being considered as partial

(García Antón, 2016)[10] was aimed at finding practical bilateral implementation among countries usually connected as they were trade partners or closely bound jurisdictions by geographical proximity (League of Nations—Fiscal Committee, 1930). It is therefore possible to say that even if the setting is bilateral, the roots of the original model convention and several of the comments introduced by the OECD and the UN aim at providing solutions for a multilateral arena.

For long, tax scholars made pleas for a multilateral tax treaty, without success.[11] One of the reasons for the failure to reach a multilateral agreement were the differences between developed and developing countries and the problems in the (fair) allocation of taxing rights between residence (mainly developed) countries and source (mainly developing) countries. Although, compared to the OECD model, the UN model allocates more taxing rights to source countries, provided that developing countries were usually perceived as source states (Lennard, 2009),[12] it rests on a compromise of alternating taxing rights between source and residence. This consideration reflects the general principle that dominates international taxation and is the setting upon which countries preserve their power struggles limiting the options for achieving multilateral cooperation. This does not mean that multilateralism is to be hindered by bilateralism, moreover then both currents will blend for international taxation. The Multilateral Instrument is an example of this tendency, as it constitutes a multilateral treaty affecting bilateral treaties with standard rules, provided the countries select those bilateral treaties as to be covered by the multilateral initiative.

In light of the aforementioned context, new tax developments cannot forego the fact that the international tax praxis rests upon bilateral treaties which according to the IMF by 2016 exceeded over 3,000 (*Tax Treaties: Boost or Bane for Development?—IMF Blog*, n.d.). The fact that the whole international tax network rests upon principles aiming at achieving the interests of single states (source and residence), and the sovereignty principle,[13] allows the interpreter to believe that the course of action to be followed for international taxation will inevitably be marked by a blending of bilateralism and multilateralism.

2.2. The Multilateral Responses to International Tax Evasion and Tax Avoidance

After the 2008 financial crisis, new support emerged to revamp the efforts for tax cooperation and transparency. Raising revenues for supporting the economies was a top priority for all crisis-affected countries. Gaining awareness about the extension of such problems allowed the G20 to insist that further investigations regarding connected issues should be handled independently by the OECD with the objective of finding once again an adequate solution or at least proposals or standards to be followed internationally. Tax cooperation was perceived as a must, since the interactions of multinational enterprises (MNEs) around the world proven to exacerbate the possibilities of facing cases of tax evasion[14] and (unacceptable) tax avoidance regarded as aggressive tax planning.[15]

Two separate regimes emerged, one mainly focused on tax evasion, the other on tax avoidance. The tax evasion regime consists principally in the exchange of information standard, which proscribes that countries have to provide all foreseeably relevant information about a taxpayer resident in another country that this other country requests to enforce its tax laws (Global Forum on Transparency and Exchange of Information for Tax Purposes, 2016). In addition, the standard mandates since 2014 that countries *automatically* exchange information on foreign taxpayers' bank accounts (e.g. number of accounts and balance) with the tax administrations of the taxpayers' countries of residence. Compliance with the standard is reviewed by the Global Forum on Transparency and Exchange of Information, which as of August 2020 has 161 member jurisdictions.

The (unacceptable) tax avoidance regime consists mainly in the outcomes of the BEPS project, published in 2015. While many parts of the published reports are mere recommendations, they also contain Four Minimum Standards, which 137 jurisdictions have committed to implement by becoming members of the BEPS Inclusive Framework and peer-review reports monitor the implementation process of the standards.

These standards mandate participating countries to abolish aspects of their tax regimes that encourage tax avoidance MNEs and oblige countries to require from MNEs with an annual revenue of more than €750 million headquartered in the country to supply a so-called country by country report. The report contains information about the MNE, such as revenue, number of employees and value of assets, on a country-by-country basis. Such information allows the tax administration to conduct a tax avoidance risk assessment and select certain companies for closer scrutiny. Further, the BEPS standard requires the country to share the report with all other countries in which the MNE has a subsidiary.

Further, the BEPS Four Minimum Standards affects bilateral tax treaties by obliging all participating states to exchange agreements between taxpayer and tax administrations (rulings) and to introduce an anti-abuse rule in their bilateral tax treaties. However, the efficacy of the BEPS standards has been called into question. Indeed, as these can generally be qualified as soft law and states need to introduce them in domestic law, actual compliance is uncertain and remains an under-researched issue.[16]

2.3. The Role of the United Nations in International Taxation

In the UN, the proposals for international taxation are being discussed and adopted by the UN Committee of Experts on International Tax Cooperation in Tax Matters. One of the authors has argued elsewhere that "in this multilateral decision-making mechanism, the role of the UN can be relevant, since it represents the developing countries, i.e. most of the countries of Latin America and African regions. However, up till now the role of the UN in respect of developing countries is limited mainly due to the lack of participation of developing countries in the initiatives of the UN, the lack of support to give the UN Committee of Experts on International Cooperation in Tax Matters (UN Tax Committee) a more important role and in the choice for South-to-South cooperation by means of partnerships between developing countries".[17]

Two examples can illustrate this limited role in international taxation. The first one is the limited response by countries regarding the BEPS questionnaire drafted by the UN Committee,[18] and the lack of support developed countries to give to the UN committee an intergovernmental status in the 2015 Addis Ababa conference.[19]

Despite this, the UN Committee continues working on issues of international taxation, including also submitting a new proposal (6 Aug. 2020) to amend bilateral tax treaties regarding the tax treatment of payments for digital services (art. 12B UN Model).[20] This proposal is presented as an alternative to the OECD Proposal to tax highly digitalized business, due to the lack of consensus among members of the BEPS Inclusive Framework. At the time of writing is not yet clear whether OECD or UN proposal will be adopted. Since there are countries that are introducing unilateral rules to tax digital services, it could be possible that the amendment presented by the UN could be easier to implement in tax treaties, than to reach a consensus in a multilateral system.

2.4. The Prospects for Deepening Multilateral Cooperation in Tough Times

While the standards on exchange of information (Global Transparency Forum) and the BEPS 4 Minimum Standards (BEPS Inclusive Framework) represent an increase of the importance of multilateral principles in taxation, these standards do not deal with the allocation of taxing rights between countries (which countries mainly deal with on a bilateral basis as introduced earlier), neither with the issue of tax competition among countries. However, members of the BEPS Inclusive Framework are currently discussing two proposals that could introduce a multilateral element in these issues.

The first proposal aims to find a solution to the tax issues resulting from the increasing digitalization of the economy. While countries' tax laws bilateral tax treaties rely to a large extent on the physical location of businesses to determine where income is generated (and where it should be taxed accordingly), digitalization increasingly enables businesses to take part in the economy of a country without physical presence (Mosquera & Heitmüller, 2019). The OECD's proposal for "revised nexus and profit allocation rules" suggests a method that could be applied to allocate income of digital companies to different countries. However, and mainly due to the lack of agreement in the content of these proposals, countries are introducing unilateral rules departing from the multilateral solution, it is expected however that these would be repealed once an aggregate solution is found.[21] Other countries have decided to wait before committing to further discussion for the adoption of any proposals.[22]

The second proposal addresses tax competition: "Tax competition" describes a practice whereby countries try to provide lower tax rates than other countries in order to attract internationally available capital. This is considered as potentially problematic, because countries are induced to discriminate between different "tax bases". While mobile bases, meaning principally companies in sectors that do not depend significantly on physical locations, would end up paying very little tax, immobile bases (workers, heavy industries etc.) might face a higher burden or public spending would be reduced. While the available empirical evidence is not definitive (Adam et al., 2013), the downward trend in corporate income tax rates (Genschel & Seelkopf, 2016) and the proliferation of corporate income tax incentives (Stausholm, 2017), paired with politicians' frequent statements that the national "tax system should be more competitive" suggests that the phenomenon is real (Latulippe, 2016). Tax competition resembles a classical prisoner's dilemma situation (Rixen, 2008, p. 18).

While earlier initiatives always stressed that countries are free to set their tax rate, the current OECD proposal for GLoBE rules aims at introducing a global minimum tax rate, which would "set a floor for tax competition" (OECD, 2019, p. 27). While countries would not be obliged to introduce such a minimum rate in their tax legislation, the proposed rules would act as an incentive to do so. Their basic idea is that either the country where an MNE is headquartered or the country where income is earned would tax income normally attributed to the other country if that other country fails to levy a tax above the globally fixed minimum rate.

In sum, the two proposals currently discussed might, if adopted, influence the allocation of taxing rights and tax rates set by countries, thereby extending the scope of multilateralism in international taxation.

A remaining question is to what extent the COVID-19 crisis affects multilateralism in taxation. First, COVID-19 means that holding meetings in person is more difficult, which might, in general, render reaching negotiated multilateral solutions more difficult. Nevertheless, for the time being, the OECD Secretariat and countries involved have continued negotiations with only little delay (Irma Johanna Mosquera Valderrama, 2020). But what about the content? How are the political pre-conditions for deepening multilateralism in taxation affected by COVID?

While many European countries provided direct cash transfers to businesses in difficulty (sometimes in form of wage subsidies), many countries with lower budgetary capacity enacted temporary tax reliefs for business. However, in the case of subsidiaries of MNEs, such tax reliefs might be rendered ineffective if the GloBE proposal is adopted (in a strong version)—which led observers doubt that many countries would currently agree on such a proposal (Swain et al., 2020).

The prospect for "pillar 1", however, might be better: many digital companies are considered as winners of the crisis (think for example about online video conferencing, delivery services, video-on-demand, etc.), which, paired with a bigger need to raise revenue in the medium term, has increased the political salience of taxing their income (OECD, 2020c, p. 6; Swain et al., 2020). Whether countries will indeed agree on a multilateral solution or whether other ways such as unilateral digital services taxes will be more prominent is, however, still open.

Within the European Union, however, the COVID-19 crisis has already led the EU Commission to propose a tax on digital services directly levied at European level, which—if adopted—would represent an unprecedented step of tax multilateralism within the European Union (see following section).

3. MULTILATERAL COOPERATION
IN THE EUROPEAN UNION

Commonly political scientists refer to the European Community as a case of success in the quest for multilateralism. Ruggie, for instance, argues, "The European Community (EC) is the undisputed anchor of economic relations and increasingly of a common political vision in the West". As such its actions and interactions at a regional level should be accounted as part of a thick multilateralism[23] providing an example of regional multilateral agreement to the extent that is possible for tax matters within the EU and in its relations with non-EU members (third countries).[24]

The following section will address the elements that support multilateral cooperation between EU member-states, as well as those that hinder a higher level of cooperation in direct taxation at the Union level. Then comments will be provided upon the role of the EU in drafting and adopting at regional and international levels generalizable principles of conduct towards direct taxation via the introduction of the EU Anti-Avoidance Package and EU fair and simple taxation, as well as the evolution of the Good Tax Governance Standard.

3.1. Achieving Multilateral Cooperation at the EU Level

The claim about a thick multilateralism at the EU level is supported by the fact that practical coordination is granted as there is a developed institutional form that works in order to solve extensive problems of member states at the Union. In short, discussions being suggested at the Economic and Financial Affairs Council (ECOFIN) are evaluated by the EU Parliament and also commented by the EU Commission. The former, enables all EU institutions to discuss broadly topics to be adopted within the same year or at least in shorter periods of time. Institutional coordination can also be harness by the EU when entering into agreements with third countries (D'Ambrosio, 2020).[25]

The institutional framework enables the creation of generalizable principles of conduct that shall be adopted by member states in their negotiations of investment treaties, commercial agreements and in general financial deals which in turn will impact direct taxation. The common ground achieved by the EU resides in the development of tax standards that provide a background upon which member states will develop their financial agreements, investment treaties and tax policies.

Basically, relations at the EU level will be envisioned with a common set of aims. The establishment of such aims is considered to be embedded in the general conception of working together to achieve broader benefits that could be applicable to all circumstances rather than specific ones (diffuse reciprocity) (Caporaso, 1992). Also, the fact that standards are being agreed in a regional setting allows member states to expect alike costs and leverage from benefits associated with the collective actions (indivisibility).[26]

Yet, while the setting is established in order to strive in multilateral tax cooperation member states preserve their right to define their domestic and international tax policies on a single basis, with a few exceptions (e.g. compliance with primary and secondary EU law). Those exceptions need to be discussed and adopted by member states following the principle of unanimity, which necessarily implies delays in the decision-making process because of the lack of consensus among member states.[27]

In January 2019, the EU Commission proposed to change decision making in direct taxation to qualified majority (European Commission., 2019, p. 15). With this proposal, the Commission aimed at changing the special legislative procedure, where the Council acts as the only legislator and the EU Parliament is a consulted body, for introducing an ordinary legislative procedure, where both bodies would co-legislate. According to the Commission, this change was needed to overcome the veto power that each member states has with regard to legislation for direct tax matters. Among other reasons, it was stated that the unanimity requirement implies that new proposals can be blocked for several years at the Council's level without being discussed, and that agreements are achieved at the "lowest common denominator level", which reduces the cohesive impact of measures or makes them rather more burdensome.[28]

On the other side, QMV would enable the Council to pass direct taxation decisions with 55% of the member states voting in favour if the voting parties represent at least 65% of the EU population. In other words, the shift would mean giving up tax sovereignty on the grounds of agreement with other member states, and especially with those whose population is significantly representative of the EU inhabitants. It is not surprising that the proposal was not adopted as states with smaller populations (e.g. Luxembourg, Ireland and the Netherlands) did not back the decision at the closed-door meeting held in February 2019.[29]

The outcome faced by the proposal to amend the decision-making process explains some of the struggles faced by the EU when it comes to achieving a multilateral engagement at the regional level. The main feature that prevents a harmonic result for direct taxation resides in the supremacy of the concept of tax sovereignty. The unanimity rule sets a dynamic that constrains a move forward into achieving a homogenous system for direct taxes. However, as long as tax standards exist, the future developments promise a better future perspective regarding a tax coordinated evolution.

3.2. Adopting Standards as a Way to Create Generalized Principles of Conduct

From 1997 onwards, EU institutions started investing into importing and exporting tax standards (I. J. M. Valderrama, 2019). In general, three elements were presented as required to be standardised among EU members: (a) transparency; (b) exchange of information (on request and automatic); and (c) fair tax competition. Explicitly this were the elements included in the Standard of Good Tax Governance as introduced by the ECOFIN in 2008, with the intention to tackle tax fraud, tax avoidance and the use of tax havens by securing their commitment to transparency and exchange of information. Since the creation of this standard, EU institutions encouraged EU states to extend the adherence of this commitment to third (non-EU).

In order to do so, the Commission issued further recommendations on 2009 and 2012 within which new guidelines were provided. On the first, it was clarified that third states to be considered for adopting the standard were EU potential candidates and third countries requesting and receiving EU development aid.[30] If these countries did not accept, they could risk to lose the support, as it could be "relocated to other countries, or in some cases even cancelled" (European Commission, 2009, pp. 9–12).

On 2012, the Commission issued an Action Plan (European Commission, 2012b)[31] and two recommendations (European Commission, 2012a), providing criteria to determine administrative conditions needed in order to adopt the standards as well as hallmarks for determining if a country was engaging into harmful tax practices. The criteria mentioned by the Commission replicated OECD's advices and made emphasis in the use of OECD accepted principles (e.g. Arm's length principle) (Valderrama, 2019).[32] Connected with this work the Commission discussed the possibility to include a blacklist for identifying the countries not willing to adopt the good tax governance standards. The list was created looking forward to terminate agreements with listed nations if a solution to their standard's adoption reluctance was not foreseeable. However, the initiative was not adopted and amendments never took place (I. J. M. Valderrama, 2019).

In 2016, the Commission issued the Anti-Tax Avoidance Package (European Parliament, 2018)[33] which Annexes entailed the process for assessing and blacklisting third countries not compliant with the criteria of EU good governance in tax matters (European Commission, 2016a). The main criteria chosen for the assessment were aligned with the considerations included under the BEPS project, among them not having implemented harmful tax regimes, being able to request the taxpayer for proof of real economic activity and fulfilling the international standards of exchange of information (European Commission, 2016b). Such an action was followed by the EU Council adopting the EU blacklist (Council of the European Union, 2017)[34] of non-cooperative jurisdictions for tax purposes.[35]

In 2018, the ECOFIN introduced the BEPS four minimum standards within the elements concerning the EU Standard of Good Tax Governance (Council of the European Union, 2018) highlighting that parties compliant with the standards are interested in improving international cooperation as well as enabling jurisdictions to collect legitimate tax revenues (Council of the European Union, 2018).

4. CRITICAL PERSPECTIVES ON THE CURRENT SYSTEM OF MULTILATERAL COOPERATION

Both the procedure and the outcomes of multilateral cooperation in tax matters have received criticism. Many criticized, for example, that although developed and developing countries are participating in the implementation of standards on information and exchange and BEPS, the agenda-setting and decision-making process for these international tax standards have taken place at OECD and G20 level or EU level which consists only of developed countries.[36]

The BEPS project was developed between 2013 and 2015 by the OECD with the political mandate of the G20, which represents mainly developed countries and some emerging economics (G20: China, India and Russia). The BEPS Inclusive Framework was introduced in 2016 looking for the participation of OECD, G20 and non-OECD, non-G20 countries.

This biased agenda setting creates doubts upon the input legitimacy[37] of the BEPS efforts vis-à-vis non-OECD, non-G20 countries as addressed by one of the authors elsewhere (Irma Johanna Mosquera Valderrama, 2015). In the past, Pistone has questioned the legitimacy of the international standard for fiscal transparency, which in his opinion was once again created by the OECD and left to be further developed by a newly created Global Forum on Tax Transparency (Pistone, 2015).

In the case of the EU, third countries, including developing countries, have been required to adopt the Standard of Good Governance as a precondition to receive EU development aid, and conclude strategic partnership agreements, free trade and economic partnership agreements. More recently, compliance with the standard determines whether a third country should be included in a common EU list of non-cooperative jurisdictions. Also, the black and grey lists adopted in 2017 by the EU Council get to be updated constantly (European Commission, 2020).

In this way, peer pressure is created for the adoption of the standards at the regional level and at the international level as the countries that belong to the Inclusive Framework allow other countries to peer review the adoption of the minimum standards (I.J. Mosquera Valderrama, 2018).

5. CONCLUSION

The evolution of multilateral cooperation in tax matters in the past 30 years is owed to the constant interaction of stakeholders[38] aiming at finding common standards for the solution of collective problems such as tax evasion and avoidance. As a general rule, the issues identified refer to the reduction of taxes collected as a result of artificial manoeuvres conducted to reduce the reported earnings in each jurisdiction entitled to tax them. These issues are supposed to gain importance in the coming years as the commercial and trade practices evolved making use of digital solutions for conducting businesses that were traced in regard to material interactions for which administrative practices were designed.

Based on this conception, international and regional efforts have been put into practice for determining generalized principles applicable to the design of countries' tax systems and their interaction among each other. One can say that between the G20, the OECD, the UN (to a lesser extent) and the EU, these principles have been introduced as standards to be adopted by nation states around the world. The constant interaction between these actors and the feedback obtained from NGOs, MNEs, civil society and media enabled nation states to move forward into their adoption.

The interplay of stakeholders can be beneficial for the tax practice as it fuels the discussions regarding revenue raise, tax policy design and tax collection procedures. Conversely, the pressure imposed upon legislative and administrative bodies to provide standards might result in the creation of overlaping terminologies, which creates confusion among stakeholders. An example of this situation was already presented by one of the authors in the past concerning the drafting of provisions for Good Tax Governance within investment treaties signed by EU member-states and third countries (I. J. M. Valderrama, 2019). It must be remembered that the consolidation of founding principles even within local or regional settings is a reverberation process that is influenced by contrasting forces in long periods of time before a formal adoption. It is in fact this mixture of ideas and interests that enables legitimate processes to take place, as the agenda setting and the implementation phases are connected and defined jointly by all the stakeholders.

Likewise, the determination of the standards introduced by the BEPS project is tainted with issues of legitimacy in their input and output (Mosquera Valderrama, 2015, p. 348) spectrums at least in consideration to non-OECD countries (mostly developing countries). Foremost, legitimacy issues could arise in the future since the pressure caused by changing circumstances (e.g. the COVID-19 pandemic) might influence the decision-making process for some of the actors at the expense of increasing the expenses for other nation states or breaching both the global tax governance cooperative aim and looking for immediate benefits opposing to tax benefits in the long run.

Some scholars might talk about a change between bilateral agreements to multilateral ones (Pistone, 2015). However, the reality seems to corroborate that both phenomena coexist and they will continue doing so, since tax standards will derive into the adoption of generalized organizing principles fuelling multilateral cooperation without eliminating completely the bilateral interactions (Avi-Yonah & Xu, 2016). Likewise, unilateral action might be expected from countries that have enough bargaining power or either preserve a prevalent position[39] and decide to exercise their power to determine their tax legislation at odds with the agreed multilateral standards.[40]

The blending between bilateralism and multilateralism is a constant from which the later avails in order to keep thriving as an institutional form for international taxation. To that extent, that the standards being agreed multilaterally will be enriched in the course of action by the diverse wordings used in bilateral or group focused interactions. Ruggie mentioned that "institutional arrangements of the multilateral form have adaptive and even reproductive capacities" (Ruggie, 1992, p. 4). Indeed, multilateralism needs to be transformed in order to better serve the needs of the stakeholders through time.

For the time being, multilateral cooperation needs to survive the power struggles that may arise in the attempt to determine a new way of taxing profits achieved by enterprises operating during the COVID-19 pandemic.[41] Alternatively, international organizations/multilateral associations might raise their influence taking the lead in defining a standard that could guide states deflecting unilaterally determined tax measures. In either way, countries will strive to raise revenues with which they will cover public expenses incurred to support employment and commercial activity during the markets' partial paralysis, as well as revenues to cover for tax incentives authorized for certain economic sectors.[42]

NOTES

1. Juliana Cubillos (PhD GLOBTAXGOV Fellow), Frederik Heitmüller (PhD GLOBTAXGOV Fellow) and Irma Mosquera Valderrama (Associate Professor and Lead Research GLOBTAXGOV Project). All three working at the Institute of Tax Law and Economics in the Faculty of Law at the University of Leiden in the Netherlands. The writing and research carried out for this Article is the result of the ERC research in the framework of the GLOBTAXGOV Project (2018–2023). This Project investigates international tax lawmaking, including the adoption of OECD and EU standards by 12 countries. *See* GLOBTAXGOV, https://globtaxgov.weblog.leide-nuniv.nl/. The GLOBTAXGOV Project has received funding from the European Research Council (ERC) under the European Union's Horizon 2020 Programme *(ERC Grant agreement n. 758671).*

2. One generally distinguishes between direct and indirect taxes. Direct Taxes are levied on the income of individuals or corporations, whereas indirect taxes are levied principally on consumption in the form of value added taxes or excise taxes. This chapter deals exclusively with multilateral cooperation aimed at direct taxes.

3. The BEPS and the Action Plan have been endorsed in the G20 meetings at Mexico (June 2012) and St Petersburg (September 2013), respectively. In the G20 meeting in St. Petersburg, G20 leaders committed to address base erosion and profit shifting, tackling tax avoidance and promoting transparency and automatic exchange of information. See in particular, para. 50 of the Declaration, where it has been stated: "In a context of severe fiscal consolidation and social hardship, in many countries ensuring that all taxpayers pay their fair share of taxes is more than ever a priority. Tax avoidance, harmful practices and aggressive tax planning have to be tackled". http://www.g20.utoronto.ca/2013/2013-0906-declaration.html

4. *See* section 2.3 of this chapter.

5. The BEPS Project contains 4 Minimum Standards that deal with harmful tax competition, tax treaty abuse, transfer pricing documentation and dispute resolution (Actions 5, 6, 13, and 14), 10 best practices and 1 multilateral instrument. Countries have committed to implement the 4 Minimum Standards by becoming members of the BEPS Inclusive Framework.

6. *See* section 2.4 of this chapter.

7. The OECD's proposals for Pillars 1 and 2 contain more than 500 pages (September 2020). *See* Section 2.4 of this chapter.

8. Rixen and Rohlfing qualified the issue as "coordination game with a distributive conflict".

9. The Fiscal Committee delivered several reports in the course of years 1927–1935. The report of the Fifth Session expressed specifically that there were a limited number of countries willing to adopt a collective solution. For an analysis upon the League of Nations, work upon a multilateral convention (García Antón, 2016).

10. García Antón highlights the following when addressing the League of Nations' initial work: "Notwithstanding the difficulties, the Committee acknowledged the fact that bilateral conventions only constitute a partial solution to the problem of double taxation" (García Antón, 2016).

11. Disregarding the Multilateral Instrument which entered into force as of 1 July 2018. See, for instance, (Thuronyi, 2000) and (Ring, 2000).

12. The UN introduced in its model measures enabling the source state to claim taxing rights under specific situations that were not addressed by the OECD in their model (Lennard, 2009).

13. The sovereignty principle confers power to the state to design and enact the tax policy based on the agreement of a social contract adopted by the people of the given jurisdiction to their elected (legitimate) legislators and governmental agencies.

14. "The OECD state that 'tax evasion' is a term that is difficult to define but which is generally used to mean illegal arrangements where liability to tax is hidden or ignored, i.e. the taxpayer pays less tax than he is legally obligated to pay by hiding income or information from the tax authorities" (Valderrama et al., 2018).

15. Tax avoidance has been defined by the OECD stating that it is "a term that is difficult to define but which is generally used to describe the arrangement of a taxpayer's affairs that is intended to reduce his tax liability and that although the arrangement could be strictly legal it is usually in contradiction with the intent of the law it purports to follow" (OECD, 2020a).

However the distinction between "acceptable tax avoidance" and "unacceptable tax avoidance" is not clearly established, Valderrama et al. recognize that "the approach towards the boundaries between accepted (legally effective) and unaccepted tax avoidance (obtaining benefits not intended by the legislator and legally ineffective due to the use of anti-avoidance doctrines) is followed by countries around the world" (Valderrama et al., 2018).

16. This research is currently carried out in the framework of the European Research Council funded project GLOBTAXGOV in 12 jurisdictions participating in the BEPS Inclusive Framework. This Project investigates international tax law making, including the adoption of OECD and EU standards by 12 countries. (*GLOBTAXGOV—*

A New Model of Global Governance in International Tax Law Making, 2020). The GLOBTAXGOV Project has received funding from the ERC under the European Union's Seven Framework Programme (FP/2007–2013) (ERC Grant agreement n. 758671).

17. See section 6.2.2.2. "Participation of the United Nations" (Irma Johanna Mosquera Valderrama, 2015).

18. Ibid; (Irma Johanna Mosquera Valderrama, 2015).

19. The proposal of the UN Tax Committee as intergovernmental body was rejected by developed countries. These countries contested the leading role of the OECD in all tax issues. See paras. 28 and 29 of the Resolution 69/313 adopted by the General Assembly on 27 July 2015. See also (Irma Johanna Mosquera Valderrama, 2015).

20. The provision's draft can be consulted at: (*TAX TREATY PROVISION ON PAYMENTS FOR DIGITAL SERVICES.Pdf*, 2020).

21. One example is the GAFA Tax—acronym of Google, Apple, Facebook and Amazon.

22. One example is the United States regarding digital taxation.

23. "Regionalism as a model of governance constitutes a thick multilateralism, that is to say, self-conscious efforts to construct regional identities by the use of multilateral identities and organizations" (García Antón, 2016).

24. Countries within the EU are typically capital exporters; hence, EU decisions tend to favour residence taxation. Nevertheless, they need to consider that their positioning depends on the good relations they have with both capital importers and exporters around the world.

25. See chapter 8 of this book to get a perspective of economic and financial consequences of the COVID19 crisis on the multilateral relations of EU member states.

26. García Antón describes indivisibility as the situation whereby "costs and benefits associated with the actions taken by the collectivity are spread among the participant actors. For instance, if peace is the action, the costs and benefits concerning its effective implementation cannot be singularized by particular states" (García Antón, 2016). *See* also (Ruggie, 1992).

27. An example of this stagnation is mentioned by I.J. Mosquera in reference to the lack of consensus between EU countries when defining the content of directives addressing direct taxation matters: "For example, the 1990s Directives on Merger Directive (90/434/EEC) and the Parent and Subsidiary Directive (90/435/EEC) took more than thirty years to be approved and have since been amended further" (I. M. Valderrama, 2020).

28. For a description of the special legislative procedures, please consult (Ramos, 2019).

29. (*Member States Shield National Vetoes on Tax Matters—EURACTIV.Com*, 2020).

30. The Commission published a communication promoting good governance in tax matters (European Commission, 2009, p. 13).

31. See also (European Commission, 2013).

32. See also (OECD, 2010).

33. The package included a plan to revise the blacklist of tax havens outside the EU, an anti-tax avoidance directive, a proposal for establishing the automatic

exchange of country-by-country reports and a recommendation to member states to revise their tax treaties.

34. See also (European Council, 2017).

35. To review the evolution of the list, please go to (European Commission, 2020) either visit (European Commission, 2016).

36. For an overview of the arguments criticizing the participation of developing countries in the agenda setting on the BEPS Project, see Irma Johanna Mosquera Valderrama (2015) and regarding the participation of developing countries in the BEPS Inclusive Framework, see Christians (2018).

37. Regarded as the participation and representation of developing countries in setting the agenda and the content of the OECD/G20 BEPS initiative. "Scharpf states that input legitimacy means that all people affected by the decision should be brought together in deliberations searching for win-win solutions on which all can agree" (Irma Johanna Mosquera Valderrama, 2015).

38. Among them, but not limited to, nation states, non-governmental organizations, international organizations, regional organizations, country associations, media and what has been defined as the Global Civil Society.

39. Which might be granted due to their affiliation to informal associations between countries as the BRICS, G20, G8 or G24.

40. This was, for example, seen before releasing the final report of the Base Erosion and Profit Shifting Action Plan where some countries decided to introduce unilateral measures deviating from the holistic and coordinated approach driven by the OECD with the project (García Antón, 2016).

41. Mainly companies that work with intangible assets or provide web platforms for online interactions. Some of which incremented their estimated profits for the year 2020 in twice of what was expected. One of this companies is Zoom, of which statistics for 2020 can be reviewed in the following webpage (Mansoor, 2020).

42. "Putting stimulus packages in place, including measures to support employment, for example, taking on the burden of unpaid salaries on behalf of companies suffering from the economic effects of COVID-19 pandemic" (OECD, 2020b).

REFERENCES

Adam, A., Kammas, P., & Lagou, A. (2013). The effect of globalization on capital taxation: What have we learned after 20 years of empirical studies? *Journal of Macroeconomics*, *35*, 199–209.

Avi-Yonah, R. S., & Xu, H. (2016). Global taxation after the crisis: Why BEPS and MAATM are inadequate responses, and what can be done about it. *University of Michigan Public Law Research Paper*, *494*.

Caporaso, J. A. (1992). International relations theory and multilateralism: The search for foundations. *International Organization*, 599–632.

Council of the European Union. (2017). *Council Conclusions adopted on 5 December on the EU list of non-cooperative jurisdictions for tax purposes and its Annex (15429/17 FISC 345, ECOFIN 1088)*. (Brussels).

Council of the European Union. (2018). *Council Conclusions adopted on 26 April on the EU Standard Provision on Good Governance in Tax Matters for Agreements with Third Countries, FISC 180, ECOFIN 364.*

D'Ambrosio, C. (2020). *Chapter 9—The European Union and the Challenges to Internal Multilateralism: A study of the economic implications of the COVID-19 crisis.* Rowman & Littlefield.

European Commission. (2009). *Communication of 28 April: Promoting Good Governance in Tax Matters, COM (2009) 201 final (at p.13).*

European Commission. (2012a). *Commission Recommendation of 6 December: Measures intended to encourage third countries to apply minimum standards of good governance in tax matters, C (2012) 8805 final (at p.4).*

European Commission. (2012b). *Communication of 6 December 2012: An Action Plan to Strengthen the Fight against Tax Fraud and Tax Evasion, COM 722 final.*

European Commission. (2013). *Commission Decision of 23 April: Commission Expert Group to be known as the Platform for Tax Good Governance, Aggressive Tax Planning and Double Taxation, OJ C120/17 (at 3).*

European Commission. (2016a). *Communication of 28 January: External Strategy for Effective Taxation, COM/2016/024 final, Annex II.*

European Commission. (2016b). *Communication of 28 January: External Strategy for Effective Taxation, COM/2016/024 final. Annexes I and II of the External Strategy For Effective Taxation.*

European Commission. (2016, September 15). *Common EU list of third country jurisdictions for tax purposes* [Text]. Taxation and Customs Union—European Commission. https://ec.europa.eu/taxation_customs/tax-common-eu-list_en

European Commission. (2019). *Communication of 15 January: Towards a more efficient and democratic decision making in EU tax policy, COM 8 final.*

European Commission. (2020). *Evolution of the EU list of tax havens.* https://ec.europa.eu/taxation_customs/sites/taxation/files/eu_list_update_18_02_2020_en.pdf

European Council. (2017, December 5). *Taxation: Council publishes an EU list of non-cooperative jurisdictions.* Taxation: Council Publishes an EU List of Non-Cooperative Jurisdictions. https://www.consilium.europa.eu/en/press/press-releases/2017/12/05/taxation-council-publishes-an-eu-list-of-non-cooperative-jurisdictions/

European Parliament. (2018). *Legislative Train Schedule, External Strategy for Effective Taxation.* https://www.europarl.europa.eu/legislative-train/theme-deeper-and-fairer-internal-market-with-a-strengthened-industrial-base-taxation/file-external-strategy-for-effective-taxation

García Antón, R. (2016). The 21st Century Multilateralism in International Taxation: The Emperor's New Clothes. *World Tax Journal, 8*(2), 147–192.

Genschel, P., & Seelkopf, L. (2016). Winners and Losers of Tax Competition. In P. Dietsch & T. Rixen (Eds.), *Global Tax Governance. What Is Wrong with It and How to Fix It* (pp. 55–76). United Kingdom: ECPR Press.

Global Forum on Transparency and Exchange of Information for Tax Purposes. (2016). *2016 Terms of reference to monitor and review progress towards transparency and exchange of information on request for tax purposes.* http://www.oecd.org/tax/transparency/documents/terms-of-reference.pdf

GLOBTAXGOV—A new model of global governance in international tax law making. (2020, October). https://globtaxgov.weblog.leidenuniv.nl/

Latulippe, L. (2016). Tax competition: An internalised policy goal. In P. Dietsch & T. Rixen (Eds.), *Global Tax Governance: What Is Wrong with It and How to Fix It* (pp. 77–100). United Kingdom: ECPR Press.

League of Nations—Fiscal Committee. (1927). *Double Taxation and Tax Evasion, Report C.216.M.85.1927.II* (p. 8). League of Nations—Fiscal Committee.

League of Nations—Fiscal Committee. (1930). *Report to the Council on the Work of the Second Session of the Committee, C.340.M.140.1930.II.*

League of Nations—Fiscal Committee. (1935). *Report to the Council of the Work of the Fifth Session of the Committee, C.252.M.124.1935.II.A.* (pp. 12–17). League of Nations—Fiscal Committee.

Lennard, M. (2009). The UN Model Tax Convention as Compared with the OECD Model Tax Convention—Current Points of Difference and Recent Developments. *Asia-Pacific Tax Bulletin, 29*, 4–11.

Mansoor, I. (2020, July 20). *Zoom revenue and usage statistics (2020)—Business of apps.* https://www.businessofapps.com/data/zoom-statistics/

Member states shield national vetoes on tax matters—EURACTIV.com. (2020). https://www.euractiv.com/section/economy-jobs/news/member-states-shield-national-vetoes-on-tax-matters/

Mosquera Valderrama, Irma Johanna. (2015). *Legitimacy and the making of international tax law: The challenges of multilateralism.* 3 World Tax Journal (2015), Journals IBFD.

Mosquera Valderrama, I.J. (2018, December 10). *Peer Review of BEPS 4 Minimum Standards: From Compliance to Learning and Contextualization presented at the International Tax Cooperation: The Challenges and Opportunities to Multilateralism organized by the Saïd Business School, University of Oxford.*

Mosquera Valderrama, Irma Johanna. (2020, May 6). Multilateralism: The Weakest Link? *GLOBTAXGOV Blog.* https://globtaxgov.weblog.leidenuniv.nl/2020/05/06/multilateralism-the-weakest-link/

Mosquera, V. I.J., & Heitmüller, F. (2019). *Corporate Tax, Digitalization and Globalization.* WEF – Platform for Shaping the Future of Trade and Global Economic Interdependence: white paper. Cologny / Geneva: World Economic Forum. http://www3.weforum.org/docs/WEF_Corporate_Tax_Digitalization_and_Globalization.pdf

OECD. (2010). *Launch of a Peer Review Process: Terms of Reference to Monitor and Review Progress towards Transparency and Exchange of Information for Tax Purposes, Global Forum on Transparency and Exchange of Information for Tax Purposes (4–9).* https://www.oecd.org/ctp/44824681.pdf

OECD. (2019). *Programme of work to develop a consensus solution to the tax challenges arising from the digitalisation of the economy* (OECD/G20 Base Erosion and Profit Shifting Project). http://www.oecd.org/tax/beps/programme-of-work-to-develop-a-consensus-solution-to-the-tax-challenges-arising-from-the-digitalisation-of-the-economy.pdf

OECD. (2020a). *Glossary of tax terms—OECD.* http://www.oecd.org/ctp/glossary oftaxterms.htm

OECD. (2020b). *OECD secretariat analysis of tax treaties and the impact of the COVID-19 crisis.* https://read.oecd-ilibrary.org/view/?ref=127_127237-vsdagpp 2t3&title=OECD-Secretariat-analysis-of-tax-treaties-and-the-impact-of-the-COVID-19-Crisis

OECD. (2020c). *Tax and fiscal policy in response to the coronavirus crisis: Strengthening confidence and resilience.* https://read.oecd-ilibrary.org/view/?ref= 128_128575-o6raktc0aa&title=Tax-and-Fiscal-Policy-in-Response-to-the-Coro navirus-Crisis

Pistone, P. (2015, September 17). *Form and substance of national tax sovereignty in the era of international tax standards presented at the 10th GREIT Annual Conference—Session one-Tax sovereignty in the era of tax multilateralism— EU BEPS; Fiscal Transparency, Protection of Taxpayer Rights and State Aid. Amsterdam.*

Ramos, E. (2019, January 11). *Decision making on EU Tax Policy* [Text]. Taxation and Customs Union—European Commission. https://ec.europa.eu/taxation_customs/ taxation/decision-making-eu-tax-policy_en

Ring, D. M. (2000). Prospects for a multilateral tax treaty. *Brook. J. Int'l L., 26,* 1699.

Rixen T. (2008). Introduction. In: The Political Economy of International Tax Governance. Transformations of the State. London: Palgrave Macmillan. https://doi. org/10.1057/9780230582651_1.

Rixen, T., & Rohlfing, I. (2007). The Institutional Choice of Bilateralism and Multilateralism in International Trade and Taxation. *International Negotiation, 12*(3), 389–414. https://doi.org/10.1163/138234007X240718

Ruggie, J. G. (1992). Multilateralism: The anatomy of an institution. *International Organization,* 561–598.

Stausholm, S. N. (2017). Rise of ineffective incentives: New empirical evidence on tax holidays in developing countries. *SocArXiv.* https://doi.org/10.31235/osf. io/4sn3k

Swain, S., Goel, S., & Goel, A. (2020, April 30). International tax law and policy amid the COVID-19 pandemic. *GLOBTAXGOV Blog.* https://globtaxgov.weblog.leide nuniv.nl/2020/04/30/international-tax-law-and-policy-amid-the-covid-19-pandemic/

Tax Treaties: Boost or bane for development?—IMF Blog. (n.d.). https://blogs.imf. org/2016/11/16/tax-treaties-boost-or-bane-for-development/

Tax treaty provision on payments for digital services. (2020, October). https:// www.un.org/development/desa/financing/sites/www.un.org.development.desa. financing/files/2020-08/TAX%20TREATY%20PROVISION%20ON%20PAY MENTS%20FOR%20DIGITAL%20SERVICES.pdf

Thuronyi, V. (2000). International Tax Cooperation and a Multilateral Treaty. *Brooklyn Journal of International Law, 26,* 1641.

Valderrama, I. J. M. (2019). The EU Standard of Good Governance in Tax Matters for Third (Non-EU) Countries. *Intertax, 47*(5), 14.

Valderrama, I. M. (2020). A New Wind Change in Direct Taxation. *German Law Journal, 21*(1), 90–95.

Valderrama, I. M., Mazz, A., Schoueri, L. E., Quiñones, N., West, C., Pistone, P., & Zimmer, F. (2018). Tools used by countries to Counteract Aggressive tax planning in light of transparency. *Intertax, 46*(2), 140–155.

Chapter 14

The UN Climate Regime: Multilateralism, Polycentricity and Divergent Energy Futures

Susann Handke

1. INTRODUCTION

The world experienced an unpredicted decline in greenhouse gas emissions in 2020. The coronavirus pandemic that spread from China to across the globe during the first quarter of 2020 brought a fast halt to economic activity. Energy-related emissions fell suddenly when governments shut down entire economies in order to stop the spread of the virus. The sudden fall in demand for oil even caused prices for oil futures turn to negative in April, when traders lost confidence in a quick recovery of the fossil-fuel-based global economy (Brower et al., 2020). The viability of pre-pandemic low-carbon transition[1] plans was also doubted amidst fiscal constraints resulting from crisis recovery packages. The years following 2020 will show whether the international community will be able to *structurally* reduce greenhouse gas emissions by deploying economic policy measures and adhering to the agreed rules-based climate cooperation that the UN climate regime institutionalises.

This chapter explores whether the UN climate regime constitutes a suitable framework to coordinate multilateral climate cooperation in the coming decades. To assess the regime's role, the chapter considers its contribution to global efforts to decarbonise energy generation. Although the UN climate regime stipulates rules for an economy-wide approach to limit the emission of several greenhouse gases that are responsible for global warming, the chapter focuses on energy and climate measures that decrease the emission of carbon dioxide (CO_2) for two reasons.

First, the energy sector is responsible for the emission of more than two-thirds of all anthropogenic greenhouse gases.[2] Second, singling out CO_2 is appropriate because this gas is primarily responsible for global warming. It is emitted when fossil fuels—crude oil, natural gas and coal—are burnt to generate energy in order to *transport* goods or people, *heat* rooms and *power* electric appliances. Accordingly, the energy sector largely contributes to the emission of CO_2.[3] Thus, transforming the way in which energy is produced is essential for any success in mitigating climate change. In many states, this transformation—described as the decarbonisation of energy generation or low-carbon transition—has been ongoing since the turn of the century, mainly driven by dovetailing national climate and energy policies.

Governments, businesses and local communities took low-carbon measures on a larger scale as a response to the adoption of the 1992 UN Framework Convention on Climate Change (UNFCCC) and especially after the 1997 Kyoto Protocol entered into force in 2005.[4] These first two treaties of the UN climate regime established a top-down approach to emissions reductions, based on negotiated emissions reduction obligations for developed states. The 2015 Paris Agreement restructured the regime, which now facilitates a hybrid form of multilateral climate cooperation. In fact, the new approach combines bottom-up elements in the form of nationally determined contributions (NDCs) to global emissions reductions with top-down international oversight tools for which the decisions of 2018 Katowice Rulebook provide detailed guidelines.

Following this volume's theme, this chapter evaluates challenges to multilateralism that relate to the recent restructuring of the UN climate regime. The chapter examines how climate multilateralism is revisited based on the polycentric nature of climate governance on which the UN climate regime relies after the adoption of the Paris Agreement. Obviously, there is a necessity to coordinate national climate and energy policies at the global level to achieve the objective of the Paris Agreement (Article 2 (1) (a))—that is, keeping global warming below 2°C compared to pre-industrial temperatures. Thus, multilateral cooperation needs to navigate both polycentric structures of climate governance and very divergent energy situations.

This chapter focuses on two forms of challenges that multilateral climate cooperation faces under the Paris Agreement. First, it considers the coordination of polycentric energy and climate governance. To show which difficulties have to be addressed in this regard, the chapter discusses the energy and climate policies of the European Union (EU), the United States and China and their respective roles in the UN climate regime. Second, the chapter examines still unsolved regulatory issues that pertain to the streamlining of the multilateral oversight tools. These procedures are vital for information sharing and strengthening global efforts to mitigate climate change. The chapter argues that the UN climate regime provides tools for creating an interactional space as part of a multilateral process that can facilitate multi-layered, polycentric climate governance.

The next section gives an overview of the theoretical framework and the methods that are used to structure the reasoning. Section 3 summarises the development of the UN climate regime. Section 4 explains the polycentric nature of governing the low-carbon energy transition and summarises the different approaches of the biggest emitters—the EU, the United States and China. Section 5 discusses which elements are essential to inform multilateral monitoring processes that the Paris Agreement establishes in order to deal with these divergent realities. It also identifies limits to international cooperation. The sixth section ponders the evolving characteristics of climate multilateralism in the post-Paris and post-pandemic era. Section 7 concludes and offers some reflections on how the findings of this chapter relate to both the practice of climate negotiations and the study of international climate cooperation.

2. THEORETICAL APPROACH: MULTILATERALISM IN A CLIMATE-CONSTRAINED WORLD

This chapter's theoretical approach is interdisciplinary. It starts with a brief legal analysis of the structural evolution of the UN climate regime that highlights the norms that will guide multilateral climate cooperation in the years to come. Then, the chapter resorts to theoretical concepts that political scientists developed, such as polycentric governance (Thiel, 2017) and discursive multilateralism (Weisband, 2000). These concepts help to assess whether the Paris Agreement, together with the decisions of the Katowice Rulebook, provides a suitable framework to coordinate international climate cooperation. This approach is particularly useful to understanding the possible challenges that climate multilateralism, as guided by the UN climate regime, will face in the near future.

The concepts of polycentricity and discursive multilateralism are deployed to assess the evolving linkage between national energy and climate policymaking and the implementation of the Paris Agreement. First, in section 4, the chapter describes the institutional landscape that comes with the low-carbon transition as a multi-layered form of governance. The features of these governance structures and their diversity across the globe are exemplified by a brief consideration of the decarbonisation of the power sector in the EU, the United States and China. It will be shown that important decisions are taken at local, sub-national and national levels. The low-carbon transition is thus an example of *polycentricity*. This chapter uses this term in an ontological sense—that is, describing a configuration of governance structures that can be observed (Thiel, 2017, pp. 56–56, 65–66). This also points to the fact that the low-carbon transition is a governed transition (Kern & Rogge, 2016,

pp. 13–17), involving governance structures and fields of policymaking that
display horizontal and vertical linkages that are shaped and maintained by
various actors with decision-making power and authority to implement policies. These governance structures reflect diverging interests, conceptualisa-
tions and imaginaries regarding the future trajectory of the energy sector *and*
related social, economic and environmental policies.

Subsequently, section 5 uses the concept of *discursive multilateralism*, as
introduced by Edward Weisband (2000), in order to assess the UN climate
regime in the context of this polycentric governance landscape. This concept
is befitting this chapter's analysis, mainly because it offers a theoretical
approach that is based on social constructivist theories, which are particularly
suited to study the interaction of states and their identities in the context of
legal norms and international regimes.

Constructivist theories consider states as agents or actors whose identities
are shaped by the norms of the regimes in which they participate. This char-
acteristic is a helpful point of departure for analysing regimes that set "benchmarks" for the evaluation of the parties' compliance with the regime's norms
in question (Broome & Quirk, 2015). These benchmarks are formulated and
traced through monitoring procedures. The analysis in this chapter will show
which oversight tools the Paris Agreement entails and how these procedures
can enable a form of discursive multilateralism in the future. This analysis
also reveals possible challenges to the effectiveness of climate multilateralism under the Paris Agreement with respect to its objective of keeping global
warming limited to 2°C compared to pre-industrial levels.

To sum up, the analysis of the chapter follows two threads. First, it considers the polycentricity of the governance structures that steer the low-carbon
energy transition. Second, it assesses oversight tools that the Paris Agreement
applies in a top-down way to promote the parties' compliance with their
commitments. Based on the findings that derive from these two analytical
threads, some conclusions can be drawn regarding the nature of the climate
multilateralism that the Paris Agreement can enable and which challenges the
parties might face in the near future.

3. GUIDING GLOBAL CLIMATE CHANGE MITIGATION

The UN climate regime was established with the adoption of the UNFCCC.
The negotiation of this treaty was part of a broader multilateral effort to
address global environmental problems in preparation of the 1992 Earth Summit[5] in Rio de Janeiro, Brazil. The structure of the UN climate regime follows the pattern of other multilateral environmental agreements. Since these
regimes usually address *global* environmental problems, they seek to engage

as many states as possible. The institutionalisation of the cooperation to solve the problem at hand begins with the adoption of a framework convention that primarily regulates procedural aspects and establishes the institutions of the regime. Subsequently, substantive specificities and concrete obligations of the states parties[6] are negotiated and delineated in additional protocols under the framework convention (Hey, 2016, pp. 87–88, 96–107).

From a legal perspective, framework conventions and their protocols are treaties under international law. They contain legally binding commitments that the parties undertake to coordinate the solution of an environmental problem. Together with the institutions—such as plenary and governance bodies—these treaties form a regime under which the states parties adopt decisions in order to guide and regulate multilateral efforts to address environmental degradation.

First efforts to coordinate and institutionalise multilateral responses to the global environmental crisis were made in the early 1970s, beginning with the 1972 Stockholm Conference on the Human Environment (Joyner, 1974, p. 357; Elliott, 1998, p. 15). Since then, the principles of international environmental law have been further developing, especially following the adoption of the 1992 Rio Declaration (Viñuales, 2015). They continue to inspire the design of multilateral environmental agreements.

The institutions and principles of the UN climate regime reflect the early conceptualisation of global warming as an environmental problem—that is, harmful emissions that affect the atmosphere. Consequently, its institutional approach derives from the experiences with other multilateral environmental agreements. This approach, together with the principles of international environmental law, largely shaped the structural evolution of the UN climate regime. As will be shown, this legacy will also be relevant for the parties' future interaction under the re-structured regime. Therefore, a brief overview of the role of principle of common but differentiated responsibilities, one of the UN climate regime's core principles, is justified at this point.

The principle of common but differentiated responsibilities seeks to facilitate differential treatment for developing states to ensure and enable their participation in the regime. The principle played an important role throughout the regime's history, especially following the rigid interpretation (Weisslitz, 2002) featured in the 1995 Berlin Mandate, which was the first decision the conference of parties, the UN climate regime's plenary body, took under the UNFCCC. This decision stipulated that developing states would be exempted from any substantive commitments that might go beyond the cooperation that the UNFCCC required. This notion determined the scope of the Kyoto Protocol, which, as a result, only lists negotiated emissions reduction targets for developed states. This top-down structure eventually failed to achieve a significant limitation of global greenhouse gas emissions.

The Kyoto Protocol's first implementation period began in 2008 and lasted until 2012. By that time, the global emissions situation had changed remarkably compared to the early and mid-1990s, mainly because after the turn of the century, China added hundreds of coal-fired power plants to supply its fast-growing industry and mega-cities with electricity. Moreover by the early 2010s, other developing states, such as India and Brazil, also joined the ranks of emerging economies. Meaningful international climate cooperation without these states' contribution became increasingly impossible. Therefore, the conference of parties in its 2011 Durban Platform called for a reconsideration of the international approach to climate change mitigation and the adoption of a new legal instrument by 2015.

Subsequent decisions of the annual conferences of parties envisaged structural changes to international climate cooperation, especially the option that the states parties derive their commitments from national policies instead of negotiating emissions reduction targets. With the adoption of the Paris Agreement, these anticipated changes became treaty law. Pursuant to Article 4 (2) of the Paris Agreement, *all* parties submit NDCs to engage in some form of climate change mitigation. The first round of NDCs were sent to the UNFCCC Secretariat ahead of the 2015 climate summit that adopted the Paris Agreement. The parties based their submissions on existing and intended national climate and energy policies. The implementation of the NDCs began in 2020, while follow-up NDCs are expected to constitute a progression to the previous ones. The first evaluation of the global emissions situation and the parties' efforts to implement their NDCs will take place in 2023.

To sum up, the Paris Agreement established a process of coordinating international climate cooperation by evaluating the progress of national climate and energy policies in terms of the treaty's objective of limiting global warming to a 1.5 to 2°C compared to pre-industrial temperature levels. This bottom-up approach to defining the parties' commitments is complemented by oversight tools that inform further conversations to foster international climate action. The next three sections discuss the intricacies of linking national policies and sub-national decision making with multilateral processes under the UN climate regime and resulting challenges for future climate action.

4. POLYCENTRICITY AND THE GOVERNANCE OF LOW-CARBON TRANSITIONS

The low-carbon transition, in contrast to previous shifts from one fuel to another, is described as a governed transition. This points to the fact that this transition is not primarily driven by the economic benefits of the new fuel (Fouquet, 2010). Instead, the motives for replacing fossil fuels with non-carbon energy resources relate to broad environmental concerns, including air pollution and the threat of climate change. Thus, the choice for non-carbon fuels, such as wind, solar and hydropower, can generally not be justified from an economic perspective, if environmental externalities are excluded. Therefore, government interference, such as fiscal incentives and financial support measures, was necessary to implement policies, at least in the early phase of the low-carbon transition (Kern & Rogge, 2016, p. 14).

Generally, the low-carbon transition of the energy generation was limited to the electricity sector during its first phase (International Energy Agency, 2016). The late 2010s witnessed initial steps to conceptualise the decarbonisation of the heating and transport sectors. In achieving these transitions, the electricity sector and its low-carbon credentials will be vital. Thus, it is warranted, for the purpose of this chapter, to focus on the decarbonisation of electricity generation.

This fuel transition took place against the backdrop of previous fuel choices and within a liberalised structure of the electricity sector. The EU, the United States and China provide examples of the challenges that governments faced when they began to implement initial measures to promote the use of renewable energy sources to produce electricity. To understand these challenges, considering the power sector's governance is particularly relevant. During the 1990s, the market liberalisation of the electricity sector, both in developed and developing states, sought to introduce more competition and relieve the sector from what was perceived as overtly expensive government control. However, liberalisation policies generally resulted in hybrid governance structures that facilitated competition, but retained some form of government intervention. In the EU, this situation was complicated by efforts of the European Commission to establish a common market for electricity and integrate the sectors of all member states. In the United States, federal oversight of the electricity sector was limited, leading to state-based governance or regional liberalisation models. In China, liberalisation measures resulted in the creation of several large state-owned enterprises by splitting the assets of the Ministry of Electric Power among these entities, functionally and geographically. Five large companies focus on the generation of electricity regionally, while the transmission component of the power sector was (very unequally) divided between two companies.

To guide the functioning of the power sector, some form of government oversight is necessary. In the EU, the European Commission and the Agency for the Cooperation of Energy Regulators regulate and coordinate the implementation of the liberalisation legislation in the member states together with national regulators, in order to create a common market for electricity. In the United States, the Federal Energy Regulatory Commission fulfils a coordinating role at the federal level. In China, independent oversight of the newly created commercial entities remains weak. The Chinese government had initially established a regulatory body, the State Electricity Regulatory Commission. Yet, in 2013, the responsibilities of this commission were taken over by the National Energy Administration, a government agency under the National Development and Reform Commission, which is China's main economic policymaking body.

Two outcomes of this restructuring process relate to future climate cooperation under the Paris Agreement. First, reform efforts in the electricity sector as described for the EU, the United States and China exemplify global trends. Restructuring policies remain incomplete from the perspective of the theory of market liberalisation, while the quality of law enforcement depends on the overall nature of economic governance and the legal system. Thus, electricity sectors across the world face very divergent regulatory environments in which they receive distinct market signals. They respond to societal demands and international environmental standards very differently.

Second, the examples of the EU, the United States and China show that more often than not the central governance level, which from the outset has been in charge of designing climate policies, lacks decision-making powers in the field of energy policy, in terms of institutional or factual competence. Obtaining the same far-reaching powers needed to adopt and implement energy legislation remains a challenge in many states. Thus, the central level is often unable to dovetail climate measures with accompanying energy policies. In the EU, many concrete energy laws and policy decisions were adopted at the national level in the member states, while in the United States, federal states largely determined the direction of their energy policies, sometimes in cooperation with neighbouring states. In China, many elements of economic planning that concern the energy sector have been transferred to the provincial level or even lower levels of decision-making.

These governance structures reflect constitutional and politico-economic specificities of the parties to the UN climate regime that seek to implement low-carbon measures. Efforts to promote the transition to renewable energy sources to generate electricity and *replace* fossil fuels thus interact with various economic, political, societal and environmental concerns.

This is where the concept of polycentricity of governance structures helps to understand the challenge of realising the low-carbon transition: to decarbonise the generation of electricity, many layers of governance—horizontal and vertical—have to coordinate their policies to arrive at consistent incentive structures. This process is complicated by shifting societal preference and politico-economic changes. In addition, during the initial phase of the low-carbon transition after the Kyoto Protocol's entry into force, in 2005, international norms had been further evolving, culminating in the adoption of the Paris Agreement.

Accordingly, the identity of states parties to the Paris Agreement is not only shaped in interaction with the norms of this treaty but also by the norms of various governance levels that inform the states parties' contributions to international climate action. The central governance level has a coordinating role between the international and subnational levels. Hence, states parties engage in multilateral processes, while their identities are in flux, regarding their interests with respect to emissions reduction measures, the deployment of renewables and socio-economic and cultural imagination of their energy futures.

5. MULTILATERAL PROCESSES, POLYCENTRIC GOVERNANCE AND DIVERGENT ENERGY FUTURES

This section explains how multilateral monitoring processes interact with polycentric governance structures and the imagination of energy futures "on the ground." Considering this interrelationship helps to contextualise the Paris Agreement's oversight tools that guide the process of international climate action to mitigate climate change.

As mentioned in section three, the parties prepared their first NDCs, based on existing and planned climate and energy policies, for submission to the UNFCCC Secretariat during the first half of 2015. For the EU, the United States and China, as the three largest emitters, the European Commission, the federal government and the State Council, respectively, drafted these national commitments. Yet, as said, these entities are unable to solely determine and enforce the implementation of the policies. A realisation of the announced climate measures requires the cooperation of various governance levels and the support of the electricity sector. From the outset, all three parties have faced difficulties in fulfilling their self-determined commitments. Thus, it remains to be seen how multilateral monitoring procedures will appreciate the phenomenon of polycentric governance structures.

In the EU, the implementation of the Paris Agreement in domestic policies and law seems to be well underway. By mid-2019, comprehensive legislation to streamline the Union's climate and energy legislation had been adopted—that is, the "Clean Energy for All Europeans" legislative package (European Commission, 2017). Furthermore, in late 2019, the European Commission presented the "European Green Deal" (European Commission, 2019). In March 2020, the member states agreed to decarbonise the Union's economy by 2050 (Council of the European Union, 2020). The EU then submitted its strategy to achieve this aim to UNFCCC Secretariat, as envisaged by Article 4 (1) and (19) of the Paris Agreement that stipulates the need to move to a carbon neutral development path from the second-half of the twenty-first century onwards.

Despite the fact that all EU member states supported this goal, Poland voiced concerns about the timeline of this trajectory, citing the fear of social disruptions in regions that heavily depend on coal production (Morgan, 2019). Indeed, the notion of a just energy transition is a vital aspect of the debate at all levels of decision making. The energy transition highlights concerns about structural change in regions whose economies depend on the fossil-fuel-based generation of energy. Other important issues are energy poverty of vulnerable segments of society and regions, and a growing divide between rural and urban constituencies that are differently affected by the implementation of low-carbon policies, in particular the deployment of renewable energy sources and long-distance electricity transmission lines.

Accordingly, various financial and socio-economic measures still have to be worked out in the coming years to address these matters. Many of these problems will have to be solved by the member states and at decision-making levels that are "closer" to the citizens. However, for the time being, the European Commission at the supranational level seems to be committed to the timely implementation of the Paris Agreement's goals in EU climate and energy legislation.

In the United States, the federal government emerged as the least reliable component in the polycentric governance structure for two reasons.[7] First, more often than not federal measures to influence the fuel mix of the electricity sector are challenged in court, questioning the constitutionality of these measures. Examples are the Clean Power Plan of the Obama administration and the Affordable Clean Energy rule of the Trump administration. Second, the issue of climate change is highly politicised in the United States. The approach of the federal government to coordinate domestic climate measures and international cooperation depends on the president's political persuasion and support in both chambers of the U.S. Congress. Therefore, federal states have become "norm sustainers" in the context of climate multilateralism (Murthy, 2019, p. 24), by implementing the NDC that the United States had submitted to the UNFCCC Secretariat in 2015 and by providing information about the progress related to these initially stated climate targets.

In China, decade-long reliance on coal to fuel rapid economic growth created a political economy that supports powerful constituencies. The economic clout of combusting coal is huge. The wealth of entire provinces and their business and political elites depends on locking in a coal-based economic growth trajectory. These interest groups communicate their message through policy measures of provincial governments or business decisions of provincial or central state-owned enterprises. The central government's economic planning needs to take into account these constituencies, which was once again reflected in the debate about the construction of additional coal-fired power plants in the period of the 14th Five-Year Plan (2021–25), China's main economic planning exercise. The coal industry voiced demands for expansion, despite the fact that by the 2010s, many existing coal-fired power plants were not operating at full capacity (Myllyvirta et al., 2020).

The parties to the UN climate regime face a variety of challenges and need to navigate divergent sets of governance levels that up to the international level guide their low-carbon transitions. Thus, when assessing efforts to mitigate climate change "on the ground," it is necessary to receive and interpret different signals, depending on the specific context of polycentric governance structures that prevail in the jurisdiction in question. Thus, the application of oversight tools needs to account for these differences when evaluating the states parties' compliance with their commitments.

Generally, the role of monitoring procedures in multilateral regimes is to provide some form of compliance control, mainly through regular reports and deliberations among the states parties, which facilitate a constant conversation to highlight best practices. This conversation also assesses the responsiveness of states to previous criticism and reveals their ambition to fulfil their commitments. Ideally, these monitoring procedures and responses of the parties cultivate a form of discursive multilateralism. They then enhance the legitimacy and effectiveness of the regime in question (Weisband, 2000, p. 644).

The Paris Agreement deviates from the previous top-down approach of UN climate regime that can be described as executive multilateralism—that is, a mode of coordinating international decision-making among government representatives that centres on government priorities and largely excludes input from the public (Zürn et al., 2007, p. 133). Instead, in Article 14, the Paris Agreement institutionalises the so-called global stocktake. This forum provides an interactional space where discursive multilateralism can be practised. It remains to be seen to what extent the various levels of polycentric energy and climate governance will be able to communicate with each other in this space.

The global stocktake considers worldwide emissions trends and takes into account national reports about the implementation of the NDC. Pursuant to Article 14, the global stocktake assesses the global emissions situation every five years, beginning in 2023. The conclusions of this stocktake will be interpreted in the context of the Paris Agreement's goal of limiting global warming to less than 2°C and the demand that the parties' successive NDCs have to constitute a progression compared to the previous one. Each state party's performance is evaluated in regular reports that are part of the transparency framework. Thus, this exchange, based on the global emissions situation and the examination of the parties' progress, can institutionalise the interaction between governance levels. Here, discursive multilateralism can take place if the parties allow it to evolve. Much will depend on practical aspects of international oversight procedures.

The Katowice Rulebook stipulates detailed guidelines for the implementation of these oversight mechanisms. The global stocktake is the most notable oversight tool. It relies on the quality of transparency framework that Article 13 of the Paris Agreement regulates, especially the submission of inventory reports. This article includes two important issues that are relevant for the conduct of the global stocktake as a multilateral monitoring process—that is, the notion of "flexibility" in Article 13 and the determination of common timeframes for the submission of NDCs.

First, the notion of flexibility is reflected in the Decision 18/CMA.1 that stipulates the guidelines for the transparency framework of Article 13 (13) of the Paris Agreement. In its second paragraph, Article 13 emphasises that flexibility should be provided to developing states. The bottom-up approach of the Paris Agreement allows states parties to self-categorise to which grouping they belong. Therefore, the transparency framework, as a monitoring tool, is essential for the functioning of the global stocktake. However, by permitting self-categorised developing states to apply flexibility "in the light of their capacities" (Decision 18/CMA.1, paras 3 (c), 4, 5, 6, 7 (c), 25, 29, 32, 34, 35, 48, 57, 58, 85, 92, 95, 102, 159, 162, 192 (c)), these provisions weaken the top-down monitoring procedures. Much will depend on how the parties interpret and incorporate flexibility when judging the credibility and accuracy of the review process and the information that the transparency framework communicates to the global stocktake.

Second, common timeframes regarding the submission of states parties' NDCs are necessary to regulate the parties' increasing mitigation obligations. However, the parties only agreed to apply common timeframes from 2031 onwards. If this decision is upheld, the implementation of the Paris Agreement will be unpredictable and uncertain for more than a decade regarding the coordination of mitigation efforts.

In fact, the delay in implementing common timeframes for the submission of successive NDCs could severely hamper the emergence of states parties' identities in the context of the restructured UN climate regime, mainly because it creates ambiguity with respect to national planning processes. Throughout the 2020s, governments will not know in which frequency the parties will have to update their NDCs during the following decade. This might negatively affect the ambition that the initial NDCs convey. It also prevents the steady development of "best practices" that the interactional space, in which discursive multilateralism takes place, can help identify.

Nevertheless, with the global stocktake, the Paris Agreement institutionalises an interactional space that can facilitate the cultivation of discursive multilateralism in the future. It remains to be seen to what extent, during annual climate negotiations, the states parties will be willing and able to strengthen the monitoring procedures by providing more clarity regarding the definition of flexibility and by advancing the implementation of common timeframes.

However, if these efforts fail or take too long the window of opportunity will be closed. It will be impossible to develop a meaningful discursive multilateralism by relying on weak monitoring procedures. Instead, most of the parties' interactions will continue to focus on the further interpretation of the notion of flexibility and the extension of the period during which the parties can determine their own timeframes for implementing their policy plans.

Under such circumstances, identity formation will be directed by the legacy of the UN climate regime—especially the rigid differentiation between developed and developing states—rather than deriving from the new bottom-up approach to multilateral climate action that the Paris Agreement introduces. Hence, the UN climate regime provides tools for creating an interactional space as part of a multilateral process that can guide climate change mitigation in structures of multi-layered, polycentric climate governance. But issues that have been insufficiently regulated in the decisions of the Katowice Rulebook have the potential to render the effect of the structural adjustments to the UN climate regime void.

6. POST-PARIS, POST-PANDEMIC CLIMATE MULTILATERALISM

The question arises how polycentricity of climate and energy governance and incomplete oversight procedures will affect the evolution of multilateral climate cooperation in the post-Paris era that will, above all, be constrained by many yet unknown post-pandemic predicaments. When considering this question, three factors need to be weighed that will influence climate multilateralism in the near future—that is, trust, accountability and time.

First, trust is indispensable in achieving any progress in international cooperation to provide for a common public good, such as climate change mitigation. The reduction of greenhouse gas emissions requires a far-reaching transformation in developed and large emerging economies. Moreover, climate change is increasingly emerging as a source of threats to national and regional security, challenging "fixed points of reference for international affairs" (Sending et al., 2020, p. 189), as well as a highly politicised issue in the public debate in many states. Thus, fact-based exchange of information and cooperation is of utmost importance. It is vital that negotiators can count on their counterparts that agreements will be honoured and relevant information will be shared in order to enhance the understanding of the climate change phenomenon and its mitigation.

The spread of the coronavirus and the Chinese leadership's reluctance to provide information about the outbreak and the severity of the disease, both in its communications at home and with international partners, have profoundly shaken the trust in its commitment to international cooperation in general. The pandemic highlighted the challenges that the international community faces when multilateral processes to a large degree rely on official reporting from China. As by far the largest emitter of greenhouse gases, China's role in international climate cooperation will be pivotal to any progress in averting dangerous climate change in the near future. Yet, confidence in information shared by the Chinese leadership can be included in the collateral damage of the pandemic. The resulting lack of trust among states parties severely hinders the development of a meaningful climate multilateralism. It also creates room for manoeuvre for other political leaders that seek to discredit multilateral efforts to combat climate change or multilateralism in general.

Second, accountability mechanisms that track governments' efforts to implement their NDCs are blurred, because of the aforementioned polycentric governance structures. In addition, some states parties will most likely continue to avoid stringent accountability norms by further delaying the introduction of common timeframes and trying to rely on a vague notion of flexibility when implementing the modalities of the transparency framework. Prolonged negotiations about small details of these provisions might become commonplace at the annual conferences of parties in the next few years.

Third, the most crucial factor is time. Humankind has only a few decades to prevent dangerous climate change and limit global warming to 1.5 to 2°C. However, the NDCs of most large emitters are insufficient to meet this threshold. In addition, it will take time to adjust the planned energy transitions to the post-pandemic situation. Many states will face fiscal constraints that might hamper the timely implementation of energy policies and climate mitigation measures, while changing social practices, such as working from home and decreased mobility, will have a long-term effect on energy use. Furthermore, the trajectory of the global economy in the post-pandemic era will remain uncertain for a prolonged period of time. Climate negotiations might not be considered the most urgent issue during the first half of the 2020s.

Nevertheless, fast progress on the commencement of the use of common timeframes and a rapid progression of successive NDCs is necessary to speed up the implementation of emissions reduction measures. It is also high time to conceptualise carbon neutrality and the principles and norms that will guide a global economy that is not driven by fossil fuels. At the time of writing there were only three decades left to nurture imaginaries of a world that was expected to emerge after 2050.

The three factors of trust, accountability and time reveal a structural weakness of the Paris Agreement—that is, the lack of a stringent compliance mechanism. Obviously, the deployment of the UN climate regime's instruments can only be as aspirational as the parties allow them to be. During the negotiation process, the parties chose not to include strong measures to enforce compliance with the commitments under the Paris Agreement. In addition, the unfinished and delayed work to determine the details of the oversight tools' implementation renders the design of the Paris Agreement's monitoring processes unnecessarily opaque. Hence, in the Post-Paris and post-pandemic era, the international community faces great challenges to accomplish meaningful multilateral climate cooperation.

7. CONCLUSION

The negotiators of the Paris Agreement succeeded in reversing a structural approach to international climate cooperation that was unable to promote climate multilateralism and begin the process of mitigating climate change at a global scale. However, the evolution of a *discursive* climate multilateralism through monitoring procedures might (again) be derailed by relatively small issues, such as the interpretation of flexibility and the application of common timeframes.

After the coronavirus pandemic caused the organisers of the conference of parties in 2020 to postpone the plenary gathering in Glasgow, United Kingdom, for one year, it is likely that these issues will be overlooked when climate negotiations will continue. The global economic crisis that the pandemic causes will delay the implementation of planned climate and energy policies. This might subsequently result in adjusted monitoring measures, thwarting constructive debates among the states parties as well as the formation of states parties' identities in interaction with the regime's norms. To avoid this outcome, the challenge for lawyers, diplomats and practitioners, who treasure the ambition that the Paris Agreement seeks to communicate, will be to identify the crucial issues and be cognisant of the slight procedural adjustments that could be responsible for even further delay in significantly reducing global greenhouse gas emissions.

Under the restructured UN climate regime, oversight tools are available, as institutionalised by the Paris Agreement and detailed in the decisions of the Katowice Rulebook. Their implementation can result in a global conversation about the path towards a decarbonised world economy that relies on polycentric governance structures, while monitoring each party's fulfilment of its successive NDCs. Yet, much will depend on the parties' willingness to thoroughly embrace the procedures that promote the emergence of a *discursive* climate multilateralism.

Practitioners and students of international climate cooperation need to become familiar with the polycentric nature of climate and energy governance and the various avenues that this polycentricity provides for the emergence of a hybrid multilateralism, especially in the light of a possible withdrawal of major actors from the Paris Agreement. Furthermore, it is vital to acknowledge the importance of tiny procedural provisions in the Katowice Rulebook, such as the definition of common timeframes and the notion of flexibility. In this context, it is necessary to acknowledge the long-lasting detrimental effect that the rigid division of developed and developing states' obligations under the Kyoto Protocol had on international climate cooperation. Being cognizant of how the definition and further elaboration of procedural matters can impact future climate cooperation can prevent the adoption of a decision by a conference of parties that might allow for a very loose application of monitoring procedures.

Finally, both practitioners and students of climate multilateralism need to acquaint themselves with the various dynamics of energy transitions at the local, subnational, national and international levels of governance. The polycentric nature of energy and climate governance limits international coordination. However, the experiences at these levels of governance also inform multilateral processes by the communication of a great variety of approaches from which best practices can be identified. These insights are essential when both gauging the room for manoeuvre in international negotiations as well as assessing the politics of international climate cooperation. No doubt, the treaties and modes of climate multilateralism have come of age, but states parties' conduct is yet far from maturity.

NOTES

1. The term decarbonisation or low-carbon transition points to the gradual replacement of fossil fuels—crude oil, natural gas, and coal—by other fuels to produce energy. This transformation of the energy system has far-reaching consequences in terms of the need to adjust infrastructure and revisit the socioeconomic, fiscal, environmental and financial links of the energy system with the rest of the economy.

2. Annex A to the Kyoto Protocol lists the following greenhouse gases: carbon dioxide (CO_2), methane (CH_4), nitrous oxide (N_2O), hydrofluorocarbons (HFCs), perfluorocarbons (PFCs) and sulphur hexafluoride (SF_6).

3. According to the International Energy Agency (2019, p. 14), from 1990, the UN climate regime's base year, to 2015, the share of energy among other sectors that mainly contribute to anthropogenic CO_2 emissions increased from 70% to 74%. In absolute numbers, energy-related CO_2 emissions increased by 12.6 $GtCO_2$ equivalent to almost 35 $GtCO_2$ equivalent from 1990 to 2015. The energy sector was responsible for 70% of all greenhouse gas emissions in 2015.

4. The first decade of the twenty-first century was a time of high oil prices and increasing air pollution in large cities in developing states, that additionally

incentivised low-carbon measures relating to energy security and environmental concerns.

5. The Earth Summit in June 1992 was a major step in the institutionalisation of multilateral efforts to address global environmental degradation. Next to the UNFCCC, several other documents were finalised as part of the preparation of the summit: Rio Declaration on Environment and Development, 14 June 1992, UN Doc. A/CONF.151/26 (vol. I); 31 ILM 874 (1992); Convention on Biological Diversity, 29 December 1993, [1993] ATS 32, 1760 UNTS 79, 31 ILM 818 (1992); and Agenda 21, https://sustainabledevelopment.un.org/content/documents/Agenda21.pdf.

6. The Earth Summit in June 1992 was a major step in the institutionalisation of multilateral efforts to address global environmental degradation. Next to the UNFCCC, several other documents were finalised as part of the preparation of the summit: Rio Declaration on Environment and Development, 14 June 1992, UN Doc. A/CONF.151/26 (vol. I); 31 ILM 874 (1992); Convention on Biological Diversity, 29 December 1993, [1993] ATS 32, 1760 UNTS 79, 31 ILM 818 (1992); and Agenda 21, https://sustainabledevelopment.un.org/content/documents/Agenda21.pdf.

7. At the time of writing, the withdrawal from the Paris Agreement that the U.S. Department of State had submitted to the UNFCCC Secretariat was not yet effective. It would be effective on 3 November 2020, one day after the presidential election in the United States.

REFERENCES

Broome, André, and Joel Quirk. "Governing the World at a Distance: The Practice of Global Benchmarking." *Review of International Studies* 41, no. 5 (2015): 819–41.

Brouwer, Derek, David Sheppard, Anjli Raval, and Gregory Meyer "What Negative US Oil Prices Mean for the Industry," *Financial Times*, 21 April 2020.

Council of the European Union. "Long-term Low Greenhouse Gas Emission Development Strategy for the European Union and Its Member States." Document 6612/20, 5 March 2020, pp. 1–6.

Elliott, Lorraine. *The Global Politics of the Environment*. Basingstoke: Macmillan, 1998.

European Commission. "Clean Energy for All Europeans Package." 20 October 2017, https://ec.europa.eu/energy/topics/energy-strategy/clean-energy-all-europeans_en.

European Commission. "The European Green Deal." 11 December 2019, COM(2019), 640 final, pp. 1–24.

Fouquet, Roger. "The Slow Search for Solutions: Lessons from Historical Energy Transitions by Sector and Service." *Energy Policy* 38 (2010): 6586–96.

Hey, Ellen. *Advanced Introduction to International Environmental Law*. Cheltenham: Edward Elgar, 2016.

International Energy Agency. "CO_2 Emissions from Fuel Combustion: Highlights." November 2019, https://iea. blob. core.windows.net/assets/eb3b2e8d-28e0–47fd-a8ba-160f7ed42bc3/CO2_Emissions_from_Fuel_ Combustion_2019_ Highlights. pdf, pp. 1–156.

International Energy Agency. *Re-powering Markets: Market Design and Regulation during the Transition to Low-carbon Power Systems*. Paris: OECD/IEA, 2016.

Joyner, Christopher C. "Stockholm in Retrospect: Progress in the International Law of Environment." *World Affairs* 136, no. 4 (1974): 347–62.

Kern, Florian, and Karoline Rogge. "The Pace of Governed Energy Transitions: Agency, International Dynamics and the Global Paris Agreement Accelerating Decarbonisation Processes?" *Energy Research and Social Sciences* 22 (2016): 13–7.

Morgan, Sam. "EU Leaders Claim Victory on 2050 Climate Goal, despite Polish Snub," *Euractiv*, 13 December 2019.

Myllyvirta, Lauri, Zhang Shuwei, and Shen Xinyi. "Analysis: Will China Build Hundreds of New Coal Plants in the 2020s?" *Carbon Brief*, 24 March 2020.

Myrthy, Sharmila L. "States and Cities as 'Norm Sustainers': A Role for Subnational Actors in the Paris Agreement on Climate Change." *Virginia Environmental Law Journal* 37, no. 1 (2019): 1–51.

Sending, Ole Jacob, Indra Øverland, and Thomas Boe Hornburg. "Climate Change and International Relations: A Five-pronged Research Agenda." *Journal of International Affairs* 73, no. 1 (2020): 183–93.

Viñuales, Jorge, ed. *The Rio Declaration on Environment and Development: A Commentary*. Oxford: Oxford University Press, 2015.

Weisband, Edward. "Discursive Multilateralism: Global Benchmarks, Shame, and Learning in the ILO Labor Standards Monitoring regime." *International Studies Quarterly* 44, no. 4 (2000): 643–66.

Weisslitz, Michael. "Rethinking the Equitable Principle of Common but Differentiated Responsibility: Differential versus Absolute Norms of Compliance and Contribution in the Global Climate Change Context." *Colorado Journal of International Environmental Law and Policy* 13, no. 2 (2002): 474–509.

Zürn, Michael, Martin Binder, Matthias Ecker-Ehrhardt, and Katrin Radtke. "Politische Ordnungsbildung wider Willen" [Forced construction of a political order]. *Zeitschrift für Internationale Beziehungen* 14, no. 1 (2007): 129–64.

LEGAL DOCUMENTS

2015 Paris Agreement—Adoption of the Paris Agreement, Decision 1/CP.21 (FCCC/CP/2015/10/Add.1), 29 January 2016.

2011 Durban Platform—Establishment of an Ad Hoc Working Group on the Durban Platform for Enhanced Action, Decision 1/CP.17 (FCCC/CP/2011/9/Add.1), 15 March 2012.

1997 Kyoto Protocol—Kyoto Protocol to the UN Framework Convention on Climate, 11 December 1997, 2303 UNTS 148, 37 ILM 22 (1998).

1995 Berlin Mandate—The Berlin Mandate: Review of the Adequacy of Article 4, paragraph 2 (a) and (b), of the Convention, Including Proposals Related to a

Protocol and Decisions on Follow-up, Decision 1/CP.1 (FCCC/CP/1995/7/Add.1), 6 June 1995.

Decision 18/CMA.1—Modalities, Procedures and Guidelines for the Transparency Framework for Action and Support Referred to in Article 13 of the Paris Agreement, Decision 18/CMA.1 (FCCC/PA/CMA/2018/3/Add.2), 19 March 2019.

United Nations Framework Convention on Climate Change, 9 May 1992, 1771 UNTS 107, 31 ILM 849 (1992).

Conclusion

Morgane B. De Clercq and Susann Handke

On 19 May 2020, the 73th WHA, the plenary body of the WHO, requested the director-general of this organisation "to initiate . . . a stepwise process of impartial, independent and comprehensive evaluation . . . to review experience gained and lessons learned from the WHO-coordinated international health response to COVID-19" (World Health Assembly 2020, para 9). This review process will include an assessment of the effectiveness of the WHO mechanisms and the application of the operationalisation of the 2005 International Health Regulations (IHR) by the member states. No doubt, the investigation team will hardly be able to answer the questions that people all over the world have about the cause and spread of the pandemic, which changed the course of their lives within only a few weeks and in many cases took the lives of their loved ones.

In fact, this WHO announcement—and likewise the final report on the matter—can only convey cautious and procedural language typical of an international organisation that relies on and coordinates the cooperation of its member states in order to deal with problems that affect the entire international community. The member states will most likely rewrite and strengthen the IHR to avoid mistakes that were made at the beginning of the outbreak.

The debate about the WHO's role illustrates the hopes and expectations that many harbour when state leaders decide to pool resources and address global challenges in a cooperative manner. Yet, it also reveals the bitter disappointment with multilateralism and deep regret about missed opportunities, when states fail to fulfil their commitments. Eventually, international cooperation under a multilateral agreement can only be as effective and forward-looking as the participating states allow and enable it to be.

Observing the watershed moment in international affairs that the 2020 coronavirus pandemic brought about, this volume sought to consider challenges to multilateral governance as well as opportunities that this form of international cooperation can provide. The volume defined a multilateral approach to global or transnational problems as a distinct form of international cooperation in the sense that several states agree on new arrangements or the involvement of existing international institutions in order to manage the response to the problem in question. Moreover, multilateral cooperation is inevitably based on solidarity and the principles and rules of international law.

Historically, this approach to solving international problems emerged during the nineteenth century and manifested itself at the end of the Second World War. For the purpose of this chapter, two distinct past periods can be identified—that is, the post-war and Cold War era and the decades that followed the Cold War. The conditions for multilateral cooperation differed considerably during these two periods (Ikenberry, 2015). The period that began with the end of the Second World War was mainly characterised by the ideological dissonance between the United States and its allies on one side and the Soviet Union on the other. This dissonance impacted many efforts to address global problems. The post-war period ended with the fall of the Berlin Wall in 1990 and the collapse of the Soviet Union in 1991.

Then, during the early 1990s, a new period of multilateral cooperation began. The end of ideological conflict between great powers resulted in a "peace dividend" in international affairs, reflected in various multilateral agreements, especially in the fields of global environmental and trade governance. Regional cooperation also expanded and was increasingly institutionalised. The various forms of multilateral efforts to foster regional integration discussed in this volume are cases in point.

The norms and institutions that were conceived during the immediate period after the end of the Cold War largely shaped the interaction among the members of the international community during the first two decades of the 21st century. Yet, rapid economic globalisation and growing interdependence resulted in many problems that existing international institutions could not adequately address. In addition, dissonance within the international community increased during the late 2010s. Bilateral relations between China and the United States rapidly deteriorated (Schell, 2020). Subsequently, the onslaught of the coronavirus pandemic accelerated many dynamics in international affairs (Haass, 2020), most notably those that had led many people to doubt the effectiveness and suitability of existing forms of multilateral arrangements. Hence, with the pandemic, a new era of multilateral cooperation began. However, the contours of this era are still undefined and uncertain.

This concluding chapter, based on the contributions in this volume, reflects on the future of multilateralism in the (post-)pandemic era. It identifies three factors that will shape the prospects for multilateral progress and determine the scope of multilateral cooperation in the future. These factors are (1) the framework of existing multilateral institutions; (2) the dynamics of international affairs, especially in the context of the further evolution of U.S.-China relations and related regional developments; and (3) widespread dismay and socio-economic uncertainty caused or exacerbated by the pandemic and global environmental degradation. The following paragraphs consider the current state of multilateralism and answer the question of how these factors might influence multilateralism in the twenty-first century.

By the late 2010s, it became clear that "the crisis of multilateralism is more about a renewal of the multilateral system rather than its end" (Lazarou, 2017, p. 7). This would imply a reset of global governance and the creation of a new "full set of formal and informal 'ideas, values, rules, norms, procedures, practices, policies, and institutions'," which would help states and people around the world to be better able to "identify, understand, and address transboundary challenges that go beyond the problem-solving capacities of individual states" (Ikenberry, 2015, p. 401; Weiss, 2014, p. 4).

The contributions in this volume highlight how multilateral organisations at the global and regional level try to deal with global threats to peace and international security. International organisations and multilateral regimes play a vital role in the coordination of policies in the fields of finance, trade and in with transnational social, health and environmental problems. This concluding chapter argues that above all knowledge and creativity are needed to fully utilise existing multilateral institutions and arrangements in the post-pandemic era.

Indeed, the pandemic affects numerous fields of global cooperation. Global health governance under the WHO is only the most obvious example. The care for and wellbeing of children and women are also cases in point. The pandemic highlights the need to critically assess international cooperation under the framework of UNICEF and UN Women.

Furthermore, the economic and financial consequences of the pandemic are going to shape the future policy agendas in the IMF and the WB. Both institutions are confronted with a fragmented system of international financing. The way in which the IMF and WB can adapt to the needs of their members following the pandemic will determine their future role. Yet, the ongoing decoupling between the United States and China will also influence international cooperation led by these two institutions.

The decoupling process between the two largest economies also redefines global trade governance. The contribution about the WTO in this volume introduced to the increasing difficulties that this organisation faces. These difficulties largely result from growing disagreements between the United States and China on the principles and rules that should govern global trade as well as domestic economic policies. The contraction in international trade that followed the beginning of the coronavirus crisis will complicate efforts to uphold and improve rules and institutional arrangements in the field of international trade. Uncertainty about the development of global economic exchanges also hampered efforts to strengthen international tax governance. Immediately after the beginning of the crisis, national governments focused on relief measures to uphold and stimulate domestic economic activity, while negotiations about initiatives to prevent tax evasion and tax avoidance took a backseat.

Regional multilateral institutions also felt the impact of the pandemic. Instruments to coordinate national approaches were insufficient or deliberately neglected during the initial weeks of the coronavirus crisis, as could be observed in the European Union, the AU and Mercosur. However, the member states of these organisations subsequently tried to reiterate their commitment to multilateral approaches when seeking to solve common problems. Most notably, the EU adopted a massive coronavirus recovery package in July 2020 (European Council, 2020). This package will bring about crucial changes to multilateral cooperation among EU member states on financial and economic policies. Mercosur also created a fund to deal with the crisis and considered institutional reforms to enhance the organisation's agenda-setting powers. Generally, the extent to which regional integration organisations will be able to overcome the distress caused by the pandemic will depend on their member states' willingness to address issues that already impeded the development of regional multilateralism prior to the crisis.

This is also relevant for the continuation of initiatives and multilateral cooperation under the umbrella of the UN. More often than not, progress in implementing forward-looking initiatives is frustrated by the fractionalisation of the organisation and the lack of coherence among different UN agencies and programmes. The pandemic aggravated these tendencies. It also is likely that the severe socio-economic consequences of the crisis will divert attention from the implementation of the Sustainable Development Goals (SDGs). Moreover, vital international climate negotiations under the UN climate regime, planned for late 2020, were postponed for one year. Important issues, such as rules that guide the transparency framework and the monitoring of emissions reduction measures, still need to be clarified. Delay in the implementation of the SDGs and uncertainty about procedural aspects of international climate cooperation could affect billions of people. Thus, both cooperation to realise the SDGs and the mitigation of climate change are essential public goods. Only multilateral efforts can deliver these global public goods.

Since the mid-1940s, multilateral cooperation in international and regional organisations or under specialised regimes has been evolving against the backdrop of structural changes in the international system during the post-war and Cold War period as well as during the decades following the end of the Cold War. The United States played a dominant role in the establishment of the post-war international order and influenced the institutional arrangements of the main institutions, such as the IMF and WB and the General Agreement on Tariffs and Trade (GATT), the WTO's predecessor. These institutions have been coordinating international financial and trade cooperation for decades.

Other actors, especially the EU and China, played an increasing role in the negotiations of the institutions and norms that shaped multilateral cooperation after the end of the Cold War. The UN climate regime is an example for the growing role of the EU as norm entrepreneur. Furthermore, the accession of China to the WTO in 2001 was a crucial milestone for the rapid economic globalisation that characterised the first two decades of the twenty-first century. Yet, other fields of policymaking lacked adequate multilateral arrangements to coordinate national policies, in order to address the multi-facetted challenges and complexities that result from ever increasing economic and security interdependence (Ikenberry, 2020). Thus, the post–Cold War international order was inadequate and deficient.

Several dynamics are going to shape the (post-)pandemic multilateralism. These dynamics began to emerge during the late 2010s. The United States cast doubt about its contribution to international organisations and cooperation efforts that it had initiated during the post-war period or greatly influenced after the end of the Cold War. Examples in this regard are its continued commitment to NATO and its role in the WTO. Since 2014, the Russian Federation has increasingly been trying to re-interpret and re-assess post–Cold War arrangements in Europe and beyond. In fact, the illegal annexation of Crimea and the establishment of the Eurasian Economic Union changed the political and economic arrangements that had evolved after 1991.

The Chinese leadership displayed growing confidence to create space that allows its preferred state-led economic model and the Chinese party state to develop without international interference. This volume includes a contribution about the AIIB. The establishment of the AIIB followed the announcement of the Belt and Road Initiative, a massive infrastructure construction scheme that would link the economies of numerous states to China via overland routes and sea transport facilities. The Chinese leadership uses quasi-multilateral forums, such as FOCAC in Africa and 17+1 in Central and Eastern Europe, to guide the implementation of the Belt and Road Initiative, by largely circumventing existing institutional arrangements of the AU and the EU. In the post-pandemic era, the AIIB might evolve as a vital lender to projects that counter economic decoupling between China and the United States or efforts by the Japanese government to "re-shore" economic activity.

The bank could be utilised to re-draft the extensive network of supply chains on the Eurasian mega-continent. In this role, the AIIB might emerge as a vital vehicle to shape the geo-economics of Asia in the decades to come.

China's growing posture in the Asia-Pacific region greatly influences the dynamics within Southeast Asia. The contribution about ASEAN in this volume emphasises that the legitimacy of this regional organisation is dependent on its positioning in the context of the Chinese leadership's involvement in regional affairs. The contribution also illustrates how internal disagreements about issues such as a unified response to the displacement of the Rohingya minority can weaken multilateral cooperation in Southeast Asia and diminish ASEAN's leading role in the region.

EU foreign policymaking is also fraught with disagreement about the Union's relations with the most important actors in international affairs. Russia's more assertive role and China's involvement in Central and Eastern Europe pose great challenges to the EU policymaking apparatus that is delineated in this volume. Despite the fact that this apparatus and the standing of the EU as international actor have great potential to (further) promote forward-looking multilateral initiatives, it remains unclear whether the Union will be able to fully realise its potential as a global actor in the post-pandemic era.

In fact, in the decades to come, international affairs, and in particular, the prospects for global multilateral cooperation, will be determined by the evolution of U.S.-China relations. Given the complexities of economic and security interdependence, it will be difficult to clearly side with one of the emerging rivals. However, growing unease is felt regarding China's role in Southeast Asia (Lee, 2020); and European states are increasingly reluctant to strengthen and institutionalise economic cooperation with the communist country, following the Chinese leadership's ever more authoritarian policies at home and undue assertiveness abroad (Pei, 2020). In the post-pandemic era, for many states, relations with China will continue to exemplify the complexities of economic interdependence.

After witnessing the Trump administration renounce multilateral cooperation in various policy fields, the international community increasingly questions the future global role of the United States. However, representatives of a younger generation of leaders in the United States vocally emphasise the importance of institutions for proper governance at home and their contribution to the provision of global public goods (Abrams, 2020). Yet, for the time being, many members of the international community are wary of expressing their allegiance to the world's two leading powers, considering their economic might and willingness to influence international affairs. Hence, in the post-pandemic era, the success of multilateralism will depend on how other actors, especially regional organisations, will be able to manage the dynamics of U.S.-China relations (Nye, 2020). Global multilateral cooperation will most likely take place in policy fields where regional trends and leadership can inform the international level and induce the United States and China to join efforts to address global challenges.

How students and practitioners of international relations will be able to identify opportunities to pursue multilateral cooperation will largely determine the nature of multilateralism in the near future. Governments rely on scholarly and policy analysis as well as procedural knowledge of the workings of international organisations. Thus, states' ability to effectuate multilateral cooperation is dependent on informed input. The contributors to this volume sought to compile a primer for students and young researchers who want to acquaint themselves with the practical side of multilateral cooperation. They deliberately chose to focus on intergovernmental organisations and regimes.

No doubt, the task of finding appropriate and timely responses to the coronavirus pandemic re-emphasised the role of states as by far the most prominent actors in international affairs. The crisis marks an important turning point in global governance. It corrects a trend that, since the 1990s, saw the emergence of ever more transgovernmental networks, arbitration bodies, multistakeholder initiatives, voluntary regulations and codes of conduct (Hale & Held, 2011, pp. 16–17). These hybrid or entirely non-governmental transnational entities and instruments were increasingly part of global efforts to respond to various economic, developmental and environmental challenges. The coronavirus pandemic, however, halted the proliferation of such institutional innovations. It remains to be seen to what extent these actors and mechanisms of transnational governance will re-emerge or adjust their operations to the changed international landscape.

With its choice for an analysis of multilateral organisations and regimes, this volume provides a distinct approach to assessing challenges to multilateral cooperation in the context of the coronavirus pandemic. The studies that the chapters present identify common patterns in the responses to the crisis and point to differences. Thus, the volume acknowledges the coronavirus crisis as a crucial moment in the development of global and regional multilateralism. It offers students and young researchers a point of departure that combines an overview of the pre-crisis challenges to the existing multilateral order with a discussion of how several institutions fared at the beginning of the crisis. The volume invites the reader to further investigate the authors' observations and ponder on the prospects of multilateralism.

As mentioned earlier, this concluding chapter highlights three factors that will shape the future of multilateralism in the years to come. These factors contextualise creative international and regional approaches to multilateral cooperation. First, *existing multilateral institutions* will primarily form the stage for multilateral cooperation in the near future. It is rather unlikely that new far-reaching global agreements will be adopted any time soon; neither will there be prominent new international organisations. Thus, extensive knowledge of existing institutions is key. Knowing the limitations and functioning of an international organisation, especially procedural matters and its organisational structure, will be ever more vital when trying to influence outcomes.

Second, the further development of *U.S.-China relations* will most likely impact many fields of international cooperation. Students and practitioners of international affairs need to be aware of this increasingly "special" relationship, in the sense that knowledge of bilateral and domestic developments (in both states) is essential to assess the room for manoeuvre that international initiatives might be able to obtain. Opportunities for multilateral cooperation must be evaluated regarding their substantive content (related to the policy field) as well as their regional or international contexts.

Third, *socio-economic and environmental uncertainties* will increasingly require (and hamper) multilateral cooperation. The coronavirus pandemic will cause socio-economic distress for many years to come. In addition, ongoing climate change and other forms of environmental degradation not only necessitate international cooperation but also impair the practical implementation of international initiatives "on the ground". For instance, the logistical inaccessibility of certain regions as a result of extreme weather events could endanger efforts to address environmental issues or provide developmental aid, while the destruction of economic livelihoods by natural disasters might need attention before other policies can be implemented. Thus, it is vital to pursue realistic approaches to multilateral cooperation and find pragmatic and credible solutions to evolving emergencies. After having endured the coronavirus pandemic, people will not be able to suffer through another global crisis that international organisations handle inappropriately. Nothing less than the legitimacy of multilateralism is at stake.

REFERENCES

Abrams, S. (2020). "American Leadership Begins at Home: The Global Imperative to Rebuild Governance and Restore Democracy". *Foreign Affairs*, 1 May, https://www.foreignaffairs.com/articles/united-states/2020-05-01/stacey-abrams-american-leadership-begins-home.

European Council (2020). Special Meeting of the European Council (17, 18, 19, 20 and 21 July 2020)—Conclusions, EUCO 10/20, 21 July, https://www.consilium.europa.eu/media/45109/210720-euco-final-conclusions-en.pdf.

Haass, R. (2020). "The Pandemic Will Accelerate History Rather Than Reshape It". *Foreign Affairs*, 7 April, https://www.foreignaffairs.com/articles/united-states/2020-04-07/pandemic-will-accelerate-history-rather-reshape-it.

Hale, T., and D. Held (2011). "Editors' Introduction: Mapping Changes in Transnational Governance." in *Handbook of Transnational Governance: Institutions and Innovations*, ed. T. Hale and D. Held (Cambridge: Polity), 1–36.

Hale, T. and D. Held, eds. (2011). *Handbook of Transnational Governance: Institutions and Innovations*. Cambridge : Polity.

Lee, H. L. (2020). "The Endangered Asian Century: America, China, and the Perils of Confrontation". *Foreign Affairs*, 4 June. https://www.foreignaffairs.com/articles/asia/2020-06-04/lee-hsien-loong-endangered-asian-century.

Ikenberry, G. J. (2020). "The Next Liberal Order: The Age of Contagion Demands More Internationalism, Not Less." *Foreign Affairs* July/August, https://www.foreignaffairs.com/articles/united-states/2020-06-09/next-liberal-order.

Ikenberry, G. J. (2015). "The Future of Multilateralism: Governing the World in a Post-Hegemonic Era". *Japanese Journal of Political Science* 16.3 (2015):, 16, 3, 399–413.

Lazarou, E. (2017). European Parliament Briefing: The future of multilateralism—Crisis or opportunity?. https://www.europarl.europa.eu/RegData/etudes/BRIE/2017/603922/EPRS_BRI(2017)603922_EN.pdf.

Nye Jr, J. S. (2020). "The U.S.-China Relationship Is at a Crossroads". *The National Interest*, 15 January, https://nationalinterest.org/feature/us-china-relationship-crossroads-114041.

Pei, M. (2020). "China's Deepening Geopolitical Hole". 16 July. *Project Syndicate*. https://www.project-syndicate.org/commentary/china-uk-huawei-ban-another-diplomatic-setback-by-minxin-pei-2020-07.

Schell, O. (2020). "The Ugly End of Chimerica: The Coronavirus Pandemic Has Turned a Conscious Uncoupling into a Messy Breakup". *Foreign Policy*, 3 April. https://foreignpolicy.com/2020/04/03/chimerica-ugly-end-coronavirus-china-us-trade-relations.

Weiss, T. (2014). Governing the World? Addressing 'Problems without Passports', Boulder, CO: Paradigm.

World Health Assembly (2020). Decision WHA73.1—COVID-19 Response, 19 May 2020.

Index

Index

About the Editors and Contributors

ABOUT THE EDITORS

Madeleine O. Hosli

Madeleine O. Hosli is a professor of political science (international relations) at Leiden University. She is director of the advanced M.Sc. International Relations and Diplomacy. Her main research interests are in international political economy, international organizations and European integration. She is author of *The Euro: A Concise Introduction to European Monetary Integration* (Lynne Rienner, 2004), co-editor of *Decision-Making in the European Union Before and After the Lisbon Treaty* (Routledge 2015) and *The Changing Global Order* (Springer 2020). She has published widely in peer-reviewed journals, including *International Organization, International Studies Quarterly, Journal of Common Market Studies, European Union Politics, Journal of European Public Policy, European Journal of Political Research* and *Review of International Organizations*.

Taylor Garrett

Taylor Garrett holds two bachelor degrees in international relations (B.A.) and modern languages (B.A.) from Northern Arizona University. She also studied international comparative politics and EU policy at Science-Politiques Toulouse. Taylor is a young academic currently pursuing an advanced master in international relations and diplomacy (M.Sc.) taught jointly by Leiden University and the Netherlands Institute of International Relations, Clingendael. She focuses on topics related to conflict transformation, identity in peace-building and the potential of blockchain technologies for humanitarian aid and development. With an experienced global perspective, she has circled the earth by the age of 23 with a mission to immerse herself in local cultures and integrate these realities into academic research. She has volunteered and worked in various countries, including Vietnam, New Zealand, Senegal and Romania. As a researcher, Taylor highly values curiosity for approaching every subject as an opportunity to discover and create awareness around the deeply rooted elements responsible for enduring interpersonal or international conflicts.

Sonja Niedecken

Sonja Niedecken holds a B.A. in European studies from Maastricht University. She is currently pursuing an advanced master in international relations and diplomacy (M.Sc.) jointly taught by Leiden University and the Netherlands Institute of International Relations, Clingendael. During her B.A., Sonja completed an exchange semester at Seoul National University where she took several graduate courses in the field of international politics, development studies and Asian studies. Her research interests are focused on EU external relations, diplomacy and development studies. She wrote her thesis on the "Influence of Civil Society Organizations on the European Development Policy". She has given workshops on the EU and related topics to high school students in the Netherlands and Germany. She gained professional experience during a development volunteer service in Uruguay and a year as a volunteer coordinator in a refugee camp in Germany.

Nicolas Verbeek

Nicolas Verbeek received a B.A. in political science, sociology and media studies from Bonn University. Furthermore, he studied geopolitics, foreign policy analysis, financial economics and economic sociology at Charles University, Prague. He is currently pursuing an advanced master in international relations and diplomacy (M.Sc.) jointly taught by Leiden University and the Netherlands Institute of International Relations, Clingendael. His academic work focuses on the U.S.-China rivalry, perception and power in foreign policy analysis, conflict mediation and the transformation of global governance structures. He is author and member of the research groups "IR-Theories and Foreign Policy Research" and "USA/Transatlantic Relations/NATO" of the Cologne Forum for International Relations and Security Policy, a Cologne-based think tank. He authored a chapter on empirical limitations of contemporary realist theory in foreign policy analysis in a book that will be published by Tectum by the end of 2020. Furthermore, he currently works on an in-depth comparison of U.S.-China relations under Obama and Trump, which will be published by Springer in early 2022.

ABOUT THE CONTRIBUTORS

Gulnara Abbas

Gulnara Abbas holds a master's degree in development studies from King's College London. She is currently a Ph.D. student at Leiden University, working on a dissertation in the area of changing paradigms in development cooperation. During her professional experience as a Researcher at the leading think tank in the Southern Caucasus and Central Asia—Center for Economic and Social Development (CESD), she co-authored a couple of publications in high impact factored journals (*Resources Policy* and *International Economics*). Gulnara participated as an expert in a project organized by the Swiss Agency for Development and Cooperation and as a project assistant in projects organized by the EU, UNDP and ADB. She also conducted scoping studies on the development cooperation priorities of the OECD-DAC members at the International Criminal Court (ICC) in the Hague as an external relations and state cooperation Intern.

Juliana Cubillos

Juliana Cubillos González is a PhD candidate in the GLOBTAXGOV Project at Leiden University's Institute for Tax Law and Economics. Since 2018, she holds an LLM in international taxation from the University of Amsterdam (UvA) and the International Bureau of Fiscal Documentation (IBFD). Prior to this achievement, she graduated as a bachelor in law and as a master in tax law from Universidad de los Andes (Bogotá Colombia). Before joining the GLOBTAXGOV project, she worked as an associate for Baker McKenzie (2012–2014) in the tax litigation team and as a tax consultant for PwC (2014–2019) focused mainly in providing advice to oil and gas companies. Within the GLOBTAXGOV project, she investigates the implementation of the BEPS Four Minimum Standards in developed countries including EU member countries.

Carolina D'Ambrosio

Carolina D'Ambrosio holds a B.Sc. in political science and economics from the University of Milan, Italy. She is currently pursuing an advanced MSc in international relations and diplomacy, jointly taught by Leiden University and the Netherlands Institute of International Relations, Clingendael. Throughout her studies, she consolidated her knowledge and skills in international policy analysis through her combined interest in political science, international relations, diplomacy, as well as international law and public economics. She conducted academic research in the fields of European integration, international law and negotiation practices, with a specific focus on Middle Eastern and African conflicts, and on European development aid initiatives. She also cultivated an incredible curiosity for transitional justice, as she developed her Bachelor's thesis on the Special Tribunal for Lebanon and on further instances of transitional justice in the country. Alongside her academic training, she matured considerable expertise in Communication and PR through her working experience as Junior Account at *BCW Global* Milan. This experience enabled her to gain extensive skills in advocacy and established her passion for political intelligence and public affairs.

Morgane De Clercq

Morgane De Clercq holds a bachelor's degree in economics and business economics (B.Sc.) with a major in macroeconomics from Maastricht University School of Business and Economics, Netherlands. She is currently pursuing an advanced master in international relations and diplomacy (M.Sc.) jointly taught by Leiden University and the Netherlands Institute of International Relations, Clingendael. She had the opportunity to deviate from her Western perspective and deepen her South-East Asian perspective during her exchange at National University of Singapore and her internship at the Embassy of the Kingdom of Belgium in Jakarta, Indonesia. Her main research interests are in international trade, development economics and international political economy. In 2019, De Clercq was invited to participate in the 12th Bali Democracy Forum (BDF), Bali, Indonesia, to discuss on the topics of democracy and inclusivity.

Yue Han

Yue Han obtained a bachelor's degree (B.A.) in journalism from Beijing International Studies University. She is currently pursuing an advanced master in international relations and diplomacy (M.Sc.) jointly taught by Leiden University and the Netherlands Institute of International Relations, Clingendael. Furthermore, she studied social psychology and Islam in Central Asia when exchanging at the University of Copenhagen. During her undergraduate studies, she focused on International Journalism. In her thesis, she analysed the political discourse of the reports of *New York Times*. Yue has interned with the largest news outlet in China, the Xinhua News Agency in Beijing. Now, she wants to deepen her critical understanding of global political dynamics. Therefore, her research interests revolve around the role of international organizations and global security issues. In her spare time, Yue has volunteered in fundraising for impoverished children in China's mountainous areas and teaching in a primary school for migrant workers' children. Yue aspires to see more, learn more and contribute more.

Susann Handke

Susann Handke is an international lawyer and sinologist, and alumna of Leiden University. She specialises in international and EU energy law and governance. Her recent publications include book chapters about the geopolitics of the energy transition and EU infrastructure governance in the context of China's economic foreign policy. In autumn 2020, she defended her dissertation on the UN climate regime at Erasmus University Rotterdam. Her Ph.D. research examined the substantive legal development of this multilateral environmental regime. It related the evolution of the regime, beginning with the 1992 UNFCCC, to trends in energy legislation and policies in the EU, the United States and China ahead of the adoption of the Paris Agreement.

Frederik Heitmüller

Frederik Heitmüller is a Ph.D. candidate in the GLOBTAXGOV project at Leiden University's Institute for Tax Law and Economics. Being educated through an interdisciplinary and intercultural political and social science study programme at the universities of Stuttgart, Bordeaux and Monterey, he believes that interdisciplinary approaches are vital to the creation of new knowledge. By participating in the GLOBTAXGOV research project, he aims to investigate the intersections of tax law, politics, (economic) development and concepts of justice and fairness.

Nandi Makubalo

Nandi Makubalo holds a B.A. degree in development studies from the Zambia Catholic University. During her studies, she worked in a non-governmental organization and in a development consultancy. While studying for her undergraduate degree, she attended a conference on the significance of international peace at the Dag Hammarskjold Institute of Peace and Conflict Studies at the Copperbelt University in Zambia. This conference awakened her interest in peace and conflict resolution. Nandi is currently a student in the International Master of African Studies at Ghent University. She has conducted an internship at the United Nations University Institute of Comparative Regional Integration Studies (UNU-CRIS) in Bruges, Belgium, in 2018 and 2019. She is author of the 2019 UNU-CRIS policy brief 'Strengthening United Nations (UN) and AU Coordination on Peace Missions' and co-author of 'The African Union in the United Nations' (in Katie Laatikainen and Karen Smith, eds., *Group Politics in UN Multilateralism,* Brill 2020).

Irma Mosquera Valderrama

Dr Irma Johanna Mosquera Valderrama is associate professor of Tax Law at Leiden University, the Netherlands and Lead Researcher of the European Research Council ERC Funded Project GLOBTAXGOV. She received her Ph.D. (cum laude) in 2007 in the Netherlands. She was also a Fulbright Scholar (PhD research) at New York University, and the University of Florida (Gainesville), United States. She is currently Programme Coordinator Limits of Tax Jurisdiction and member of the Research Board, Leiden Law School. Since August 2019, she is a member of the EPPJMO-PROJECT Digitalization of Tax Administrations (DIGITAX) in the EU in cooperation with several partners (main applicant the Fundacion Universitaria San Pablo-CEU—Universidad CEU Cardenal Herrera). She is also a member of the Reference Group (Policy & Operations Evaluation Department [IOB] Dutch Ministry of Foreign Affairs) evaluating the Dutch government policies and activities to strengthen tax systems in developing countries in the period 2012–2019. She is a member of the International Law Association Study Group on International Tax Law and Member Council for International Multidisciplinary Cooperation of Mendel University in Brno, Czech Republic. She is also a member of the International Fiscal Association and of the Dutch Fiscal Association.

Before joining Leiden, she was working as tax adviser (PwC, Hamelink & Van den Tooren), lecturer (University of Utrecht, Erasmus University, the Hague University of Applied Sciences) and postdoctoral researcher (International Bureau of Fiscal Documentation IBFD, Netherlands). She was also a member of the international research project entitled "Sustainable Tax Governance in Developing Countries through Global Tax Transparency" (DeStaT), financed by the Research Council of Norway. Her areas of expertise are international tax law and comparative tax law in developed and developing countries and more recently exchange of information and BEPS related issues in developing countries.

Dimitra Protopsalti

Dimitra Protopsalti holds a master's degree (M.A.) in political analysis of public and European policies from University of Crete. She is currently pursuing an advanced master's in international relations and diplomacy (M.Sc.) jointly taught by Leiden University and the Netherlands Institute of

International Relations, Clingendael. Her area of research included the Euro-Mediterranean relations whilst her master's thesis analysed the relations of Spain and the Maghreb countries on bilateral and multilateral levels. While obtaining a bachelor's degree (BEd) in preschool education and volunteering in the Hellenic Red Cross, she has developed an interest in the human rights sector, with a focus on humanitarian aid. This interest was boosted during her exchange semester at Complutense University of Madrid, Spain. Other academic interests include peace building, peace-keeping and conflict resolution. Dimitra has always strived to reach across borders and immerse herself in foreign cultures through her work in order to gain as much multicultural experience as possible in her career and academic life. Consequently, she has also served as a youth worker throughout Europe as part of the Erasmus+ programme.

Amber Scheele

Amber Scheele holds a B.Sc. in management, society and technology from the University of Twente. She pursued an advanced master in international relations and diplomacy (M.Sc.) jointly taught by Leiden University and the Netherlands Institute of International Relations, Clingendael. She is an intuitive young professional, skilled in international negotiations, public administration, international and external European Union relations and economic policy. As the Ambassador of University of Leiden (2020–2021) to the European Union Career Services, Amber strives to continuously challenge herself in order to contribute to a more accepting and collaborative mentality within international relations. Her interests in cultures, global governance and the geopolitical landscape of Latin-America as well as the European Union have led her to many international opportunities abroad. Amber's drive, curiosity and open-mind have expanded and diversified her problem-solving abilities.

Rizwan Togoo

Rizwan Rafi Togoo completed his B.A. (Hons) in international relations at Asia Pacific University (APU) in Kuala Lumpur, Malaysia. Furthermore, he interned at the Malaysian chapter of Global Peace Foundation (GPF), where he worked in the department of Corporate and Strategic Partnerships. He is currently pursuing an advanced masters in international relations and diplomacy at Leiden University jointly taught by Leiden University and the Netherlands Institute of International Relations, Clingendael. During his internship with GPF, he worked on humanitarian projects in rural villages in Malaysia that are inhabited by the indigenous population. His research interests are refugee crisis, migration, politics and society in Asia, the role of non-state actors in international affairs and the Kashmir conflict. As a bachelor's degree student at APU, he wrote his thesis about the human security of Rohingya refugees in Malaysia. Rizwan's family comes from the most militarized zone in the world, that is, Kashmir, and he aspires to tell stories of his people to the rest of the world.